SCALING METHODS

SCALING
METHODS

Peter Dunn-Rankin

University of Hawaii at Manoa

LEA LAWRENCE ERLBAUM ASSOCIATES, PUBLISHERS

1983   Hillsdale, New Jersey   London

Lawrence Erlbaum Associates, Inc., Publishers
365 Broadway
Hillsdale, New Jersey 07642

Library of Congress Cataloging in Publication Data

Dunn-Rankin, Peter.
  Scaling methods.

  Bibliography: p.
  Includes index.
  1. Scale analysis (Psychology)   2. Scaling (Social
sciences)   3. Attitude (Psychology)—Testing. I. Title.
[DNLM: 1. Attitude.   2. Personality Assessment.
3. Psychometrics—Methods.   BF 39 D923s]
BF39.D83 1983   303.3'8'0287   83-11515
ISBN 0-89859-203-8

Printed in the United States of America
10 9 8 7 6 5 4 3 2 1

This book is dedicated to
Pat, Yoshie, Ken, F. J., and Saint

Contents

Preface

This text is written for people in the behavioral sciences who desire to analyze data that result from subjective responses. This group includes teachers who wish to appraise children's affective reactions to their educational environment (a student's liking for school, for example); social scientists who feel that attitudes are an important variable in their research; educators who feel that some measure of motivation is an important adjunct to achievement; sociologists who wish to generate hypotheses about the latent factors underlying social values; or psychologists who wish to define the underlying dimensions of perception.

In recent years books on scaling attitudes or the measurement of perception have concentrated on the psychometrician's view of measurement rather than on the user's view. This text addresses itself to general or *lay* practitioners in the social sciences who are interested in the measurement and representation of attitudes (in this case attitude is a synonym for subjective assessment of all kinds, i.e., values, interests, perceptions, etc.). The more advanced reader may also consult Cliff (1973) and Carroll and Arabie (1980).

The text is a product of a graduate class the author has taught in the measurement of qualitative data for the past 15 years. The methods outlined have been chosen because they: (1) will handle most data analysis problems; (2) have proven to be useful; (3) are relatively easy to comprehend; and (4) have functional computer solutions. Over the past decade newer methods of clustering and multidimensional scaling have proliferated. Most of these methods have been tried by the author and incorporated as a methodology if they proved to offer something substantially unique or useful to the analysis of subjective data.

Part I of this text introduces two major purposes for the analysis of psychological objects. A psychological object is any variable or object for which some degree of attitude, sentiment, or perception can be measured. These purposes are: (1) to produce estimates of the distance between each pair of objects and (2) to produce a simplified representation of the objects (i.e., draw a parsimonious picture [a map] of the data). Such objectives can have useful consequences. The consequences vary from enhancing the validity of attitude- or perception-measuring instruments, to the discovery of new relationships underlying a set of objects, to the testing of hypothetical models of relationships among a set of psychological objects. Part I also provides an introduction to the types of tasks that an experimenter can use. It details the major ways in which initial measures of proximity can be obtained from data that result from responses to the objects of interest.

The next three parts of the book explain the various methodologies. Because the methods start with unidimensional techniques, move to graphic displays and clustering, and end with multidimensional analyses, a gradual progression from simple representations to more complex is involved. The author has found that if students learn the early techniques first, the latter methods are more easily assimilated.

The text follows the pedagogy of ''instruction by example.'' Thus each chapter introduces: (1) the theory surrounding the particular methodology; (2) a computationally simple example; (3) a ''real-world'' application; and (4) references to a computer solution. The book may be used as a basis for a one-semester course in the measurement of qualitative data or as a handbook. Because each method is a complete unit, the reader may turn directly to the chapter that explains a specific methodology. The reader may find that the examples make interesting reading because most have not been previously published. In Part V an introduction to computer usage is provided so that such solutions can be obtained by the uninitiated. Examples of computer solutions for each method or measure presented along with FORTRAN source programs are also provided in Part V.

The author is indebted to his students, Ruth Robison, Gerald Knezek, Burt Furuta, Jean Holtz, Martha Crosby, Eddie Wong, Sue Atkins, Bob Bloedon, Mike Furlong, Roger Moseley, Kay Hiraki, Ferd Britton, Odette Villanueva, Joy McClarty, Mildred Higashi, Jan Moriyama, Carol Smith, Cham Nong Vilbulsri, John Hills, John Anderson, Gerald Roberts, Debbie Bennett, Gilbert Fujiyoshi, Xenia Montenegro, and Margaret Donovan for their creative efforts incorporated in this text. Special thanks to professors Frank Carmone, Donald Veldman, and Douglas McRae for permission to reproduce some of their FORTRAN source programs. A debt of gratitude persists to Yoshie Kaneshiro for her continuing support and secretarial help. Thanks to Professor Vidya Bushan for his careful reading of the manuscript. Special thanks to Ralph Freese for his help on Inter-judge Differences and to Derek Dunn-Rankin for his careful reading of the manuscript.

Peter Dunn-Rankin

SCALING METHODS

FOUNDATIONS

In Part I definitions of scaling and dimensional representation are provided and the fundamental difference between judgments and choices is explored. In addition the ordered sequence, objects → tasks → proximity measures → computer solutions is explained. Each step is an important ingredient in the process of attitudinal measurement.

1 Process of Relative Measurement

INTRODUCTION

Scaling consists of ordering things in some meaningful way such as labeling the units on a thermometer. One very cold winter's night, Fahrenheit made a mark on a glass tube containing mercury. He called this point zero. He knew that if the mercury ever became that low again it would be very cold. He had, in fact, attached significant if *relative* meaning to the height of the mercury on a wintry night.

Afterward, the mercury heights for freezing and boiling water were also indicated on the tube. The distance between the freezing and boiling marks was divided into 180 equal parts or units. The "very cold day" mark was observed to be 32 of these units below the freezing point of water. Each unit was called a degree and the "very cold day" mark was arbitrarily designated as zero. Thus the freezing point of water was given as 32°F or 32 degrees on the Fahrenheit scale and the boiling point became 212°F.

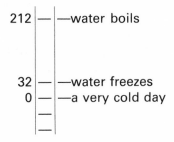

Meaning is attached to the numbers 32 and 212. One can think of 32 as an informative distance away from 212 because each temperature reading represents a logical extreme with regard to water. These extremes provide meaning to the degree units that are ordered on the tube. Taken altogether the units constitute a scale. Fahrenheit temperature values, however, remain relative to where the zero was initially placed.

PSYCHOLOGICAL OBJECTS

While the objects in the previous case are mercury heights that vary under temperature changes, scaling in the social sciences deals with *psychological* objects. *Psychological objects* can be tangible, such as chairs and postcards, but they can also be almost anything that is perceived by the senses and that results in some cognitive affect. Psychological objects can be colors, words, tones, and sentences as well as houses, gold stars, and movie stars. Psychological objects are most often sentences or statements, such as "There will always be wars" or "I hate war." With young children the objects are often pictures. In marketing analysis, psychological objects are the products of industry: cars, soap, TV's, and toothpaste.

Likert's (1932) suggestion that psychological objects (statements) should be chosen so that people with different points of view will respond to each statement differently is still valuable. He suggests that statements may vary widely in emphasis although their content remains similar. Thus the statements:

"I would recommend this course to a friend."

and

"This is the worst course I have ever taken."

should evoke different responses but remain generally evaluative in nature or dimensionality. Specifically the following criteria for selecting attitude statements can be used:

1. Avoid statements that refer to the past rather than to the present.
2. Avoid statements that are factual or capable of being interpreted as factual.
3. Avoid statements that may be interpreted in more than one way.
4. Avoid statements that are irrelevant to the psychological object or continuum under consideration.
5. Avoid statements that are likely to be endorsed by almost everyone or no one (your instrument may include a few such statements to ascertain endpoints of a scale.)

6. Select statements that are believed to cover the entire range of the effective scale of interest.
7. Keep statements simple, clear, and direct.
8. Statements should be short (rarely exceeding 20 words).
9. Each statement should contain only one complete thought.
10. Avoid universals such as all, always, none, and never.
11. Avoid complex and compound sentences.
12. Avoid double negatives.
13. Avoid difficult words.

Scaling is concerned with classes of objects about which people can manifest some attitude. Usually the experimenter wishes to know the relationship among the objects; that is, how far apart they are and in what relative directions the objects may lie. Generally, our own familiar Euclidean space provides a framework within which numbers can be assigned to objects in a relative but meaningful way.

This use of Euclidean space is demonstrated by the scaling of lowercase letters of the English alphabet (letters are the psychological objects) on a unidimensional or linear scale in terms of their similarity to specific target letters (Dunn-Rankin, 1968). (See Fig. 5.6.) Note that when the letter *a* is used as a target the other letters are scaled in their perceived similarity to *a* as follows:

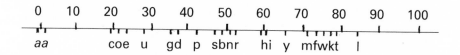

In this scale the letter *l* is seen as least similar to the target letter *a*, whereas *o*, *e*, and *c* are judged much closer to *a*. Relative meaning can be attached to the ends of the scale (i.e., the numbers 0 and 100). In this case they represent the unlikely prospect of having every one of the judges (315 second- and third-grade children) indicate that one letter was most like the target letter *a* and that one other letter was least like the target letter *a* (when presented with all possible pairs of letters and asked to make a judgment about similarity). In this scale the distance between *a* and *c* is shorter than the distance between *a* and *y*. One can infer from the scaling technique that *y* is probably considered more different from *a* than *c* when making these comparisons.

Distances are not a necessary requisite for a scale. One could select a set of objects for which order is the scale. If, for example, the following math problems were presented to a group of school children they would be well ordered in difficulty:

(1) $2 + 2 =$

(2) $24 - 16 =$

(3) $375.5 \div 4 =$

(4) $\dfrac{4!}{2!(4 - 2)} =$

(5) $\dfrac{d(3x^2 + 4)}{dx} =$

Each succeeding problem is more difficult than the one before it. The questions or psychological objects constitute a scale based on difficulty and the numbers (the ranks) have been assigned in a meaningful way. If we score a 1 for each correct answer and 0 for an incorrect answer, the pattern of ones and zeros over the five questions tells us where the student is on this math difficulty scale. Thus a person who has the pattern 11110 is farther along on the scale than the student with scored responses of 11000.

SPATIAL REPRESENTATION

Spatial representation has two objectives. Its major function is *description*. Hopefully, for scientists, this description is parsimonious. Effective representation may then lead to the generation of hypotheses about the relations among the objects. For example, a set of statements reflecting student attitudes toward instructors was given to classes of college seniors. Based on the student responses a measure of similarity (Pearson's correlation, *r*) was found between each pair of statements. By utilizing the most positive measures of relationship (see Chapter 11) the representation given in Fig. 1.1 was determined.

This picture of the relationships among the statements is revealing because it illustrates that most of the statements impinge on the general evaluation statements. Clusters of statements identified as motivational, affective, and cognitive aspects of instruction, although generally unrelated to each other, all contribute to general evaluation.

JUDGMENTS OR CHOICES

One must initially decide the measurement objectives of a particular study or experiment. If a psychological scale is to be constructed then the responses to the objects must be *judgments* of similarity. Subjective *preference* among objects is used when a description of the data is desired instead of a scale, or when it is felt that the sample is an accurate representation of some population, or both. Thus, the two main kinds of responses that subjects can make are: (1) judgments; and (2) choices (preferences).

Figure 1.2 presents a diagrammatic outline for attitudinal measurement. First the psychological objects are chosen. The selection is dictated by the interests of the experimenter. (Suggestions for the construction of attitude statements are given on page 4.) Once the objects have been obtained or formulated they are presented in a task (a taxonomy of tasks is found in Chapter 2). If the task requires judgments, unidimensional or multidimensional methods are used to scale the objects. From this analysis a subset of the objects may be chosen and the objects formulated into a psychological scaling instrument. These instruments can then be presented to the target group(s) and their responses scored (see Chapter 10). Should judgments of similarity between tangible objects, such as letters, odors, and sounds, be obtained in several dimensions, the distance between the objects can be used in future studies as specific measures of similarity. Should preferences instead of judgments be obtained, a descriptive analysis occurs directly. Such analyses can generate or test hypotheses.

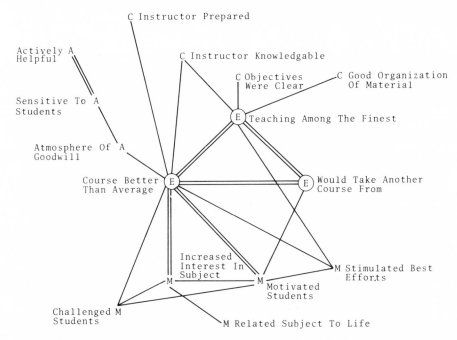

FIG. 1.1. Graphic similarity analysis of correlations among teacher evaluation items. Double lines indicate $r > .80$; single lines indicate $r > .70$. Notice clusters of items C (cognitive), A (affective), and M (motivational), which are unrelated to each other but impinge on the E (general evaluative) items.

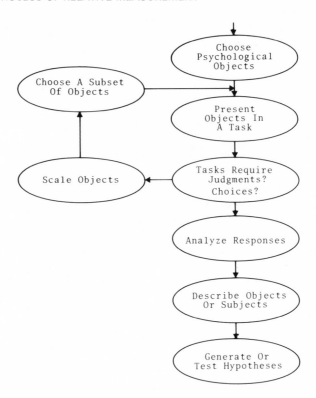

FIG. 1.2.   Diagrammatic representation of attitudinal measurement.

QUALITATIVE OR QUANTITATIVE DATA

As Marascuilo and McSweeney (1977) have suggested, statistical variables can be of two types: qualitative or quantitative. Qualitative variables can be ordered or unordered and are variables whose states are defined by a set of mutually exclusive subclasses defined in verbal terms. Examples include sex, race, and attitude toward _____. The first two variables would contain unordered subclasses male/female and Caucasians/Asians, for example. Attitude, however, assumes order (strongly agree, agree, disagree, strongly disagree), as do variables like social class (high, medium, low). Quantitative variables are variables whose values are determined by counting or measuring. Such measures might include height, weight, and I.Q.

Measures of perceptions and attitudes are generally relative and subjectively determined. Most often attitude scales, therefore, are derived from qualitative data. It is the purpose of this text to describe the most effective methods for handling such data but this does *not* rule out the use of these methods with quantitative scores where they have wide applicability.

2 Tasks Used in Assessing Subjective Perception

Psychological objects can be any object about which subjects have some perception or attitude. A taxonomy of tasks for assessing people's judgments or choices about psychological objects is provided below.

Types of Tasks	Examples
1. Placing or Grouping	Clustering: "Put the similar ones together."
2. Naming or categorizing	Opinion polls: "Do you agree or disagree?"
3. Ordering	Judging a contest: "Who is the best?"
4. Quantifying	Fixing a price: "I say it's worth $20."
5. Combinations	Ordered categories: Good ___x___ Bad

(The example for row 4 / 5 also shows the word *onions* above the "Good ___x___ Bad" line.)

The examples provided in this chapter are short and designed as introductions to the tasks. By consulting the index actual examples of instruments can be found in the body of the text.

PLACING OBJECTS

Placing

Placing tasks are ones in which minimal constraints are made on the subjects in determining the similarity between objects. This can be valuable because no a priori judgments about the underlying dimensions are given and the experimenter is thus able to obtain a scale or measurement that is free from experimental bias. Suppose, for example, the dimensions and relative positions of similarity among six geometric shapes is desired by the experimenter.

One task may be to present the objects on a level surface and to record: (1) the length of time each object is looked at; (2) the length of time they are handled; or (3) the distance they are apart after handling.

Another relatively unstructured task would be to present the subject with a number of objects (for example, the words *sea, sky, sun, red, blue,* and *ice* typed on cards) and a round flat surface to place them on. The subject is asked to move the objects around on the surface until he or she is satisfied with their position. The positions of the objects may be obtained by overlaying a grid on the surface, or using one already imbedded in the surface. The relative positions of the objects, noted in terms of x and y coordinates, can then be used to determine the dissimilarity or distance between the centers of the objects using the well-known formula for distance.

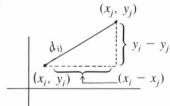

$$d_{ij} = \sqrt{(x_i - x_j)^2 + (y_i - y_j)^2}$$

(See also page 31.)

Example: A circle 18 in. in diameter is placed before the subject. The subject is asked to place cutout members of a family (father, mother, son, daughter) on the circle. After such placement, coordinates of the center (centroid) of the figures are established on a grid imbedded lightly on the circle; distances between objects are obtained using the coordinates.

GROUPING OR CLUSTERING

Clustering consists of placing similar objects together in groups or sets. Example: Subjects are given the letters of the English alphabet—abcdefghijklmnopqrstuvwxyz—each printed on a small card; the task is to place similar-looking letters together. As shown, Subject 1 groups the letters into different and fewer clusters than Subject 2.

Subject 1

Clusters	aceos	bdpgq	fklt	ij	jmnu	vwx	y	r
Cluster Number	1	2	3	4	5	6	7	8

Subject 2

Clusters	ceo	as	bd	pgq	ft	klh	ji	mw	nu	vxyz	r
Cluster Number	1	2	3	4	5	6	7	8	9	10	11

After a *number* of subjects have responded, the proportion of times that any two letters are grouped together constitutes a measure of their similarity (see page 36). Thus, the similarity between any two objects i and j equals the *frequency with which i and j are found in the same groups* divided by the number of subjects. (See also Fig. 2.1.)

Please circle the numbers of each word that you identify as having something in common. Then describe the basis for this grouping on the right side of the page.

Grouping #   1

---

(1) check
2. clock   The characteristic that the encircled words
3. crank   have in common is:
4. cloak
5. clack   all begin with ch
6. creak   and end with k.
7. crock
8. clink
9. croak
10. cluck
11. crack
12. cleek
(13) chuck
(14) chock
15. click
16. crook
(17) chick
(18) chalk
(19) cheek
(20) chink
21. creek
22. clerk
23. crick

(Note: Ten more grouping pages followed this one subject's responses have been recorded.)

FIG. 2.1.   An example of an instrument used in clustering or sorting.

NAMING OBJECTS (CATEGORIZING)

The set of categories is predetermined. Subjects are asked to place an object in a category. For example, a poll is taken and subjects are asked to indicate whether they will sign or not sign a petition about the president's policy on the war. In this case the petition on war policy is the psychological object and the categories are "would sign" and "would not sign." Specifically:

In a recent poll the following results were obtained:

Would Sign	Would Not Sign
48	42

Objects may also be categorized under *specific labels* such as "put all the round ones together."

ORDERING OBJECTS (RANKING)

Direct Ranking

Simple ranking consists of assigning integers 1 to k to k objects, indicating order of preference or judgment.

Example: Given the following job occupations, subjects are asked to order the objects on the basis of their personal desirability.

Garbage Man
Janitor
Mailman
Policeman
Fireman

Ranks for Occupations (k)

		G	J	M	P	F
	A	5	3	4	2	1
Subjects (n)	B	3	4	2	3	1
	C	4	5	3	2	1
	D	4	5	3	1	2
	E	3	5	2	4	1

Rank values (RV) assigned to the jobs and then summed over a number of respondents provide a basic scale of interest for each job (see Simplified Rank

Method of Scaling, page 55). ($RV = k + 1 - R_k$ where k = the number of objects and R_k is the rank of object k; for example, the Rank Value [RV] for mailman [M] for subject A is $RV = 5 + 1 - 4 = 2$)

Conditional Ranking

One of the objects or stimuli is taken as a standard. Subjects are asked to choose which of the (k–1) remaining objects is most similar to the standard; then which of the (k–2) objects is most similar, etc. until all of the objects have been ranked.

Pairs

The subjects or judges are presented the preference objects in all possible pairs and asked to make judgments of similarity and choices between the pairs. Example: the following five objects

are presented in all possible ($^k_2$) or [$k(k - 1)/2$] = 10 ways. The judges may then choose which of each pair has a salient characteristic such as angularity, or they may indicate their preference, or they may do both. In the example the circled objects were chosen as most angular in each pairing.

The votes may be counted for each object and a rank order for the objects results from the rank values provided by the sum of the votes for each object. Incomplete rank values, indicated by ties, may occur (due to circularity; see Chapter 6) when objects are not consistently voted upon. From the foregoing example the votes are as follows:

objects

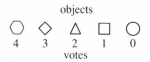

Triadic Comparisons

In making triadic comparisons the objects are formed in all possible ($_3^n$) triples. In this situation the subject is asked to judge which two objects of each triple are most alike and which two are least alike. A set of scores can then be formed from the number of times that any object is judged more like one of a pair. Example: Four objects—*chuck, chock, check, chunk*—formed in all possible ways [$k(k − 1)(k − 2)$]/6 = 4 triples.

1. chuck, chock, check
2. chuck, chock, chunk
3. chuck, check, chunk
4. chock, check, chuck

(In each triple the subjects are asked to judge which two words are most alike and which two least alike.)

Suppose the judgments for a single subject are as follows:

	Most Alike	Least Alike	Remaining
1.	chock–check	chuck–chock	chuck–check
2.	chuck–chunk	chunk–chock	chuck–chock
3.	chuck–chunk	chunk–check	chuck–check
4.	chock–check	check–chunk	chock–chunk
Score:	2	0	1

A matrix (array of scores) for each subject can be formed in which choices are weighted giving 2 points for pairs most alike, 0 for pairs least alike, and 1 for the remaining pairs. The summed scores represent measures of similarity. By subtracting the similarity score from a constant (in this case 5), distances can be formed, and in this case the objects may be approximately arranged in two dimensions as follows:

	Similarity				Distance = (5 − similarity)			
	chuck,	chock,	check,	chunk	chuck,	chock,	check,	chunk
chuck	—				—			
chock	1	—			4	—		
check	2	4	—		3	1	—	
chunk	4	1	0	—	1	4	5	—

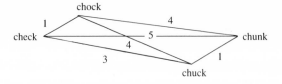

This diagram provides a close approximation to the matrix of distances. The scores for a number of subjects may be summed and averaged and then analyzed in a variety of ways. The data may also be handled as proportions (Torgerson, 1958).

Ranking Pairs

This task consists of ranking pairs of objects whose subsequent scores can be used in multidimensional scaling. For example, if the objects are *man, woman, boy,* and *girl,* six pairs are created and the pairs ranked on judgments of similarity (1 most similar, 6 least similar):

Pairs	Similarity Rank
man–woman	4
boy–girl	3
boy–man	2
boy–woman	5
girl–man	6
girl–woman	1

These ranks may be used, in a matrix of the objects, as direct estimates of distance. For example:

	Man	Woman	Boy	Girl
M	—			
W	4	—		
B	2	5	—	
G	6	1	3	—

Tetrads (Pairs of Pairs)

Pairs of pairs may be formed. Using the objects of the previous example this would be $6(5)/2 = 15$ pairs of pairs. For example:

man–woman or man–boy

man–woman or man–girl

man–woman or woman–boy

man–woman or woman–girl

man–woman or boy–girl

man–boy or man–girl

man–boy or woman–boy

man–boy or woman–girl

man–boy or boy–girl

man–girl or woman–boy

man–girl or woman–girl

man–girl or boy–girl

woman–boy or woman–girl

woman–boy or boy–girl

woman–girl or boy–girl

The 15 "pairs of pairs" can be handled like other paired data. Asking for example, which of each pair is most similar. Such data are useful in looking at the dimensions of *relationships*. Because the pairs increase dramatically with the number of variables this may restrict the use of pairs of pairs. For example, 11 objects generate 1485 pairs of pairs.

Arranging Pairs

It has been customary to arrange the objects in pairs according to the method outlined by Ross (1934). Table A in the Appendix presents balanced orders for the presentation of pairs for odd numbers of objects from 5–17. For even numbers the next higher odd sets of pairs is used, striking out all pairs containing the nonexistent odd object. Ross' pairing for five objects is as follows:

$$K = 5. \qquad 1\text{--}2, \ 5\text{--}3, \ 4\text{--}1, \ 3\text{--}2, \ 4\text{--}5, \ 1\text{--}3, \ 2\text{--}4, \ 5\text{--}1, \ 3\text{--}4, \ 2\text{--}5$$

Pair arrangement may be randomized if care is taken to randomize both the order of the pairs and positions of the objects in the pairs.

Partial Ranks

Gulliksen and Tucker (1961) illustrate a compromise between direct ranking and complete paired comparisons. This scheme involves the use of Balanced Incomplete Block (BIB) designs. Table I in the Appendix shows six designs for various numbers of objects. Cochran and Cox (1957) provide many others. Because it becomes increasingly fatiguing to respond to more than 15 objects that are paired in all possible ways, incomplete block designs can be used. Suppose, for example, students are asked to decide their preference for seven adjectives: (1) powerful, (2) wise, (3) rich, (4) sociable, (5) healthy, (6) honest, and (7) famous. For each row of the BIB using $t = 7$ objects and $k = 3$ ranks, a ranking task is created. Once the ranks for the objects in each row are obtained, the array of paired comparisons for all objects can be derived. Creating this array (matrix) would ordinarily mean that $(7)(6)/2 = 21$ pairs of objects would have to be compared. Asking subjects to make seven ranks of three objects may be an easier task than making choices over 21 pairs. A BIB design for the seven objects in blocks of three (see Table I) is formed as follows:

1. famous __1__ powerful __3__ rich __2__
2. powerful __3__ wise __1__ sociable __2__
3. wise __1__ rich __3__ healthy __2__
4. rich __1__ sociable __3__ honest __2__
5. sociable __3__ healthy __1__ famous __2__
6. healthy __1__ honest __2__ powerful __3__
7. honest __3__ famous __1__ wise __2__

In this example a subject has ranked each row of three adjectives from 1 to 3 in order of preference. By using the rank orders a complete paired matrix of preferences can be derived because each object has been compared with all other objects. The preference matrix is then formed by placing a 1 wherever a certain column object is ranked higher than a row object and a zero otherwise.

If a person's ranks among the seven adjectives were (as shown above)

1	3	2
3	1	2
1	3	2
1	3	2
3	1	2
1	2	3
3	1	2

their converted matrix would look as follows:

		Column Adjectives						
		P	W	R	S	H	Ho	F
	P	—	1	1	1	1	1	1
Row	W		—					1
Adjectives	R	1		—		1		1
	S	1	1		—	1	1	1
	H	1				—		
	Ho	1	1			1	—	1
	F					1		
	Sum	0	5	3	1	5	2	5
					Votes			

In this case the subject ranked and voted most often for famous (F), wise (W), and healthy (H), least often for powerful (P).

One of the author's students Bert Furuta has written a Fortran computer program to convert the partial ranks of a balanced incomplete block design (BIB) into the complete paired comparisons over the same set of variables. The writeup and listing for this program is provided in Chapter 20.

QUANTIFYING OBJECTS (NUMERICAL ASSIGNMENT)

Number Assignment

In making numerical assignments the task can be relatively unstructured. The subject may be given an object and asked to provide a number to go with it. Suppose, for example, the objects are *red, ice, blue, sky, salt, sun,* and *sea;* we could ask for a number that indicates preference or value. The subject might respond as follows:

red	−5
ice	20
blue	23
sky	40
salt	15
sun	135
sea	160

Sometimes the experimenter may wish to restrict the range of the numbers to values between 0 and 100, or 1 and 7, or −4 to +4, and so on. Magnitude estimation has been most effectively explored by Stevens (1951). Usually such scores are standardized or transformed in some way for each individual.

Ratio Estimation

Another method of estimation is *ratio* estimation (Ekman, 1963). In this method the subject is asked to estimate what percent of "A" is contained in "B" and conversely what percent of "B" is contained in "A." Suppose, for example, the letters *o, b,* and *l* are used as stimuli. Subjects are then asked, "Graphically, how much of *o* is contained in *b,* how much of *l* is in *b,*" and so on. The ratios are as follows: *o* in *b, b* in *o, o* in *l, l* in *o, b* in *l, l* in *b.* The results for a single subject are given in the following matrix:

		Column		
		o	*b*	*l*
	o	—	.40	.00
Subject A row	*b*	.90	—	.90
	l	.05	.40	—

The matrix is read, "How much of the column object is contained in the row object?" Thus Subject A estimated 90% of *o* was contained in b but only 40% of *b* was contained in *o.*

This array of data is therefore *asymmetrical* because the column by row entries are not equal to the row by column values. Such array data are generally averaged (using the mean or median) over a number of subjects. The resulting mean ratios are then converted to scalar products (see page 33) and factor analyzed. There are also more recent methods for handling asymmetrical sets of data (Harshman, 1978).

Similarity Between Pairs of Objects

Similarity between objects may also be qualitatively judged and values directly assigned; for example (in this example values are restricted to integers 1 through 5):

These data can be formed into a *symmetrical* array of similarities and subsequently analyzed:

	◯	⬡	▢	△	▱
◯		5	3	3	3
⬡	5		2	1	1
▢	3	2		3	2
△	3	1	3		3
▱	3	1	2	3	

Latency

The length of time it takes to respond is sometimes used as a measure of similarity. In perceptual research this usually requires some sort of shutter and a timing device. Two objects (letters, words, pictures, etc.) are hidden behind a shutter. When the stimuli are exposed a clock starts. The subject is asked to indicate whether the stimuli are the same or different by pressing one of two switches. Once a switch is pressed the clock stops. If the average latency, for example, for the letters b and h is .80, whereas the latency for o and l is .50, one may assume that b and h are more similar than o and l.

COMBINATIONS

Categorized Ratings

It is conceivable that many combinations of the previous task types could be made. Ordered-category scales, however, are the most frequent combination. In this task order is implied by bipolar adjectives that constitute a frame of reference for judgments or choices. Whole numbers are often provided as category definitions. (See Examples 1 and 2 that follow.)

Ordered Categories

In this example the subject checks ($\checkmark$) the appropriate position on the line. In example 2, the subject circles the appropriate number.

Semantic Differential

The ordered category task can be reversed if there are a large number of bipolar adjectives and only a few objects. For example:

The semantic differential (Osgood, Suci, & Tannenbaum, 1957) is a good example of this combination task.

Likert Scale

The Likert (1932) task has minimal definitions of categories in which order is implied. For example:

Pairing and Quantifying

In this case the objects are paired but instead of indicating only choice or preference, degree of preference is also obtained. If, for example, you have four applicants for a job, the applicants can be paired and a degree of preference for each made. For example:

Applicants = Mary—Alice—Grace—Pat

*Mary—Alice	4	Alice—Grace	5
Mary—Grace	2	Alice—Pat	3
Mary—Pat	7	Grace—Pat	6

*circled object is preferred

An array which shows degree of preference can then be established and analyzed.

	M	A	G	P	
M	—		2	7	
A	4	—	5	3	(column is preferred over row)
G			—	6	
P				—	
Σ	4	0	7	16	

In this case the column sums suggest the relative preference for applicant Pat. Combining quantification and preference is an effective way to obtain information. The similarity estimates between the pairs results in a configuration of the objects and the preference data indicate the subjects' position with regard to the map or configuration of the objects.

Clustering, Pairing, and Quantifying

Once a number of objects have been clustered into groups the groups may be paired in all possible ways and measures of similarity assigned to the paired groups. If, for example, one clusters the following words—*ice, blue, sea, sky, salt*—as follows:

(1) (ice, salt)
(2) blue
(3) (sea, sky)

The clusters may be paired and rated as follows:

(ice, salt)—blue	3
(ice, salt)—(sea, sky)	3
blue—(sea, sky)	6

The clusters may then be arranged in a similarity matrix and analyzed.

	Similarity		
	1	*2*	*3*
1			
2	3	—	
3	3	6	—

By converting the similarities to distance by subtracting from a constant larger than the maximum rating (say 10), a picture of the relationship among the three clusters can be drawn.

(ice–salt)

7   7

4

(sea, sky)   blue

Clustering prior to pairing is a way of reducing the number of objects so that using paired comparisons becomes a reasonable technique. Usually the centroid object of a cluster is chosen to represent the group in the pairing.

DISCUSSION

The combinations presented here are ones that have been found most useful to the author. The examples given are small and the analysis rudimentary. The reader should explore other combinations of tasks.

Two Useful Tasks

Two tasks with high potential for analysis consist of: (1) estimating similarities between pairs of objects; and (2) ordered category ratings.

The first task might look as follows:

Word Pairs	Degree of Meaning Similarity							
	0	1	2	3	4	5	6	
1. rose—rows	___	___	X	___	___	___	___	1.
2. rose—date	___	___	___	X	___	___	___	2.
3. rose—ate	___	X	___	___	___	___	___	3.
4. rows—date	X	___	___	___	___	___	___	4.
5. rows—ate	X.	___	___	___	___	___	___	5.
6. date—ate	___	___	___	___	___	___	X	6.

A check is placed in appropriate box on the right. Responses for a Subject are shown.

The second task might look as follows:

	Strongly Agree	Agree	Undecided	Disagree	Strongly Disagree
1. The instructor appears well organized.	(SA)	A	U	D	DS
2. The instructor is interested in the subject.	SA	(A)	U	D	DS
3. This course has improved my cognitive skills.	(SA)	A	U	D	DS
4. Morale in class has been positive.	SA	(A)	U	D	DS
5. The instructor is sensitive to student feelings.	SA	A	(U)	D	DS

Subject A's responses have been circled.

Both of these tasks can be used to create similarity matrices about the objects. Only the first, however, can be used to analyze the responses of a single subject. This is because, in estimating similarity between pairs of objects the estimates can be directly placed into an object by object matrix. For example:

	Subject A			
	Words			
	rose	*rows*	*date*	*ate*
rose				
rows	2			
date	3	0		
ate	1	0	6	

This simple matrix can be explored multidimensionally or several matrices can be averaged and analyzed.

In the second task, however, a single subject's responses

Subject A $\begin{cases} 1 & 2 & 3 & 4 & 5 & \text{Item Number} \\ \text{SA} & \text{A} & \text{SA} & \text{A} & \text{U} & \text{Response} \\ 5 & 4 & 5 & 4 & 3 & \text{Weight} \end{cases}$

are insufficient for multidimensional analysis and many responses are required before relationships between the items can be analyzed.

Ranking versus Rating

Because the most widely used methods for obtaining *direct* judgments of similarity are ranking and rating, it is worthwhile to investigate whether or not the separate scaling of ranking and rating responses to the same pairs of psychological objects achieves the same results. (See Ranking, page 15 and Similarity Rating Between Pairs, page 19).

The rating task usually involves assigning estimates of similarity for each pair of objects on a scale of some stated range, whereas ranking calls for the stepwise ordering of pairs of objects in terms of increasing or decreasing similarity. Past experience indicates that although ranking maximizes the transitivity (ordering) of pairs, it is the more demanding of the two tasks (takes more time). The difficulty it presents increases dramatically with an increase in the number of psychological objects. Rating, on the other hand, seems to be less demanding, requiring a shorter time for completion. In order to determine whether rating can substitute adequately for ranking, judgments of similarity using both rating and ranking methods must be compared. One such study was done using all pairs of seven campus places (Villanueva & Dunn-Rankin, 1973). The seven campus "places" were: *classroom, dormitory, library, cafeteria, gymnasium, theater,* and *laboratory*. The sequence of pairs, as they appeared in the rating sheet and the ranking pile, followed the optimum presentation order recommended by Ross (1934) and was the same for both tasks and for all S's.

For the rating task, each subject was instructed to assign any number from zero to 100 to each pair according to how similar the two places appeared. The most similar pair would have the highest rating, whereas the most dissimilar would have the lowest rating. The 100-point rating scale was chosen because of its familiarity and relatively wide range. For the ranking task, each subject (S) was instructed to sort the pairs initially into two piles consisting of (1) similar and (2) dissimilar pairs of objects. This initial sorting procedure had previously been found effective in simplifying the ranking task (Green & Carmone, 1970). The subject was next instructed to rank order the pairs in both piles according to the similarity between the two paired "places" on each card. The position at any one pair in the pile from the most similar to the most dissimilar determined its rank. The similarity configurations derived from both methods were then matched.

The authors concluded that with *sophisticated* judges and *familiar* objects, both methods produce similar configurations under multidimensional scaling, and so rating can be substituted for ranking. Under similar conditions, the use of the rating method will economize the time and effort needed for tasks requiring judgment of similarity. Because the tediousness of the ranking task increases the occurrence of undesirable response sets and random responding, particularly with young subjects, it seems worthwhile to investigate whether rating can also substitute accurately for ranking among children.

DATA TYPES AND ASSOCIATED PROCEDURES

The data that are collected after the presentation of different kinds of tasks can be identified as consisting of four major forms. (See Shepard, 1972a,b for a more complete discussion.) These forms of data are Dominance, Profile, Proximity, and Conjoint. See Chapter 20 for specific source programs and examples.

Dominance Data

One subject, object, or group is chosen, preferred, or judged over another (i.e., it dominates). The data may be directly ranked. Pairs may be formed and indirectly ranked by judgment or preference for one object of each pair. Pairs of pairs may be formed and indirectly ranked.

Analysis of dominance data could use one or more of the following methods and corresponding computer programs described in this text.

Method	Benefits	Program
Variable Stable Rank	Simple to use and understand. Scaled objects can be compounded statistically. Can handle direct ranks and preference.	
Thurstone Case V	Normality assumptions met. Analysis of variance scale reliability.	
Circular Triad Analysis	Analysis of circularity.	
Preference Vector Fitting	Multidimensional. Description of space and direction of individuals paired preference.	

Profile Data

Subjects respond to or are evaluated by a set of variables or stimuli. Objects or variables may also be scored. The variables can be quantitative, binary, or qualitative. Ordered categories fit this data type. By interrelating the columns or rows of this basic data matrix (subjects by variables) a *proximity data* set can be formed between objects or subjects.

Analysis of profile data could be directly handled by one or more of the following programs:

Method	Benefits
Successive Intervals Scaling	Weights category widths under normality assumptions.
Guttman's Scalogram	Scales data based on order; provides measures of scalability.
Ordered Category	Easy to create; uses item analysis techniques in revision.

Proximity Data

The data are some form of similarity, confusion, association, correlation, or distance measures between pairs of objects or subjects. The data can be drawn from profile information or by methods of direct appraisal and assessment.

Analysis of proximity data could use one or more of the following programs:

Method	Benefits
Graphic Similarity	Lack of assumptions concerning object relations; insightful; hand calculation is easy.
Metric Hierarchical	Provides a metric index for group similarity.
Nonmetric Hierarchical	Uses order relations to provide maximum and minimum clusters.

Partitions (K mean)	Fits best group specification.
Metric divisive	Can accomodate large numbers.
Factoring	Provides orthogonal description of space; well known; statistically viable.
MDS	Few assumptions; can be used on a few subjects or objects; great flexibility.
Individual differences scaling	Provides description or object space; weights subjects on dimensions.

Conjoint Data

The position of a point in a matrix is represented by its value in two or more simple dimensions. Thus a point could represent a person with regard to health, sociability, and intelligence at the same time. Although a program such as KYST handles conjoint data, its analysis is not discussed in this text.

TABLE 2.1
Procedures Associated with Data Types

Methods	Dominance	Data Type Profile	Proximity
Unidimensional			
Variance Stable Rank	*		
Case V	*		
Successive Intervals		*	
Guttman Sealing		*	
Clustering			
Graphic Similarity			*
Metric-Agglomerative-Hierarchical			*
Nonmetric-Agglomerative-Hierarchical			*
Partitioning-K means iterative			*
Metric diversive			*
Multidimensional			
Factoring			*
Fitting Preference Vectors	*		
Multidimensional scaling	*		
Individual differences scaling	*		*
Preference mapping	*	*	

Table 2.1 summarizes which procedures in this text are used to handle the first three data types.

3 Measures of Proximity

Proximities are numbers that tell how similar or different objects are. A great number of proximity measures are available that relate to the tasks and types of data that have been presented. These can be categorized as measures of: (1) correlation; (2) distance; (3) direct estimates of similarity; and (4) association. In order to analyze a set of objects by clustering or multidimensional scaling, some measure of similarity or dissimilarity between all the pairs of the objects is needed.

CORRELATION

$$r_{xy} = \frac{\Sigma\, XY - (\Sigma\, X\, \Sigma\, Y/N)}{\sqrt{\{\Sigma\, X^2 - [(\Sigma\, X)^2/N]\}\{\Sigma\, Y^2 - [(\Sigma\, Y)^2/N]\}}}$$

The Pearson Product Moment Correlation is the most common measure of similarity (see Factor Analysis Chapter 15). The measure can be applied to an $N \times K$ (subjects by objects) set of raw data to generate a square $K \times K$ (object by object) symmetric matrix of correlations (r_{xy}). (A symmetric matrix is a square array of numbers whose entries above the diagonal equal those below the diagonal.) Because information in a symmetric matrix is redundant, sometimes only the upper or lower triangle of entries is used.

The procedure is graphically illustrated as follows:

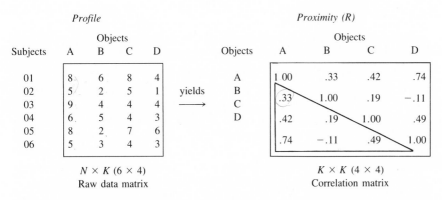

FIG. 3.1.   An illustration of how profile data yields a matrix of proximities (correlations) between objects (variables).

In this example the four columns of objects are intercorrelated in all possible ways. In the *R* matrix the lower triangle is outlined.

Sometimes the *subjects* are intercorrelated using the objects as profile information. Care must be taken in this instance because two subjects can be highly correlated (because their profile has the same pattern) yet differ widely in the level of their scores. This is true, for example, with subjects 01 and 02 in Fig. 3.1.

01	8	6	8	4
02	5	2	5	1
Difference	3	4	3	3

In this case the difference between the two profiles is relatively large yet they correlate highly $r = .97$. Should such difference in profile weight be important, other measures must be obtained, such as, the sum of the absolute differences

$$\sum_{i=1}^{K} \left| X_i - Y_i \right|$$

or some measure of Euclidean distance.

The significance of the Pearson correlation (significance means a correlation so large that it wouldn't occur very often by chance, i.e., 5 times in 100) can be estimated by the following formula:

$$\text{Significant } r_{.05} \cong \frac{2}{\sqrt{N+2}}$$

If $N = 14$ pairs the approximate correlation needed is $2/\sqrt{16}$ or .50. A t test can be used to find the significance of r at other probability levels.

Kendall's Tau Correlation

Kendall's (1952) tau (a measure of similarity) has special relevance for measuring proximity because it is a rank order correlation coefficient with fewer assumptions than Pearson's r. It can be applied to ordered category scales and it forms the base for other widely used measures of association, such as Goodman–Kruskal's gamma (γ). In r_{tau} all possible pairs of scores are compared for each variable separately. When $+1$ is assigned to concordant pairs and -1 to discordant pairs the tau coefficient can be calculated by finding the sum of the products of the concordant or discordant scores in the two sets of pairings and dividing by the number of possible pairs $\binom{N}{2}$. (A pair is concordant if the numbers associated with each pair are in ascending rank order, otherwise the pair is discordant.)

Suppose the following rank data are given:

	Achievement	Maturation
S_1	2	3
S_2	1	2
S_3	3	4
S_4	4	6
S_5	6	5
S_6	5	1

The six subjects can be paired in $\binom{6}{2}$ or 15 ways and scored as follows:

	S_1S_2	S_1S_3	S_1S_4	S_1S_5	S_1S_6	S_2S_3	S_2S_4	S_2S_5	S_2S_6	S_3S_4	S_3S_5	S_3S_6	S_4S_5	S_4S_6	S_5S_6
ACH	-1	$+1$	$+1$	$+1$	$+1$	$+1$	$+1$	$+1$	$+1$	$+1$	$+1$	$+1$	$+1$	$+1$	-1
MAT	-1	$+1$	$+1$	$+1$	-1	$+1$	$+1$	$+1$	-1	$+1$	$+1$	-1	-1	-1	-1
Product	$+1$	$+1$	$+1$	$+1$	-1	$+1$	$+1$	$+1$	-1	$+1$	$+1$	-1	-1	-1	$+1$

(C) Number of positive products = 10 by summing the positive scores

and

(D) Number of negative products = 5 by summing the negative scores

$$S = C - D = 10 - 5 = 5 \text{ (See Appendix, Table E, for significance of } S).$$

$$\text{Kendall's tau} = \frac{S}{\binom{N}{2}} = \frac{5}{15} = .33$$

Wilcoxon & Wilcox (1964) have shown that S can also be calculated graphically. In this case one of the set of scores is rank ordered. Lines are drawn connecting numbers of equal rank in the two sets of data. The number of intersections (or inversions of the second set) called I is doubled and subtracted from $\binom{N}{2}$, or

$$S = \binom{N}{2} - 2I$$

For example

	Achievement	Motivation
S_2	1	2
S_1	2	3
S_3	3	4
S_4	4	6
S_6	5	1
S_5	6	5

$I = 5$, $S = 15 - 2(5)$ or $S = 5$

A computer program (KENTAU) has been written to calculate Kendall's rank correlations and is documented in chapter 20.

Gamma Correlation

Gamma is simply the number of concordant products minus the number of discordant products divided by the sum of the concordant and discordant products or

$$\gamma = \frac{N_C - N_D}{N_C + N_D}$$

If there are no ties in the data, gamma (γ) will equal tau. If ties are present gamma will be greater than tau.

DISTANCES

Measures of distance are dissimilarity measures of proximity. They can solve the problem of similar profile patterns that vary in magnitude. The distance measure between two points in a plane is

$$d_{ij} = \sqrt{(X_i - X_j)^2 + (Y_i - Y_j)^2}$$

Distance calculations are often applied to a profile of standardized scores.

$$z_i = \frac{x_i - \bar{x}}{s} \qquad s = \text{std. dev.}$$

The Mahalanobis d^2 statistic, however, standardizes the variables before calculating the Euclidean distance by dividing each dimensional difference by the variance of that variable. For example:

$$d_{ij}^2 = \frac{(X_i - X_j)^2}{s_x^2} + \frac{(Y_i - Y_j)^2}{s_y^2}$$

The formula for Euclidean distance can be generalized for r dimensions using the following formula

$$d_{ij} = \left[\sum_{t=1}^{r} (X_i - X_j)^2 \right]^{1/2}$$

where t runs from 1 to r dimensions and $\frac{1}{2}$ indicates the square root of the sums of the squared differences.

In these cases the data are in some form of an N by K matrix that yields a square symmetric matrix of distances. Using the data from Fig. 3.1, we have the following Euclidean distances between the *subjects*.

		K Subjects								Subjects				
		1	2	3	4	5	6		1	2	3	4	5	6
Objects								Subjects						
	A	8	5	9	6	8	5	1	—					
	B	6	2	4	5	2	3	2	6.6	—				
N	C	8	5	4	4	7	4	3	4.6	5.5	—			
	D	4	1	4	3	6	3	4	4.7	5.9	3.3	—		
								5	4.6	6.2	4.2	5.6	—	
			$N \times K$ (4 × 6)					6	5.9	2.4	4.2	2.2	5.3	—
			Raw data matrix											

$K \times K$ (6 × 6)
D matrix

A more general formula of distance, called the Minkowski metric, can be written as follows:

$$d_{ij(p)} = \left[\sum_{t=1}^{r} |X_{it} - X_{jt}|^p \right]^{1/p}$$

When $p = 2$ the formula is equal to Euclidean distance. If $p = 1$, the formula reduces to:

$$d_{ij} = \sum_{t=1}^{r} |X_{it} - X_{jt}|$$

commonly known as the city block metric. A computer program (DISSIM) has been written to calculate distances and is documented in Chapter 20.

SCALAR PRODUCTS

Distances and correlations can be related by using scalar products. In order to understand how distances and correlations can be related it is necessary to review the law of cosines. Remembering that in a right triangle the cosine equals the length of the adjacent side divided by the length of the hypotenuse,

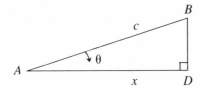

$$\cos \theta = \frac{x}{c} \text{ and } x = c \cos \theta.$$

Given the distances between three points, A, B, and C as shown in Fig. 3.2,

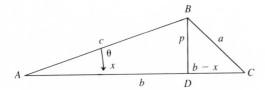

FIG. 3.2.   Triangle created by points A, B, and C.

$c^2 = x^2 + p^2$	In Δ ABD	1
$p^2 = c^2 - x^2$		2
$p^2 = a^2 - (b - x)^2$	In Δ BCD	3
$c^2 - x^2 = a^2 - (b - x)^2$	substituting for p^2 in (2)	4
$a^2 = c^2 - x^2 + (b - x)^2$		5
$a^2 = c^2 + b^2 - 2bx$	From (1) substituting $c \cos \theta$ for x	6
$a^2 = c^2 + b^2 - 2bc \cos \theta$		7

and

$$bc \cos \theta = \frac{c^2 + b^2 - a^2}{2} \qquad\qquad 8$$

We know therefore that the distance (a) between two points (B and C) can be obtained by knowledge of the length of two vectors (that terminate at B and C) that have the same origin and by knowing the size of the angle included between the two vectors.

The left-hand side of Equation 8 is called the scalar product and is often taken as a substitute for the correlation between the two points represented by the vectors. The correlation is sometimes written

$$r_{ij} = h_i h_j \cos \theta_{ij} \qquad (h = \text{length of vector})$$

when the data have been standardized.

If two vectors are of unit (1.000) length and the angle between them is acute, then the cosine of the included angle should directly reflect their correlation. For example

if

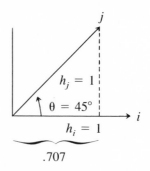

then

$$r_{ij} = \cos 45° = .707$$

If a perpendicular is drawn from the end of unit vector h_j to h_i its projection represents the scalar product.

An evaluation of the scalar product and therefore the correlation can be made with only a knowledge of the distance between the objects. Suppose, for example, one knew only the distances between objects i, j, and k as follows:

$$d_{ij} = 10$$

$$d_{ik} = 8$$

$$d_{jk} = 6$$

Suppose also that interest is in the scalar product between j and k (call this value b_{jk}).

From step 8 we know that

$$b_{jk} = \frac{1}{2}(d_{ij}^2 + d_{ik}^2 - d_{jk}^2)$$

$$= \frac{1}{2}(10^2 + 8^2 - 6^2)$$

$$= 64$$

Sketching the distances using a compass reveals the configuration shown in Fig. 3.3.

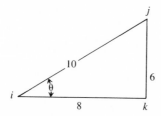

FIG. 3.3.   Illustration of equality between b_{jk} and scalar product.

Measuring θ we find it to be 37°. Therefore

$$b_{jk} = d_{ij}d_{ik} \cos 37°$$

$$= (10)(8)(.8)$$

$$= 64$$

A specific distance (d_{jk}) can be found by:

$$d_{jk} = \sqrt{d_{ij}^2 + d_{ik}^2 - 2b_jk}$$

$$= \sqrt{100 + 64 - 2(64)}$$

$$= 6$$

Several methods in multidimensional scaling convert similarities to distances to scalar products because the algebra associated with their solutions is amenable to this measure of proximity. The methods may also calculate the scalar product based on the *coordinates* of the two points. This scalar product

$$b_{jk} = \sum_t^r x_{jt}x_{kt}$$

is known as the dot product, and x_j and x_k are the coordinates of objects j and k on dimension t. The sum of the cross products of the coordinates, b_{jk}, provides the scalar product. In the foregoing triangle, if the coordinates of j are $(8, 6)$ and of k are $(8, 0)$ (i is at the origin) then $b_{jk} = 8 \cdot 8 + 6 \cdot 0 = 64$.

A computer program has been written to calculate scalar products. See SCALAR, chapter 20.

DIRECT ESTIMATION

Usually direct estimates of similarity are gathered in some form of pairwise comparisons. Instead of asking for simple preference or judgment, degrees of preference are sought by the experimenter. In this case a square matrix of similarity is obtained from the pairwise data. Direct estimates can be obtained by a numerical assignment, ratio estimation, or measures of latency (see page 17).

Example: Given four objects *A, B, C,* and *D* paired in all possible ways. If two subjects make direct estimates of similarity between each pair of objects their raw data might look as follows:

Estimates of Similarity

| | \multicolumn{6}{c}{*Pairs*} |
	AB	*AC*	*AD*	*BC*	*ED*	*CD*
Subject 01	7	4	1	5	2	6
Subject 02	5	5	2	6	3	7

For each subject a matrix of direct similarities results

| | \multicolumn{4}{c}{*Subject 1*} | | \multicolumn{4}{c}{*Subject 2*} |
	A	*B*	*C*	*D*		*A*	*B*	*C*	*D*
A					*A*				
B	7				*B*	5			
C	4	5			*C*	5	6		
D	1	2	6		*D*	2	3	7	

These data can be analyzed together by averaging the scores, or analyzed separately for each subject, or both.

ASSOCIATION

In free clustering where subjects are asked to group similar objects together, different subjects may include the same objects in their groups. Should two objects be frequently placed together by the subjects the assumption is that they are similar. An index of this similarity is the proportion of times any two objects are found in the same group. Suppose, for example, five subjects group the words shown as follows:

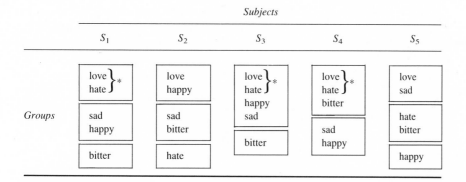

Because love and hate are put together in a group by three of the five subjects the similarity score is 3/5 or .60.

A matrix of all the proportions for the foregoing data is as follows:

	1 love	2 hate	3 sad	4 happy	5 bitter
1 love	—				
2 hate	.60	—			
3 sad	.40	.20	—		
4 happy	.40	.20	.60	—	
5 bitter	.20	.40	.20	.00	—

Other less commonly used overlap estimates include:

1. The sum of the minimum estimated percentage between two variables or categories.

$$\sum_{i=1}^{K} X_i \text{ or } Y_i \text{ where } X \text{ or } Y \text{ is minimum}$$

For example:

Subject n	X Real Life	Y Ideal Life	Min. (X or Y)
1. Work	50%	30%	30%
2. Play	25%	50%	25%
3. Rest	25%	20%	20%
Σ	100%	100%	75%

The 75% represents the similarity between a real and ideal life for subject n.

2. The percentage of overlap between two variables.

Σp_{ij} where i or j is minimum $= \%$ overlap

	i	j	Min. (i or j)
1	.6	.3	.3
2	.2	.2	.2
3	.2	.3	.2
4	0	.2	0
			.7 Σ min. proportions (measure of association)

For example, estimated time spent for various activities over a 24-hour period are given in the following table:

	Ideal	Real	Minimum
Teaching	3	3	3
Recreation	3	3	3
Writing	1	1	1
Research	3	1	1
Eating	1	1	1
Sleeping	8	8	8
Entertainment	2	2	2
Travel	½	1	½
Social	2	1	1
Misc.	½	3	½
	24	24	22

% overlap   22/24 = relationship between
ideal and real

A computer program (PEROVER) has been written to calculate the percent overlap and is documented in Chapter 20.

GOWER'S SIMILARITY MEASURE

Gower (1972) has defined a general measure of similarity between two subjects or objects that can combine qualitative, binary, and quantitative data. The measure can be used independently on a set of scores of a single type or on a mixture of scores. This index is

$$\text{Similarity}_{ij} = S_{ij} = \frac{\sum\limits_{k=1}^{r} s_{ijk}}{\sum\limits_{k=1}^{r} w_{ijk}}$$

s_{ijk} = similarity measure between objects i and j for k variables

w_{ijk} = weight associated with each i, j, and k

The weights (w_{ijk}) are usually 1 for each variable so that the $\Sigma\ w_{ijk}$ for all variables will ordinarily be the number of different variables r. If a comparison is not valid, or variable k is unknown or absent for one or both of the objects being compared, then the w_{ijk} is equal to 0. s_{ijk} is computed as follows:

Binary: s_{ij} = 1 if values of variable are same for both objects.

Qualitative: s_{ij} = 1 if same quality is present in both objects.

Quantitative $s_{ij} = 1 - \dfrac{|x_{ik} - x_{jk}|}{R_k}$ where x is the score and R is the range of the variable k.

If, for example, subjects are measured on IQ, reading score, sex, and ethnic origin as follows:

	Quantitative		Binary	Qualitative
Subjects	IQ	Reading	Sex*	Ethnic Origin
1	100	50	1	Caucasian
2	90	50	2	Japanese
3	110	45	1	Japanese
4	115	60	2	Filipino
5	130	54	1	Caucasian

*1 = male, 2 = female

The similarity between each pair of subjects can be calculated. The similarity between Subjects 1 and 2 is used as an example.

Measure	Variable		$s_{12_{(k)}}$	w_{12_k}	s_{12_k}/w_{12_k}
(1) Quant:	IQ	$s_{(12)_1} = 1 - \dfrac{100 - 90}{40} = $	.75	1	.75
(2) Quant:	Reading	$s_{(12)_2} = 1 - \dfrac{50 - 50}{15} = $	1.0	1	1.0
(3) Binary:	Sex	$s_{(12)_3} = 0$	0	1	0
(4) Qual:	E.O.	$s_{(12)_4} = 0$	0	1	0
	Sum			4	1.75

$$S_{12} = \frac{\sum_{k=1}^{4} S_{12_{(k)}}}{\sum_{k=1}^{4} w_{12_{(k)}}} = \frac{1.75}{4} = .44$$

Table 3.1 presents all the pairwise measures of similarity for these data.

TABLE 3.1
Set of S_{ij} Measures

	1	2	3	4	5
1	—				
2	.44	—			
3	.60	.54	—		
4	.24	.43	.22	—	
5	.75	.07	.48	.31	—

A number of computer programs are useful in establishing measures of proximity (similarity or distance). Most programs require that the data be translated from raw form (subject by object data) into some form of proximity matrix (usually object by object).

The most common measure of similarity used is Pearson's r correlation. All computer centers have programs to calculate this similarity measure between pairs of objects. Not so common is the calculation of Kendall's tau although it is found in SAS and SPSS (see page 30). The program KENTAU is detailed in Chapter 20. GOWER and SCALAR, less common algorithims for measuring similarity are documented in Chapter 20. Distance measures are not as common and the program DISSIM provides this index. A listing is provided as a guide. Measures of association are even less available. PEROVER should be easily adaptable (also detailed in Chapter 20). The next chapter introduces another measure of distance based on the difference between judges who do free clustering.

4 Interjudge Differences Following Free Clustering

This chapter is concerned with measuring and displaying distributions of differences among judges following free clustering. By using a computer to generate random distributions of differences the probability distributions for $k = 3$ to 20 objects were determined and are presented in Table J in the Appendix. Theoretical analyses are used to create general formulas for the mean and standard deviations of the differences for varying k. The results should have value for assessing interjudge reliability and for analyzing object similarity matrices because the responses of groups of different judges could be analyzed separately.

OBJECT SIMILARITY

Measuring object similarity using the method of free clustering is gaining in popularity. Instructions are usually simple, and because no structure is imposed on the subject's selection, response bias is reduced. More importantly, measures of object similarity derived from the judges' clustering can be adequately analyzed by the methods of multidimensional scaling.

Subjects are usually asked to judge or select objects that are most similar and form them into groups or clusters. The number of clusters is variable and an object by itself can constitute a cluster. Suppose there are k objects and n judges and let $a, b, c,$ and d denote typical objects while i and j are typical judges. We number the clusters of each judge; $i(a)$ denotes the number of the cluster into which judge i places object a. A measure of proximity or similarity between any two objects is found by calculating their "percent overlap," that is, the number of times the judges have placed the objects in the same group divided by the number of judges. More formally:

if

$$i(a) = i(b), \text{ then } x_i^{(ab)} = 1$$

if

$$i(a) \neq i(b), \text{ then } x_i^{(ab)} = 0$$

$$S_{ab} = \sum_{i=1}^{n} \frac{x_i^{(ab)}}{n}$$

See measures of Association Chapter 3 for examples.

DISTRIBUTIONS OF INTERJUDGE DIFFERENCES

The differences among judges' free-clustering behavior, however, has not been fully explored. Often, judges will *not* cluster objects in similar ways. It is a question of interest whether some judges should be excluded or separated from the rest and the analysis done over separate sets of judges.

One way to determine the difference between two judges is to pair the objects in all possible $\binom{k}{2}$ ways and create a vector or matrix of ones and zeros for each judge by providing a score of one when paired group numbers are the same and zero otherwise (the same group numbers occur when the objects have been placed in the same group). The difference between two judges is simply the sum of the squared or absolute differences between these matrices (Boorman & Arabie, 1972). More formally X is a function of two judges, i and j, defined by

$$d_{ij} = X(i, j) = |\{(a, b) : 1 \leq a < b \leq k \text{ and } i(a) = i(b) \text{ and } j(a) \neq j(b)$$
$$\text{or } i(a) \neq i(b) \text{ and } j(a) = j(b)\}|$$

Notice $X(i, j)$ simply counts the number of pairs of objects that one judge thought were similar and the other did not. If we let

$$X_{ab}(i, j) = \begin{array}{l} 1 \text{ if } i(a) = i(b) \text{ and } j(a) \neq j(b) \\ 1 \text{ if } i(a) \neq i(b) \text{ and } j(a) = j(b) \\ 0 \text{ otherwise} \end{array} \tag{1}$$

then

$$d_{ij} = X(i, j) = \sum_{1 \leq a < b \leq k} X_{ab}(i, j). \tag{2}$$

where d_{ij} is the dissimilarity between judges i and j.

DISTRIBUTIONS OF RANDOM DIFFERENCES

Suppose three objects are to be clustered. Any time a judge groups two or more objects together the members of the cluster become indistinguishable. The chance probability of the difference between two judges can be determined by assuming a random uniform distribution of letters, each representing an object. If two or more identical letters are randomly drawn they constitute a random cluster. For three objects ($k = 3$) the letters A, B, and C represent the objects. If one assumes random selection with replacement, k^k or 27 different arrangements of the letters can occur. Table 4.1 presents the complete enumeration of possible differences between two judges for $k = 3$ objects.

Because $k = 3$ there are three possible letters (A, B, and C) that can be selected randomly. If one draws an A on each of three consecutive trials, all objects form one cluster. This is also true if a B is drawn in three consecutive trials. The partition (A, A, A) generates the same random clustering as (B, B, B). There are, therefore, only five possible groupings of three objects: (A, A, A); (A, A, B); (A, B, A); (B, A, A); and (A, B, C). The sum of differences between each pair of different arrangements can be 0, 1, 2, or 3.

Table 4.2 presents the cumulative probability distributions derived from the enumeration of differences in Table 4.1. Table 4.2 suggests that if one judge places three objects together in one group, and another groups each element or object separately, the difference between these two clusterings would not occur very often by chance. That is, it would only occur with a probability of .049.

Because most objects to be clustered are presented randomly, the order in which the objects are selected to be placed together is not considered important. Thus, if there are five objects, A, B, C, D, E, and one judge chooses to place B and C together first and another judge puts B and C together last, the two clusterings are not considered to be different. In this study an object is restricted to be a member of only one group. That is, an object does not share group membership.

Although the probability of a particular combination can be theoretically determined, the probability distribution of the differences between any two cluster combinations is more difficult. This is because a combination such as $AABBC$ is the same as $BBAAC$ under free clustering but is not the same under rules for permutations. Thus the differences are not isomorphic to the distributions of similar elements in a specific clustering. Determining the exact probability distributions of interjudge differences does not seem feasible because as k increases, the number of possible pairs of differences increases dramatically. Therefore, Monte Carlo methods were used to calculate distributions of random differences for k objects from 3(1) 20, 25, and 30.

Table J in the Appendix presents these Monte Carlo distributions in cumulative probability form. These distributions were generated using the uniform random digit generator from the IMSL Library (1980).

TABLE 4.1

Possible Distribution of Differences in Free Clustering when k = 3

Possible Clusters	AAA	BBB	CCC	AAB	AAC	BBA	BBC	CCA	CCB	ABA	ACA	BAB	BCB	CAC	CBC	BAA	CAA	ABB	CBB	ACC	BCC	ABC	ACB	BAC	BCA	CAB	CBA
AAA	0	0	0	2	2	2	2	2	2	2	2	2	2	2	2	2	2	2	2	2	2	3	3	3	3	3	3
BBB	0	0	0	2	2	2	2	2	2	2	2	2	2	2	2	2	2	2	2	2	2	3	3	3	3	3	3
CCC	0	0	0	2	2	2	2	2	2	2	2	2	2	2	2	2	2	2	2	2	2	3	3	3	3	3	3
AAB	2	2	2	0	0	0	0	0	0	2	2	2	2	2	2	2	2	2	2	2	2	1	1	1	1	1	1
AAC	2	2	2	0	0	0	0	0	0	2	2	2	2	2	2	2	2	2	2	2	2	1	1	1	1	1	1
BBA	2	2	2	0	0	0	0	0	0	2	2	2	2	2	2	2	2	2	2	2	2	1	1	1	1	1	1
BBC	2	2	2	0	0	0	0	0	0	2	2	2	2	2	2	2	2	2	2	2	2	1	1	1	1	1	1
CCA	2	2	2	0	0	0	0	0	0	2	2	2	2	2	2	2	2	2	2	2	2	1	1	1	1	1	1
CCB	2	2	2	0	0	0	0	0	0	2	2	2	2	2	2	2	2	2	2	2	2	1	1	1	1	1	1
ABA	2	2	2	2	2	2	2	2	2	0	0	0	0	0	0	2	2	2	2	2	2	1	1	1	1	1	1
ACA	2	2	2	2	2	2	2	2	2	0	0	0	0	0	0	2	2	2	2	2	2	1	1	1	1	1	1
BAB	2	2	2	2	2	2	2	2	2	0	0	0	0	0	0	2	2	2	2	2	2	1	1	1	1	1	1
BCB	2	2	2	2	2	2	2	2	2	0	0	0	0	0	0	2	2	2	2	2	2	1	1	1	1	1	1
CAC	2	2	2	2	2	2	2	2	2	0	0	0	0	0	0	2	2	2	2	2	2	1	1	1	1	1	1
CBC	2	2	2	2	2	2	2	2	2	0	0	0	0	0	0	2	2	2	2	2	2	1	1	1	1	1	1
BAA	2	2	2	2	2	2	2	2	2	2	2	2	2	2	2	0	0	0	0	0	0	1	1	1	1	1	1
CAA	2	2	2	2	2	2	2	2	2	2	2	2	2	2	2	0	0	0	0	0	0	1	1	1	1	1	1
ABB	2	2	2	2	2	2	2	2	2	2	2	2	2	2	2	0	0	0	0	0	0	1	1	1	1	1	1
CBB	2	2	2	2	2	2	2	2	2	2	2	2	2	2	2	0	0	0	0	0	0	1	1	1	1	1	1
ACC	2	2	2	2	2	2	2	2	2	2	2	2	2	2	2	0	0	0	0	0	0	1	1	1	1	1	1
BCC	2	2	2	2	2	2	2	2	2	2	2	2	2	2	2	0	0	0	0	0	0	1	1	1	1	1	1
ABC	3	3	3	1	1	1	1	1	1	1	1	1	1	1	1	1	1	1	1	1	1	0	0	0	0	0	0
ACB	3	3	3	1	1	1	1	1	1	1	1	1	1	1	1	1	1	1	1	1	1	0	0	0	0	0	0
BAC	3	3	3	1	1	1	1	1	1	1	1	1	1	1	1	1	1	1	1	1	1	0	0	0	0	0	0
BCA	3	3	3	1	1	1	1	1	1	1	1	1	1	1	1	1	1	1	1	1	1	0	0	0	0	0	0
CAB	3	3	3	1	1	1	1	1	1	1	1	1	1	1	1	1	1	1	1	1	1	0	0	0	0	0	0
CBA	3	3	3	1	1	1	1	1	1	1	1	1	1	1	1	1	1	1	1	1	1	0	0	0	0	0	0

TABLE 4.2
Probability of Cluster Differences
when k = 3

d	f	p	cp
0	153	.210	.999
1	216	.296	.789
2	324	.444	.493
3	2̸6̸	.049	.049

$\sigma^2 = .740$

NCE OF DIFFERENCES

distributions of interjudge differences

dges is $d_{ij} = \Sigma X_{ab}$ where $X_{ab}(i, j)$ is
gle pair (a, b) of the k objects is

and b together and $1 - (1/k)$ is the
d b together. The constant 2 results
.

) (if $(a, b) \neq (c, d)$) the variance of
$X_{ab})^2$ and $X_{ab}^2 = X_{ab}$]:

$$\frac{\cdots}{k^4}$$

$$= \frac{k^5 - 4k^4 + 7k^3 - 6k^2 + 2k}{k^4}$$

$$= k - 4 + \frac{7}{k} - \frac{6}{k^2} + \frac{2}{k^3}$$

These derivations for μ and σ^2 are so close to the means and variances of the sample distributions that one can conclude that the sample distributions are accurate reflections of the cumulative probabilities of true chance differences (for $k = 15$, $\mu = 14.0625$ and $\bar{X} = 14.068$, for example).

Comparison with the Normal Distribution

If the distributions of differences were normally distributed, then the theoretical mean and variance could be used with any suitable normal probability table to test for significant differences. Figure 4.1 illustrates the distribution of 20,000 chance differences when $k = 20$ objects and 30 objects, respectively. The upper tail distribution for 30 objects is quite close to the normal curve. It is suspected that as k increases the tail distributions will become increasingly normal. For k less than 30 the sample distributions will require larger differences to be declared significant at standard alpha levels than the normal distribution of differences using the true mean and variance.

Calculations of the sample skewness and kurtosis of interjudge differences for $k = 5, 10, 15, 20, 25,$ and 30 objects suggest that as k increases these moments tend toward their normal values. It is also possible to derive these moments theoretically. Further studies, however, are needed to assert normality for the distribution of differences with large values of k ($k > 50$).

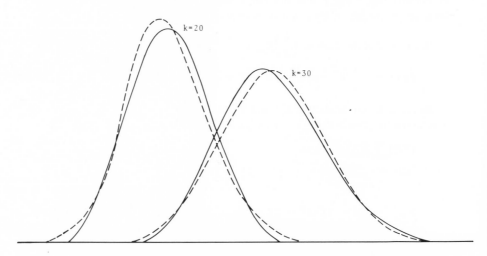

FIG. 4.1.   The distribution of 20,000 chance differences when $k = 20$ and 30 objects, respectively. Dotted curve represents the normal distribution of the same data.

APPLICATION: HOW JUDGES CLUSTER 11 WORDS

How can the derived information be applied? Once a clustering experiment is performed how may the judges be compared? An example may be illustrative.

Fifteen graduate students clustered 11 words that began with the letter a. The words (a, as, at, and, $aged$, $army$, $away$, $areas$, $almost$, $admits$, $aiming$) were typed on IBM prestige elite type on small slips of paper and presented randomly. Directions were "Put the words you think are similar together in groups. You may form as many or as few groups as you wish." Table 4.3 provides the basic data. The entries are cluster numbers. The judges a to o are listed vertically and the words represent the columns.

Before analyzing the differences among the judges the similarities among the objects was ascertained. Percentage overlap values derived by comparing the pairwise columns of objects were formed. These are presented in Table 4.4. The object similarities were analyzed by multidimensional scaling (Kruskal, 1964), and a two-space configuration of the objects is shown in Fig. 4.2. It can be seen that the objects have been classified largely on the basis of their length.

Did the judges, however, generally agree in their clustering behavior? Table 4.5 provides the differences (d_{ij}) among all pairs of judges based on definitions given in this chapter. Because there are 11 objects, reference to Table J in the Appendix shows that a difference of 15 or greater would occur less than 5 times in 100 by chance. Given this frame of reference there appear to be real dif-

TABLE 4.3
Group Membership Identification Numbers for 11 Words
Beginning with the Letter a. The 15 Adult Respondents are
Listed by Letter from a to o in the Left-Hand Margin.

	a	$admits$	$aged$	$almost$	$aiming$	and	as	at	$areas$	$army$	$away$
a	1	2	3	2	4	3	1	1	5	6	6
b	1	2	3	2	2	1	1	1	3	2	2
c	1	2	1	2	2	3	1	1	3	3	3
d	1	2	3	4	4	1	5	6	7	8	8
e	1	2	3	4	4	1	5	6	7	8	8
f	1	2	3	3	4	5	1	6	7	8	8
g	1	2	2	2	2	3	1	1	2	2	2
h	1	2	3	4	5	6	7	7	8	9	9
i	1	2	3	2	4	5	1	6	4	4	4
j	1	2	3	4	5	2	1	1	2	6	6
k	1	2	3	2	4	1	1	1	3	5	5
l	1	2	3	4	2	3	1	1	3	3	3
m	1	2	3	2	4	5	1	1	6	7	5
n	1	2	3	2	4	5	1	1	6	7	7
o	1	2	3	2	2	3	1	1	3	2	3

TABLE 4.4
Percent Overlap Scores for 11 Words Beginning with the Letter a.
Data is Based on 15 Adult Subjects' Free Clustering.

	a	admits	aged	almost	aiming	and	as	at	areas	army	away
a	1.000	0.0	0.067	0.0	0.0	0.267	0.800	0.667	0.0	0.0	0.0
admits	0.0	1.000	0.067	0.600	0.333	0.067	0.0	0.0	0.133	0.200	0.133
aged	0.067	0.067	1.000	0.133	0.067	0.200	0.067	0.067	0.333	0.133	0.200
almost	0.0	0.600	0.133	1.000	0.400	0.0	0.0	0.0	0.067	0.200	0.133
aiming	0.0	0.333	0.067	0.400	1.000	0.0	0.0	0.0	0.133	0.267	0.200
and	0.267	0.067	0.200	0.0	0.0	1.000	0.133	0.133	0.267	0.133	0.267
as	0.800	0.0	0.067	0.0	0.0	0.133	1.000	0.733	0.0	0.0	0.0
at	0.667	0.0	0.067	0.0	0.0	0.133	0.733	1.000	0.0	0.0	0.0
areas	0.0	0.133	0.333	0.067	0.133	0.267	0.0	0.0	1.000	0.267	0.333
army	0.0	0.200	0.133	0.200	0.267	0.133	0.0	0.0	0.267	1.000	0.867
away	0.0	0.133	0.200	0.133	0.200	0.267	0.0	0.0	0.333	0.867	1.000

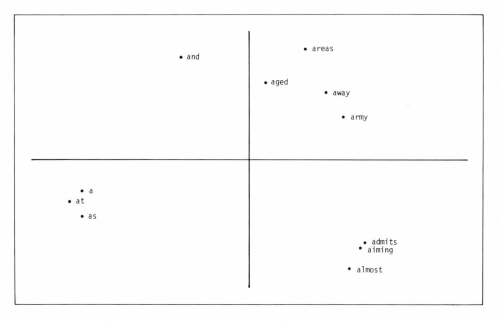

FIG. 4.2.   Multidimensional plot of 11 words beginning with *a*. Percentage overlap data were derived from free cluster responses of 15 adults.

TABLE 4.5
Lower Triangular Matrix of Differences between 15 Judges
Following Their Clustering of 11 Words

	a	*b*	*c*	*d*	*e*	*f*	*g*	*h*	*i*	*j*	*k*	*l*	*m*	*n*
						Subjects								
b	13.													
c	11.	18.												
d	7.	14.	14.											
e	7.	14.	14.	0.										
f	5.	16.	14.	4.	4.									
g	20.	13.	21.	23.	23.	21.								
h	4.	15.	13.	3.	3.	3.	22.							
i	8.	15.	13.	9.	9.	7.	16.	8.						
j	5	16.	12.	8.	8.	6.	21.	5.	11.					
k	5.	8.	14.	8.	8.	8.	21.	7.	11.	8.				
l	10.	19.	9.	15.	15.	13.	18.	12.	14.	11.	13.			
m	3.	14.	10.	8.	8.	6.	21.	5.	9.	6.	6.	11.		
n	1.	12.	10.	6.	6.	4.	19.	3.	7.	4.	4.	11.	2.	
o	11.	12.	12.	16.	16.	16.	15.	15.	15.	14.	14.	9.	10.	12.

ferences among the judges. The difference matrix was also analyzed by multidimensional methods. This result is presented as Fig. 4.3. Figure 4.3 suggests that judge G is somewhat different from the other judges. Next to each judge or small group of judges is placed the results of his or her grouping strategy. The plane is divided by judges who group words into just a few clusters and those who place words into many clusters. A scrutiny of the "north–south" dimension suggests that judges have difficulty with the word *and*. Some see it as a short word, some see it as a medium-sized word, and the rest are undecided.

DISCUSSION

Because scaling is relative, it is helpful to have an objective means of comparing the differences among judges. Intuitively, however, it seems that the null hy-

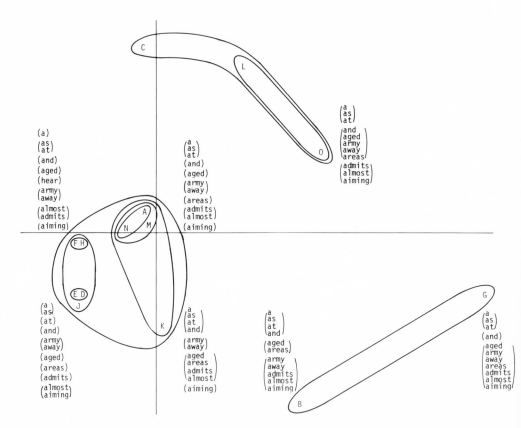

FIG. 4.3.   The nonmetric multidimensional scale analysis of differences among judges following the free clustering of 11 words. A hierarchical clustering is superimposed on the two-dimensional solution. Representative clustering strategies are shown adjacent to letters representing judges or small groups of judges.

pothesis of chance differences could make unreasonable assumptions about experiments of this type. While unlikely it seems apparent that someone could put all the words together in one cluster based on ideas such as ''they are all words, they all begin with *a,* they are all familiar, and so forth.'' Someone else, on the other hand, could defend a clustering of 11 separate groups contending that ''they all have different meanings, etc.'' The chance probability of this difference between two such judges (a difference of 55) is almost impossible, yet its occurrence in the real world is reasonably possible.

Assuming that distributions of differences become normal after k reaches 30, then multiple comparison methods could be applied to lower triangular matrices of differences because the true variance is known. Thus, groups of judges significantly different from each other could be analyzed separately, or outlying judges could be excluded from subsequent analyses of the objects. In the foregoing example, one might wish to exclude subject G or group all similar judges together and analyze the objects over these separate groups.

A computer program has been written to calculate percentage of overlap between objects (PEROVER) and another program to find interjudge distances (JUDGED) (See Chapter 20).

II ■■ UNIDIMENSIONAL METHODS

In Part II, four major unidimensional methods are presented. Despite recent advances in multidimensional scaling, unidimensional methods have value because of their simplicity and versatility, and because they are amenable to hand-calculated solutions. It is theoretically just as advantageous to create three separate unidimensional scales as it is to derive three dimensions from one multidimensional analysis. In fact, one methodology can serve as a check on the other. (Judgments rather than preferences are more frequently used in unidimensional methods.)

Each of the unidimensional methods presented offers something unique to scaling analysis. With *rank scaling* it is simplicity and tests of significance. In *comparative judgment* it is meeting normality assumptions about attitude. *Scalogram analysis* provides an "order" definition of scaling. In *ordinal categories,* profile data is handled instead of paired data. Under this category Likert scaling is explored more fully.

5 Rank Scaling

The variance stable rank method of scaling (Dunn-Rankin, 1965, Dunn-Rankin & King, 1969) is an adaptation of a two-way analysis of variance by ranks. In other words it is a nonparametric subject by treatment analysis in which the treatments are the psychological objects that are scaled. The basic assumption of the method is that the scale values are proportional to the sum of the ranks assigned by the judges to each of the objects. In this method the maximum and minimum possible rank totals, for a given number of judges and objects, act as a convenient and interpretive frame of reference within which the objects are scaled. A linear transformation of these two extreme rank totals into 100 and zero, respectively, defines the limits of the scale.

METHOD: DUNN-RANKIN'S VARIANCE STABLE RANK SUMS

The psychological objects can be ranked directly or the ranks can be determined from the votes given to the objects when they are arranged in all possible pairs and a choice made of the most preferred of each pair. Complete ordering can also be derived from partial ranking procedures.

A group of second-grade children were asked what they most preferred as a reward after a job was well done; an *A,* a *100,* a *gold star* (GS), or the word *excellent* (Ex). For these children the objects were formed in all $[K(K - 1)/2]$

55

possible pairs. The circled objects in Fig. 5.1 indicate the preferred choice in each pairing for Subject 1. The figure also shows the preference values for Subject 1. These values are found by summing the votes for each different object. In this case three choices or votes were made for a 100, two votes for an A, 1 vote for the *gold star,* and no preference for the word *Excellent.* The 3, 2, 1, and 0 rank *values* are the reverse of the rank *order* of the objects but are utilized in this position so that the value associated with the most preferred object has the largest magnitude.

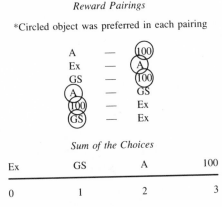

Reward Pairings

*Circled object was preferred in each pairing

A	—	(100)
Ex	—	(A)
GS	—	(100)
(A)	—	GS
(100)	—	Ex
(GS)	—	Ex

Sum of the Choices

Ex	GS	A	100
0	1	2	3

FIG. 5.1.   Subject 1's preference for the objects is shown and the rank values obtained by counting the choices for each subject.

Table 5.1 shows the rank values obtained for 24 subjects over the same objects. After obtaining the rank value totals (R_k), the Scale Values (SV) are obtained by dividing each vote total by the maximum vote possible and multiplying by 100. These values and a unidimensional graph are presented at the bottom of Table 5.1.

Discussion

The scale scores obtained by this simplified rank method can be utilized in traditional ways and are strikingly isomorphic with values obtained under Thurstone's Case V model (Thurstone, 1927; see page 79).

Smith (1968) showed, in a study of 19 actual paired comparison matrices varying in size from 4–21 items, a decidedly linear distribution regardless of the number of items in the matrix. The correlations between the actual distribution and the theoretical uniform distribution varied between .967 and 1.00. This indicates that purposeful judgments tend to create *uniform* distributions of responses. The idea of using rank totals as scale scores has been suggested in a

TABLE 5.1
Calculation of Scale Values (SV) from Sum of the Rank Values

Subjects	Min	Ex	GS	A	100	max
1	0	0	0	2	3	3
2	0	0	1	3	2	3
3	0	0	1	2	3	3
4*	0	1	1	1	3	3
5	0	3	2	0	1	3
6	0	0	1	2	3	3
7	0	1	0	3	2	3
8	0	0	3	2	1	3
9	0	0	1	3	2	3
10*	0	2	0	2	2	3
11	0	1	0	2	3	3
12	0	1	0	3	2	3
13	0	0	1	3	2	3
14	0	3	2	0	1	3
15	0	1	0	2	3	3
16	0	0	1	3	2	3
17	0	3	0	2	1	3
18	0	0	1	2	3	3
19	0	0	3	2	1	3
20	0	0	3	1	2	3
21*	0	2	0	2	2	3
22	0	0	1	3	2	3
23	0	0	1	2	3	3
24	0	0	1	2	3	3
Sums (R_k)	0	18	25	49	52	72 (N (K-1))
SV ($100\ R_k/R_{max}$)	0	25	34.7	68.1	72.2	100

*Circular triads present (in such cases the procedure assigns the mean of the three rank values to each of the items involved).

Graph of Reward Preference Scale Values

slightly different form by Mosteller (1958). Guilford (1954) and Rummel (1964) have also proposed related techniques.

TESTS OF SIGNIFICANCE

If tests of significance are considered to be an important part of the scaling process then a sufficient number of judges (N) need to be selected. This will ensure that the objects have the opportunity to be significantly different. In Table 5.2 are the sample sizes necessary at the .01, .05, and .10 probability levels. For the (K) and alpha levels not listed a solution can be obtained by solving for N in the following formula where Q is taken from the values by Harter (1959) or Dixon and Massey (1969).

$$N = \frac{Q_\alpha^2(K)(K + 1)}{12}$$

When tests of significance are incorporated into the scaling process, variance stable scales of paired comparison data can be constructed. The rank method has units that are equal in a *variance stable* sense. They are variance stable because a difference between rank sums has the same probability of occurrence wherever the rank totals (and the scaled scores) may be located. In scaling we are usually interested in all the possible comparisons that can be made between the objects. Utilizing rank totals in the scaling process provides the opportunity to examine significant differences between pairs of psychological objects.

The nonparametric method of multiple comparisons (Wilcoxon & Wilcox, 1964) concentrates on detecting differences between treatments and in this case is analogous to the Tukey method of multiple comparisons. This method declares that objects with significantly large rank sum differences will have significantly different means.

Dunn-Rankin and Wilcoxon (1966) investigated the true distribution of the range of rank totals, that is, the distribution of the differences between the rank

TABLE 5.2
Number of Judges Necessary to Insure the Possibility
of K Items Being Significantly Different

Items	*Number of Judges*		
	.01	*.05*	*.10*
3	17	11	9
4	33	19	18
5	53	38	31
6	80	57	47
7	112	82	68
8	150	111	92
9	194	145	123
10	244	184	157
11	301	228	195
12	364	278	239
13	434	333	287
14	511	394	341
15	594	461	400

sums. The study determined the exact probability values necessary when using small numbers of judges and objects. Appendix, Table H presents critical values of the rank sum differences where K (objects) and N (judges) are less than or equal to 15. The study also was able to verify that the normal approximation to this distribution is accurate when the number of judges or objects is greater than 15. Thus, the probability can be easily calculated for N or $K > 15$.

Calculation of the critical range for the sample of 24 subjects shown in Table 5.1 is illustrated below. The critical range is the product of the expected standard deviation $E(S) = \sqrt{N(K)(K + 1)/12}$ and the studentized range (Q_a) for K objects and infinite degrees of freedom at the alpha level chosen.

The $E(S)$ is $\sqrt{N(K)(K + 1)/12}$ and $Q_a = W/S$ is the studentized range for K treatments and infinite df. For $N = 24$, $K = 4$ and $P = .05$, the

$$\text{Critical Range} = E(S) \cdot Q_{.05}$$
$$= \sqrt{\frac{24(4)(5)}{12}} \cdot 3.633$$
$$= \sqrt{40} \cdot 3.633$$
$$= 22.98$$
$$= 23$$

An illustration of the calculation of the significant range for 24 judges and four objects where the .05 probability level is chosen is illustrated here.

The values of the studentized range ($Q_a = W/S$) have been extensively tabled by Harter (1959) or may be found in Dixon and Massey (1969). Appendix, Table G, presents the Q_a values for $K = 3$(to)15. In this example the .05 probability level has been chosen and the critical range is 23. Table 5.3 presents a matrix of rank differences for the data for Table 5.1, in which the significant values have been starred. Calculation of scalability indexes is also shown.

The number of possible significant pairs is determined by using N times the integers 1 (to) K as the rank sums and testing how many of those paired sums are significantly different. These sums represent the maximum possible scale scores. Note that when the number of judges (N) exceeds the critical range [$Q_a \cdot E(S)$], the relative scalability index (RSI) equals the scalability index.

DISCUSSION

Multiple comparison tests of significance would appear to be a useful adjunct to the scaling process for the following reasons:

TABLE 5.3
Matrix of Rank Differences and Calculation
of the Scalability Index (SI)

	100	A	GS	Ex
R_i	52	49	25	18
52	—			
49	3	—		
25	27*	24*	—	
18	34*	31*	7	—

*Significant at the .05 level (critical range = 23)

$$\text{Scalability Index} = \frac{\text{No. Sig. Different Pairs}}{K(K-1)/2}$$

$$SI = 4/6$$

$$= .67$$

$$\text{Relative Scalability Index} = \frac{\text{No Sig. Different Pairs}}{\text{No Possible Sig. Different Pairs}}$$

$$RSI = 4/6$$

$$= .67$$

1. Tests of significance can provide help in making decisions about whether two objects come from the same population of stimuli. In the example presented, the 100 and the A were scaled very close to each other. The difference between the sums for A and 100 is three. The small difference of three or less has an extremely high probability of occurrence by chance so that the observed difference is likely just a chance difference. Thus the 100 and the A (which can be categorized as adult approval rewards) could be chosen to represent one category of reward preference on alternate forms of an instrument that compares adult approval with independence rewards. That is, a child might be asked whether he or she preferred an "A" to "*being free to do what he or she liked*" on one form and whether he or she preferred a "100" to "*being free to go outside*" on another.

2. Significance tests can create categories of stimuli that may be considered discrete. In Likert scaling, for example, the categorical descriptions could be tested to see that they were significantly different as well as equally spaced. Bashaw and Anderson (1968) scaled adverbial modifiers of the type used in Likert scales and were able to show that elementary and secondary school students could distinguish *pretty much* from *quite*. Students were unable, however, to see significant differences between *rather* and *pretty much*.

3. Significance tests can be used to build an index of scalability for psychological objects somewhat analogous to Guttman's coefficient of reproducibility. One index consists of a ratio of the number of significantly different pairs of objects to the total number of possible pairs. In the illustration provided in this chapter (see bottom of Table 5.3) there were four significantly different pairs out of six. This resulted in a scalability index of .67.

A relative scalability index (Knezek, 1978) can also be calculated by forming the ratio of the significantly different pairs over the number that could be significantly different. The denominator is found by: first using the $N(K - 1)$ values as the maximum possible scale scores, then testing these pairs of values for significance, and finally counting the number of significant pairs.

Such indices can be utilized to quantify the ability of different groups of people to distinguish between psychological objects.

4. By solving for N in the following formula: $N = Q_a^2(K)(K + 1)/12$, the number of judges (N) necessary to insure that all objects have a possibility of being significantly different at the particular alpha level chosen can be determined. In the example provided a sample size of 22 is called for by the formula.

To summarize, this method of scaling has value because:

1. It is simple and easy to use.
2. It allows scaling along a continuum with meaningful endpoints.
3. Its scale values correlate highly with those obtained by other techniques.
4. It allows for tests of significance between the items.

APPLICATION 1: DIRECT RANKING OF AUTHORITY

In his doctoral dissertation Moseley (1966) wished to determine scale values for statements that reflected the authority given to administrators to make decisions. He had 98 company executives compare and judge 13 different decision situations by direct ranking (see Fig. 5.2). Scaled results are provided in Table 5.4.

Moseley then created a final Authority Scale by combining statements whose rank differences were not significantly different (see Table 5.5). He then used this scale during interviews with comptrollers and was able to place the results of the interview effectively into one of the six distinct categories.

By assigning scores to persons interviewed in different companies Moseley was able to test differences between the authority viewpoints of comptrollers and supervisors. He also tested the differences among the degrees of authority given by different companies.

Instructions:

Assume that Mr. Jones is an executive in the Omega Company. The company is faced with the decision of whether or not to adopt a new operating procedure. Below is a list of the various ways in which Mr. Jones might participate in making that decision.

In the column on the extreme left, place the number 1 in front of the situation which you believe provides Mr. Jones with the most authority. Place the number 2 in front of the situation which you believe provides him with the second greatest degree of authority. Continue until you finally place the number 11 in front of the situation which provides him with the very least authority.

You should think of Mr. Jones' authority in terms of the degree to which he could make the decision in each of the situations.

It may be difficult to choose between some of the alternatives for a particular ranking, but each must be assigned a different rank number.

Your Final Answer	Scratch Work Column	Decision Situation – the decision is made by:
		Mr. Jones' superior and/or others, but without Mr. Jones participating.
		A formal committee. Mr. Jones is chairman. His superior is not on the committee.
		A formal committee. Mr. Jones is on the committee, but is not chairman. His superior is not on the committee.
		A formal committee. Mr. Jones is chairman. His superior is on the committee.
		Mr. Jones and others, but not in a formal committee Mr. Jones' superior participates.
		Mr. Jones and one other person who is not Mr. Jones' superior.
		Mr. Jones.
		A formal committee. Mr. Jones is on the committee, but is not chairman. His superior is on the committee as a member.
		Mr. Jones and others, but not in a formal committee. Mr. Jones' superior does not participate.
		A formal committee. Mr. Jones' superior is chairman. Mr. Jones is a member of the committee.
		Mr. Jones jointly with his superior.

FIG. 5.2. An example of the ranking instrument used by Moseley to create an authority scale.

TABLE 5.4
Authority Ranking Questionnaire Scale Scores and Ranks*

Decision Situation (Who makes the decision)	Rank	Scale Score
Executive	1	100
Executive jointly with one other	2	82
Committee, executive chairs, superior not on committee	3	74
Executive jointly with two or more others	4	57
Committee, executive chairs, superior is on committee	5	52
Executive jointly with superior	6	49
Committee, executive member, superior is not on committee	7	48
Executive jointly with others and superior	8	38
Committee, executive member, superior is on committee	9	30
Committee, executive member, superior chairs	10	21
Superior and/or others	11	0

TABLE 5.5
Decision-Making Authority Scale

Authority Index Score	Decision Situation (Who makes the decision)		Authority Description
100	Controller		Unilateral
75	Controller jointly with one other	Maximum Shared	
	Committee, controller chairs, superior not on committee		
50	Controller jointly with two or more others	Intermediate Shared	s h a r e d
	Controller jointly with superior		
	Committee, controller member, superior not on committee		
35	Controller jointly with others and superior	Moderate Shared	
25	Committee, controller member, superior is on committee	Minimum Shared	
	Committee, controller member, superior chairs		
0	Superior and/or others		No

APPLICATION 2: DIRECT RANKING OF COUNSELOR
ROLES

Furlong, Atkinson, and Janoff (1980) developed a list of 14 elementary school counselor roles such as program planning, counseling, pupil appraisal, and disciplinarian. Fifty-four counselors ranked the list in two ways: (1) the order in which they actually spend their time; and (2) the amount of time they would actually like to spend practicing each of the roles. Figure 5.3 shows the results of this scaling. The authors concluded that a primary function of counseling, namely evaluation, is the least preferred actual and ideal activity for elementary counselors.

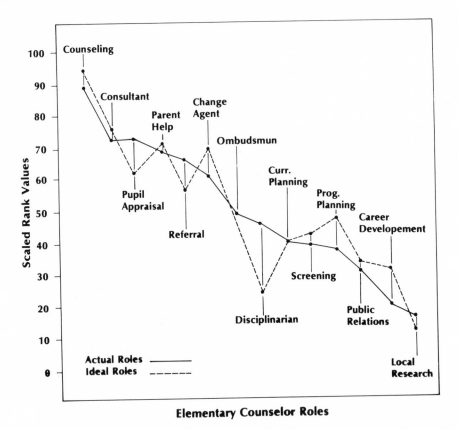

FIG. 5.3. Difference between actual and ideal roles for 54 counselors. The largest difference between roles occurs for Disciplinarian. Least desirable role is Local Research.

APPLICATION 3: LETTER SIMILARITY SCALES

Dunn-Rankin (1968, 1978) has scaled lowercase letters of the English alphabet using the Simplified Rank Method (see Figs. 5.4 and 5.5). In this case the objects were paired and votes (rank values) obtained.

The author has written a computer program, RANKO (see Chapter 20) to do simplified rank scaling from ranks or paired preference data (Dunn-Rankin, 1966).

FIG. 5.4.   Letter similarity instrument (one of 21 pages).

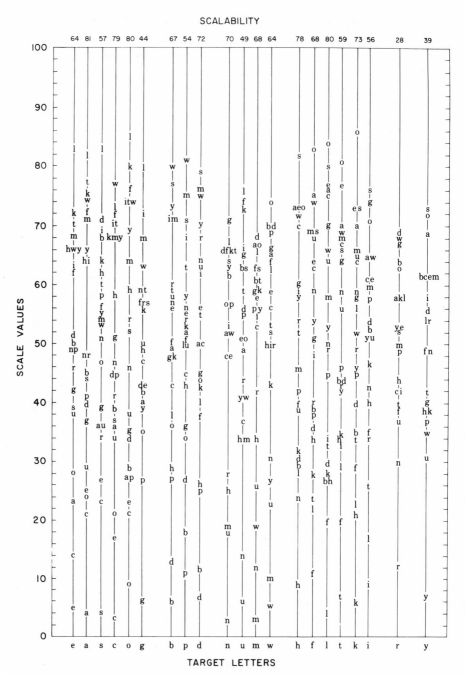

FIG. 5.5.   (Caption on opposite page)

FIG. 5.5.   LETTER-SIMILARITY SCALES were constructed by the author on the basis of a letter-discrimination test in which 21 lowercase letters were matched in pairs to determine their relative similarity to one another (See Fig. 5.4). The cumulative choices made by 315 second- and third-grade children over all 210 possible pairings were then analyzed, and sets of linear scale values were assigned to the letters in terms of their relative similarity to each target letter. (The comparatively infrequent letters not included in the study were j, q, v, x, and z.) In the arbitrary frame of reference in which the letters are plotted here zero indicates no error in choosing a letter most like the target letter, and 100 indicates no error in choosing the letter most unlike target letter. The scales are organized by similar letter groups (*colored bands*).

6 Circular Triads: Distributions and Applications

Circular triads are proposed as a basis for determining object scalability and individual judge (subject) consistency when using complete paired comparisons data. In this chapter: the theoretical rationale for the measurement process is developed, circular triad distribution characteristics are explored, and several measurement indices are derived.

THEORY: DISTRIBUTIONS OF INTRANSITIVITY

Circular triads are formed whenever intransitive pairwise choices occur. If a subject is presented with all possible pairs of three objects, *A, B,* and *C,* for example, and is asked on each occasion to judge which member of the pair is preferred, then a preference pattern of the following type may result:

where → means *is preferred to*. This preference pattern is called a circular triad. The first object is preferred to the next, whereas the remaining object is preferred to the first. There is no indication of which object is most or least preferred.

Whenever a circular triad exists, a nonlinear ordering has taken place. When *no* circular triads occur in a set of paired data a linear ordering results. Because all *intransitive* preference patterns, involving more than three objects, can be decomposed into circular triads (Kendall & Babington–Smith, 1939), the number of circular triads can serve as an index of intransitivity in complete paired comparisons data.

Judge Circular Triads (JCT)

Kendall and Babington–Smith were the first to formalize the use of circular triads in psychological measurement. They suggested that the relative consistencies of judges (subjects) could be determined by counting the total number of circular triads each judge produced in the course of making choices among all possible pairs of objects. The authors were unable to determine *exactly* how inconsistent any *one* judge was because the exact probability distributions of *Judge Circular Triads* (JCT) for more than eight objects were unknown. Kendall and Smith, however, were able to derive formulas for the maximum values and the first four moments (measures of variability) of judge circular triad distributions. These formulas are shown below:

$$\text{Maximum}_{JCT} = \frac{K^3 - K}{24} \quad \text{for odd } K \tag{1}$$

$$\text{Maximum}_{JCT} = \frac{K^3 - 4K}{24} \quad \text{for even } K \tag{2}$$

$$\text{Mean}_{JCT} = \frac{1}{4}\binom{K}{3} = \frac{K(K-1)(K-2)}{24} \quad \text{for } K \geq 3 \tag{3}$$

$$\text{Variance}_{JCT} = \frac{3}{16}\binom{K}{3} = \frac{K(K-1)(K-2)}{32} \quad \text{for } K \geq 4 \tag{4}$$

$$\text{Skewness}_{JCT} = \frac{-3}{32}\binom{K}{3}(K-4) = \frac{-K(K-1)(K-2)(K-4)}{64}$$

$$\text{for } K \geq 5 \tag{5}$$

$$\text{Kurtosis}_{JCT} = \frac{3}{256}\binom{K}{3}\left\{9\binom{K-3}{3} + 39\binom{K-3}{2}\right.$$

$$\left. + 9\binom{K-3}{1} + 7\right\}$$

$$= \frac{K(K-1)(K-2)}{512}\left[\frac{3(K-3)(K-4)(K-5)}{2}\right.$$

$$\left. + \frac{39(K-3)(K-4)}{2} + 9(K-3) + 7\right] \quad \text{for } K \geq 6$$

where K = number of objects, and $\binom{K}{j}$ indicates the number of possible combinations for K objects taken j at a time.

Kendall and Babington–Smith also developed a method for calculating the number of judge circular triads from a vector containing a judge's total preference for each object. (Kendall, 1955, later simplified the formula.) In addition, the writers reported derivations for a measure of judge consistency, the Coefficient of Consistence. These formulas are:

$$JCT_i = \frac{K(K-1)(2K-1)}{12} - \frac{\sum_{j=1}^{K} a_{ij}^2}{2} \tag{7}$$

$$Consistence_i = 1 - \frac{24(JCT_i)}{K^3 - K} \quad \text{for odd } K, \text{ and} \tag{8}$$

$$Consistence_i = 1 - \frac{24(JCT_i)}{K^3 - 4K} \quad \text{for even } K \tag{9}$$

where K = number of objects, JCT_i stands for the total number of circular triads produced by $judge_i$, and a_{ij} = number of times $judge_i$ preferred $object_j$. The last two formulas can be derived from:

$$Consistence_i = 1 - \frac{JCT_i}{Maximum_{JCT}} \tag{10}$$

which is a form of reliability statement now common in psychological measurement.

Many researchers have developed or tested methods for approximating the JCT probability distributions. Most notable is the work of David and Starks (David, 1959, 1963; Starks & David, 1961; Starks, 1958). They extended knowledge of the exact JCT distributions from seven to eight objects and found a particular chi-square approximation to be the best of the then popular approximations for eight or fewer objects. By using computer processing, verification of the exact JCT distributions for three through seven objects and the simulation of JCT distributions for eight through twenty objects has been made (Dunn-Rankin, Knezek, & Abalos, 1978). Critical lower tail values of judge circular triads for five through 20 objects can be found in the Appendix, Table B.

METHOD: KNEZEK'S TESTS FOR CIRCULARITY

Suppose one conducts a complete paired comparison experiment and is interested in analyzing the circularity that occurs. What can be done?

1. One can test whether the total circularity that occurs for all the judges across all the objects is less than one would expect by chance. (Knezek, 1978).

(The test should generally be significant at conventional .05 alpha levels. The experimenter may, therefore, use $\alpha \leq .20$, for example)

2. One can test whether an *individual* judge has significantly fewer circular triads, across all objects, than is expected by chance. This can be accomplished by comparing the number of JCTs to the appropriate critical lower tail value listed in Table B in the Appendix or by referring to the true distribution, which has been tabled for 3–20 objects (Table C). (Experience has shown that a test against chance may not be viable for most objects and judges at conventional alpha levels.)[1]

3. If one is reluctant to use the null hypothesis of chance differences, one can test whether an *individual* judge has a significantly greater number of circular triads than the group average. Because most circular triad group data are normally distributed, a standard z test for circular triads can be made. Mean and standard deviation values for the z can be calculated directly from JCT data through conventional techniques. If the shape of the distribution is in doubt, a test for normality can also be made.

4. One may wish to know whether a particular *object* is involved in significantly less circularity across the judges than would be expected by chance. A conservative probability figure can be obtained using Cheybshev's inequality:

$$P\left\{ |OCT - Mean_{OCT}| > d \right\} \leq \frac{Variance_{OCT}}{d^2} \tag{11}$$

where d is chosen by the experimenter, OCT = object circular triads and

$$Mean_{OCT} = \left(\frac{K^2 - 3K + 2}{8} \right) N \tag{12}$$

and

$$Variance_{OCT} = \frac{3}{4} Mean_{OCT}. \tag{13}$$

(Gnedenko & Khinchin, 1962). Mean $_{OCT}$ and Variance$_{OCT}$ are obtained from the derivations by Knezek (1978) and d is the absolute deviation of a particular number of object circular triads from the theoretical mean. N is the number of judges and K is the number of objects. The resulting probability will be two-tailed and should be halved for the hypothesis described. In cases where $N \times K \geq 16$, a z test using the mean and variance values described previously is

---

[1]Given a set of 15 whole numbers paired in 105 possible ways and asked which number in each pair is the larger, it is reasonable to expect even a young student to make consistent choices resulting in few circular triads. Because zero circular triads in this case is an extraordinary occurrence by chance $p < .00000000000001$, the example serves to remind us that if the data are highly discriminable and the dimension of judgment well defined, logical, not chance choice generally will follow.

suitable. (Experience indicates that the number of circular triads involving a specific object will usually be small and that the test against chance may not be useful if conventional (.05, .01) levels are used.)

5. One may wish to test, therefore, whether a specific *object* is involved in more or less circularity than other objects, that is, a relative test. In this case the z statistic can be used after calculating (using conventional formulas) the mean and standard deviation of object circular triads for a particular set of data.

6. Experience has shown that circular triads are sometimes associated with a particular pair of objects, and these circularities are often unidirectional. Therefore, one may wish to test whether the direction of the preferences between two objects involved in a large amount of circularity is significantly greater than expected by chance. Here the traditional binomial test can be employed:

$$P(X \geq S) = \sum_{X=S}^{T} \binom{T}{X} p^X (1-p)^{T-X} \tag{14}$$

(Gnedenko & Khinchin, 1962) where T = the number of times a particular pair of objects is involved in a circular triad (the number of trials), S = the larger number of single direction occurrences (the number of successes), $p = .5$ = the random probability of each preference being in the direction with the larger number of occurrences (the probability of success on each trial), and X is a random variable that can take on any value within the range of the distribution. Because the value yielded is a one-tailed probability, it should be doubled whenever a specific directionality is not hypothesized. (A computer program is usually necessary to count directional circularity. This is provided in Chapter 20).

7. It is helpful to calculate the coefficient of variation (variance/mean) among object circular triads for each pair of objects involved in circularity. This determines whether circularity is evenly distributed across the judges. A large coefficient indicates that only a few judges are involved in the circularity for that particular pair of objects, whereas a small coefficient shows the circularity is widely distributed.

APPLICATION: CIRCULARITY AMONG ADJECTIVE PAIRS

An example may serve to illustrate some of the procedures described in the foregoing section. In a recent study (Dunn-Rankin et al., 1978), 15 adjectives were selected on the criterion that all were socially desirable. All adjective pairs were presented and 39 high school students were asked to choose the trait preferred in each case (Fig. 6.1 and Fig. 6.2 illustrate the instrument used).

The resulting rank ordering and scale values based on rank sums (Dunn-Rankin & King, 1969) were:

Powerful	Famous	Good-Looking	Rich	Generous	Courteous	Just	Good-Humored	Considerate	Sociable	Successful	Honest	Intelligent	Loving		Healthy
↓	↓	↓	↓	↓	↓	↓	↓	↓	↓	↓	↓	↓	↓		↓

30	40	50	60	70

Based on circular triads, several more detailed analyses were performed on the data.

1. *Overall Circularity.*   Although words thought to be close to each other in social desirability were chosen with hopes that high circularity would be produced, the adjectives instead proved to be highly scalable. Only 1343 judge circular triads were produced by the 39 judges. This is far fewer than the average of 113.75 times 39 or 4436.25 expected by chance (see Formula 3). This rare probability also applies to the average of all judges' Coefficients of Consistence which is C = .754 (1343/39 = 34.43; C = 1 − 24(34.43)/5360) using formula 8.

2. *Absolute Judge Consistency.*   Most of the judges were highly consistent in their choices. There was, however, at least one exception. One judge produced 107 circular triads, relatively close to the 113.75 (see Formula 3) expected by chance. Because the number produced is greater than the $p = .05$ critical

DIRECTIONS

On the following page you will find 105 pairs of words. For each pair of words, you are to choose one according to your own preference. Underline your choice for each pair of words.

For example:

5) Healthy or Sociable

If you prefer to be sociable rather than be healthy, then underline the word Sociable.

Thus,

5) Healthy or Sociable

There is no time limit for this task, so take your time!

FIG. 6.1.   Directions for selecting adjective pairs.

WHAT WOULD YOU RATHER BE?

1) Good-Looking or Sociable
2) Healthy or Good-Looking
3) Generous or Just
4) Honest or Famous
5) Healthy or Sociable
6) Generous or Courteous
7) Successful or Just
8) Powerful or Good-Looking
9) Loving or Courteous
10) Loving or Generous
11) Just or Rich
12) Healthy or Successful
13) Healthy or Honest
14) Good-Humored or Loving
15) Powerful or Loving
16) Successful or Generous
17) Good-Humored or Famous
18) Considerate or Honest
19) Intelligent or Healthy
20) Considerate or Healthy
21) Healthy or Powerful
22) Powerful or Courteous
23) Honest or Good-Humored
24) Powerful or Intelligent
25) Intelligent or Loving
26) Healthy or Rich
27) Just or Considerate
28) Healthy or Courteous
29) Intelligent or Famous
30) Intelligent or Sociable
31) Loving or Intelligent
32) Rich or Successful
33) Famous or Considerate
34) Rich or Good-Humored
35) Good-Humored or Sociable
36) Rich or Powerful
37) Considerate or Just
38) Just or Powerful
39) Good-Humored or Considerate
40) Good-Humored or Considerate
41) Famous or Rich
42) Loving or Honest
43) Rich or Honest
44) Considerate or Successful
45) Intelligent or Courteous
46) Rich or Intelligent
47) Famous or Powerful
48) Famous or Just
49) Good-Humored or Intelligent
50) Considerate or Generous
51) Successful or Famous
52) Courteous or Just
53) Successful or Courteous
54) Loving or Healthy
55) Rich or Generous
56) Just or Loving
57) Sociable or Courteous
58) Sociable or Successful
59) Good-Humored or Powerful
60) Good-Looking or Just
61) Considerate or Intelligent
62) Honest or Generous
63) Sociable or Honest
64) Sociable or Loving
65) Courteous or Considerate
66) Successful or Good-Looking
67) Rich or Courteous
68) Good-Humored or Just
69) Intelligent or Generous
70) Famous or Loving
71) Powerful or Sociable
72) Loving or Rich
73) Generous or Healthy
74) Generous or Famous
75) Honest or Good-Looking
76) Considerate or Powerful
77) Generous or Powerful
78) Good-Humored or Good-Looking
79) Good-Looking or Loving
80) Good-Looking or Considerate
81) Courteous or Good-Humored
82) Courteous or Good Humored
83) Successful or Good-Humored
84) Good-Looking or Generous
85) Powerful or Honest
86) Honest or Successful
87) Powerful or Successful
88) Good-Looking or Intelligent
89) Healthy or Just
90) Loving or Successful
91) Generous or Sociable
92) Loving or Considerate
93) Just or Sociable
94) Sociable or Considerate
95) Rich or Good-Looking
96) Famous or Healthy
97) Intelligent or Honest
98) Courteous or Honest
99) Famous or Sociable
100) Just or Honest
101) Courteous or Good-Looking
102) Successful or Intelligent
103) Healthy or Good-Humored
104) Good-Looking or Famous
105) Rich or Sociable

FIG. 6.2.   105 pairs of adjectives presented to 39 high school students.

74

value of 96 shown in Table B of Appendix, the null hypothesis of random choices cannot be rejected for this judge. (The estimated actual probability of 107 or fewer JCTs is .24). One can assume this judge was guessing or doubt the subject's competence. In either case, the judge's data should probably be removed from the analysis.

3. *Relative Judge Consistency.* In this area, a strong case can again be made against the aforementioned judge. The relative reliability of two other judges can also be questioned. The first judge's 107 circular triads, standardized utilizing the mean and standard deviation of all JCTs, transformed to a z score of +3.1. The other two judges produced 88 circular triads, each equivalent to a z score of +2.29. All these scores are significantly inconsistent at the .05 level, according to the group distribution under the assumption of the applicability of the standard normal curve. (A Kolmogorov–Smirnoff test uncovered no deviation [$p = .05$] from normality in the data.) It is possible therefore to justifiably remove the choices of all three judges from the analysis.

4. *Absolute Object Scalability.* The object involved in the greatest number of circular triads (sociable) was subjected to this test. If $N \times K \geq 16$, the distribution of the OCT will be approximately normal, therefore, a z test was used. The 370 object circular triads for "sociable" were equivalent to a theoretical z score of -3.21, with a probability level of less than .001, where

$$z = \frac{OCT_K - (N \cdot Mean_{OCT})}{N \cdot SD_{OCT}}$$

or

$$\frac{370 - (39 \cdot 22.75)}{39 \cdot 4.13} = -3.21.$$

(as z values approach zero, objects are less scalable). The null hypothesis of random scalability would therefore be rejected. Because "sociable" was found to be scalable, all other objects, that have fewer circular triads, would also be highly scalable.

5. *Relative Object Scalability.* Three objects were selected for this test. They were the two with the highest number of circular triads and the one with the lowest. Using the mean and standard deviation of the entire group of object circular triads, z scores of $+2.28$, $+1.24$, and -1.83 were derived for "sociable," "intelligent," and "powerful," respectively. "Sociable" deviates significantly ($p = .05$) from the circularity of others in the group, whereas the remaining two objects do not. If the goal was improvement of the scale of social desirability, the word "sociable" would be eliminated from the scale.

6. *Pairwise Circularity.* A large number of circular triads (101) were found to be associated with the pair of objects "sociable" and "rich." Because this number was much larger than the average value of 38.37 for all pairs involved in circular triads, and because 80 of these 101 involvements were in the direction of

"sociable" being preferred to "rich" (binomial probability = 0.0, Formula 14), the pair was singled out for further study. The word "rich" was found to be involved in only about the average number of circular triads, whereas "sociable," as previously stated, was involved in a significantly greater amount of circularity than the remainder of the objects in the group. These facts, in combination with consideration of a low coefficient of variation for "sociable" (1.22 versus a mean of 1.49), lead to the conclusion that the word "sociable" is often preferred to "rich," "rich" is preferred to many other words, and these words are then preferred to "sociable." Removal of the word "sociable" should destroy this potential intransitivity, leading to an improvement in a linear scale of social desirability.

DISCUSSION

The analysis of data through circular triads should be especially appropriate whenever the concept of judge or subject reliability does not depend on inter-judge agreement. Data from instruments such as the Edwards Personal Preference Schedule (EPPS, Edwards, 1959) might meet this requirement. Circular triad analysis of EPPS data would determine the degree to which individuals were consistent in their personality choices, as well as allow determination of the overall consistency of the group. The first test is not possible in the more popular types of reliability measures, whereas the second test (with the present procedure) allows for the possibility of perfect consistency even if the ordering of the objects for every judge is unique.

Tests of type 3 and type 5 can possibly be conducted more accurately using analysis of variance. If one is willing to assume that a particular set of circular triad data is normally distributed although the theoretical distributions are not, then all assumptions required for analysis of variance are met. A test for normality should probably precede the use of analysis of variance on a set of data.

Knezek (1978) has written a computer program, TRICIR, to aid in the analysis of circular triads (see Chapter 20).

7 Comparative Judgment

L. L. Thurstone (1927) provided a rationale for ordering objects on a psychological continuum. Psychological objects are stimuli for which some reaction takes place within the sensory system of the individual, the objects could be a beautiful girl, a telephone's ring, sandpaper, sugar water, or nitrous oxide. They could also include visual statements, such as ⟨stop⟩ , ''I hate school,'' or patriot.

THEORY: REACTIONS ARE NORMALLY DISTRIBUTED

Thurstone postulated that for any psychological object: (1) our reactions to such stimuli were subjective; and (2) our judgment or preference for an object may vary from one instance to another. Thurstone suggested that, although we may have more or less favorable reactions to a particular psychological object, there was a most frequent reaction to any object or stimulus. The most frequent reaction is called the *modal* reaction. The mode can be based on repeated reactions of a single individual or the frequency of the reactions of many subjects.

Thurstone assumed that reactions to various stimuli were normally distributed. Because the normal curve is symmetrical, the most frequent reaction (the mode) occupies the same scale position as the mean. Thus the mean can represent the scale value for the particular psychological object.

Scale values can be acquired, however, only within a relative frame. Thus it is necessary to have at least two objects so that a comparison can be made. In this case Thurstone assumed that the reactions to each object would be normally distributed and, additionally, that the variance of the reactions around each mean would be the same for both objects. Figure 7.1 illustrates this case.

Suppose i and j are two psychological objects that are to be judged on a

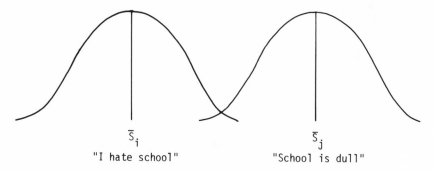

$$\bar{s}_i$$
"I hate school"

$$\bar{s}_j$$
"School is dull"

FIG. 7.1.   Theoretical distribution of responses about two different psychological objects.

continuum of positive affect toward school. Suppose i is "I hate school," and j is "Sometimes school is dull."

We might ask a group of subjects to judge which statement is more favorable toward school attendance. If 80% of the subjects choose j as more favorable than i and therefore 20% choose i as more favorable than j, we might argue that the average reaction to j should be higher on a scale than the average reaction to i, or $\bar{s}_j > \bar{s}_i$. The separation between $\bar{s}_j$ and $\bar{s}_i$ is a function of the number of times j is rated over i. Using paired comparisons we can count the votes and get proportions of preference. If, with 50 subjects, j (Sometimes school is dull.) is chosen 40 times over i (I hate school.), then the proportion is 40/50 or .80.

The proportions in this method, however, can be expressed as normal deviates (i.e., (z) standard scores can be obtained for proportions). In this case the normal deviate $(z_{ij}) = .84$ (for $p = .80$). The scale separation between two psychological objects can be made in terms of this normal deviate, that is $z_{ij} = \bar{s}_j - \bar{s}_i$. Diagrammatically we can say that somewhere on the continuum of "attitude toward school attendance" that j and i are separated by a distance of .84 as follows:

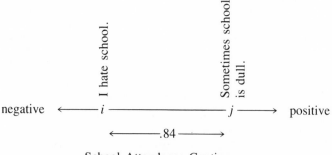

School Attendance Continuum

Note that despite the fact that the mean of the distribution of responses around the stimuli will never actually be known the *difference* between any two means can be obtained if one makes the assumption of normality mentioned previously. Thurstone's use of the normal deviate as a measure of distance is justified in the following way: The reader probably remembers that the test of the difference between means of two normal distributions is:

$$z_{12} = \frac{\bar{X}_1 - \bar{X}_2}{\sqrt{S_1^2 + S_2^2 - 2rS_1S_2}}$$

where

$\bar{X}$ = mean

S = standard error

r = correlation

Thurstone solves this equation for the difference as follows:

$$\bar{X}_1 - \bar{X}_2 = z_{12}\sqrt{S_1^2 + S_2^2 - 2rS_1S_2}$$

By letting the means, $\bar{X}_1$ and $\bar{X}_2$, represent the scale values of two stimuli (the mean and the mode are the same in a normal distribution), and by assuming the items to be uncorrelated (i.e., $r = 0$), the formula reduces to

$$\bar{X}_1 - \bar{X}_2 = z_{12}\sqrt{S_1^2 + S_2^2}$$

By assuming that the variances of response are equal for the two items the value under the radical becomes a constant and in this case (Thurstone's Case V) the formula reduces to

$$\bar{X}_1 - \bar{X}_2 = z_{12} \cdot \text{constant}$$

Although the constant can take on any value, it is generally chosen to be one (1).

METHOD: THURSTONE'S CASE V

Thurstone's procedure for finding scale separations starts with the votes derived from some paired comparison schedule of objects. The votes can be accumulated in a square array by placing a 1 in each row and column intersection in which the column object is judged or preferred over the row object. Suppose that four objects, A, B, C, and D, are paired in all possible ways and one subject responds as follows:

Votes	Pairs	Matrix			
			A	B	C	D

Votes	Pairs		A	B	C	D
3	$\underline{A}$ B	A	—	0	0	0
	$\underline{A}$ C					
	$\underline{A}$ D	B	1	—	0	0
2	$\underline{B}$ C					
	$\underline{B}$ D	C	1	1	—	0
1	$\underline{C}$ D					
		D	1	1	1	—
			3	2	1	0

In each pair the underlined item was favored.

A matrix can accumulate a large number of different subjects' responses to the objects. In the fictitious example that follows, the first table (Table 7.1) contains the frequency of choices of 100 subjects to the psychological objects *Cafeteria, Gymnasium, Theater, Library, Classroom*. The subjects were asked to judge the importance of each to their college education. The objects were paired in the 10 possible ways and votes accumulated in a frequency matrix.

Initially the column sums are found (Table 7.1) and if the sums are not in order (as shown) the rows and columns of the matrix are rearranged so that the column sums are ordered from smallest to largest. The rearranged matrix follows in Table 7.2. Under the variance stable or simplified rank method we would proceed directly to use the sum of the votes as scale scores. But, under Thurstone's rationale, the individual frequencies are converted to proportions as shown in Table 7.3.

TABLE 7.1
Accumulated Frequency Matrix, n = 100

			i		
	Cl	*Ca*	*Gy*	*Li*	*Th*
Cl	—	20	30	35	10
Ca	80	—	30	40	20
Gy	70	70	—	45	15
Li	65	60	55	—	25
Th	90	80	85	75	—
Sum	305	230	280	195	70

Note. Each entry contains the votes of column objects over the row objects.

A proportion of .50 is placed on the diagonal of this matrix under the assumption that any object judged against itself would receive a random number of

TABLE 7.2
Ordered Frequency Matrix

	Th	Li	Gy	Ca	Cl
Th	—	75	85	80	90
Li	25	—	55	60	65
Gy	15	45	—	70	70
Ca	20	40	30	—	80
Cl	10	35	30	20	—
	70	195	200	230	305

votes. The expectation is that 50% of the time the subject would choose the column object and 50% of the time the row object.

TABLE 7.3
Proportions = f_{ij}/N

	Th	Li	Gy	Ca	Cl
Th	.50	.75	.85	.80	.90
Li	.25	.50	.55	.60	.65
Gy	.15	.45	.50	.70	.70
Ca	.20	.40	.30	.50	.80
Cl	.10	.35	.30	.20	.50

Next the proportions are converted to normal deviates by reference to the normal distribution (see Appendix, Table D) as shown in Table 7.4.

TABLE 7.4
Normal Deviates

	1 Th	2 Li	3 Gy	4 Ca	5 Cl
Th	.00	.67	1.03	.84	1.28
Li	-.67	.00	.13	.25	.38
Gy	-1.03	-.13	.00	.52	.52
Ca	-.84	-.25	-.52	.00	1.17
Cl	-1.28	-.38	-.52	-1.17	.00

Finally, the differences between column stimuli are found as shown in Table 7.5. If the data are complete the differences between the column sums of the normal deviates in Table 7.4 are equal to the sums of the column differences.

TABLE 7.5
Column Differences

Statements	2-1 Li-Th	3-2 Gy-Li	4-3 Ca-Gy	5-4 Cl-Ca
	.67	.37	-.19	.44
	.67	.13	.12	.13
	.90	.13	.52	.00
	.59	-.27	.52	1.17
	.90	-.14	-.55	1.17
Sum	3.73	.22	.42	2.91
n	5	5	5	5
Average	.746	.044	.084	.582

Knowing the differences among the objects we can assign scale values to each by accumulating the differences or distances among them. Thus, we let:

		Scale Values
Theater	(Th) =	= .00
Library	(Li) = 000 + .75	= .75
Gymnasium	(Gy) = 000 + .75 + .04	= .79
Cafeteria	(Ca) = 000 + .75 + .04 + .08	= .87
Classroom	(Cl) = 000 + .75 + .04 + .08 + .58	= 1.45

A graphical representation can be made as follows:

Th		Li	Gy	Ca		Cl	
↓		↓	↓	↓		↓	
.00		.75	.79	.87	1.00	1.45	2.00

Should proportions greater than .98 occur in the data they are reduced to .98. This is similarly true for proportions less than .02, which are made equal to .02. The reason for this restriction is that normal deviations for extreme proportions usually result in an extreme distortion of the scale values (100% equals infinity, for example). If data are missing the entries are left blank and no column differences are found for the blank entries. Averages of column differences are then found by dividing by an n reduced by the number of incomplete entries. The Case V method requires assumptions of equal dispersion of reactions and uncorrelatedness between judgments of different objects. If these assumptions cannot be met some other method or case may have to be used. The Case V is the simplest of the various cases that Thurstone explored.

RELIABILITY

A test of the effectiveness of any linear scale can be based on the ability of the scale scores to recapture the original proportions or frequencies used to produce the scale. Traditionally (for the Case V model) this is done by converting the z-scale values to obtained proportions (p^1). That is, finding differences between all pairs of z scale values and converting each difference into a proportion. Then the average difference between the original (p) and obtained proportions (p^1) is calculated. A measure, called the average deviation (AD) of the two sets of proportions, is then used as the index of scalability. Smith, in her master's thesis, in 1968, did a Monte Carlo study of the distribution of the AD and confirmed its relationship to Mosteller's (1951) χ^2 test.

Gulliksen and Tukey (1958) have attacked the problem of scale reliability using analysis of variance because they wished to answer the question of how effectively the scale scores account for variability in responses (i.e., what percentage of the total variance is accounted for). In this case the traditional definition of reliability $r_{tt} = 1 - (S_e^2/S_T^2)$ (where S_e^2 = error variance and S_T = total variance) is used as an index of scalability. The computer program COMPPC calculates such reliability measures based on an analysis of variance model in which the mean square within is substituted for the error variance in the general formula for reliability. Specifically the original proportions (p) are compared to proportions (p^1) derived from the scale values. This is accomplished by transforming each proportion to an arc-sine value in radians θ or θ'. $\theta = 2 \arcsin \sqrt{p}$. The difference between the Σ of $(\theta_{ij} - \theta'_{ij})^2/[k(k - 1)/2]$ is the error variance (s_e^2), where elements are taken for $j < i$. The total variance (s_T^2) is equal to $\Sigma (\theta - \bar{\theta})^2/[k(k - 1)/2]$. Thus r and r^2 can be calculated.

APPLICATION: TOURS FOR EAST–WEST CENTER STUDENTS

C. Vilbursri, one of the author's students, asked East–West Center students in Hawaii to indicate their preference for activity tours as part of the social events program of the center. Seven tours were paired in all possible ways according to the procedures outlined by Ross (1934). Figure 7.2 is an example of the instrument used. Subjects were asked to underline the preferred activity.

Ninety-two subjects representing 17 countries responded (61 males and 31 females). Vilbursri used Thurstone's Case V method to scale the tours. Table 7.6 briefly illustrates the analysis. It seems clear that the students preferred the active tours over the passive ones. In Table 7.6 the differences between column sums

---

Types of Activities

I. *Tours*: Underline the activity you prefer to participate in each pair.

1.   Polynesian Cultural Center *or* Paradise Park
2.   Hawaiian Wax Museum *or* Honolulu Academy of Arts
3.   Dole Pineapple Plantation *or* Sea Life Park
4.   Paradise Park *or* Bishop Museum
5.   Honolulu Academy of Arts *or* Polynesian Cultural Center
6.   Sea Life Park *or* Hawaiian Wax Museum
7.   Bishop Museum *or* Dole Pineapple Plantation
8.   Paradise Park *or* Honolulu Academy of Arts
9.   Polynesian Cultural Center *or* Sea Life Park
10.   Hawaiian Wax Museum *or* Dole Pineapple Plantation
11.   Honolulu Academy of Arts *or* Bishop Museum
12.   Sea Life Park *or* Paradise Park
13.   Dole Pineapple Plantation *or* Polynesian Cultural Center
14.   Bishop Museum *or* Hawaiian Wax Museum
15.   Honolulu Academy of Arts *or* Sea Life Park
16.   Paradise Park *or* Dole Pineapple Plantation
17.   Polynesian Cultural Center *or* Hawaiian Wax Museum
18.   Sea Life Park *or* Bishop Museum
19.   Dole Pineapple Plantation *or* Honolulu Academy of Arts
20.   Hawaiian Wax Museum *or* Paradise Park
21.   Bishop Museum *or* Polynesian Cultural Center

FIG. 7.2.   Example of a paired activity instrument.

are used instead of finding the sum of the column differences. Because the data are complete the result is the same.

Gulliksen (1958) has written a computer program, COMPPC, which provides scale scores and reliability indices (see Chapter 20).

TABLE 7.6
Results of Scaling 7 Activities Preference Judged by 92 Subjects
(61 males and 31 females)

FREQUENCY MATRIX, F

Activities*	6	3	7	5	2	1	4
6	46.000	52.000	61.000	61.000	68.000	74.000	73.000
3	40.000	46.000	59.000	59.000	61.000	64.000	73.000
7	31.000	33.000	46.000	52.000	52.000	52.000	61.000
5	31.000	33.000	40.000	46.000	46.000	47.000	58.000
2	24.000	31.000	40.000	46.000	46.000	48.000	64.000
1	18.000	28.000	40.000	45.000	44.000	46.000	60.000
4	19.000	19.000	31.000	34.000	28.000	32.000	46.000

PROPORTION MATRIX, P

Activities*	6	3	7	5	2	1	4
6	0.500	0.565	0.663	0.663	0.739	0.804	0.793
3	0.435	0.500	0.641	0.641	0.663	0.696	0.793
7	0.337	0.359	0.500	0.565	0.565	0.565	0.663
5	0.337	0.359	0.435	0.500	0.500	0.511	0.630
2	0.261	0.337	0.435	0.500	0.500	0.522	0.696
1	0.196	0.304	0.435	0.489	0.478	0.500	0.652
4	0.207	0.207	0.337	0.370	0.304	0.348	0.500
SUMS	2.272	2.630	3.446	3.728	3.750	3.946	4.728

NORMAL DEVIATE MATRIX, Z

Activities*	6	3	7	5	2	1	4
6	0.0	0.164	0.421	0.421	0.640	0.856	0.817
3	-0.164	0.0	0.361	0.361	0.421	0.513	0.817
7	-0.421	-0.361	0.0	0.164	0.164	0.164	0.421
5	-0.421	-0.361	-0.164	0.0	0.0	0.028	0.332
2	-0.640	-0.421	-0.164	0.0	0.0	0.055	0.513
1	-0.856	-0.513	-0.164	-0.028	-0.055	0.0	0.391
4	-0.817	-0.817	-0.421	-0.332	-0.513	-0.391	0.0
SUMS	-3.319	-2.309	-0.131	0.586	0.657	1.225	3.291
N	7	7	7	7	7	7	7
MEANS	-0.474	-0.330	-0.019	0.084	0.094	0.175	0.470
SCALE VALUES	0.0	0.144	0.455	0.558	0.568	0.649	0.944
	6	3	7	5	2	1	4

* 1 = Sea Life Park   2 = Paradise Park   3 = Dole Pineapple Plantation
4 = Polynesian Cultural Center   5 = Bishop Museum
6 = Hawaiian Wax Museum   7 = Honolulu Academy of Arts

AD = .022

8 Ordered Categories

When the number of objects becomes increasingly large, greater than 20, for example, the number of pairs necessary for rank- or paired-comparison methods becomes unwieldy (for 20 objects, $20(19)/2 = 190$ pairs). Although some experimenters have asked subjects to compare 50 (1,225 pairs) and 70 (3,660 pairs) items such studies are atypical and usually involve single items in the comparison rather than statements.

The most popular unidimensional method of attitude measurement involves ordered categories. In this method the judges are asked to place items in a fixed number of categories, usually 2, 3, 4, 5, 7, 9, or 11. A typical example of this format is given in Table 8.1.

In this case a unidimensional scale of attitude toward reading is proposed for these eight statements. Judges are asked to indicate the degree of positive affect toward reading for each statement by marking appropriately. It is clear that the format can accommodate a great many statements, as it calls for only one action per statement by each judge. It is the accumulation of the responses of a number of judges that provides the data for creating the scale.

Because the formulation of pilot instruments of this type is easily made, abuses of the ordered category method are frequently found. Some of the more common abuses follow. First, it is rare that judgments are sought by the experimenter. Rather the category headings contain degrees of personal agreement. If the use of such an instrument is to be valid one must speculate that agreement and judgment are similar and that the trial sample is similar to the final population. These two speculations are not always justified. Secondly, the statements formulated are seldom unidimensional in character yet are analyzed as if they were. Thirdly, the assumption of equality of intervals is made. That is, the value of the

TABLE 8.1
Example of Ordered Category Rating Scale

	Positive						Negative
	7	6	5	4	3	2	1
1 I try reading anything I can get my hands on.	____	____	____	____	____	____	____
3 When I become interested in something I read a book about it.	____	____	____	____	____	____	____
2 I read when there is nothing else to do.	____	____	____	____	____	____	____
7 I don't read unless I have to.	____	____	____	____	____	____	____
4 I have never read an entire book.	____	____	____	____	____	____	____
5 I seldom read anything.	____	____	____	____	____	____	____
6 I almost always have something I can read.	____	____	____	____	____	____	____
8 I only read things that are easy.	____	____	____	____	____	____	____

distance between 5 and 4 and the distance between 4 and 3 (in Table 8.1) is assumed to be equal and is usually assigned a value of 1. The following pages describe various attempts at eliminating the potential abuses from ordered category methods.

METHOD 1: GREEN'S SUCCESSIVE CATEGORIES

The scaling method of successive intervals (Green, 1954) is an attempt to accommodate more items than other unidimensional techniques and, in addition, to estimate the distance or interval between the ordered categories.

When a number of judges have marked the items a distribution of judgments for each item is created (see, for example, Table 8.2). In this method the average of the normal deviates assigned to the cumulative proportions of responses in each category represents the scale score of the item but only after each deviate is subtracted from the category boundary. As in the Case V model (previous chapter), variances around scale values are assumed to be equal.

TABLE 8.2
Frequencies of Response by 15 Judges to Reading
Attitude Statements

	Negative						Positive
Statements	1	2	3	4	5	6	7
1	0	0	1	3	3	1	7
2	2	1	3	4	0	1	4
3	0	0	0	1	1	5	8
4	8	4	1	2	0	0	0
5	10	4	0	0	1	0	0
6	0	2	0	1	1	4	7
7	8	4	1	0	1	1	0
8	4	5	0	4	1	0	1

The boundaries of the intervals are located under the assumption that the judgments for each item are distributed normally. In order to analyze the items under the cumulative normal distribution, the categories are numbered from least to most favorable and the cumulative frequency distributions are found, as in Table 8.3.

TABLE 8.3
Cumulative Frequency Distributions

	1	2	3	4	5	6	7
1	0	0	1	4	7	8	15
2	2	3	6	10	10	11	15
3	0	0	0	1	2	7	15
4	8	12	13	15	15	15	15
5	10	14	14	14	15	15	15
6	0	2	2	3	4	8	15
7	8	12	13	13	14	15	15
8	4	9	9	13	14	14	15

These frequencies are then converted to cumulative probabilities, as shown in Table 8.4. Any probabilities greater than .98 or less than .02 are rejected and the cumulative proportions are converted into normal deviates by referring to areas of normal distributions (see Table 8.5). z values (normal deviates) are found in Table D in the Appendix.

The differences between the categories for each item are found and the average of the differences is equal to the boundary between the two columns. For missing entries no differences are found and the average is found for those items for which a difference is available. See Table 8.6.

TABLE 8.4
Cumulative Proportions

	Categories						
	1	*2*	*3*	*4*	*5*	*6*	*7*
1	—	—	.07	.27	.47	.53	1.00
2	.13	.20	.40	.67	.67	.73	1.00
3	—	—	—	.07	.13	.47	1.00
4	.53	.80	.87	1.00	1.00	1.00	1.00
5	.67	.93	.93	.93	1.00	1.00	1.00
6	—	.13	.13	.20	.27	.53	1.00
7	.53	.80	.87	.87	.93	1.00	1.00
8	.27	.60	.60	.87	.93	.93	1.00

TABLE 8.5
Unit Normal Deviates (z scores)

	Categories						
	1	*2*	*3*	*4*	*5*	*6*	*7*
1			-1.47	-.61	-.08	.08	
2	-1.13	-.84	-.25	.44	.44	.61	
3				-1.47	-1.13	-.08	
4	.08	.88	1.13				
5	.44	1.48	1.48	1.48			
6		-1.13	-1.13	-.84	-.61	.08	
7	.08	1.48	1.48	1.48			
8	-.61	.26	.26	1.13	1.48	1.48	

TABLE 8.6
Matrix of Differences

Items	2-1	3-2	4-3	5-4	6-5
1	—	—	.86	.53	.16
2	.29	.59	.69	.00	.17
3	—	—	—	.34	1.05
4	.80	.25	—	—	—
5	1.04	.00	.00	—	—
6	—	.00	.29	.23	.69
7	1.40	.00	.00	—	—
8	.87	.00	.87	.35	.00
Sum	4.40	.84	2.71	1.45	2.07
n	5	6	6	5	5
Average	.88	.14	.45	.29	.41

The averages in the bottom row of Table 8.6 are the distances or intervals between the categories. By setting the first boundary arbitrarily as $B_1 = 0$, the remaining boundaries can be computed by summing the boundaries cumulatively from left to right as follows:

$B_1 = .00$ $= .00$

$B_2 = .00 + .88$ $= .88$

$B_3 = .00 + .88 + .14$ $= 1.02$

$B_4 = .00 + .88 + .14 + .45$ $= 1.47$

$B_5 = .00 + .88 + .14 + .45 + .29$ $= 1.76$

$B_6 = .00 + .88 + .14 + .45 + .29 + .41$ $= 2.17$

A comparison between an equal interval assumption and the boundaries obtained can be shown by dividing the sum 2.17 by 5. This yields an interval of approximately .43.

This illustrates that the boundary between 1 and 2 is quite long whereas the boundary between 2 and 3 is fairly small.

In order to obtain the scale scores, the normal deviate values (given in Table 8.5) are subtracted from the category boundaries. In this case the first boundary is taken as zero and no values are found for column 7. Table 8.7 shows this calculation. The row sums are then averaged.

These scale values or scores indicate that the reading items should be arranged as follows:

TABLE 8.7
Boundaries Minus Column Normal Deviates

Items	B_1-1	B_2-2	B_3-3	B_4-4	B_5-5	B_6-6	Sum	n	Scale Val. Avg.
1	–	–	2.49	1.98	1.72	1.99	8.08	4	2.02
2	1.13	1.72	1.27	.93	1.22	1.46	7.53	6	1.26
3	–	–	–	2.84	2.79	2.13	7.76	3	2.58
4	-.08	-.08	-.11	–	–	–	-.37	3	-.12
5	-.44	-.60	-.46	-.11	–	–	-1.81	4	-.45
6	–	2.91	2.15	2.21	2.27	1.99	10.43	5	2.08
7	-.08	-.60	-.46	-.11	–	–	1.29	4	-.32
8	.61	.62	.76	.24	.18	.59	2.80	6	.46

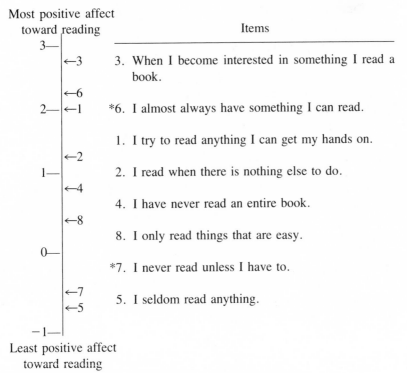

Most positive affect
toward reading   Items

3—
        ←3   3. When I become interested in something I read a
                     book.

      ←6
2—   ←1   *6. I almost always have something I can read.

                  1. I try to read anything I can get my hands on.

      ←2
1—   2. I read when there is nothing else to do.

      ←4
                  4. I have never read an entire book.

      ←8
                  8. I only read things that are easy.

0—
                *7. I never read unless I have to.

      ←7
                  5. I seldom read anything.
      ←5

−1—

Least positive affect
toward reading

Starred items may be deleted from final scale.

The experimenter may wish to delete items close together on the scale. In this case the experimenter might eliminate items 6 and 7 from the final scale.

Discussion

If an ordered category instrument contained a large number of items it may be expected that the instrument contains more than one unidimensional scale. If this is the case the multidimensional methods of clustering, factor analysis, or multi-dimensional scaling methodologies may be used (see Parts III and IV). An especially effective presentation of such analysis is given by Napier (1972).

METHOD 2: LIKERT'S SUMMATED RATINGS

Likert (1932) argues that: (1) the category intervals are generally equal; (2) preference categories should be established immediately; and (3) the judgment phase of creating a scale should be replaced by item analysis techniques. These three arguments mean that in Likert scaling the strength of a person's *preference* about *all* the psychological objects replaces the direction and intensity of the *specific objects* that a respondent has *judged*. Surprisingly, both successive intervals and Likert scaling, when carefully applied, often yield similar results. Because Likert scaling is easier, it is more popular.

The methodology of Likert scaling is as follows: The objects are chosen and unit values are assigned to each ordered category; for example, the integers 1 through 5. After subjects respond by checking or marking one of the categories for each item, an $N \times K$ (subject by item) matrix of information is generated as shown in Table 8.8. Each subject's categorical value is provided in the body of the table.

Next, item analyses are performed on the data. The mean (item difficulty) and standard deviation of each item are calculated and the Pearson r correlations of each item with the total score on all items is found. This correlation acts as a discrimination index for each item. That is, if the item correlates highly with the total score it is internally consistent and should be retained. In Table 8.8, responses to item 1 correlate $-.11$ with the total scores and the item should be eliminated. Item 1 also has low variability. Finally, a split-half reliability is found or Cronbach's alpha reliability coefficient (Cronbach, 1951). Items are eliminated on the basis of poor internal consistency, very high or low endorsement, or lack of variability.

Discussion

Initial item selection for ordered category scaling can be aided by the guidelines prescribed in Chapter 1, page 4. One should be careful to avoid "foldback"

TABLE 8.8
Example of Raw Data Matrix of "Likert" Responses

Subjects	Items						Total Score
	1	*2*	*3*	*4*	*5*	*6*	
01	2	2	3	3	2	5	17
02	1	2	3	4	3	5	18
03	1	1	1	5	5	5	18
04	2	3	3	2	2	5	17
05	2	2	2	2	2	5	15
06	2	2	2	4	3	3	16
07	2	3	1	3	2	4	15
08	1	1	3	3	3	5	15
09	1	2	3	3	3	5	17
10	2	3	3	4	3	5	20
r total	-.11	.20	.31	.55	.42	.51	
mean	1.60	2.10	2.40	3.30	2.80	4.70	
S.D.	.52	.74	.84	.95	.92	.67	

where   1 = Strongly Agree, 2 = Disagree, 3 = Undecided, 4 = Agree, 5 = Strongly Agree

analysis in which a selection of discriminating items is used to predict differences in the sample from which the items were originally selected. (See Blumenfeld, 1972; "I am never startled by a fish" at the end of this chapter.)

The steps used in creating an ordered category scale are as follows:

1. Decide on the number of dimension(s). (If more than one see multidimensional methods.)
2. Collect objects (observe criteria table, page 4; make pilot instrument).
3. Make a semantic description and exclude semantic outliers (see page 99).
4. Present instrument to judges; obtain their judgments.
5. Find item statistics (mean [proportion passing], S.D., r with total test score).
6. Run on TSCALE (see Chapter 20) for successive intervals.
7. Revise scales.

In the finished scale the category continuum is changed to one of agreement–disagreement instead of judgment.

EXAMPLE: REMMER'S GENERAL SCALE

H. H. Remmers popularized the use of the ordered category scale and produced general scales (Fig. 8.1). It is interesting to note that Silance and Remmers include some very extreme statements to insure that all possible representations are available in the final scale.

APPLICATION: REVISING A FOREIGN LANGUAGE ATTITUDE SCALE

Joy McClarty one of the author's students, selected A Foreign Language Attitude Scale for revision because it was designed to measure a single factor. A casual inspection of the items, however, suggests the presence of one or more incongruent items. The scale is designed to measure "attitude toward learning a (particular) foreign language" yet it contains items like "I would like to be a (Japanese) teacher," and "Everyone in school should take a foreign language." The original scale is given in Table 8.9.

Two hundred and thirty-one high school students (grades 7–12) taking their first year of high school Japanese responded to the scale. Many of these students were of Japanese ancestry and/or had attended Japanese language schools in their elementary school years.

              Please fill in the blanks below. (You may leave the space for your name blank.)

Name_____ _ Boy Girl (circle one) Date_____
Grade_____ __ What occupation would you like to follow?_____

Directions:
        Following is a list of statements about school subjects. Place a plus (+) sign
before each statement with which you agree with reference to the subjects listed at
the left of the statements.

math	English	science	art	
				1. I am crazy about this subject
				2. The very existence of humanity depends upon this subject.
				3. If I had my way, I would compel everybody to study this subject.
				4. This subject is one of the most useful subjects I know.
				5. I believe this subject is the basic one for all school courses.
				6. This is one subject that all Americans should know.
				7. This subject fascinates me.
				8. The merits of this subject far outweigh the defects.
				9. This subject gives pupils the ability to interpret life's problems.
				10. This subject will help pupils socially as well as mentally.
				11. This subject makes me effecient in school work.
				12. There are more chances for developing high ideals in this subject.
				13. This subject is interesting.
				14. This subject teaches methodical reasoning.
				15. This subject serves the needs of a large number of boys and girls.
				16. All methods used in this subject have been thoroughly tested.
				17. This subject has its merits and fills its purpose quite well.
				18. Every year more students are taking this subject.
				19. This subject aims mainly at power of execution or application.
				20. This subject is not based on untried theories.
				21. I think this subject is amusing.
				22. This subject has its drawbacks, but I like it.
				23. This subject might be worth while if it were taught right.
				24. This subject doesn't worry me in the least.
				25. My likes and dislikes for this subject balance one another.
				26. This subject is all right, but I would not take any more of it.
				27. No student should be concerned with the way this subject is taught.
				28. To me this subject is more or less boring.
				29. No definite results are evident in this subject.
				30. This subject does not motivate the pupil to do better work.
				31. This subject had numerous limitations and defects.
				32. This subject interferes with developing.
				33. This subject is dull.
				34. This subject seems to be a necessary evil.
				35. This subject does not hold my interest at all.
				36. The average student gets nothing worth having out of this subject.
				37. All of the material in this subject is very uninteresting.
				38. This subject can't benefit me.
				39. This subject has no place in the modern world.
				40. Nobody likes this subject.
				41. This subject is more like a plague than a study.
				42. This subject is all bunk.
				43. No sane person would take this subject.
				44. Words can't express my antagonism towards this subject.
				45. This is the worst subject taught in school.

FIG. 8.1.   A scale for measuring attitude toward any school subject.

TABLE 8.9
Foreign Language Attitude Scale

1 - do not agree at all 2 - agree a little bit 3 - agree quite a bit 4 - agree very much

1.   I would like studying Japanese.
2.   I would like to learn more than one foreign language.
3.   I like to practice Japanese on my own.
4.   Most people enjoy learning a foreign language.
5.   Everyone in school should take a foreign language.
6.   Japanese is interesting.
7.   It is too bad that so few Americans can speak Japanese.
8.   Anyone who can learn English can learn Japanese.
9.   I would like to travel in a country where Japanese is spoken.
10. The way Japanese people express themselves is very interesting.
11. Japanese is an easy language to learn.
12. I would like to be a Japanese teacher.
13. I would like to take Japanese again next year.
14. The Japanese I am learning will be useful to me.
15. I would like to know Japanese-speaking people of my own age.
16. Students who live in Japanese-speaking countries are just like me.
17. I'm glad Japanese is taught in this school.
18. My parents are pleased that I'm learning Japanese.
19. I like to hear Japanese people talk.
20. Japanese is one of my most interesting subjects.
21. Studying Japanese helps me to understand people of other countries.
22. I think everyone in school should study a foreign language.
23. Americans really need to learn a foreign language.
24. What I learn in Japanese helps me in other subjects.
25. Learning Japanese takes no more time than learning any other subject.
26. Sometimes I find that I'm thinking in Japanese.
27. My friends seem to like taking Japanese.
28. I'm glad that I have the opportunity to study Japanese.
29. I use Japanese outside the classroom.
30. I'm looking forward to reading Japanese books on my own.
31. I would like to study more Japanese during the next school year.
32. Japanese is one of the most important subjects in the school curriculum.

Because the attitude scale is relatively complex (containing 32 sentences), it was decided to use the design of semantic description given by Levy and Guttman (1975) as an initial attempt at obtaining unidimensionality. In this technique, an effort is made to classify statements subjectively by semantic dimensions. Although Guttman recommends using this technique primarily for the construction of trial items, it seems reasonable to define items using this method ''after the fact.'' (See Table 8.10.) A model sentence denoting the exact attitude being ''measured'' by the scale was set up and each sentence compared to it. The semantic bipolar categories used were: (1) self versus other; (2) like or value versus dislike or not valued; (3) study versus use; (4) Japanese versus foreign language; (5) alone versus in class; and (6) presently versus later. This technique provided a fairly stable framework with which to compare the items. Low or incongruent sums indicate items that lack content or semantic validity.

Item mean and standard deviations for the total group are given in Table 8.11 as well as correlations between each item and the total score. In this case items 4, 16, and 25 have low internal consistency.

TABLE 8.10
Semantic Description of Attitude Statements
(after Guttman)

model:	I	Like	To Study	Japanese	(qualifier)	sum
1.	x	x	x	x		4
2.	x	x	x	f.l.		3
3.	x	x	x	x	on my own	4-
4.	people	x	x	f.l.		2
5.	everyone	should	x	f.l.		1
6.	(I)	interest	—	x		3
7.	Americans	should	speak	X		1
8.	Anyone	can	learn	x		1
9.	x	x	travel	x		3
10.	(I)	interest	speech	x		2
11.	x	easy	learn	x		2
12.	x	x	teach	x		3
13.	x	x	x	x	next year	4-
14.	x	useful	x	x		3
15.	x	x	meet	x		3
16.	x	am like	—	x		3
17.	x	x	x	x		4
18.	parents	x	x	x	by me	3-
19.	x	x	hear	x		3
20.	(I)	interest	x	x		3
21.	x	helpful	x	x		3
22.	everyone	should	x	f.l.		1
23.	Americans	need	x	f.l.		1
24.	x	helpful	x	x		3
25.	x	easy	x	x		3
26.	x	—	think	x		3
27.	friends	x	x	x		3
28.	x	x	x	x		4
29.	x	use	—	x	out of class	3-
30.	x	x	read	x	on my own	3-
31.	x	x	x	x	next year	4-
32.	(I)	important	x	x		3

Abbreviations: x (same as head of col.), f.l. = foreign language, (I) = implied "I",
    "—" = neither a part of nor negated by the sentence (counted as an
    "x" for sums).

Sum = the number of "x"s (followed by a minus sign if additionally qualified).

TABLE 8.11
Item Means and Standard Deviations for Total Group

	Total	
Item	Mean	SD
1	2.86	.74
2	2.78	1.67
3	2.15	.84
4	2.70	.86
5	2.96	1.11
6	3.20	.81
7	2.77	.99
8	2.63	1.03
9	3.00	1.03
10	3.20	.87
11	2.34	.88
12	1.39	.65
13	3.24	1.05
14	3.45	.73
15	2.87	.89
16	2.87	.92
17	3.45	.72
18	3.60	.65
19	2.77	.86
20	2.49	.88
21	2.54	.99
22	3.03	.95
23	3.06	.97
24	1.86	.85
25	2.46	1.09
26	1.98	.90
27	2.43	.92
28	3.36	.75
29	2.22	.82
30	2.36	.96
31	3.20	1.01
32	3.25	.89

A final descriptive technique is made by scaling the items. Although many scaling techniques are available, the method of successive intervals (see Fig. 8.2) was selected as a representative. It was felt that after the good items had been selected by other methods, it might be desirable to incorporate only those that provided an approximation to an equal interval scale. It is felt that effective features of various unidimensional scaling methods should be used collectively. In this example, using the semantic description of Guttman, the item analysis of Likert, and the method of successive intervals, a final scale was chosen. (See Table 8.12.)

Shaw and Wright (1967) provide a complete text of ordered category scales (see also Robinson, Rusk, & Head, 1969a,b,c).

Veldman (1967) has written a series of programs for the analysis of ordered category data; TSCALE and TESTAT are useful (see Chapter 20). In addition, KENTAU can be used to intercorrelate items.

TABLE 8.12

The Revised Scale

Possible directions: Select the three statements with which you most nearly agree.

A.	Japanese is one of the most important subjects in the school curriculum. (32)
B.	I'm looking forward to reading Japanese books on my own. (30)
C.	Japanese is one of my most interesting subjects. (20)
D.	I like studying Japanese. (1)
E.	I would like to study more Japanese during the next school year. (31)
F.	I would like to take Japanese again next year. (13)
G.	Japanese is interesting. (6)
H.	I'm glad that I have the opportunity to study Japanese. (28)
I.	I'm glad that Japanese is taught in this school. (17)
J.	My parents are pleased that I'm learning Japanese. (18)

Note: Because of the similarity of wording in items E and F and in items H and I, it may be desirable to either scramble the item order or to eliminate one of each pair.

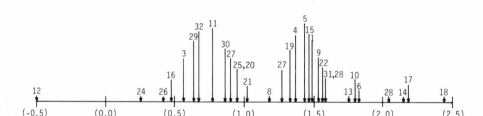

Successive Interval (T-Scale)

Note: Scale begins at -.50. Each increment equals .10.

FIG. 8.2.   Successive Interval Scale of Attitude Toward Teaching Japanese

---

'I AM NEVER STARTLED BY A FISH'

by Warren S. Blumenfeld
Georgia State University

Most of us would probably agree that, in the area of managerial selection, what is lacking most is the availability of valid non-cognitive predicators. Further, most would agree that tailor-made, special keys are to be preferred to universal, general keys. The combination of the two seems desirable and appropriate. However, as Kurtz pointed out so well in 1948, too often the wishes and hopes of the practitioner and/or the consumer manifest themselves in a strange form of selective perception in the evaluation of effectiveness of such keys, i.e., the acceptance of self-fulfilling "research" *via* foldback design.

Purpose. The purpose of this research was to develop and validate concurrently a special tailor-made key for a relatively new and exciting personality instrument in a group of potential managers. A secondary (sic) purpose of this research was to point out once again the specious, spurious, fallacious, but fascinating results that are obtained when cross-validation does not follow item analysis.

Data Collection. The subjects, criterion, and instrument follow.

The subjects in this experiment were 126 management majors in an introductory management course at Georgia State University. The instrument administration was presented to them as an example of a "scientific" selection technique (very much as charlatans present their wares to unwary personnel and marketing executives). From all indications, it was accepted as such (just as it is usually accepted by "hard-nosed businessmen"). These subjects may be viewed as entry level managers, or at least potential managers, i.e., personnel and marketing executives, hard-nosed businessmen, etc., etc.

The criterion in this study was self-reported grade point average of the subjects.

The relatively new and exciting (if not sensational) personality instrument used in this study was the *North Dakota Null-Hypothesis Brain Inventory* (*NDNHBI*), conjured up and conceived by (Art) Buchwald (1965) with a sharp tongue and a great deal of cheek in answer to the problems of face validity encountered by the *Minnesota Multiphasic Personality Inventory.* The *NDNHBI* consists of 36 statements of a non-cognitive nature to which the respondent indicates either true or false as being descriptive of himself. Since the inventory is so "special" and will no doubt be of interest, the items are presented here:

1. I salivate at the sight of mittens.
2. If I go into the street, I'm apt to be bitten by a horse.
3. Some people never look at me.
4. Spinach makes me feel alone.
5. My sex life is A-okay.
6. When I look down from a high spot, I want to spit.
7. I like to kill mosquitoes.
8. Cousins are not to be trusted.
9. It makes me embarrassed to fall down.
10. I get nauseous from too much roller skating.
11. I think most people would cry to gain a point.
12. I cannot read or write.
13. I am bored by thoughts of death.
14. I become homicidal when people try to reason with me.
15. I would enjoy the work of a chicken flicker.
16. I am never startled by a fish.
17. My mother's uncle was a good man.
18. I don't like it when somebody is rotten.
19. People who break the law are wise guys.
20. I have never gone to pieces over the weekend.
21. I think beavers work too hard.
22. I use shoe polish to excess.
23. God is love.
24. I like mannish children.
25. I have always been disturbed by the sight of Lincoln's ears.
26. I always let people get ahead of me at swimming pools.
27. Most of the time I go to sleep without saying goodby.
28. I am not afraid of picking up door knobs.
29. I believe I smell as good as most people.
30. Frantic screams make me nervous.
31. It's hard for me to say the right thing when I find myself in a room full of mice.
32. I would never tell my nickname in a crisis.
33. A wide necktie is a sign of disease.
34. As a child I was deprived of licorice.
35. I would never shake hands with a gardener.
36. My eyes are always cold.

In the original article, Buchwald presented a differential psychometric scatter scoring system for placement in either the

continued

Never startled . . .

continued

Peace Corps, the Voice of America, or the White House. In the current research, as indicated by the purpose, an appropriate configuration which concurrently related to an external criterion was developed and quasivalidated.

Data Analysis. There were three phases to the data analysis of this research, i.e., (1) item analysis, (2) foldback, and (3) cross-validation.

The 36 items in the *NDNHBI* were item analyzed using the procedure described by Lawshe and Baker (1950) with an external criterion of self-reported grade point average. A skew in the criterion distribution categories necessitated that the high and low "halves" of the criterion group be of different sizes. In the item analysis, there were 48 in the high group, and 28 in the low group. Alpha of .10 was used to identify the "discriminating" items for inclusion in the "special" key.

To prove to the proponents of the instrument (of which there were a few) and to those who really "wanted" the key to work (several students with an apparent clinical bent), the items surviving the item analysis were applied to the answer sheets of the item analysis group. The concurrent validity was documented by biserial correlation.

For those more interested in the best (rather than the most fulfilling) estimate of the relationship between the derived key and the external criterion of self-reported grade point average, the items surviving the item analysis were scored in holdout groups of 25 high answer sheets and 25 low answer sheets. Again, biserial correlation was obtained to quantify the relationship between the special key and the criterion.

Results

The item analysis procedure identified 9 items (chance would have been 4) which discriminated between the high and low groups at or beyond the .10 level. The reader will no doubt be interested in which items "came through," particularly as the potential for *post hoc* interpretations and insights are nearly infinite. The items (and their weights) in the special key were:

1. (−) My sex life is A-okay.
2. (+) When I look down from a high spot, I want to spit.
3. (−) I think most people would cry to gain a point.
4. (+) I am never startled by a fish.
5. (+) My mother's uncle was a good man.
6. (+) I don't like it when somebody is rotten.
7. (+) I have never gone to pieces over the weekend.
8. (+) Most of the time I go to sleep without saying goodby.
9. (+) It's hard for me to say the right thing when I find myself in a room full of mice.

Applying these 9 items back upon the original sample, the obtained biserial correlation was .78. This is clearly off zero beyond the .05 level,—most encouraging to all, and completely satisfactory, convincing, and conclusive to some (Kurtz, 1948). (Consider here for a moment those of your acquaintance and/or your employ using this foldback design and at this point mouthing such quasiprofessional, and sage things as "of course, these results should be interpreted with some caution").

Unfortunately, when the 9-item key was applied to the holdout sample of 50, the encouraging coefficient of .78 shrank slightly. In fact, it shrank back to .07 (*not* significantly off zero at the .05 level). Too bad; pity; so many of the items seemed to have so much construct validity, and were *so rich* in potential for *post hoc* interpretations and insights, e.g., "I am never startled by a fish."

Discussion and Conclusions

Little if any discussion seems necessary; Cureton's classic paper (1952) has been re-trotted out and executed. It seems clear once again that (1) the application of a key to the control group is the acid test of the quality of a key and (2) the (re)application of a key to the original group is but a half-acid test. To a sophisticated group like this, this would seem to be "coals to New Castle"; however, as an industrial psychologist in a business school dealing with students of business administration (and naive practitioners and consumers of business administration), it is painfully clear to me that the foldback design still remains very much in vogue. (After all, it has such obvious marketing advantages.) I think it appropriate to continue to beat home the point of cross-validation, i.e., let's have no more of this half-acid research.

In conclusion, the foldback design is not (necessarily) dead; it is very much alive and doing quite well among the malicious and the naive in the general business world.

And frankly, I *am* always startled by a fish—particularly when the "fish" turns out to be a personnel or marketing executive.

"Quasi-successful concurrent validation of a special key for a relatively new and exciting personality instrument in a group of potential managers: or, I am never startled by a fish." Paper read at the meeting of the Georgia Psychological Association, Macon, May 1972. Reprinted from Industrial Psychologist Newsletter, May 1972, with permission from the author.

9 Guttman Scaling

THEORY: MAINTAINING ORDER

Louis Guttman (1944, 1950) described a unidimensional scale as one in which the subjects' responses to the objects would place individuals in perfect order. Ideally persons who answer several questions favorably all have higher ability than persons who answer the same questions unfavorably. Arithmetic questions make good examples of this type of scale.

Suppose elementary school children are given the following addition problems:

$$
\begin{array}{llllllllll}
(1) & 2 & (2) & 12 & (3) & 28 & (4) & 86 & (5) & 228 \\
 & +3 & & +15 & & +24 & & +88 & & +894
\end{array}
$$

It is probable that if subject *A* responds correctly to item 5 that he or she would also respond correctly to items 1, 2, 3, and 4. If subject *B* can answer item 2 and not item 3, it is probable that he or she can answer item 1 correctly but would be unable to answer item 4 and 5. By scoring 1 for each correct answer and 0 otherwise, a profile of responses can be obtained. If the arithmetic questions form a perfect scale, then the sum of the correct responses to the five items can be used to reveal a person's scale type in terms of a series of ones and zeros. In our example:

| | *Items* | | | | | |
	1	*2*	*3*	*4*	*5*	*Sum*
Subject A has scale type →	1	1	1	1	1	= 5
Subject B has scale type →	1	1	0	0	0	= 2

Given a perfect scale, the single summed score reveals the scale type. Thus a single digit can be used to recreate all the responses of a subject to a set of items that constitute a perfect scale.

With five questions and scoring the item as correct or incorrect there are only six possible scale types. These are:

		Scale Type				*Score*
1	1	1	1	1	1	5
2	1	1	1	1	0	4
3	1	1	1	0	0	3
4	1	1	0	0	0	2
5	1	0	0	0	0	1
6	0	0	0	0	0	0

$$\text{———————continuum ———————} \longrightarrow$$

Although there exist 32 possible arrangements of five ones and zeros, only six of these form scale types. In general the number of scale types for dichotomously scored data is $(K + 1)$, where K is the number of objects. Although the perfect Guttman scale is unlikely to be found in practice, approximations to it can be obtained by a careful choice of items and careful analysis of a set of pilot subjects' responses to a larger number of items than are to be used in the final scale.

METHOD: GOODENOUGH'S ERROR COUNTING

In a method sometimes known as scalogram analysis (Edwards, 1957), a set of psychological objects is selected. The objects should be ones that will differentiate subjects with varying attitudes or perceptions about the objects along some single dimension. Suppose the following six statements have been chosen and 12 subjects' responses have been obtained in the form of Agreement or Disagreement to these statements. Do these statements constitute a Guttman Scale along the dimension of attitudes toward school?

TABLE 9.1
Array of Responses to Statements

Subjects	A		B		C		D		E		F	
	A	D	A	D	A	D	A	D	A	D	A	D
1		x	x		x		x		x			x
2	x		x		x			x		x		x
3	x			x		x		x		x	x	
4	x		x			x		x		x		x
5		x		x	x		x		x			x
6		x	x			x	x		x			x
7		x	x			x		x	x			x
8		x	x		x			x		x		x
9	x		x			x	x		x		x	
10		x	x		x		x			x		x
11		x		x	x			x		x		x
12		x	x		x			x	x			x

Statements	Agree	Disagree
A. School is OK.	____	____
B. I come to school regularly.	____	____
C. I think school is important.	____	____
D. It is nice to be in school.	____	____
E. I think school is fun.	____	____
F. I think school is better than a circus.	____	____

The initial data are found in Table 9.1. Subjects respond (A) agree or (D) disagree.

TABLE 9.2
Response Data in the Form of Ones and Zeros

Subjects	A	B	C	D	E	F	Scores
1	0	1	1	1	1	0	4
2	1	1	1	0	0	0	3
3	1	0	0	0	0	1	2
4	1	1	0	0	0	0	2
5	0	0	1	1	1	0	3
6	0	1	0	1	1	0	3
7	0	1	0	0	1	0	2
8	0	1	1	0	0	0	2
9	1	1	0	1	1	1	5
10	0	1	1	1	0	0	4
11	0	0	1	0	0	0	1
12	0	1	1	0	1	0	3
	4	9	4	5	6	2	33

The basic data are arranged in a table of ones and zeros in which one (1) stands for agree and zero (0) for disagree, as shown in Table 9.2, and the rows and columns are summed.

It is convenient to rearrange the table in order of the row and column sums. The errors from the scale types are calculated by subtracting the profile of ones and zeros for each subject from the perfect scale type with the same summed score. For example:

							Sum
Perfect Scale Type	1	1	1	1	1	0	5
Subject 9	1	0	1	1	1	1	5
Difference		1				−1	

The sum of the absolute value of each difference is the error. In this case $1 + |-1| = 2$ errors. These two steps are illustrated in Table 9.3.

TABLE 9.3
Rearrangement of Table by Magnitude of Row and Column Sums

Subjects	B	C	E	D	A	F	Sum	Error
9	1	0	1	1	1	1*	5	2
1	1	1	1	1	0	0	4	0
2	1	1	0*	0	1*	0	3	2
5	0*	1	1	1*	0	0	3	2
6	1	0*	1	1*	0	0	3	2
10	1	1	0*	1*	0	0	3	2
12	1	1	1	0	0	0	3	0
3	0*	0*	0	0	1*	1*	2	4
4	1	0*	0	0	1*	0	2	2
7	1	0*	1	0	0	0	2	2
8	1	1	0	0	0	0	2	0
11	0*	1*	0	0	0	0	1	2
	9	7	6	5	4	2	33	20

*Indicates error

The total possible number of errors is equal to the product of N subjects and K objects or in this case N·K = 12·6 or 72 possible errors. An estimate of how accurately the particular arrangement approximates a perfect scale is to take the ratio of the found errors to the maximum number of possible errors. Subtracting this ratio from 1.000 renders a coefficient of the scale's ability to reproduce the scores based on the row sums. In this case the coefficient is

$$1 - \frac{20 \text{ total errors}}{72 \text{ possible errors}} = .723$$

It seems apparent that the items do not form a close approximation to a true scale. Item C (I think school is important.) has six errors, of a possible 12, so it is reasonable to eliminate this item. After eliminating item C the responses to the remaining items are organized as follows:

TABLE 9.4
Rearrangement of Table Based on Errors

Subjects	B	E	D	A	F	Sum	Error
9	1	1	1	1	1	5	0
1	1	1	1	0	0	3	0
6	1	1	1	0	0	3	0
12	1	1	0	0	0	2	0
7	1	1	0	0	0	2	0
2	1	0*	0	1*	0	2	2
4	1	0*	0	1*	0	2	2
10	1	0*	1*	0	0	2	2
5	0*	1	1*	0	0	2	2
3	0*	0*	0	1*	1*	2	4
8	1	0	0	0	0	1	0
11	0	0	0	0	0	0	0
	9	6	5	4	2	26	12
p	.75	.50	.42	.33	.17		
q	.25	.50	.58	.67	.83		

In this second reorganization (Table 9.4), 12 errors occur (note that four of these occur with Subject 3. This subject's data should be checked for accuracy in following instructions, for errors in coding, etc.). In this new arrangement, a coefficient of the ability of the column sums to reproduce all the responses accurately is $1 - \Sigma$ Errors/$(N \cdot K)$ or $1 - \frac{12}{60} = .80$. This index, called the *coefficient of reproducibility* (CR), has been slightly improved by deleting item C from the analysis. Because further deletion appears not to be of benefit (that is, does not increase the coefficient of reproducibility) no more rearrangements are performed.

A test of the effectiveness of a reproducibility coefficient must be made in light of the minimal reproducibility possible given the average proportion of agree and disagree responses in each column of Table 9.4. By averaging the maximum of p or q in each column, the *minimal marginal reproducibility* (MMR) can be obtained. Thus the sum of $(.75 + .50 + .58 + .67 + .83)/5 = .67$. The difference between a CR of .80 and the MMR of .67 is .13. This number is the *percentage of improvement* (PI). A coefficient of scalability (CS) is found by dividing the percentage of improvement by, one (1) minus the minimum marginal reproducibility $(1 - MMR)$, (i.e., the possible improvement that could be made). In this case the coefficient of scalability is $.13/.33 = .39$.

To recapitulate these indices:

Example
values

(1)   The coefficient of reproducibility (CR) $= 1 - \dfrac{\Sigma\, e}{NK}$ .80

(2)   The minimum marginal reproducibility (MMR) =

$\dfrac{\sum\limits_{i=1}^{K} p_i \text{ or } q_i}{K}$ where p or q is maximum   .67

(3)   The percentage of improvement (PI) = CR − MMR   .13

(4)   The coefficient of scalability (CS) $= \dfrac{\text{PI}}{1 - \text{MMR}}$ .39

Guttman has stated that a scale with a CR < .90 cannot be considered an effective approximation to a perfect scale. Further study suggests that a CR of .93 approximates the .05 level of significance. Other sources suggest that the CS should be greater than .60. In this example, none of these cases hold and the items cannot be said to constitute a Guttman scale.

It is also possible to assign a coefficient of reproducibility to a given subject. This coefficient may be obtained by subtracting the subject's profile from a perfect scale vector with the same score. The sum of the absolute differences divided by K items and subtracted from 1 gives the CR_i for the subject chosen. For example:

$K = 9$	1	2	3	4	5	6	7	8	9	
Scale type	$Y = 1$	1	1	1	1	1	0	0	0	Score = 6
Subject's vector	$X = 1$	1	1	0	1	1	1	0	0	Score = 6
				1			−1			

$CR_i = 1 - [(|1| + |-1|)/9] = 1 - 2/9 = .7778$

APPLICATION 1: CLOZE TESTS IN READING

F. J. King (1974) has utilized scalogram analysis (Guttman Scaling) to grade the difficulty of cloze tests. A cloze test asks the subject to complete passages in which a specific set of words has been deleted. It has been suggested that a system for getting children to read materials at their appropriate reading level must be capable of locating a student on a reading level continuum so that he can read materials at or below that level. This is what a cloze test is designed to do.

King constructed eight cloze passages ordered in predicted reading difficulty. If a student answered seven of 12 items on a certain passage correctly he was given a score of one, if he had fewer than seven correct answers he received a score of zero. A child's scale score could vary from zero to eight, a score for each of the eight passages.

If the test passages form a cumulative scale, then scale scores should provide a description of performance. A scale score of 4, for example, would have this vector

11110000

and this would indicate that a student could read text material at the fourth level and below. By constructing a table to show the percentage of students at each scale level who passed each test passage King was able to indicate that "smoothed" scale scores were capable of producing the score vectors with considerable accuracy.

Once the scalability of the passage was determined, King related the reading difficulty of the test passages to the difficulty level of the materials in general. Thus he was able to indicate which material a child could comprehend under instruction.

APPLICATION 2: ARITHMETIC ACHIEVEMENT

D. M. Smith (1971) applied Guttman Scaling to the construction and validation of arithmetic achievement tests. He first broke simple addition into a list of 20 tasks and ordered these tasks according to hypothesized difficulty. Experimental forms containing four items for each task were constructed and administered to elementary school children in grades 2–6. Smith reduced his 20 tasks to nine by testing the significance of the difference between the proportion passing for each pair of items. He chose items that were different at $\alpha \leq .05$ for his test. The nine tasks were scored by giving a one (1) each time three or more of the four parallel items for that task were answered correctly and a zero (0) otherwise. These items were analyzed using the Goodenough technique. The total scale score for each subject was defined as the number of the item that preceded two successive failures (zeros). Thus a subject with the following vector

```
1  2  3  4  5  6  7  8  9    Tasks
1  1  1  0  1  1  0  0  0    Subject's vector
                      Second zero
```

would have a scale score of 6.

Table 9.5 shows the coefficients of reproducibility obtained by Smith on the addition tests for three schools and five grades.

The high coefficients of reproducibility indicate that a student's scale score

TABLE 9.5
Obtained Coefficients of Reproducibility

Grade	Shadeville	Sopchoppy	Both
2	.9546	.9415	.9496
3	.9603	.9573	.9589
4	.9333	.9213	.9267
5	.9444	.9557	.9497
6	.9606	.9402	.9513
All	.9514	.9430	.9487

accurately depicts his or her position with regard to the tasks necessary in solving addition problems. For this reason Smith's results can be used: (1) to indicate the level of proficiency for a given student; (2) as a diagnostic tool; and (3) to indicate the logical order of instruction.

Anderson (1966) has written a useful program for the analysis of Guttman Scale Data. BMD, BMDP, and SPSS also have routines for this analysis (see Chapter 20).

10 Scoring Unidimensional Scales

Once a unidimensional scale of psychological objects has been established subjects can be located on the scale in several ways:

NAMING OR PAIRING

The simplest method is to ask the subject to name the statement(s) or object(s) that he or she most agrees with or most approves. The subject is then given the scale values of the objects named. Some experimenters prefer to average the weights or values of three or more objects agreed upon. They use the mean or median of the scale of the objects that are agreed with. This becomes the scale score for the subject. If, for example, there are nine objects with the following scale values,

Objects	Scale Values	Objects Agreed with by Subject i	Score for Subject i	
			Median	Mean
A	90	x	81	86
B	85			
C	81	x		
D	76	x		
E	64			
F	53			
G	47			
H	22			
I	16			

the subject would have a score of either 81 or 86.

Edwards (1957) has proposed pairing all the scaled objects and giving the subject a score of one (1) for every object of a pair he or she selects that agrees with the scaled order of the objects. Suppose four objects are scaled using some unidimensional technique as follows:

Objects	A = 40 B = 30 C = 20 D = 10	Scale Value

The pairs AB, AC, AD, BC, BD, and CD are formed and the subject chooses one object in each pair he most agrees with. If he chooses A > B in the first pair he scores one (1) point because A (40) has a higher scale value than B (30). Should he choose A > B > C > D he would have a score of 6, or the maximum score.

AGREEMENT CATEGORIES

More frequently categories of agreement are established for the scaled objects. Values are assigned to the categories (the values are usually ordered integers). The related category weight for each item responded to is multiplied by the object's scaled value. The sum of these products is taken as the subject's score on the dimension. For example:

	Scale Value	SA	A	D	SD	Score
		Categories				
		Weights				
		4	3	2	1	
1. I hate wars.	5.0	x				20 (4 × 5.0)
2. Wars should be abolished.	4.0	x				16 (4 × 4.0)
3. There will always be wars.	3.0			x		6 (2 × 3.0)
	TOTAL					30

In Likert scoring the objects are all given equal weight, namely, unity (1). Ordered categories of agreement are established, and given ordered integer values. Positive statements are usually given high value for strong agreements. For example:

	5	4	3	2	1	Category value
	SA	A	U	D	SD	Degrees of agreement
						U stands for undecided
(A) School is good.			x			Subject's item score is 4

Negative statements are reversed in scoring. Reverse scoring is calculated by subtracting the category value from $K + 1$ categories: Thus a distinction is made between rank order of the category and the score assigned on the basis of the direction of the statement. For example:

	5	4	3	2	1	Category value
	SA	A	U	D	SD	Degrees of agreement
(B) I hate school.			x			Subject's item score is $(5 + 1) - 4 = 2$

A subject's total score is simply the sum of all his or her item scores or their average.

Guilford (1954) weights items from 1–9 based on the correlation (r) of the item with the total score. The higher the item correlation, the greater the weight associated with that item.

DISCUSSION

In establishing objects for Likert scoring (in the case where objects have been previously scaled by some other method), the objects should have some symmetry around a neutral object. If one assumes a normal distribution for the scale values, then objects should be closer together at the extremes of the scale and well spread near the center or neutral position when equal scale values are assumed.

If the distance between a neutral item ($z = 0$) and an extreme item ($z = .98$) is divided by the number of objects, and proportions are assigned to these z scores and plotted linearly, then the linear plot reveals how items should be selected in order for them to have unit weight in Likert scoring.

Suppose, for example, only positive objects are needed, then the following z values and related proportions would be obtained

	z	p
(1) A neutral item	0	.50
(2) A moderate item	.5	.69
(3) A very positive item	1.0	.84

(4) A fairly extreme item	1.5	.93
(5) An extreme item	2.0	.98

Plotting the proportions linearly results in:

(1)	(2)		(3)	(4)	(5)
↓	↓		↓	↓	↓
.5	.69	.75	.84	.93	.98

The selection of scaled objects could therefore approximate this distribution.

The Likert summed scores have the advantage of greater differentiation among respondents because a larger range among the scores may occur than with other methods. Likert scoring is easy and computer programs are available for finding such sums (TESTAT, Veldman, 1967).

The GSO SCALE is an example of an attempt to normalize responses (see Fig. 10.1). In this case the category definitions are used to spread the responses of the students into a more nearly normal distribution. A score of 5, for example, is given for professors rated in the upper 5% of all professors, whereas a score of 4 is given to instructors rated in the upper 25%, and so on. It is theoretically more difficult to give a professor a score of 5 than a 4, for example.

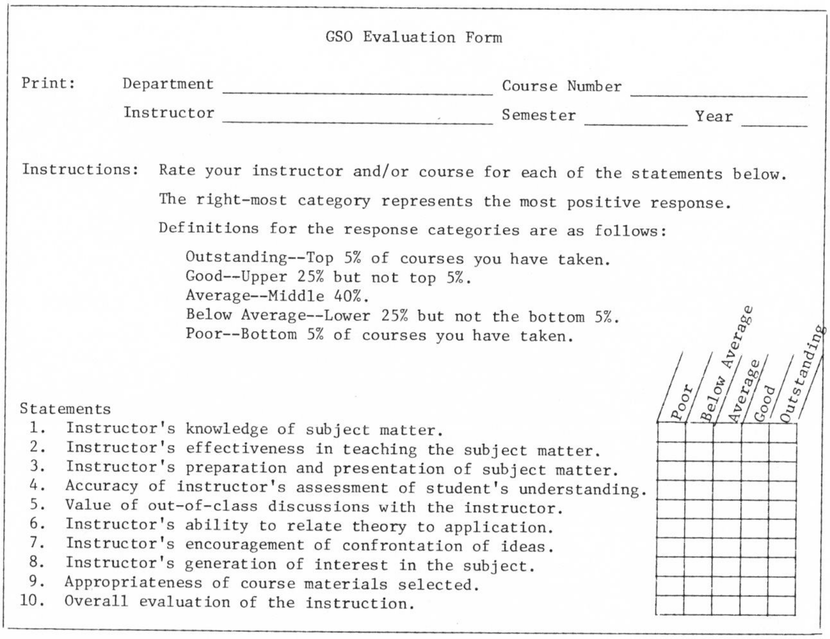
GSO Evaluation Form

Print: Department ______ Course Number ______

Instructor ______ Semester ______ Year ______

Instructions: Rate your instructor and/or course for each of the statements below.
The right-most category represents the most positive response.
Definitions for the response categories are as follows:

Outstanding--Top 5% of courses you have taken.
Good--Upper 25% but not top 5%.
Average--Middle 40%.
Below Average--Lower 25% but not the bottom 5%.
Poor--Bottom 5% of courses you have taken.

Statements	Poor	Below Average	Average	Good	Outstanding
1. Instructor's knowledge of subject matter.					
2. Instructor's effectiveness in teaching the subject matter.					
3. Instructor's preparation and presentation of subject matter.					
4. Accuracy of instructor's assessment of student's understanding.					
5. Value of out-of-class discussions with the instructor.					
6. Instructor's ability to relate theory to application.					
7. Instructor's encouragement of confrontation of ideas.					
8. Instructor's generation of interest in the subject.					
9. Appropriateness of course materials selected.					
10. Overall evaluation of the instruction.					

FIG. 10.1. An example of a scale that attempts to spread subject's responses by using specific definitions for response categories.

EXERCISES FOR PART II

1. Scale by the simplified rank method.
   Subjects (Chinese East-West Grantees, 10 males, 10 females)
   Psychological objects = purposes for dressing

	MALE						FEMALE				
	Prevent Colds	For Beauty	Prevent Injury	Enhance Rank	Reduce Exposure		– Colds	+ Beauty	– Injury	+ Rank	– Exposure
Sa	A	B	C	D	E	Sa	A	B	C	D	E
1	5	3	1	2	4	1	2	5	1	4	3
2	4	3	1	2	5	2	3	2	4	1	5
3	5	1	2	3	4	3	2	5	1	4	3
4	4	3	5	1	2	4	3	5	4	1	2
5	4	3	5	1	2	5	5	3	2	1	4
6	5	2	3	1	4	6	4	3	1	2	5
7	3	4	5	1	2	7	2	5	1	4	3
8	5	2	4	1	3	8	4	3	1	2	5
9	2	1	3	5	4	9	1	5	2	3	4
10	5	4	1	3	2	10	3	5	2	1	4

2. Scale by Thurstones Case V Method

   Psychological dimension = Degree of "eternal truth"

   1. Nothing lasts
   2. There are no great men.
   3. Progress is an illusion.
   4. You can't make anyone love you.
   5. You only keep what you give away.

	PAIRS									
SUBJECT	1-2	1-3	1-4	1-5	2-3	2-4	2-5	3-4	3-5	4-5
S_1	1	1	1	1	2	2	1	2	2	2
S_2	1	1	1	1	2	2	2	2	2	2
S_3	1	2	2	2	2	2	2	1	1	2
S_4	1	1	1	1	1	2	1	1	1	1
S_5	1	1	1	2	1	1	2	2	2	2
S_6	1	1	1	2	2	2	1	1	2	2
S_7	1	2	1	2	2	2	2	1	2	2
S_8	2	2	2	1	1	1	1	2	1	1
S_9	1	1	1	1	1	2	2	1	2	2
S_{10}	1	1	1	1	1	2	2	1	2	2

3. Scale by method of successive intervals (T scale)

Psychological dimension = Play evaluation

OBJECT

1. This play is a masterpiece.
2. I am delighted with this play.
3. This play is fairly interesting.
4. This play is too obvious.
5. This play is dull.
6. I thoroughly dislike this play.

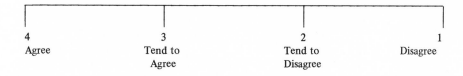

4	3	2	1
Agree	Tend to Agree	Tend to Disagree	Disagree

SCORE MATRIX

SUBJECTS	OBJECTS					
	1	2	3	4	5	6
S_1	3	3	3	2	2	1
S_2	4	4	2	2	2	1
S_3	2	2	1	1	1	1
S_4	3	2	2	2	2	2
S_5	4	4	4	2	1	1
S_6	3	3	3	2	2	2
S_7	4	4	4	1	1	1
S_8	4	3	2	2	2	2
S_9	1	1	1	2	2	4
S_{10}	4	4	3	3	1	1

4. Find the scale values using the Goodenough technique for Guttman scaling.

Psychological dimension = school importance

A.   I come to school every day.
B.   I come to school often.
C.   I try to do extra school work.
D.   I attend school activities.
E.   I join school clubs.
F.   I run for school offices.

Subjects respond agree (A) or disagree (D)

	ITEMS											
	A		B		C		D		E		F	
SUBJECTS	A	D	A	D	A	D	A	D	A	D	A	D
1		x	x		x		x		x			x
2	x		x		x			x		x		x
3	x			x	x			x		x	x	
4	x		x		x			x		x		x
5		x		x	x		x		x			x
6		x	x		x		x		x			x
7		x	x		x			x	x			x
8		x	x		x			x		x		x
9	x		x			x	x		x		x	
10		x	x		x		x			x		x
11		x		x	x			x		x	x	
12		x	x		x			x	x			x

Exercises

You may use computer solutions.

1. Scale by the simplified rank method.

J	ITEMS						J	ITEMS					
	A	B	C	D	E	F		A	B	C	D	E	F
1	1	2	3	4	5	6	7	1	3	2	5	4	6
2	2	3	5	4	6	1	8	2	3	1	5	4	6
3	3	4	2	5	1	6	9	1	2	3	4	5	6
4	1	2	3	4	5	6	10	4	3	2	1	5	6
5	4	2	3	1	5	6	11	3	2	1	4	5	6
6	5	1	2	3	6	4	12	1	2	3	4	5	6

2. Find the scale under Thurstone's Case V Method.

F MATRIX

	A	B	C	D	E
A	-	2	3	6	5
B	8	-	1	4	6
C	7	9	-	0	3
D	4	6	4	-	5
E	5	4	7	5	-

3. Find the Scale values of the items by the method of successive intervals.

							ITEMS					
	1	2	3	4	5	6	7	8	9	10	11	12
S_1	4	4	3	4	4	3	3	4	4	4	4	3
S_2	4	4	3	4	4	3	2	4	4	4	3	3
S_3	4	4	3	4	3	3	2	4	2	4	3	3
S_4	3	4	2	4	3	4	2	4	2	4	3	3
S_5	3	3	2	3	2	4	2	4	2	4	3	3
S_6	3	3	2	3	2	4	1	4	2	3	2	3
S_7	3	3	1	3	1	2	1	4	2	3	2	2
S_8	3	3	1	2	1	2	1	2	1	3	2	2
S_9	3	2	1	2	1	2	1	2	1	2	2	3
S_{10}	3	2	1	1	1	1	1	1	1	2	1	2

Four categories are: Agree, Tend to Agree, Tend to Disagree and Disagree (A, TA, TD, D)

4. Find the scalability of the following objects using the Goodenough Technique.

	ITEMS						ITEMS			
SUBJECTS	A	B	C	D	SUBJECTS	A	B	C	D
	+ -	+ -	+ -	+ -		+ -	+ -	+ -	+ -
1	x	x		x	x	7	x	x	x		x
2	x	x		x	x	8	x	x		x	x
3		x x		x	x	9		x	x	x	x
4		x	x	x	x	10	x		x	x	x
5	x	x	x		x	11	x	x	x		x
6	x	x	x		x	12	x	x		x	x

5. Test whether the following items form a Guttman Scale by presenting the items to a group of students.

ED.D. EXAMINATION IN ED PSY

Instructions

1. On the following pages two categories of "terms" are presented—measurement and statistics. Using a seven point scale, where the value "1" denotes no knowledge of the term whatsoever and the value "7" denotes mastery of the term at an "I could teach this well" level, *rate your knowledge of each term* by checking the appropriate scale value (1-7) to the right of each item.

2. *Within each of the four categories,* the proctor will select 3 items. You are to write a paragraph which indicates your mastery of these terms. (The paragraph is an adequate illustration of your understanding of the term.)) Write the name of the category and the number of term on the paper provided.

MEASUREMENT

		1	2	3	4	5	6	7	
1.	individual differences scaling	—	—	—	—	—	—	—	1.
2.	factor analysis	—	—	—	—	—	—	—	2.
3.	discriminant function	—	—	—	—	—	—	—	3.
4.	orthogonal rotation	—	—	—	—	—	—	—	4.
5.	multidimensional scaling	—	—	—	—	—	—	—	5.
6.	hierarchical clustering	—	—	—	—	—	—	—	6.
7.	communality	—	—	—	—	—	—	—	7.
8.	shrinkage	—	—	—	—	—	—	—	8.
9.	reliability of different scores	—	—	—	—	—	—	—	9.
10.	biserial correlation	—	—	—	—	—	—	—	10.
11.	scalogram analysis	—	—	—	—	—	—	—	11.
12.	Cronbach's alpha	—	—	—	—	—	—	—	12.
13.	Kendall's tau	—	—	—	—	—	—	—	13.
14.	cumulative frequency distribution	—	—	—	—	—	—	—	14.
15.	Likert scale	—	—	—	—	—	—	—	15.
16.	psychophysics	—	—	—	—	—	—	—	16.
17.	phi correlation	—	—	—	—	—	—	—	17.
18.	pt. biserial correlation	—	—	—	—	—	—	—	18.
19.	standard error of measurement	—	—	—	—	—	—	—	19.
20.	$S_{xy}\sqrt{1 - r_{tt}^2}$	—	—	—	—	—	—	—	20.
21.	item discrimination	—	—	—	—	—	—	—	21.
22.	standardization sample	—	—	—	—	—	—	—	22.
23.	concurrent validity coefficient	—	—	—	—	—	—	—	23.
24.	curricular validity	—	—	—	—	—	—	—	24.
25.	split half reliability	—	—	—	—	—	—	—	25.
26.	T score	—	—	—	—	—	—	—	26.
27.	objective test	—	—	—	—	—	—	—	27.
28.	bar graph	—	—	—	—	—	—	—	28.
29.	the 12 edge	—	—	—	—	—	—	—	29.
30.	3rd quartile	—	—	—	—	—	—	—	30.

STATISTICS

		1	2	3	4	5	6	7	
1.	mode	—	—	—	—	—	—	—	1.
2.	median	—	—	—	—	—	—	—	2.
3.	random sample	—	—	—	—	—	—	—	3.
4.	scatter plot	—	—	—	—	—	—	—	4.
5.	statistic	—	—	—	—	—	—	—	5.
6.		—	—	—	—	—	—	—	6.
7.	negative skew	—	—	—	—	—	—	—	7.
8.	Pearson's r	—	—	—	—	—	—	—	8.
9.	$\Sigma(X-\bar{X})^2$	—	—	—	—	—	—	—	9.
10.	$p < .05$	—	—	—	—	—	—	—	10.

11.	uniform distribution	—	—	—	—	—	—	—	11.
12.	F ratio	—	—	—	—	—	—	—	12.
13.	homogeneity of variance	—	—	—	—	—	—	—	13.
14.	chi square	—	—	—	—	—	—	—	14.
15.	Fisher's z	—	—	—	—	—	—	—	15.
16.	leptokurtic	—	—	—	—	—	—	—	16.
17.	homoscedasticity	—	—	—	—	—	—	—	17.
18.	binomial test	—	—	—	—	—	—	—	18.
19.	prove: $\Sigma(x-\bar{x})(y-\bar{y}) = \Sigma xy - \dfrac{\Sigma x \Sigma y}{N}$	—	—	—	—	—	—	—	19.
20.	mean square	—	—	—	—	—	—	—	20.
21.	sampling distribution	—	—	—	—	—	—	—	21.
22.	t-test	—	—	—	—	—	—	—	22.
23.	non-parametric statistics	—	—	—	—	—	—	—	23.
24.	Wilcoxon Signed Ranks Test	—	—	—	—	—	—	—	24.
25.	analysis of variance	—	—	—	—	—	—	—	25.
26.	df	—	—	—	—	—	—	—	26.
27.	$r_{12 \cdot 3} = \dfrac{r_{12} - r_{13}\, r_{23}}{\sqrt{1 - r_{13}^2}\ \ 1 - r_{23}^2}$ partial correlation	—	—	—	—	—	—	—	27.
28.	second order interaction	—	—	—	—	—	—	—	28.
29.	the scree test	—	—	—	—	—	—	—	29.
30.	covariance analysis	—	—	—	—	—	—	—	30.
31.	trend analysis	—	—	—	—	—	—	—	31.
32.	multiple correlation	—	—	—	—	—	—	—	32.
33.	Smirnov goodness of fit	—	—	—	—	—	—	—	33.
34.	multiple regression	—	—	—	—	—	—	—	34.
35.	eta	—	—	—	—	—	—	—	35.
36.	power	—	—	—	—	—	—	—	36.
37.	suppressor variable	—	—	—	—	—	—	—	37.
38.	Neuman-Keuls multiple range	—	—	—	—	—	—	—	38.
39.	MANOVA	—	—	—	—	—	—	—	39.
40.	Sheffe's multiple comparisons	—	—	—	—	—	—	—	40.

CLUSTERING

The clustering methods are introductory to the more sophisticated methods of multidimensional scaling. As opposed to the creation of unidimensional scales, clustering methods are generally more descriptive in nature. They have value because of their simplicity and lack of assumptions. Cluster analysis is a general term for those methods that attempt to group objects or individuals together that are generally more similar or have some specific similar characteristic(s). The methods covered in this section are ones that the author has found to be useful and that cover the major techniques. These methods include graphic similarity analysis, single and complete linkage clustering, divisive clustering, and K-means iterative clustering. The essential function of these methods is data reduction and description, but they can be useful in some forms of hypothesis generation or hypothesis testing by uncovering hidden structure.

It is useful to cluster the items routinely in any ordered category instrument. Clustering provides information on the probable dimensionality of the instrument and pictorially isolates items that do not belong.

The simpler clustering methods do not provide estimates of similarity between the objects that are grouped or between the groups. Measures of distance between objects or groups is handled in Part III.

The typical analysis for clustering is as follows:

1. Objects are gathered.
2. Proximities between all the objects are obtained.
3. Objects are grouped together based on a measure of proximity.
4. A graphical picture of the groups that have been formed is created.

11 Graphing Proximities

METHOD 1: WAERN'S GRAPHIC SIMILARITY ANALYSIS

This technique, proposed by Waern (1972) is one of the simplest methods for analyzing a matrix of similarities among the members of a set of objects. In this method the magnitude of the similarity measures is analyzed in stepwise fashion. Initially, the experimenter sets some absolute or relative standards of magnitude under which he or she makes pairwise choices of objects.

If the standard for clustering is levels of significance for correlations, the experimenter may choose conventional .01, .05, and .10 levels. One may also choose cutoff values for each step that include certain small percentages of the pairwise similarity data. For example, steps that include 5% of the highest similarity values at each step might be chosen. That is, steps would be chosen such that the top 5% of all similarity data values would be included in step 1, the second 5% would make up step 2, and so on.

Generally, however, the former conventional system is used. A search for all pairwise correlations that reach the .01 level is made as a first step. These selections are mapped in the two-dimensional space of a plain sheet of paper and connected by heavy black lines. Next the correlations at the .05 level are placed, using dashed lines, and finally those at the .10 level, using dotted lines.

If correlations are found with negatively worded items, the original scoring of these items should be reversed so that similar items will be correlated positively. The typical correlation between two items such as ''I like school'' and ''school is worthless'' would be negatively correlated under normal scoring or weighting. Reversing the scoring means that ''I like school'' and ''school is *not* worthless'' would be positively correlated. Suppose, for example, the data of Table 11.1 are available:

TABLE 11.1
Matrix of Similarities

	A	B	C	D
A				
B	.5**			
C	.2	.2		
D	.1	.4*	.5**	

$*p \leq .05$
$**p \leq .01$

First, objects A and B (S_{AB} = .5) and C and D (S_{CD} = .5) are connected by heavy black lines as follows:

A————B   D————C

Next, B and D (S_{BD} = .4) are connected by a dotted line as shown.

A————B-----------D————C

Because C is not significantly related to A and B it is placed away from them. Thus a pictorial chain of the stimuli results.

Clusters of points can also be formed when a set of stimuli are mutually similar. The data in Table 11.2 illustrate this type of plot.

TABLE 11.2
Similarity Estimates for Six Stimuli

	b	d	p	q	x	z
b						
d	.9*					
p	.8*	.9*				
q	.8*	.8*	.8*			
x	.20	.3	.3	.2		
z	.10	.2	.1	.2	.8*	—

$*p$ .05

In this case the data may be mapped as follows:

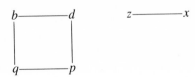

Some subjectivity is necessary in this analysis but the results can be revealing and rewarding because subtle connections between cluster and chains may be lost in more conventional methods such as factor analysis and multidimensional scaling. The technique is particularly useful in interpreting the results from other more technical methods. Fig. 1.1 illustrates Waern's method using correlations between statements on teacher evaluation (see page 6).

APPLICATION: GRAPHING LETTER SIMILARITY

Waern (personal communication, 1973) analyzed the similarity between 21 lowercase letters of the English alphabet. Her resulting plot follows:

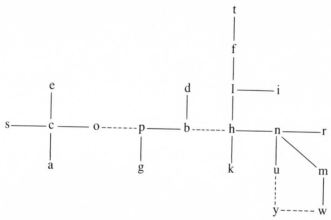

The similarities were based on the similarity scales in Fig. 5.6. Paired values from that scale were rank ordered. This graph is an effective representation of the data.

Heavy lines (————) indicate scale score separations ≤ 20 whereas dotted lines (---------) indicate separations > 20.

METHOD 2: MCQUITTY'S ELEMENTARY LINKAGE ANALYSIS

Elementary linkage analysis is a method of clustering. It can be used to cluster any objects (people or items) that have distinctive cluster characteristics.

Advantages of elementary linkage analysis are: its speed, its objectivity, and its provision for investigating a particular theoretical position. A 15-variable matrix can be analyzed into objectively determined "types" in 5 to 10 minutes. Furthermore, all elementary linkage analysis operations require only pencil and paper. This method of analyzing a correlation matrix has been proposed by McQuitty (1957). His method is as follows:

1. Underline the highest (absolute) entry in each column of the matrix.

2. Select the highest entry in the matrix. Write the variable code on a piece of paper with reciprocal arrows; for example: A ⇔ B. Call this the first type.

3. Select all those variables (objects or subjects) that are most like members of the first type by reading across the *rows* containing the first two variables (A and B) and selecting previously *underlined* entries in these rows. Write down these variable codes and connect them to the related variable by a single arrow; for example: A ⇔ B ← C. Call these variables (C) first cousins.

4. Select all those variables that are like the first-cousin variables. Write them down with connecting arrows; for example:

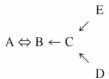

Call these variables (D and E) second cousins.

5. Search for higher order cousins until no more exist.

6. Exclude all variables already classified and repeat steps two to five. Increment the type number by one for each time through the steps.

7. Repeat these steps until all variables are classified.

An example is illustrated (Table 11.3).

TABLE 11.3
Intercorrelations of Test Scores of High School Students

	Reading	Spelling	Algebra	Geometry	Chemistry	History
Reading		.72	.12	.27	.20	.63
Spelling	.72		.16	.40	.12	.56
Algebra	.12	.16		.64	.48	.10
Geometry	.27	.40	.64		.50	.21
Chemistry	.20	.12	.48	.50		.14
Histroy	.63	.56	.10	.21	.14	

Linkage results: R   ⇔   S   A   ⇔   G

         ↑   ↑

         H   C

       Type (Factor?) I   Type (Factor?) II

First the highest values were underlined in each column. The correlation (.72) between spelling (S) and reading (R) is initially selected as type I (R<==>S). A review of the Reading and Spelling rows reveals one other underlined correlation (.63) between History (H) and Reading (R). History becomes a first cousin. As no other underlined correlation exists in these two rows, a search is made for the next highest correlation not already utilized. This occurs between Algebra and Geometry ($r = .64$). This initiates the second type, to which Chemistry is attached.

APPLICATION: GROUPING EVALUATION ITEMS

Montenegro (1978) intercorrelated 34 items of a student evaluation instrument that had been presented to 315 undergraduate students at the University of Hawaii. The items are presented in Fig. 11.1. The correlations are presented in Table 11.4. Figure 11.2 illustrates the linkage analysis of the correlation. This analysis reveals the clustering and correlation pattern of the evaluation items.

TABLE 11.4
Intercorrelations Between Evaluative Items

R MATRIX	1	2	3	4	5	6	7
1		0.6154	0.1849	0.4824	0.3507	0.4016	0.3980
2			0.3494	0.5464	0.4681	0.4373	0.4011
3				0.2005	0.3751	0.1924	0.1880
4					0.4008	0.3484	0.4103
5						0.2893	0.2834
6							0.2965
7							
8							
9							
10							
11							
12							
13							
14							
15							
16							
17							
18							
19							
20							
21							
22							
23							
24							
25							
26							

(continued)

TABLE 11.4 (continued)
Intercorrelations Between Evaluative Items

R MATRIX	8	9	10	11	12	13	14
1	0.3744	-0.5187	0.2870	0.5449	0.5430	0.6161	0.4879
2	0.4359	-0.5384	0.3940	0.4747	0.5130	0.6434	0.5162
3	0.1957	-0.1041	0.2067	0.0696	0.1866	0.1891	0.2268
4	0.3026	-0.4521	0.3030	0.2840	0.3635	0.5409	0.3911
5	0.3108	-0.3242	0.4904	0.2217	0.2506	0.3399	0.3350
6	0.3268	-0.4153	0.2811	0.3366	0.3622	0.4069	0.3983
7	0.3346	-0.4638	0.3221	0.2414	0.3508	0.4561	0.3669
8		-0.3993	0.2655	0.4003	0.4160	0.4022	0.4476
9			-0.3053	-0.4459	-0.4267	-0.5789	-0.4318
10				0.2843	0.2162	0.3005	0.3391
11					0.4841	0.5073	0.4629
12						0.5646	0.5109
13							0.4982
14							
15							
16							
17							
18							
19							
20							
21							
22							
23							
24							
25							
26							
27							
28							
29							
30							
31							
32							
33							
34							

TABLE 11.4 (continued)

Intercorrelations Between Evaluative Items

R MATRIX	15	16	17	18	19	20	21
1	-0.4409	0.2116	0.4601	0.2770	0.2009	0.3758	0.3989
2	-0.5050	0.1377	0.4240	0.3057	0.1995	0.4248	0.3092
3	-0.1407	0.0022	0.1130	0.2020	-0.0322	0.1607	0.1414
4	-0.4997	0.2227	0.3073	0.2814	0.2418	0.4903	0.2617
5	-0.3811	0.0259	0.2137	0.2234	0.0285	0.2754	0.2778
6	-0.2779	0.1544	0.2981	0.3186	0.1893	0.3417	0.3049
7	-0.4067	0.2828	0.3022	0.3283	0.2198	0.4076	0.2799
8	-0.3055	0.0149	0.3913	0.3051	0.1791	0.2758	0.3950
9	0.5059	-0.2532	-0.3785	-0.2671	-0.2530	-0.4486	-0.3996
10	-0.3252	-0.0566	0.2171	0.2231	-0.0223	0.2820	0.1997
11	-0.4031	0.1317	0.4960	0.3001	0.2840	0.3446	0.4531
12	-0.3920	0.1765	0.4611	0.3811	0.1754	0.4196	0.3273
13	-0.5692	0.2519	0.3978	0.3472	0.2972	0.4950	0.3932
14	0.4428	0.0515	0.4132	0.3024	0.1428	0.2965	0.4622
15		0.1297	-0.3081	-0.1985	-0.1839	-0.3028	-0.3475
16			0.2220	0.2476	0.3247	0.2673	0.1402
17				0.3183	0.3270	0.2760	0.5286
18					0.3077	0.4076	0.2677
19						0.2397	0.2650
20							0.2917
21							
22							
23							
24							
25							
26							
27							
28							
29							
30							
31							
32							
33							
34							

TABLE 11.4 (continued)

Intercorrelation Between Evaluative Items

R MATRIX	22	23	24	25	26	27	28
1	-0.5508	0.4732	0.6419	0.3512	0.2374	0.3747	0.2338
2	-0.6206	0.5494	0.6039	0.4260	0.2314	0.4068	0.2326
3	-0.1841	0.1980	0.1251	0.1568	0.0732	0.1517	0.1006
4	-0.5455	0.4811	0.5143	0.3995	0.1632	0.4433	0.1579
5	-0.3505	0.2628	0.2502	0.2853	0.1140	0.3986	0.1099
6	-0.4154	0.3221	0.4324	0.3354	0.1866	0.2183	0.2963
7	-0.4606	0.2609	0.3700	0.3750	0.1034	0.3579	0.0048
8	-0.3648	0.3194	0.3944	0.3519	0.1779	0.3278	0.2056
9	0.6336	-0.4814	-0.5402	-0.3333	-0.2172	-0.3677	-0.1513
10	-0.2856	0.2812	0.2014	0.2996	0.0939	0.4467	0.0708
11	-0.4283	0.4499	0.5352	0.3146	0.4226	0.3234	0.2398
12	-0.4760	0.4128	0.6138	0.3426	0.2943	0.3547	0.3004
13	-0.6955	0.5459	0.7038	0.3803	0.3091	0.4137	0.1893
14	-0.5435	0.4049	0.5361	0.3537	0.2522	0.3565	0.3099
15	0.6324	-0.4419	-0.4766	-0.3261	-0.1804	-0.3494	-0.0532
16	-0.2447	0.1380	0.2354	0.0560	0.1794	0.0879	-0.0014
17	-0.3811	0.4537	0.4940	0.2960	0.2756	0.2941	0.1713
18	-0.3682	0.2930	0.3735	0.3183	0.3012	0.2987	0.0527
19	-0.2697	0.3343	0.3383	0.2160	0.3598	0.1078	-0.0019
20	-0.4412	0.3955	0.4667	0.3403	0.2576	0.3609	0.0676
21	-0.4557	0.3321	0.4264	0.2559	0.3201	0.2838	0.1855
22		-0.5068	-0.5655	-0.3132	-0.2401	-0.3521	-0.1696
23			0.6149	0.2915	0.2855	0.2801	0.0994
24				0.4290	0.3601	0.3622	0.2271
25					0.2952	0.3982	0.2457
26						0.2806	0.2715
27							0.1310
28							
29							
30							
31							
32							
33							
34							

TABLE 11.4 (continued)
Intercorrelation Between Evaluative Items

R MATRIX	29	30	31	32	33	34
1	0.3655	0.4000	0.4776	0.6327	0.3581	0.3565
2	0.4584	0.4280	0.4581	0.6278	0.4029	0.3663
3	0.2431	0.1615	0.1494	0.1783	0.1620	0.0927
4	0.4727	0.3173	0.3615	0.5575	0.4405	0.3513
5	0.3365	0.2813	0.2558	0.2399	0.2961	0.1747
6	0.2473	0.3087	0.3007	0.3895	0.3021	0.3199
7	0.3230	0.2446	0.3184	0.4079	0.2343	0.3076
8	0.3262	0.3262	0.3504	0.4156	0.2867	0.2680
9	-0.3710	-0.2981	-0.4081	-0.4996	-0.3307	-0.3680
10	0.4889	0.3232	0.1750	0.2813	0.3120	0.1397
11	0.2231	0.4550	0.5299	0.4815	0.2072	0.3511
12	0.3647	0.3846	0.4331	0.5526	0.3249	0.3785
13	0.4382	0.3766	0.4618	0.6243	0.3909	0.3907
14	0.2741	0.3607	0.4739	0.4706	0.3084	0.3307
15	-0.3958	-0.2812	-0.3492	-0.4408	-0.3683	-0.3715
16	0.1450	0.0330	0.2093	0.2653	0.1005	0.2219
17	0.2627	0.3540	0.4088	0.4765	0.2681	0.3525
18	0.2663	0.2379	0.3763	0.2967	0.1976	0.2357
19	0.0773	0.2152	0.3971	0.3066	0.0876	0.2410
20	0.3084	0.3229	0.2785	0.4707	0.2628	0.2429
21	0.2340	0.3185	0.4551	0.3609	0.2635	0.2643
22	-0.3861	-0.3711	-0.4303	-0.5333	-0.3840	-0.4052
23	0.3032	0.2943	0.4453	0.5047	0.2847	0.3042
24	0.2891	0.4007	0.5492	0.6798	0.3182	0.3884
25	0.3442	0.2806	0.2883	0.4284	0.3135	0.2801
26	0.1297	0.3306	0.5233	0.3106	0.1463	0.2809
27	0.5966	0.2900	0.2962	0.4443	0.4785	0.3017
28	0.1521	0.3049	0.2793	0.3087	0.1883	0.2439
29		0.3087	0.2693	0.4245	0.6046	0.3380
30			0.5281	0.4230	0.2497	0.3732
31				0.5561	0.2901	0.4045
32					0.4407	0.3923
33						0.2510
34						

FIG. 11.1.   Items of an evaluation survey.

BIRTHDATE _____ _____ _____
                     MO   DAY   YR

Student Evaluation of Educational Psychology

For each of the 34 statements mark one of the response categories – 1 = strongly disagree, 2 = disagree, 3 = uncertain, 4 = agree, or 5 = strongly agree. Each column from left to right corresponds to a category.

Please make any additional comments on the reverse side of the IBM answer sheet.

1 = STRONGLY DISAGREE

2 = DISAGREE

3 = UNCERTAIN

4 = AGREE

5 = STRONGLY AGREE

1. The instructor motivated students.
2. The instructor increased my interest in this subject matter area.
3. The instructor cited current or up-to-date information on the subject matter.
4. I developed significant skills in the field.
5. The instructor related the subject matter to real-life or out-of-class situations.
6. The instructor posed questions and issues that were challenging to the students.
7. The objectives of the course were clear.
8. The instructor adapted effectively to changes in the classroom situation.
9. The way this course was taught, it was a waste of time.

10. I can now see implications of the subject matter in my own life.
11. There was an atmosphere of mutual goodwill between the instructor and the members of the class.
12. The instructor prepared, integrated, and summarized subject matter effectively.
13. This course was better than average.
14. The instructor had the ability to make difficult concepts more easily understood.
15. I would not recommend this course to a friend.
16. The instructor promptly informed students of the results of written tests and assignments.
17. The instructor was sensitive to students' feelings and problems.
18. The instructor had extensive knowledge of the subject matter.
19. The instructor was available to students for consultation or assistance.
20. Choice and organization of course materials (e.g., text, readings, extra-class activities) were of high calibre.
21. The instructor showed respect for student opinions and comments.
22. Overall, I would rank this course as one of the *worst* I have taken.
23. I would take another course from this instructor even if it were not required.
24. Considering everything, I would rate this instructor's teaching among the finest I have experienced.
25. The instructor was interested in developing the students' professionalism.
26. The instructor showed up for class and kept appointments with students.
27. I can now identify and appraise judgments and values that enter into making decisions in this field.
28. The instructor reviewed the subject matter when test results showed poor performance.
29. I can now confront new problems and use general ideas or practical techniques from this course to solve them.
30. The instructor's approach to the class was flexible.
31. The instructor was actively helpful when students had difficulty.
32. The instructor stimulated me to put forth my best effort in this course.
33. When people discuss topics in the field, I can now recognize when they are using good or poor arguments.
34. Evaluation of student performance was adequate and fair.

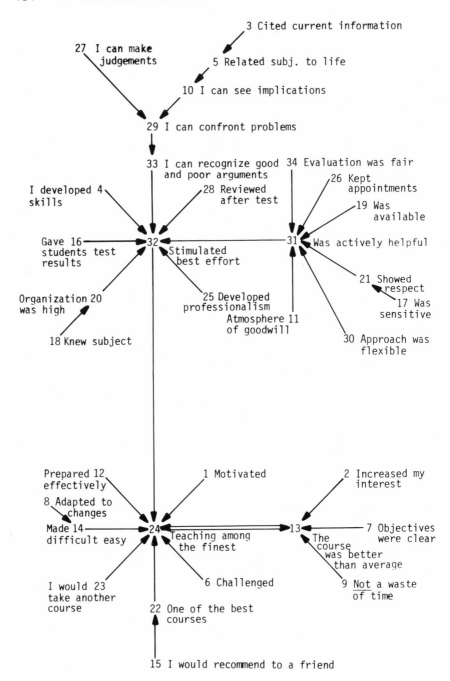

FIG. 11.2.   Elementary linkage analysis on 34 evaluation items. Only one type with many cousins is revealed.

DISCUSSION

Graphic methods can be quickly applied to any form of proximity matrix. Proximities can be correlations, distances, and so on. Nearly every computer center has packaged programs that routinely calculate correlations. Computer programs that calculate these measures could be modified to print only values of a certain size, relative size, or significance. This would aid the graphic methods in that the selection of relevant variables would be easier.

12 Agglomerative–Hierarchical Methods

THEORY: SUCCESSIVE COMBINING

Agglomerative methods of clustering begin with the calculation of the similarity or distance matrix. Objects which are most similar or which are not far apart are grouped together. The objects are reduced in stepwise fashion by forming new groups of similar objects at each step. The process is continued until all the objects are formed into a single group. The graphic representation of this process is called a tree or dendogram.

METHOD 1: WARD'S MINIMUM SUMS OF SQUARES

Ward (1963) uses the "sum of squares" as the criterion for inclusion of objects in a group. The sum of squares, a measure of variation, is given by

$$SS = \Sigma(X - \bar{X})^2 = \Sigma X^2 - \frac{(\Sigma X)^2}{N}$$

At each stage of the clustering a SS is calculated for every possible pair of objects and the pair is chosen which provides the minimum sum of squares. Suppose paired distances between the following objects (their scale scores) are as follows:

136

OBJECT	DISTANCE BETWEEN OBJECTS d	SCALE VALUE	VALUE^2
1		0	0
	} 2		
2		2	4
	} 2		
3		4	16
	} 4		
4		8	64
	} 2		
5		10	100
	} 4		
6		14	196
		38	380

$$SS_{TOT} = \Sigma \, X^2 - \frac{(\Sigma \, X)^2}{N}$$

$$= 380 - \frac{(38)(38)}{6}$$

$$= 139.4$$

Initially each object is considered a group consisting of a single member. Next all possible pairwise groups are formed and the pair that has the smallest SS forms the first group. The process is repeated with $K - 1$ groups until all the objects are in a single group. For the foregoing data, the steps are as follows:

1st Step

15 Pairs	1–2,	1–3,	1–4,	1–5,	1–6,	2–3,	2–4,	2–5,	2–6,
SS	2	8	32	50	98	2	18	32	72

	3–4,	3–5,	3–6,	4–5,	4–6,	5–6
	8	18	50	2	18	8

(For example, the sum of the squares for objects 1 and 2 is calculated as $(0 - 1)^2 + (2 - 1)^2 = 2$, where 1 is the mean of the group $(0 + 2)/2 = 1$.) Because the pairs 1–2, 2–3, and 4–5 have equally small sums of squares, the choice is arbitrary in this case. Objects 1 and 2 are chosen simply because they are first.

By calling 1 and 2 a new group $A(12)$ the six original objects or groups have been reduced to five:

A, 3, 4, 5, 6,
(1,2)

In the second stage of clustering there are $\binom{5}{2}$ or 10 pairings:

2nd Step

	A–3,	A–4,	A–5,	A–6,	3–4,	3–5,	3–6,
	(1,2)	(1,2)	(1,2)	(1,2)			
SS	8	35	56	115	8	18	25

	4–5,	4–6,	5–6
	2	18	8

(The SS for A–3 is calculated $(0 - 2)^2 + (2 - 2)^2 + (4 - 2)^2 = 8$, where $(0 + 2 + 4)/3 = 2$ is the mean.)

Now 4 and 5 are grouped ($SS = 2$). Calling this new group B (4,5), four groups remain:

A,	3,	B,	6
(1,2)		(4,5)	

There are six pairs in the third stage.

3rd Step

	A–3,	A – B,	A–6,	3–B,	3–6,	B–6
	(1,2)	(1,2)(4,5)	(1,2)	(4,5)		(4,5)
SS	8	68	115	19	25	9

Now A and 3 are combined. Calling this new group $C(1,2,3)$ we have groups

C,	B,	6
(1,2,3)	(4,5)	

Next the sums of squares for these three groups are calculated.

4th Step

	C – B,	C –6,	B –6
	(1,2,3)(4,5)	(1,2,3)	(4,5)
SS	35	115	9

Finally, B and 6 are combined. Calling them new group D, only groups C and D are left to combine and this combination is called E.

This analysis can be summarized in a dendogram as follows:

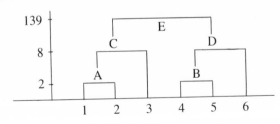

Because the increase in *SS* to combine *C* and *D* is relatively large the experimenter may wish to stop clustering after step 4. The final clusters can be ordered on the horizontal axis from left to right and the size of *SS* on the vertical axis. A smooth curve is then plotted at the height of the *SS* for each clustering. A good rule of thumb is that when the rise and run are equal, further clustering is unnecessary.

For example:

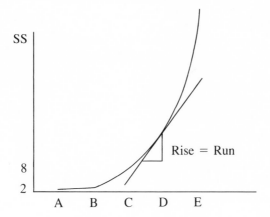

When starting with a similarity or distance matrix it can be shown (Anderberg, 1973) that the pairwise distance measures are proportional to the calculated sums of squares between all pairs of objects. The entries in the distance matrix (without summing the squares), therefore, may be taken as the *first step* in Ward's method.

Ward (personal communication, 1980) relates that for job classification and task analysis, percentage of overlap is used more often than distance (*d*) as a measure of similarity.

APPLICATION: GROUPING STUDENTS ON REWARD PREFERENCE

Dunn-Rankin, Shimizu, and King (1969) studied the reward preference of fifth- and sixth-grade children. They had students respond to a paired comparison task involving five kinds of reward: Adult Approval (AA), Competitive Rewards (C), Peer Approval (P), Independence Rewards (I), and Consumable (eatable) Rewards (CR). A child would be asked, for example, whether he or she would rather have an Excellent on his or her paper (AA) or some candy (CR) (see Fig. 12.1).

The 10 possible pairs were repeated four times and the summed votes pro-

Which one of each pair do you like best?

1.	Teacher writes "100" on your paper.	A
	Be first to finish your work.	C
2.	Package of bubble gum.	E
	Students ask you to be on their team.	P
3.	Be free to do what you like.	I
	Teacher writes "100" on your paper.	A
4.	Students ask you to be on their team.	P
	Be first to finish your work.	C
5.	Be free to do what you like.	I
	A package of bubble gum.	E
6.	Teacher writes "100" on your paper.	A
	Students ask you to be on their team.	P
7.	Be first to finish your work.	C
	Be free to do what you like.	I
8.	A package of bubble gum.	E
	Teacher writes "100" on your paper.	A
9.	Students ask you to be on their team.	P
	Be free to do what you like.	I
10.	Be first to finish your work.	C
	A package of bubble gum.	
11.	Be the only one that can answer a question.	C
	Candy	E
12.	Friends ask you to sit with them.	P
	Be free to go outside.	I
13.	Candy.	E
	Teacher writes "A" on your paper.	A.
14.	Be the only one that can answer a question.	C
	Be free to go outside.	I
15.	Teacher writes "A" on your paper.	A
	Friends ask you to sit with them.	P
16.	Be free to go outside.	I
	Candy.	E
17.	Friends ask you to sit with them.	P
	Be the only one that can answer a question.	C
18.	Be free to go outside.	I
	Teacher writes "A" on your paper.	A
19.	Candy.	E
	Friends ask you to sit with them.	P

FIG. 12.1. Reward preference inventory. Counts of (A) Adult approval, (C) Competitive Rewards, (E) Eatables, (P) Peer Approval, and (I) Independence Rewards are summed and constitute a profile.

FIG. 12.1. (*Continued*)

20.	Teacher writes "A" on your paper.	A
	Be the only one that can answer a question.	C
21.	Have only your paper shown to the class.	C
	Teacher writes "very good" on your paper.	A
22.	Classmates ask you to be a class leader.	P
	Ice Cream.	G
23.	Teacher writes "very good" on your paper.	A
	Be free to play outside.	I
24.	Have only your paper shown to the class.	C
	Classmates ask you to be class leader.	P
25.	Ice cream.	E
	Be free to play outside.	I
26.	Classmates ask you to be class leader.	P
	Teacher writes "very good" on your paper.	A
27.	Be free to play outside.	I
	Have only your paper shown to the class.	C
28.	Teacher writes "very good" on your paper.	A
	Ice cream.	E
29.	Be free to play outside.	I
	Classmates ask you to be class leader.	P
30.	Ice cream.	E
	Have only your paper shown to the class.	C
31.	A soft drink.	E
	Have your paper be the best in the class.	C
32.	Be free to work on something you like.	I
	Friends ask you to work with them.	P.
33.	Teacher writes "excellent" on your paper.	A
	A soft drink.	E
34.	Be free to work on something you like.	I
	Have your paper be the best in the class.	C
35.	Friends ask you to work with them.	P
	Teacher writes "excellent" on your paper.	A
36.	A soft drink.	E
	Be free to work on something you like.	I
37.	Have your paper be the best in the class.	C
	Friends ask you to work with them.	P
38.	Teacher writes "excellent" on your paper.	A
	Be free to work on something you like.	I
39.	Friends ask you to work with them.	P
	A soft drink.	E
40.	Have your paper be the best in the class.	C
	Teacher writes "excellent" on your paper.	A

TABLE 12.1
Major Preference Profile Groups of 5th and 6th Grade UES Children
with Related Behavioral and Ethnic Variables

	Profile					Variables					Step	
AA	C	P	I	CR	Sex	Ethnic Origin	Grade	SES	IQ		Math	Reading
						Group 1						
16	5	8	17	14	0	0	6	3	133		258	259
16	9	8	14	13	1	N	5	6	131		233	252
11	8	11	18	12	1	0	5	6	141		257	264
9	4	11	20	16	1	N	6	6	127		267	279
10	4	11	20	15	1	N	6	2	139		261	263
14	6	13	14	13	1	N	6	6	115		244	258
12	8	10	12	18	1	0	5	3	137		254	259
11	6	7	16	20	1	0	6	3	129		265	267
12	5	7	16	20	1	0	6	5	140		252	283
16	12	8	20	4	0	0	5	6	137		253	267
14	11	5	20	10	1	N	6	0	121		251	253
						Group 2						
16	4	20	12	8	0	0	5	5	134		263	273
15	6	20	13	6	0	0	5	6	141		251	261
11	9	20	16	4	0	0	5	5	152		258	276
12	8	20	16	4	0	0	6	2	135		266	296
12	8	19	17	4	0	0	6	5	133		249	251
14	8	19	15	4	1	0	6	6	138		263	287
12	7	18	18	5	0	0	6	6	141		269	291
18	6	14	13	9	0	0	5	2	131		244	260
16	6	15	17	6	0	0	5	4	110		249	267
15	10	12	15	8	1	0	5	3	120		240	242
17	9	11	17	6	0	0	6	6	125		251	259
18	7	11	16	8	1	0	6	5	131		259	266
						Group 3						
17	13	17	9	4	0	0	6	6	109		244	248
17	11	17	9	6	0	0	5	3	129		256	261
15	13	20	8	4	1	0	5	5	131		261	273
20	10	15	11	4	0	N	5	3	130		257	255
19	11	14	11	5	1	N	5	6	125		245	267
19	11	15	11	4	0	N	6	4	107		245	256
18	11	16	11	4	0	0	5	5	126		253	273
18	12	16	10	4	0	0	6	5	88		245	251
17	12	15	12	4	1	0	5	3	111		254	262
17	10	15	13	5	0	N	6	2	123		263	271
20	10	13	12	5	0	0	6	3	99		251	257
19	11	13	13	4	0	0	6	0	100		258	252
19	10	12	11	8	0	0	5	6	125		230	255
10	8	15	10	8	0	N	6	5	99		266	255

TABLE 12.1 (*Continued*)

Group 4

20	16	12	7	5	0	0	5	3	121	239	242
19	16	13	7	5	1	0	6	5	100	243	254
19	17	12	7	5	0	N	5	6	109	238	237
19	16	13	6	6	0	0	5	1	118	243	262
20	16	12	8	4	1	0	5	6	120	239	256
20	16	12	8	4	1	0	6	3	102	250	260
19	16	12	9	4	0	0	6	3	126	249	261
19	16	13	8	4	0	N	5	5	108	240	255
19	17	12	8	4	1	0	6	3	112	258	267
17	18	12	8	5	0	N	5	6	127	245	242
20	13	15	8	4	0	0	5	3	115	245	261
20	13	14	9	4	0	0	6	6	146	261	257
19	15	14	8	4	0	0	6	5	112	243	252
20	14	14	8	4	1	N	6	4	126	240	247
18	14	14	10	4	0	N	6	5	139	270	271
18	14	14	7	7	1	N	5	5	113	244	259
20	14	11	11	4	1	N	6	0	111	263	266
18	14	12	11	5	0	0	5	5	119	257	260
19	15	11	11	4	1	0	6	6	120	249	267
19	14	9	14	4	1	0	5	6	117	247	262
16	15	10	13	6	1	0	6	3	112	249	255
19	17	9	11	4	0	N	5	6	127	252	267
17	13	12	14	4	0	N	5	6	134	251	263
16	14	13	13	4	0	0	6	5	123	266	264

Summary Table

Group	AA	C	P	I	CR	N	Males	Orientals	Grade 6	SES	IQ	Step Math	Read.
1	13	7	9	17	14	11	9	6	7	4.2	131.8	254.1	264-0
2	15	7	17	15	6	12	3	12	6	4.6	132.6	255.2	269.1
3	18	11	15	11	5	14	3	9	7	4.0	114.4	252.0	259.7
4	19	15	12	9	5	24	10	15	12	4.4	119.0	249.2	257.8
			Total	61		25		42	32	4.3	123.0	251.9	261.6

vided a reward preference profile for each subject. The profiles were intercorre-lated and the correlation values were used in Ward's method to cluster the subjects. A final selection of four groups was made and these groups are present-ed in Table 12.1.

Table 12.1 illustrates that reward preference is related to a variety of variables in different ways. The mean profiles for each group illustrate that ability and achievement (judged by SCAT and STEP tests) are related to high scores for independence rewards. Lower achievement is related to a professed desire for adult approval. A theory of relative satiation for these rewards is postulated.

Veldman (1967) has written an algorithm (HGROUP) for Ward's clustering method. (see Chapter 20).

METHOD 2: JOHNSON'S NONMETRIC SINGLE AND COMPLETE LINK

In Johnson's (1967) nonmetric clustering method similarities are converted to distances. Distances are either measured to the closest member in a cluster or the farthest member of a cluster. As in most clustering methods, the basic steps are as follows:

1. Gather and establish a data matrix.
2. Calculate a distance matrix between pairs of objects.
3. Join the closest objects into a cluster.
4. Join the next closest pair of objects (using the closest or farthest member of a cluster to represent that cluster).
5. Continue until all objects are in a single cluster.

Suppose that five objects are to be grouped hierarchically and that the matrix of distances (d_{ij}) between the objects has been calculated as shown in Table 12.2.

In this case it is easy to see that objects 4 and 5 should be clustered first, as the distance between these two objects is the smallest in the table ($d_{45} = 1$). Thus objects 4 and 5 are united into a single group. Under the complete linkage method sometimes known as the "farthest neighbor" method the *maximum* distances between elements of the new group and each of the remaining objects are obtained.

$$d_{(45)1} = \max (d_{14}, d_{15}) = 10 = d_{15}$$

$$d_{(45)2} = \max (d_{24}, d_{25}) = 7 = d_{25}$$

$$d_{(45)3} = \max (d_{34}, d_{35}) = 6 = d_{35}$$

TABLE 12.2

	1	2	3	4	5
1	–				
2	4	–			
3	6	3	–		
4	8	5	2	–	
5	10	7	6	1	–

These maximum distance values are now entered into a reduced matrix of distances as shown in Table 12.3, reduced by eliminating the minimum values of

TABLE 12.3

	1	2	3	(45)
1	–			
2	4	–		
3	6	3	–	
(45)	10	7	6	–

rows 4 and 5.

This table is now examined for its smallest entry, which occurs for objects 2 and 3. These objects are united into a single group and the maximum values from this new entry are determined.

$$d_{(23)1} = \max (d_{12}, d_{13}) = 6 = d_{13}$$

$$d_{(23)(45)} = \max (d_{24}, d_{25}, d_{34}, d_{35}) = 7 = d_{25}^*$$

*From original matrix.

These are now placed in the third reduced matrix, shown in Table 12.4.

The smallest entry in this matrix is $d_{(23)1}$. When these two groups are united only two entries are left to finally unite. A dendogram of the process is given in Fig. 12.2.

TABLE 12.4

	1	(23)	(45)
1	–		
(23)	6	–	
(45)	10	7	–

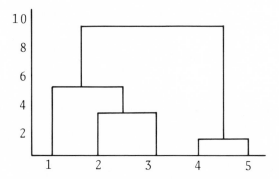

FIG. 12.2. Dendogram of complete linkage clustering.

In the single-link method, the smallest or minimum distances to the potential entries of the reduced matrix is used instead of the maximum, otherwise the procedure is the same. The single-link method has a strong theoretical rationale in the biological sciences. Practice shows that the complete-link method is more effective with social science data.

When using distances, most methods of analysis must satisfy the following properties:

1. The distance between any two objects is symmetrical (i.e., $d(xy) = d(yx)$).
2. The distance between x and y is zero only if $x = y$.
3. If x, y, and z are three objects, the distances between the three objects must form a triangle (i.e., $d(x, z) \leq d(x, y) + d(y, z)$). This last condition is called the triangle inequality. Sometimes when this condition is not satisfied a constant may be added to each value to fulfill the third condition. It is known, for example, that the psychological distance between the letters o and l is considered to be much larger than the sum of the psychological distances of o and b, and b and l. Schematically:

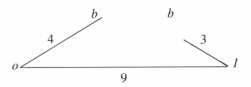

Thus, in raw form, the distances do not form a triangle. By adding 3 to each distance the inequality can be solved as follows:

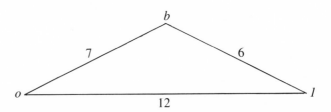

Usually the minimum constant required to satisfy the triangle inequality for all triples in an entire matrix is added to each distance.

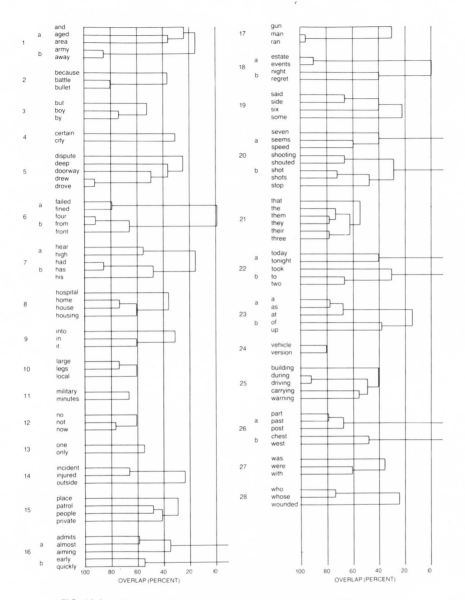

FIG. 12.3. Clustering of visually similar words results from a different kind of study, in which the test subjects were given a newspaper article containing approximately 100 words and were asked to group together words they thought looked most alike. Such findings, organized into hierarchical tables such as this one, indicate that there are four basic features adults perceive as being important in determining whether words are visually similar: similar beginning letters, similar word length, similar word endings, and similar internal letters or letter combinations. Of these four factors similar beginning letters appear to be the most important, a finding that is confirmed by other studies.

147

APPLICATION: WORD SIMILARITY

Nonmetric hierarchical clustering has been used to cluster both letters and words. Dunn-Rankin (1978) was able to show that in addition to the first letter, the length of a word is an important consideration in visual perception. In this case 100 words from a newspaper article were grouped in clusters independently by 34 college students. The percentage of overlap matrix (number of times words were grouped together divided by total number of subjects) was clustered using the complete linkage method of Johnson. Figure 12.3 shows the results of this clustering.

Johnson's (1967) nonmetric method is available from the Bell Telephone Laboratory, Murray Hill, New Jersey (see Chapter 20). It can also be found in the (1976) SAS package of programs.

13 Partitioning

If researchers could see as well in n dimensions as they can in two, partitions of data points into a specified set of clusters could be done visually. In the two-dimensional example that follows (Fig. 13.1), a good solution may be obtained by a simple inspection and placement of the data. For illustrative purposes, however, an objective solution is sought that is analogous to solutions obtainable for a larger number of data points measured on a larger number of variables or dimensions.

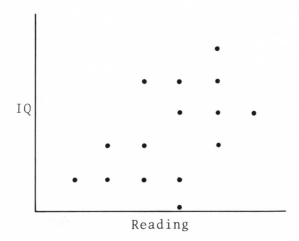

FIG. 13.1.   Data to be clustered into two groups.

THEORY: GROUPING BASED ON PROXIMITY TO CENTROID

The minimum distance method is as follows:

1. The data are initially assigned to one of a prespecified number of clusters. This assignment can be made at random or sequentially or by some other method.
2. The mean or centroid of the original clusters is determined.
3. Each data point is put into a new cluster with the closest mean or centroid to that data point.
4. The centroids of the new clusters are computed.
5. Alternate steps 3 and 4 until no data points change membership.

In this example, classification into two groups is prespecified (i.e., the number of groups [2] in the partitioning is indicated prior to the analysis).

A random assignment (coin flip) placed the subjects into *two* groups. The centroids of these two groups are calculated by averaging the independent coordinates of all the points in each group. That is, the mean of IQ values for each random group yields the IQ coordinate of the centroid for each group and the mean of reading values for each group yields the reading coordinate of the centroid for each group. Figure 13.2 shows the initial random assignment and the centroids of the two random groups.

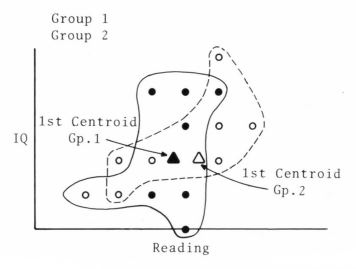

FIG. 13.2.   Random grouping and centroids.

The distances from all the data points to these two centroids were measured and points were reassigned based on the minimum distance to one of the two initial centroids (first iteration). The resulting groupings and the new centroids are shown in Fig. 13.3. The process is repeated or iterated (second iteration) using the new centroids. Figure 13.4 shows the final solution to this problem, as no new reassignment is possible (see Table 13.1).

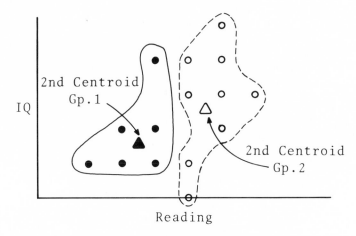

FIG. 13.3. First iteration and new centroids.

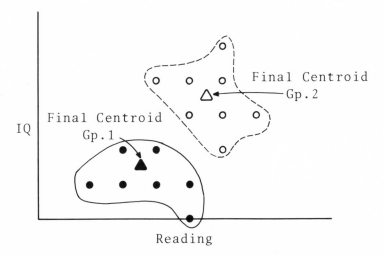

FIG. 13.4. Final assignment and final centroids.

TABLE 13.1
Scores of Reading and IQ and Iterative Group Assignment

Subjects	Reading	IQ	Random Grouping	1st Iteration	2nd Iteration
1	4	0	1	2	1
2	1	1	1	1	1
3	2	1	2	1	1
4	3	1	1	1	1
5	4	1	1	2	1
6	2	2	2	1	1
7	3	2	2	1	1
8	5	2	2	2	2
9	4	3	1	2	2
10	5	3	2	2	2
11	6	3	2	2	2
12	3	4	1	1	2
13	4	4	1	2	2
14	4	4	1	2	2
15	5	5	2	2	2

METHOD: *K*-MEANS ITERATIVE

The term "*k*-means iterative clustering" is understandable when we realize that *k* is the number of groups and thus the number of means that are prespecified. When dealing with many variables, over which a number of objects or subjects are to be classified, it is useful to employ a minimum variance criterion as a substitute for minimum distance. The "*k*-means" procedure is an attempt to minimize the variance within each cluster and consequently to maximize the variance between clusters. The sum of the squares of the distances of each point, within a cluster, from the centroid of that cluster, provides a within measure of variance. If, by relocating the data points, the sums of squares can be reduced, the relocation takes place. Cluster solutions of this type have been called minimum variance partitions. The sum of squares can be written

$$\sum_{i=1}^{g} \sum_{j=1}^{n_i} \sum_{k=1}^{p} (X_{ijk} - X_{i \cdot k})^2$$

where g is the number of clusters, n_i is the number of observations in the *i*th cluster, and p is the number of variables.

For example: Consider a set of objects divided into two groups, say x and y. If an object belongs to x it will be called x; if it belongs to y it will be called y.

The means of each group are

$$\bar{x} = \frac{\Sigma\, x}{N_{(x)}} \quad \text{and} \quad \bar{y} = \frac{\Sigma\, y}{N_{(y)}}$$

The Grand Mean (M) will be equal to

$$M = \frac{\Sigma\, x + \Sigma\, y}{N_{(x)} + N_{(y)}}$$

Then, the Total sum of squares of all x and y from the grand mean (M) is equal to

$$T = \Sigma\, (x - M)^2 + \Sigma\, (y - M)^2$$

Within each group the sum of squares is

$$W_{(x)} = \Sigma\, (x - \bar{x})^2 \quad \text{and} \quad W_{(y)} = \Sigma\, (y - \bar{y})^2$$

The sum of squares Between the weighted means of each group equals

$$B = N_{(x)}(\bar{x} - M)^2 + N_{(y)}(\bar{y} - M)^2$$

From traditional analysis of variance we know that

$$T = W + B \quad\quad \text{where } W = W_{(x)} + W_{(y)}$$

This may be shown graphically as follows in which

■ = x values   O = y values   ▲ = grand mean

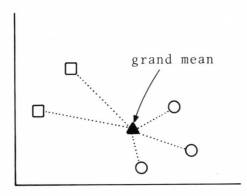

grand mean

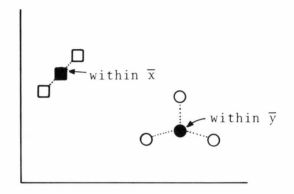

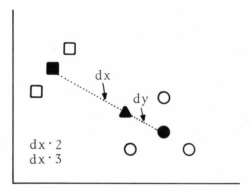

In comparing various partitions of the objects it is reasonable to try to minimize $|W_{(i)}|$. This is one of the options in the MICKA "k-means" partitioning program.

APPLICATION: MODALITY PREFERENCE IN READING

Donavan, in 1977, attempted to preclassify children into three modality groups (auditory preference]AP], visual preference [VP], and no preference, [NSMP] based on diagnostic test scores using k-means iterative clustering (Everitt, 1974). In this study the investigator did not specify the basis for classification. The procedure used was the minimization of the within cluster variance and the distance criterion was Mahalanobis, d^2 (Mahalanobis d^2 is essentially a standardized distance). That is, the squares of the x- and y-axis differences are divided by the variances of x and y prior to summation or

$$d_{AB}^2 = \frac{(X_A - X_B)^2}{\sigma_x^2} + \frac{(Y_B - Y_A)^2}{\sigma_y^2}$$

A clinical identification of modality preference groups was compared with this cluster analysis. The clinical classification identified 36 VP pupils, 29 of whom were found in Cluster 2. Nineteen AP pupils were identified clinically, and 14 were found in Cluster 1. This indicates that 78% of AP and VP learners were statistically identified through cluster analysis. Clinical procedures identi-

TABLE 13.2
Means of Classification Variables for the
Three Clusters Identified by Mikca

Variables	Cluster 1 (N=32)	Cluster 2 (N=44)	Cluster 3 (N=31)
	AP	VP	NSMP
Illinois Test of Psycho-linguistic Abilities			
Visual Sequential Memory	37.03	38.38	28.93
Auditory Sequential Memory	44.46	32.47	33.77
Gates MacGinitie Readiness Skills Test			
Listening	4.78	4.05	4.19
Auditory Discrimination	6.06	5.64	5.06
Visual Discrimination	6.34	5.86	5.03
Following Directions	4.34	4.06	3.67
Letter Recognition	7.15	7.06	6.61
Visual-Motor Coordination	6.06	6.50	5.35
Auditory Blending	5.25	5.15	4.83
Word Recognition	6.43	6.25	5.77

Italic values indicated auditory tests.

fied 52 pupils as having NSMP; 20 were found in Cluster 3. The total number of clinical identifications predicted by cluster analysis was 63, or 58%.

McRae (1971) has written a computer program to do *k*-means iterative clustering, MIKCA (See Chapter 20). *K*-means clustering is also part of the scientific analysis system (1976) (SAS) package of programs as well as the (1977) BMD software program package.

14 Hierarchical–Divisive Methods

THEORY: SUCCESSIVE SPLITTING

Hierarchical divisive methods of clustering start with all the objects in one cluster. This cluster is then subdivided into two clusters. Then one of these clusters is subdivided resulting in three clusters. Next one of the three clusters is subdivided, and so on. The process continues until the N original objects are all separate clusters. Divisive clustering usually produces clusters in which all the members within a cluster are very similar. These are called monothetic classifications.

METHOD: HOWARD–HARRIS' SPLITTING BY LARGEST VARIANCE

The Howard–Harris method (Blashfield & Oldenderfer, 1978) selects the variable, in the set of variables, that has the largest variance. All subjects or objects with scores greater than the mean of this variable are placed in one group and all subjects with scores less than the mean are placed in another group. The method then uses a k-means iterative solution to determine the membership of the two clusters. Next, the variable in the two clusters that has the largest variance is selected and its mean used to subdivide the high and low scores in that cluster. A k-means solution is then applied to these two clusters to produce a three-cluster solution. The process is repeated until some preset number of clusters is reached.

The Howard-Harris program is valuable because it can be applied to as many as 2000 subjects and as many as 20 variables.

APPLICATION: GROUPING HAM RADIOS

J. Hills, one of the author's students, had 10 ham radio operators rate the similarity between six equipment manufacturers. The radio manufacturers included Icom, Yaesu, Kenwood, Collins, Drake, and Ten Tech. The raw and standardized data are provided in Tables 14.1 and 14.2.

TABLE 14.1
Raw Data—Means—Variances of Ratings on Ham Radios

		Subjects									
		1	2	3	4	5	6	7	8	9	10
Incom	1	4.00	1.00	3.00	3.00	2.00	4.00	1.00	3.00	2.00	1.00
Yaesu	2	3.00	3.00	2.00	3.00	1.00	3.00	6.00	4.00	3.00	4.00
Kenwood	3	5.00	3.00	6.00	3.00	4.00	2.00	3.00	2.00	4.00	3.00
Collins	4	6.00	6.00	5.00	6.00	6.00	6.00	5.00	5.00	3.00	6.00
Drake	5	1.00	5.00	4.00	5.00	3.00	5.00	2.00	6.00	3.00	5.00
Ten Tech	6	2.00	3.00	1.00	1.00	5.00	1.00	4.00	1.00	6.00	2.00
		3.50	3.50	3.50	3.50	3.50	3.50	3.50	3.50	3.50	3.50

TABLE 14.2
Standardized Proximities for Ratings on Ham Radios

		1	2	3	4	5	6	7	8	9	10
		1.71	1.61	1.71	1.61	1.71	1.71	1.71	1.71	1.26	1.71
Incom	1	.29	-1.56	-.29	-.31	-.88	.29	-1.46	-.29	-1.19	-1.46
Yaesu	2	-.29	-.31	-.88	-.31	-1.46	-.29	1.46	.29	-.40	.29
Kenwood	3	.88	-.31	1.46	-.31	.29	-.88	-.29	-.88	.40	-.29
Collins	4	1.46	1.56	.88	1.56	1.46	1.46	.88	.88	-.40	1.46
Drake	5	-1.46	.93	.29	.93	-.29	.88	-.88	1.46	-.40	.88
Ten Tech	6	-.88	-.31	-1.46	-1.56	.88	-1.46	.29	-1.46	1.99	-.88

Howard—Harris divisive clustering was utilized to group the manufacturers.

The two-group solution was as follows—from Split No. 1:

1	2
Icom	Collins
Yaesu	Drake
Kenwood	
Ten Tech	

and a three-group solution was as follows—from Split No. 2:

1	2	3
Icom	Collins	Ten Tech
Yaesu	Drake	
Kenwood		

Hills was able to make sense of the three-group solution because Group 1 were all Japanese manufacturers, Collins and Drake were similar U.S. companies, and Ten Tech was a new company.

Carmone and others have programmed the Howard-Harris divisive method (see Chapter 20).

GENERAL DISCUSSION ON CLUSTERING

Number of Clusters

Although an appraisal of the cluster solution (number of clusters) in Wards' method can be made based on the size of the sums of squares (see page 136), two other methods can be employed. One is to split the original data and cluster both sets. If the clustering is similar in both cases, it can be concluded that a reliable solution has been obtained.

Another method is to use an outside criterion consisting of a set of predictor variables. This method has the following steps: (1) Select a reasonable range of groups. (2) Sequentially predict group membership using discriminant function analysis (multiple regression used to predict membership into varying numbers of clusters). The χ^2 value for each cluster solution divided by the resulting degrees of freedom can be used as a selection index (i.e., where χ^2/df is maximum).

Graphing

All clustering should be presented pictorially in order for the information to be easily understandable. The basic clustering dendogram can be thought of as a mobile. In this mobile each horizontal bar is free to rotate around the connecting vertical line. Figure 14.1 is taken from Fig. 12.3 and consists of words beginning with the letter h. In Fig. 14.2, a rearrangement has been made so as to afford a better pictorial contrast between short and long words.

Chambers and Kleiner (1980) have suggested different ways of displaying the results of clustering. The dendogram can be altered by shortening the end lines (Fig. 14.3) or by straight line connection to the nodes (points of departure from a continuous line; see Fig. 14.4).

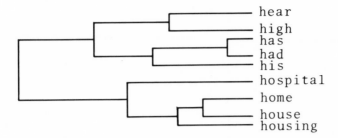

FIG. 14.1.   Basic dendogram.

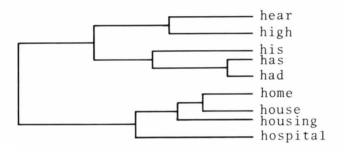

FIG. 14.2.   Mobile modification.

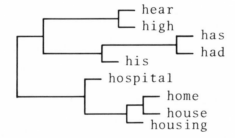

FIG. 14.3.   Dendogram with shortened lines.

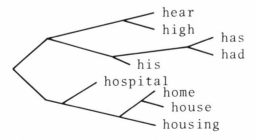

FIG. 14.4.   Dendogram constructed by straight lines.

TABLE 14.3
Intercorrelations Among Wechsler Subtests

	1	2	3	4	5	6	7	8	9	10	11
information	1.00	0.60	0.58	0.53	0.60	0.52	0.41	0.47	0.37	0.40	0.43
vocabulary	0.60	1.00	0.49	0.49	0.57	0.46	0.36	0.45	0.35	0.35	0.38
arithmetic	0.58	0.49	1.00	0.46	0.51	0.51	0.42	0.42	0.41	0.47	0.50
similarities	0.53	0.49	0.46	1.00	0.55	0.51	0.31	0.36	0.28	0.30	0.35
comprehension	0.60	0.57	0.51	0.55	1.00	0.53	0.34	0.42	0.33	0.36	0.39
sentences	0.52	0.46	0.51	0.51	0.53	1.00	0.36	0.35	0.30	0.34	0.38
animal house	0.41	0.36	0.42	0.31	0.34	0.36	1.00	0.38	0.36	0.43	0.38
picture	0.47	0.45	0.42	0.36	0.42	0.35	0.38	1.00	0.44	0.42	0.45
mazes	0.37	0.35	0.41	0.28	0.33	0.30	0.36	0.44	1.00	0.48	0.46
gemetric design	0.40	0.35	0.47	0.30	0.36	0.34	0.43	0.42	0.48	1.00	0.48
block design	0.43	0.38	0.50	0.35	0.39	0.38	0.38	0.45	0.46	0.48	1.00

EXERCISES FOR PART III

1. Given the following similarity matrix (Table 14.3), cluster the data using McQuitty's simple linkage analysis.
2. Graph the similarity matrix (Table 14.4) using the method of Waern.
3. Cluster the data of Table 14.3 using Ward's *h*-Group technique.
4. Cluster the data of Table 14.3 using Johnson's non-metric method.
5. Find the best three groups in two dimensions using *k*-means iterative analysis on the data of Table 14.4.
6. Find the 5 most divsive clusters in the data of Table 14.3.

7. Analyze the following matrix of r's to determine its dimensions.

	A	*B*	*C*	*D*	*E*
A	—				
B	.84	—			
C	.32	.47	—		
D	−.71	−.65	−.30	—	
E	−.63	−.87	−.43	.85	—

r Matrix

One of the author's students analyzed the similarities among common statistical textbooks. He did this by measuring the percentage of pages in each of seven texts devoted to 42 statistical concepts. The texts were authored by Snedecor and Cochran; McNemar; Dixon and Massey; Hays; Glass and Stanley; Ferguson; and Edwards. The percentage overlap matrix between these texts is presented as Table 14.4.

TABLE 14.4
Percentage of Concept Overlap Between Statistical Textbooks

	S & C	*McNemar*	*D & M*	*Hays*	*G &S*	*Ferguson*	*Edwards*
S & C	—						
McNemar	.50630	—					
D & M	.40463	.54633	—				
Hays	.53941	.577150	.59591	—			
G & S	.41026	.52036	.54973	.62189	—		
Gerguson	.54913	.56383	.59032	.61032	.55946	—	
Edwards	.51057	.55241	.49855	.51194	.49880	.63326	—

IV MULTIDIMENSIONAL METHODS

Part IV presents the four most useful multidimensional scaling methodologies. The technique of factor analysis, traditionally developed and utilized with tests of ability and achievement, has also been applied extensively to the reduction of matrices of proximities. Restrictive assumptions of linearity between variables and homogeneity of variance as well as the multiplicity of factors generated, however, allow the simpler assumptions underlying multidimensional scaling to be utilized in a different and generally more parsimonious description of a data matrix. Preference mapping and individual differences scaling are extensions of factor and multidimensional scaling analyses that provide insights into how individuals differ with regard to the same psychological objects.

15 Factor Analysis

Factor analysis attempts to simplify a large body of data by identifying or discovering categories of variables. These categories are called structures, dimensions, or more commonly factors. It is, statistically, an analysis of the interdependence between variables and can be used to (1) describe, (2) fulfill hypotheses, or (3) discover new relationships.

THEORY: REDUCTION OF THE CORRELATION MATRIX

Factor analysis starts with a correlation matrix (R) derived from a set of responses of N subjects to K variables or stimuli. (A matrix is a rectangular or square arrangement of data.) All the columns of the raw data matrix are intercorrelated by pairs to produce the square matrix of correlations as illustrated in Fig. 15.1. The standard or Z score representing the raw score is equal to the raw score minus the mean divided by the standard deviation or

$$Z_i = \frac{X_i - \bar{X}}{S} \tag{1}$$

Pearson's correlation is defined as the average cross product of the standardized scores.

$$r_{ij} = \frac{\Sigma Z_i Z_j}{N} \tag{2}$$

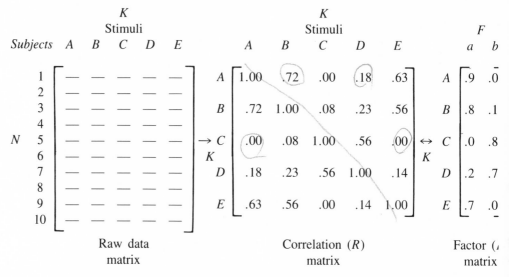

FIG. 15.1.   Illustration of how an ($N \times K$) raw data matrix yields a ($K \times K$) correlation matrix. This matrix is then resolved into a smaller ($k \times f$) factor matrix. The process of obtaining the factor matrix is explained in this chapter (see page 000).

The raw score Pearson's correlation formula is given in Chapter 3. The raw score formula standardizes the data as part of its calculation.

Each entry of the correlation matrix (R) is a measure of the relationship between two stimuli as perceived by the subjects. Because science is constantly trying to simplify a complex array of data, it is one purpose of factor analysis to present the information contained in a correlation matrix in more concise terms. Almost all the information in the correlation matrix in Fig. 15.1, for example, is contained in the simple factor matrix to its right. To understand that this is so the reader only needs to sum the *cross products* of the elements in all pairs of rows of the factor matrix. Taking variables A and B, for example, the sum of the cross products is $(.9)(.8) + (.0)(.1) = .72$, which is the correlation between variables A and B. Other correlations may be found similarly.

Summing the cross products of the factor loadings to recreate the correlation matrix is a verbal description of the fundamental factor theorem

$$[F] \cdot [F'] = [R]$$

where F is the factor matrix, F' is called the transpose matrix of F, and R is the correlation matrix. Written out for the example of Fig. 15.1, this matrix multiplication appears as follows:

$$
\begin{array}{c}
\\
A \\
B \\
C \\
D \\
E
\end{array}
\begin{array}{c}
F \\
\begin{bmatrix}
.9 & .0 \\
.8 & .1 \\
.0 & .8 \\
.2 & .7 \\
.7 & .0
\end{bmatrix}
\end{array}
\quad x \quad
\begin{array}{c}
F' \\
\begin{bmatrix}
.9 & .8 & .0 & .2 & .7 \\
.0 & .8 & .8 & .7 & .0
\end{bmatrix}
\end{array}
\quad = \quad
\begin{array}{c}
R \\
\begin{bmatrix}
.81 & .72 & .00 & .18 & .63 \\
.72 & .65 & .08 & .23 & .56 \\
.00 & .08 & .64 & .56 & .00 \\
.18 & .23 & .56 & .53 & .14 \\
.63 & .56 & .00 & .14 & .49
\end{bmatrix}
\end{array}
$$

In this case the diagonal elements of R contain the sums of the squares of the factor loadings in each row of F. The sum of the squares is known as the communality. The communality for variable B, for example, is $.8^2 + .1^2 = .65$. The communality is the total variance accounted for by the components of a particular variable that are also found in other tests or variables. This is sometimes known as common variance.

Once the factor matrix F has been determined, its elements can be plotted and analyzed spatially as shown in Fig. 15.2.

If we knew, for example, that tests C and D were tests of arithmetic and A, B, and E were tests of reading, then psychological meaning could probably be attached to this two-dimensional representation. As Cattell (1962) has suggested, what is meant by factors is nothing more than the dimensions of the space required to contain a certain set of correlations. It is therefore the central problem in factor analysis to find a dimensional (factor) matrix that is the simplest and most meaningful explanation of a larger matrix of correlations.

The elements in the factor matrix are called factor coefficients or factor loadings. They can derive meaning from basic assumptions surrounding test

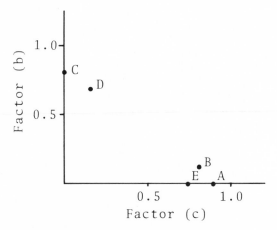

FIG. 15.2.   Plot of variables of the factor matrix.

scores and test variance. First, a test score is assumed to be the sum of a number of components. A particular intelligence test score may, for example, consist of the *sum* of separate contributions made by *v*erbal and *n*umerical ability, plus a component *s*pecific to that particular test plus a component due to *e*rror. Symbolically, after standardization, this assumption can be written as follows:

$$Z_{\text{test}} = Z_v + Z_n + Z_s + Z_e, \tag{3}$$

Z_v and Z_n, the numerical and verbal components, are called common factor components because they are dimensional elements found in common with the other tests of intelligence. The extent to which two tests are related depends on the extent to which their common factor components are similar but does not include the specific or error components.

The assumption of additivity of the components of a total score can be more formally stated as follows:

$$Z_t = aZ_a + bZ_b + cZ_c + \cdots + qZ_q + sZ_s + Z_e + \cdots \tag{4}$$

$$\text{common components} \qquad \text{specific} \quad \text{error} \\ \text{component} \quad \text{component}$$

where $a, b, \ldots, q$ are weights assigned to each component.

Equation (4) is expressed in standard (z) form. This equation states that a total test score is a weighted summation of *common factor* scores plus a *specific component* plus an *error component*. (Guilford, 1954, p. 476). The assumption may also be applied to the variance of the scores.

$$\sigma_t^2 = \sigma_a^2 + \sigma_b^2 + \sigma_c^2 + \cdots + \sigma_q^2 + \sigma_s^2 + \sigma_e^2 + \cdots \tag{5}$$

The total variance of the scores on a test or variable may also be subdivided into three general types—common, specific, and error variance. *Common variance* is that portion of the total variance that correlates with other variables. *Specific variance* is that portion of the total variance which does not correlate with any other variable. "*Error variance* is chance variance, due to errors of sampling, measurement, . . . and the host of other influences which may contribute unreliabilities [Fruchter, 1954, p. 45]."

If we divide all terms of Equation 5 by the total variance σ_t^2, we get

$$\frac{\sigma_t^2}{\sigma_t^2} = \frac{\sigma_a^2}{\sigma_t^2} + \frac{\sigma_b^2}{\sigma_t^2} + \frac{\sigma_c^2}{\sigma_t^2} + \cdots + \frac{\sigma_q^2}{\sigma_t^2} + \frac{\sigma_s^2}{\sigma_t^2} + \frac{\sigma_e^2}{\sigma_t^2} \tag{6}$$

Each component of variance can now be expressed as a proportion of the total variance. For convenience, simpler terms are substituted for the proportions. The variance equation then becomes

$$1.00 = a_x^2 + b_x^2 + c_x^2 + \cdots + q_x^2 + \overbrace{s_x^2 + e_x^2}^{u_x^2 \quad \text{uniqueness}} \tag{7}$$

$$\underbrace{}_{\text{communality } (h_x^2)} \qquad \underset{\text{specificity}}{\overset{\text{error}}{\uparrow \qquad \uparrow}}$$

Here we call h_x^2 "communality." *Communality* is defined as the *sum* of the proportions of common factor variance in the scores.

Uniqueness (u_x^2) is the portion of the total variance that is not shared in common with any other variable. And *specificity* (s_x^2) is the proportion of specific variance in a test or variable.

$$u_x^2 = s_x^2 + e_x^2 = 1 - h_x^2 \tag{8}$$

The factor coefficients or loadings exist as correlations (i.e., square roots of variance components). They must be squared, therefore, in order to provide estimates of variance. For the example given in Fig. 15.1, the sum of the squares of the factor loadings is calculated to obtain h^2 or the communality that is an estimate of how well the factors account for the variance in each test (see Table 15.1).

The total variance of each test is equal to 1.00. For five tests the total is 5.0 or 100%. If the factor loadings in each column are squared and then summed, the result is a measure of the variance accounted for by each factor. These measures can be made meaningful by dividing each sum by the total variance (i.e., 5.0). Thus in Table 15.1, the sums of the squared factor loadings are 1.98 and 1.14, respectively. The proportion of variance they account for is 1.98/5 = .40 = 40% and 1.14/5 = .23 = 23%. Taken together the two factors account for 63% of the total variance. Thus 37% of the variance is unique and is either due to error or is specific to particular tests or both.

TABLE 15.1
Accounting for Variance Using Factor Loadings

Variables	Common Factor Loadings a	b	Common Factor Variance a^2	b^2	Communality Communality $a^2 + b^2 = h^2$	Unique $u^2 = 1\text{-}h^2$	Total
Test A	.9	.0	.81	.00	.81	.19	1.0
Test B	.8	.1	.64	.01	.65	.35	1.0
Test C	.0	.8	.00	.64	.64	.36	1.0
Test D	.2	.7	.04	.49	.53	.47	1.0
Test E	.7	.0	.49	.00	.49	.51	1.0
Sums			1.98	1.14	3.12	1.88	5.0

% Variance accounted for = 40% + 23% = 63% + 37% = 100%

Reliability (r_{tt}) is defined as $1 - \sigma_e^2/\sigma_t^2 = 1 - e_x^2$. Therefore, if the reliability of a test is known some estimate of the error can be made because $r_{tt} = 1 - e_x^2 = a_x^2 + b_e^2 + c_x^2 + \cdots + q_x^2 + s_x^2$. Suppose, for example, the reliability of test A was known as $r_{tt} = .88$ then $e_x^2 = 1 - .88$ or .12 and $u_x^2 - e_x^2 = s_x^2$ or, for Test A, $.19 - .12 = .07$. Thus 7% of the variance is specific variance.

An important derivation from these additivity assumptions and from the definition of r_{ij} in Equation 2 shows that the correlation between any two variables or tests is equal to the sum of the cross products of their common factor loadings, i.e.,

$$r_{ij} = a_i a_j + b_i b_j + \ldots + q_i q_j \tag{9}$$

where i and j represent variable or Tests 1 and 2 respectively.

METHOD: THURSTONE'S CENTROID

The centroid method of factor analysis (Thurstone, 1947) is only one of several possible solutions that account for the variance in a set of correlations. It is presented here because it may be followed computationally and because it displays most of the problems of any factor analytic solution.

The centroid technique uses the column sums of the original correlation matrix R as the basis for approximations to the first factor loadings. The method next attempts to recreate the original correlations from the approximate loadings using

$$r'_{ij} = a_i a_j$$

where r'_{ij} is the recreated correlation and a_i and a_j are two factor loadings.

By adding the column entries of the correlation matrix and dividing each column sum by the square root of the grand sum of all the correlations, the relative contribution of each variable (i.e., the factor loadings) can be approximated. The reason that this is so can be illustrated as follows:

Take, for example, the simple case of a single factor, a_i. The factor matrix for this case has only one column. Assuming that there are n tests or rows in the factor matrix, it would appear as below:

$$[F]_{\substack{\text{one} \\ \text{factor}}} = \begin{bmatrix} a_1 \\ a_2 \\ a_3 \\ \cdot \\ \cdot \\ \cdot \\ a_n \end{bmatrix}$$

The correlation matrix associated with this factor matrix can be obtained, as before, using the fundamental factor theorem $[F] \cdot [F'] = [R]$ or

$$
\underset{[F]}{\begin{bmatrix} a_1 \\ a_2 \\ a_3 \\ \cdot \\ \cdot \\ \cdot \\ a_n \end{bmatrix}}
\quad
\underset{[F']}{\begin{bmatrix} a_1 & a_2 & a_3 & \cdots & a_n \end{bmatrix}}
\quad = \quad
\underset{[R]}{\begin{bmatrix} a_1 \cdot a_1 & a_1 \cdot a_2 & \cdots & a_1 \cdot a_n \\ a_2 \cdot a_1 & a_2 \cdot a_2 & & \\ & a_3 \cdot a_2 & a_3 \cdot a_3 & \\ & & & \\ & & & \\ a_n \cdot a_1 & a_n \cdot a_2 & & a_n \cdot a_n \end{bmatrix}}
$$

The correlation matrix is symmetric. For example, taking the column (or row) sum of Column 2 yields

$$r_2 = a_1 \cdot a_2 + a_2 \cdot a_2 + a_3 \cdot a_2 + \cdots + a_n \cdot a_2$$

where r_2 represents the column sum of Column 2. In general the column sum of the jth column is:

$$r_j = a_1 \cdot a_j + a_2 \cdot a_j + a_3 \cdot a_j + \cdots + a_n \cdot a_j$$

The column sums r_j can be written more concisely as:

$$r_j = a_j \cdot \sum_{i=1}^{n} a_i$$

The grand sum (T) is defined as the sum of all column sums:

$$T = r_1 + r_2 + r_3 + \cdots + r_n$$

or

$$\sum_{j=1}^{n} r_j = T$$

This can also be written

$$T = a_1 \cdot \sum_{i=1}^{n} a_i + a_2 \cdot \sum_{i=1}^{n} a_i + a_3 \cdot \sum_{i=1}^{n} a_i + \cdots + a_n \cdot \sum_{i=1}^{n} a_i$$

or factoring out

$$\sum_{i=1}^{n} a_i,$$

$$T = \sum_{i=1}^{n} a_i \cdot \sum_{j=1}^{n} a_j$$

note that

$$\sum_{i=1}^{n} a_i = \sum_{j=1}^{n} a_j$$

since the indexes i and j both go from 1 to n. Thus

$$T = \left(\sum_{i=1}^{n} a_i \right)^2 = \left(\sum_{j=1}^{n} a_j \right)^2$$

Therefore

$$\sqrt{T} = \sum_{i=1}^{n} a_i = \sum_{j=1}^{n} a_j$$

Remembering that

$$r_j = a_j \cdot \sum_{i=1}^{n} a_i \quad \text{and} \quad \sqrt{T} = \sum_{i=1}^{n} a_i$$

It is clear that

$$\frac{r_j}{\sqrt{T}} = \frac{a_j \cdot \sum_{i=1}^{n} a_i}{\sum_{i=1}^{n} a_i} = a_j \tag{*}$$

So, for single factor matrices the factor matrix (or vector) can be determined exactly from the correlation matrix by simply dividing the column sums of the correlation matrix by the square root of the grand sum. For problems with more than one factor this relation, (*) does not hold exactly but is used as a first approximation to the factor loadings.

In order to understand the centroid methodology, an outline is provided in Fig. 15.3. An example is provided in Tables 15.2–15.6. In Table 15.2, the column sums are shown and the first factor loadings are obtained through division of $\sqrt{T}$. A new correlation matrix R^1 is created from the first approximation by finding the pairwise products of the factor loadings. (See Tables 15.3 and 15.4.)

The entries of the recreated correlation matrix (R^1, Table 15.3,) are subtracted from the original entries in R and the differences (the residual matrix, Table 15.4) are then treated in a similar manner (i.e., the second factor loadings are approximated.)

Original Correlation Matrix R	(1) Original correlation matrix (R) with an estimate of communality in the diagonal. Col sums and 1st factor loadings are calculated. Sums of col correlations are proportional to factor loadings when divided by $(\Sigma r_j) = \sqrt{T}$
Col sums = r_j	
1st factor loadings $a_j = r_j/\sqrt{T}$	
Correlation Matrix created by cross products of 1st factor loadings $a_j a_k$ R′	(2) A new correlation matrix (R′) is created by the product FF′ where F contains only one factor, i.e., the cross products of the 1st factor loadings are found.
Residual or Reduced Correlation Matrix found by R* = R − R′ R*	(3) The new matrix is subtracted from the original to see how well the correlations were recaptured. The difference is a residual correlation matrix (R*).
Reflected Residual Matrix Rows and Column elements signs are changed to maximize column sums R*⁻	(4) Rows and columns of residual matrix are reflected. (Signs are changed in order to maximize the average of the factor loadings and account for maximum variance. This can be checked by summing all the correlations minus the diagonals and maximizing this sum. Row sums and second factor loadings are calculated.
r_j^{*-} Col Sums	Sign of the second factor loadings are changed to match the original signs of the residual matrix R*

FIG. 15.3.   An outline of the centroid method of factor analysis.

FIG. 15.3. *(Continued)*

$$b_j = r_j^* / \sqrt{r^*}$$

2nd factor loadings

(5) The factors are plotted in a plane.

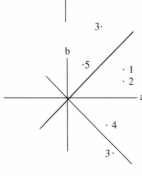

(6) The axes are rotated to maximize contrast in the factor loadings.

(7) The new loadings are read from their projections onto the new axes.

If the grand sum of the correlations, minus the diagonal elements, is negative, it is necessary to reflect some rows and columns by changing their signs, that is, the sign of each element in the row or column. Reflection continues until the sum of the column sums ($\Sigma\ r_j = T$) is as large as possible. (Reversing the signs of all the elements in a row and column of the correlation matrix means that you must reverse the signs of the loadings in the corresponding row of the factor matrix.) In the example Rows and Columns 3 and 4 are reflected.

The centroid of a set of points is the average of the coordinates of those points (In our case, it is the average of the factor loadings.). Because moving the centroid away from the origin makes the *factor* account for more variance, rows and columns of the correlation matrix are reflected (signs changed) in order to make the column sums most positive and increase the variance accounted for by that factor.

If the rank of the matrix (number of independent columns or rows) is two (as is the case in examples given here) the tests can be located in a plane, using the factor loadings as coordinates. There are, however, no specific reference axes

Example of Centroid Method of Factor Analysis

An estimate of the communality is placed in diagonal.

.81	.72	.00	.18	.63
.72	.65	.08	.23	.56
.00	.08	.64	.56	.00
.18	.23	.56	.53	.14
.63	.56	.00	.14	.49

r_j 2.34 2.24 1.28 1.64 1.82

$a_j = r_j /$ T

a_j = First Factor loadings

a_j =   .76   .73   .42   .54   .60

TABLE 15.2
Elements of Correlation Matrix Including
Estimates of the Commonality

r_j = the column sums

$\Sigma r_j = 9.32 = T$, $T = 3.05$

centroid $= \dfrac{T}{j}$ = .61

R'

	.76	.73	.42	.54	.60
.76	.58	.55	.32	.41	.46
.73	.55	.53	.31	.39	.44
.42	.32	.31	.18	.23	.25
.54	.41	.39	.23	.29	.32
.60	.46	.44	.25	.32	.36

TABLE 15.3
Recreation of Correlations from
First Factor Loadings by [F] · [F']

R*
R-R' = 1st Residual

1	.23	.17	-.32	-.23	.17
2	.17	.12	-.24	-.16	.12
3	-.32	-.24	.46	.33	-.25
4	-.23	-.16	.33	.24	-.18
5	.17	.12	-.25	-.18	.13

Sum .02 .01 -.04 .00 -.01
Sum less diagonal -.21 -.11 -.50 -.24 -.14

TABLE 15.4
Residual Correlation Matrix

It seems reasonable to change signs of rows and columns 3 and 4 to obtain largest total sum.

Changing sign of 3 and 4

			*	*	
	.23	.17	.32	.23	.17
	.17	.12	.24	.16	.12
*	.32	.24	+.46	+.33	.25
*	.23	.16	+.33	+.24	.18
	.17	.12	.25	.18	.13

	1.12	.81	1.60	1.14	.85
b_j	.48	.34	(.68)	(.49)	.36

TABLE 15.5

R*- Reflected Residual Matrix.
Signs of rows and columns 3 and 4
are reversed. All entries are now
positive

r_j^* $\Sigma r_j^* = 5.52$ T = 2.35

$b_j : r_j^* / T^*$

Principal Axes Factor Loadings

a_j	b_j
1 .76	.48
2 .73	.34
3 .42	-.68
4 .54	-.49
5 .60	.36

TABLE 15.6

The signs of the loadings of test 3 and 4 in factor b are made negative since they were reflected in the correlation matrix.

Rotated Loadings

a_j	b_j
.04	.90
.13	.79
.80	-.04
.71	.16
.05	.70

The original loadings are rotated 55° clockwise. See Fig. 15.5

available from which the points can be plotted or upon which the factor loadings can be projected. Once the column sums of R have been divided by $\sqrt{T}$, however, the values become projections of the test vectors on the centroid or principal axis. (The column sums)/$\sqrt{T}$ or first factor loadings are the first or x-axis coordinates of the test points. The key to the centroid method is that the first principal axis must be defined so as to pass through the origin and a point (the centroid) that maximizes the variance accounted for by the first factor loadings. Calculation of the centroid's is made by *averaging* the first factor loadings (in the example the average = .61). An effort is made, by changing signs within the correlation matrix, to maximize this average, thereby making the residuals as small as possible. That is, the origin and the centroid determine the first axis. The second axis is placed at right angles to the first centroid axis under the

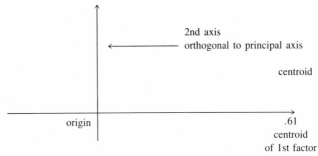

FIG. 15.4.   Projections of test vectors on the principal axis or controid vector.

assumption that the factor loadings are uncorrelated (Fig. 15.4). The second factor loadings are determined from the residual correlation matrix. These are the second or y-axis coordinates.

Once two axes are available the tests can be plotted as vectors and points in a two-dimensional diagram as shown in Fig. 15.5.

Thurstone has stated that there are two major steps in factor analysis. The first is to convert the correlations into a factor matrix using an initial arbitrary frame of reference and the second is to rotate the frame into a simplifying position. This second step means that a new set of orthogonal axes is fitted by eye to the data points in such a way as to maximize the contrast in the factor loadings. For the data reported in Fig. 15.5, it appears that this maximization occurs when axes are rotated clockwise approximately 55°. New factor loadings are then read from the new axes.

Once the number of degrees of rotation has been determined the new exact loadings can be obtained by using $\hat{a}_i = a_i \cos \theta - b_i \sin \theta$ where ^ means new or rotated loadings.

$$\hat{b}_i = a_i \sin \theta + b_i \cos \theta$$

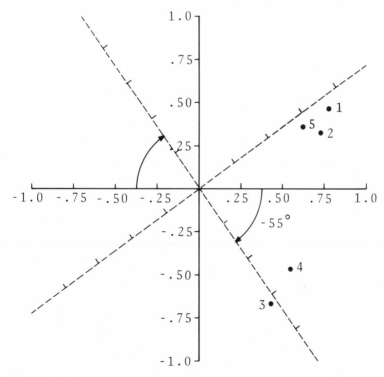

FIG. 15.5.   Right-angled (orthogonal) rotation of −55°.

For this example,

$$\cos 55° = .57 \qquad \sin 55° = 82$$

$$\cos -55° = +.57 \qquad \sin -55° = -.82$$

For the unrotated loadings of Table 15.6, followed by a rotation of those loadings 55° clockwise, the new *exact* loadings are calculated as follows:

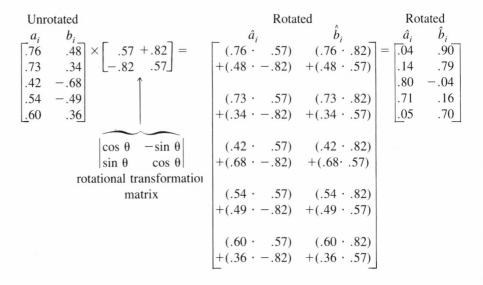

VECTOR REPRESENTATION

If the factor matrix is known, the square root of any commonality ($\sqrt{h_i^2} = h_i$) is a linear representation of the ith test's common variability. This variability can be represented by a vector of length equal to h_i. For the data of Table 15.1, the vector lengths are drawn as follows:

	h_1^2	h_i				
1	.81	.90				
2	.65	.80				
3	.64	.80				
4	.53	.73				
5	.49	.70				
			0	.25	.50	.75	1.00

It is known that the correlation between two variables (see page 34) is equal to the product of their vector lengths and the cosine of the angle included between them or

$$r_{ij} = h_i h_j \ \cos_{ij} \qquad (10)$$

For the correlation matrix of Table 15.2, the vector configuration that follows is an accurate representation, as it fits the scalar product definition of Equation 10. For example: $r_{1,5} = (.90)(.70)(\cos 6.5°) = .63$

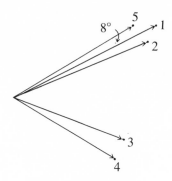

Vector Configuration

Note that this vector configuration is close to the configuration obtained using factor loadings and then axes rotation. The factor loadings are a linear combination of the columns of the correlation matrix. The correlation matrix therefore determines the length of the test vectors and their angular separation. It does not, however, locate the reference axes. It does not say where the configuration should be placed.

Discussion

The centroid method is used here for illustrative purposes. Other factor solutions (such as principal components) used to reduce the array of data in a correlation matrix to a smaller factor matrix take advantage of the algebra associated with matrix theory. A principal concept in this theory is the rank of the matrix. If a larger correlation matrix can be accurately represented by a factor matrix of just two columns the *rank* of the correlation matrix is said to be two. Fortunately, given any matrix, and using computers, there are standard methods for defining its rank or approximate rank (Harman, 1967; Rummel, 1970).

Factor analysis is a popular technique but the assumptions of linearity and normality of the data restrict its application where curvilinear or nonmetric assumptions are more tenable. Specific problems associated with linear factor analysis include:

1. Should 1's be placed in the diagonal of the correlation matrix? Putting a 1 in the diagonal indicates that the experimenter is interested in all the variance, specific and error as well as common. Placing some other value in the diagonal indicates that an estimate of the communality is available and is meaningful. The largest row correlation or squared multiple correlations (SMC) have been suggested as the best value to place in the diagonal. (See Harman (1970) for a good discussion.)

2. How many factors should be extracted? Kaiser (1958) suggests that if the sum of the squares of the factor loadings (called eigenvalues) is less than one (1) little is to be gained by extracting further factors. Cattell (1962) has suggested

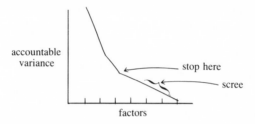

FIG. 15.6.   Example of the scree test for factor extraction. For a good discussion see Rummel, 1970.

that the decision to continue or not should be based on what is called the scree test. The scree test consists of plotting the factors in equal intervals against the variance accounted for by each factor. When the line plot ceases to drop dramatically (i.e., becomes linear), factoring should stop. See Fig. 15.6.

3. What kind of rotation to perform. Usually the general factor that emerges before rotation is not as interesting or interpretable as a solution that can be obtained by rotating the axes in order to contrast the factor loadings more effectively. Rotation can be done by hand, plotting each pairwise set of factor coefficients and then "trying out" various axes in order to obtain meaning. This method is time-consuming and difficult for more than two factors. If the purpose of the analysis is "look and see" versus "theory defense" automatic rotational procedures are available.

The most popular rotational procedure is Kaiser's orthogonal (right-angled) varimax rotation. This process attempts to rotate the axes so as to maximize the variance accounted for by each factor. This can be done by minimizing the sum of the rectangular areas encompassed by the coordinates of the points and the axes from which they are drawn. In Fig. 15.7, for example, the areas A and B are larger than in Fig. 15.8 (i.e., rotation reduced the total area).

Oftentimes the question is raised whether to use varimax *orthogonal* rotation or an *oblique* rotation. If it is felt that groups of correlated objects or tests are likely to result, then oblique rotation, in which the right-angled properties of the coordinate axes are no longer maintained, can be used.

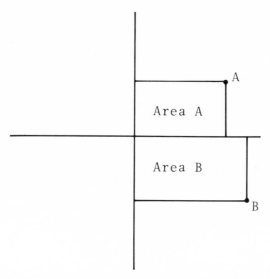

FIG. 15.7. Original areas before rotation.

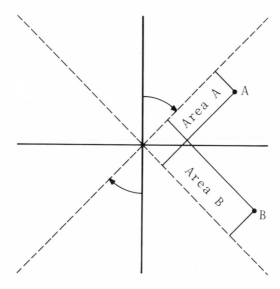

FIG. 15.8. Reduced areas following rotation.

TABLE 15.7
Principal Components Analysis

VAR.	EST COMMUN.	FACTOR	EIGENVALUE	PCT	CUM PCT
V1	.59698	1	2.37665	47.5	47.5
V2	.54754	2	1.48606	29.7	77.3
V3	.32582	3	.45203	9.0	86.3
V4	.35285	4	.41886	8.4	94.7
V5	.42103	5	.26640	5.3	100.0

SMR (Squared Multiple R)

FACTOR MATRIX USING PRINCIPAL FACTOR WITH ITERATIONS

	FACTOR 1	FACTOR 2
V1	.87216	-.21992
V2	.80008	-.09836
V3	.18602	.72991
V4	.37389	.67186
V5	.67925	-.17148

13 ITERATIONS FOR CONVERGENCE

VAR.	COMMUN.	FACTOR	EIGENVALUE	PCT	CUM PCT
V1	.80903	1	2.03657	65.5	65.5
V2	.64980	2	1.07161	34.5	100.0
V3	.56737				
V4	.59119				
V5	49079				

VARIMAX ROTATED FACTOR MATRIX
AFTER ROTATION WITH KAISER NORMALIZATION

	FACTOR 1	FACTOR 2
V1	.89865	.03810
V2	.79488	.13404
V3	-.03000	.75264
V4	.16662	.75061
V5	.69994	.02948

TRANSFORMATION MATRIX

	FACTOR 1	FACTOR 2
FACTOR 1	.95842	.28535
FACTOR 2	-.28535	.95882

The correlational data from Fig. 15.1 were run using the SPSS program for principal components analysis, a factor analytic method. Squared multiple correlations were used as estimates of the communality and two factors were extracted. This was followed by a varimax rotation. The result is shown in Table 15.7. This solution is very close to the centroid result presented in this chapter.

APPLICATION: SEMANTIC DIFFERENTIAL ON SELF-CONCEPT

One of the author's students, J. Moriyama used factor analysis to derive four factors from ordered category scales (semantic differentials) presented in Fig. 15.9. She then tested differences between the attitudes of two different generations of Japanese immigrants to Hawaii on the concepts "male and female Americans of Japanese ancestry."

The 40 subjects of this study were randomly selected; 20 second-generation Japanese–Americans (10 male, 10 female) and 20 third-generation Japanese–Americans (10 male, 10 female). All subjects had lived in Hawaii all their lives. The age of Nisei subjects ranged from 36 to 64 years old. The age of the Sansei subjects ranged from 19- to 26-years-old.

The attitudes were scaled using a modified version of Osgood's (1957) semantic differential. Thirty bipolar adjectives were chosen by the experimenter and each subject was asked to rate the concept of Americans of Japanese ancestry (male/female).

All subjects' responses on both male and female concepts were collected and run through a principal components factor analysis using the Veldman's (1967) Routine FACTOR. Four factors whose eigenroots (sums of the squares of the factor loadings) exceeded 1.0 were extracted and rotated (Table 15.8). The first factor is identified as *activity/interaction*. The identification was made by listing the bipolar adjectives that had fairly high loadings on it: sociable–unsociable, extrovert–introvert, active–passive, rugged–delicate, loud–soft, brave–coward, passionate–frigid. The second factor appears to be a typical "*stereotype*" kind of factor. The scales that load on it are: graceful–clumsy, safe–dangerous, artistic–inartistic, pleasant–unpleasant, happy–sad, thrifty–wasteful, trusting–suspicious. These scales suggest adjectives generally used to describe the Japanese. The third factor is perceived to be a *calm* and *goodness* on which load the scales: simple–complex, trusting–suspicious, honest–dishonest, calm–excited, relaxed–tense. Finally, the fourth factor is the *ability* factor: quick–slow, rich–poor, successful–unsuccessful, strong–weak, intelligent–stupid, sharp–dull.

The program FACTOR also reported each subject's scores (z-scaled) on the four factors. These factor scores were then analyzed in a three-way analysis of variance.

Instruction:

The purpose of this questionnaire is to measure the meanings of certain concepts to various people by having them judge them against a series of descriptive scales. In taking this inventory, please make your judgments on the basis of what these things mean to *you*. On the following pages you will find a different concept to be judged and beneath it a set of scales. You are to rate the concept on each of these scales in order.

If you feel that the concept at the top of the page is *very closely related* to one end of the scale, you should place your check-mark as follows:

UNFAIR: __X__ : ___ : ___ : ___ : ___ : ___ : ___ : FAIR

or UNFAIR: ___ : ___ : ___ : ___ : ___ : ___ : __X__ : FAIR

If you feel that the concept is *quite closely related* to one or the other end of the scale, you should place your check-mark as follows:

STRONG: ___ : __X__ : ___ : ___ : ___ : ___ : ___ : WEAK

or STRONG: ___ : ___ : ___ : ___ : ___ : __X__ : ___ : WEAK

If the concept seems only *slightly related* to one side as opposed to the other side, then you should check as follows:

ACTIVE: ___ : ___ : __X__ : ___ : ___ : ___ : ___ : PASSIVE

or ACTIVE: ___ : ___ : ___ : ___ : __X__ : ___ : ___ : PASSIVE

If you consider the concept to be *neutral* on the scale, or if the scale is *completely irrelevant*, then you should place your check-mark in the middle space:

SAFE: ___ : ___ : ___ : __X__ : ___ : ___ : ___ : DANGEROUS

Place your check-marks in the middle of the spaces and not on the boundaries. Work at fairly high speed through this inventory. Do not worry or puzzle over individual items. It is your first impressions about the items that we want.

This questionnaire has been designed to survey attitudes and opinions of Americans of Japanese ancestry living in Hawaii. The purpose is to obtain your point of view concerning Americans of Japanese ancestry. The information is these questionnaires is absolutely confidential. No individual names or data will be reported. Do not, therefore, sign your name on this document. However, please fill in the necessary information below:

Sex: _____ Generation: _____ (issei, nisei, sansei, yonsei, etc.)

Age: _____

a. under 20	b. 20-25	c. 26-30	d. 31-35	e. 36-40
f. 41-45	g. 46-50	h. 51-55	i. 56-60	j. over 60

FIG. 15.9. Instructions and ordered category scales (semantic differential) for measuring attitudes toward Americans of Japanese ancestry.

FIG. 15.9. (*Continued*)

AMERICANS OF JAPANESE ANCESTRY (male)

GOOD: ___ : ___ : ___ : ___ : ___ : ___ : ___ : BAD

INDEPENDENT: ___ : ___ : ___ : ___ : ___ : ___ : ___ : DEPENDENT

STRONG: ___ : ___ : ___ : ___ : ___ : ___ : ___ : WEAK

SIMPLE: ___ : ___ : ___ : ___ : ___ : ___ : ___ : COMPLEX

CLEAN: ___ : ___ : ___ : ___ : ___ : ___ : ___ : DIRTY

EDUCATED: ___ : ___ : ___ : ___ : ___ : ___ : ___ : IGNORANT

LOUD: ___ : ___ : ___ : ___ : ___ : ___ : ___ : SOFT

SUCCESSFUL: ___ : ___ : ___ : ___ : ___ : ___ : ___ : UNSUCCESSFUL

PLEASANT: ___ : ___ : ___ : ___ : ___ : ___ : ___ : UNPLEASANT

PASSIONATE: ___ : ___ : ___ : ___ : ___ : ___ : ___ : FRIGID

HAPPY: ___ : ___ : ___ : ___ : ___ : ___ : ___ : SAD

SHARP: ___ : ___ : ___ : ___ : ___ : ___ : ___ : DULL

SAFE: ___ : ___ : ___ : ___ : ___ : ___ : ___ : DANGEROUS

ARTISTIC: ___ : ___ : ___ : ___ : ___ : ___ : ___ : INARTISTIC

RELAXED: ___ : ___ : ___ : ___ : ___ : ___ : ___ : TENSE

QUICK: ___ : ___ : ___ : ___ : ___ : ___ : ___ : SLOW

BRAVE: ___ : ___ : ___ : ___ : ___ : ___ : ___ : COWARDLY

THRIFTY: ___ : ___ : ___ : ___ : ___ : ___ : ___ : WASTEFUL

RICH: ___ : ___ : ___ : ___ : ___ : ___ : ___ : POOR

TRUSTING: ___ : ___ : ___ : ___ : ___ : ___ : ___ : SUSPICIOUS

ACTIVE: ___ : ___ : ___ : ___ : ___ : ___ : ___ : PASSIVE

HONEST: ___ : ___ : ___ : ___ : ___ : ___ : ___ : DISHONEST

RUGGED: ___ : ___ : ___ : ___ : ___ : ___ : ___ : DELICATE

SOCIABLE: ___ : ___ : ___ : ___ : ___ : ___ : ___ : UNSOCIABLE

FRIENDLY: ___ : ___ : ___ : ___ : ___ : ___ : ___ : HOSTILE

GRACEFUL: ___ : ___ : ___ : ___ : ___ : ___ : ___ : CLUMSY

INTROVERT: ___ : ___ : ___ : ___ : ___ : ___ : ___ : EXTROVERT

CALM: ___ : ___ : ___ : ___ : ___ : ___ : ___ : EXCITABLE

INTELLIGENT   ___ : ___ : ___ : ___ : ___ : ___ : ___ : STUPID

FIG. 15.9. (*Continued*)

AMERICANS OF JAPANESE ANCESTRY (female)

GOOD: ____ : ___ : ___ : ___ : ___ : ___ : ___ : BAD

INDEPENDENT: ___ : ___ : ___ : ___ : ___ : ___ : ___ : DEPENDENT

STRONG: ___ : ___ : ___ : ___ : ___ : ___ : ___ : WEAK

SIMPLE: ___ : ___ : ___ : ___ : ___ : ___ : ___ : COMPLEX

CLEAN: ___ : ___ : ___ : ___ : ___ : ___ : ___ : DIRTY

EDUCATED: ___ : ___ : ___ : ___ : ___ : ___ : ___ : IGNORANT

LOUD: ___ : ___ : ___ : ___ : ___ : ___ : ___ : SOFT

SUCCESSFUL: ___ : ___ : ___ : ___ : ___ : ___ : ___ : UNSUCCESSFUL

PLEASANT: ___ : ___ : ___ : ___ : ___ : ___ : ___ : UNPLEASANT

PASSIONATE: ___ : ___ : ___ : ___ : ___ : ___ : ___ : FRIGID

HAPPY: ___ : ___ : ___ : ___ : ___ : ___ : ___ : SAD

SHARP: ___ : ___ : ___ : ___ : ___ : ___ : ___ : DULL

SAFE: ___ : ___ : ___ : ___ : ___ : ___ : ___ : DANGEROUS

ARTISTIC: ___ : ___ : ___ : ___ : ___ : ___ : ___ : INARTISTIC

RELAXED: ___ : ___ : ___ : ___ : ___ : ___ : ___ : TENSE

QUICK: ___ : ___ : ___ : ___ : ___ : ___ : ___ : SLOW

BRAVE: ___ : ___ : ___ : ___ : ___ : ___ : ___ : COWARDLY

THRIFTY: ___ : ___ : ___ : ___ : ___ : ___ : ___ : WASTEFUL

RICH: ___ : ___ : ___ : ___ : ___ : ___ : ___ : POOR

TRUSTING: ___ : ___ : ___ : ___ : ___ : ___ : ___ : SUSPICIOUS

ACTIVE: ___ : ___ : ___ : ___ : ___ : ___ : ___ : PASSIVE

HONEST: ___ : ___ : ___ : ___ : ___ : ___ : ___ : DISHONEST

RUGGED: ___ : ___ : ___ : ___ : ___ : ___ : ___ : DELICATE

SOCIABLE: ___ : ___ : ___ : ___ : ___ : ___ : ___ : UNSOCIABLE

FRIENDLY: ___ : ___ : ___ : ___ : ___ : ___ : ___ : HOSTILE

GRACEFUL: ___ : ___ : ___ : ___ : ___ : ___ : ___ : CLUMSY

INTROVERT: ___ : ___ : ___ : ___ : ___ : ___ : ___ : EXTROVERT

CALM: ___ : ___ : ___ : ___ : ___ : ___ : ___ : EXCITABLE

INTELLIGENT ___ : ___ : ___ : ___ : ___ : ___ : ___ : STUPID

TABLE 15.8
Varimax Factor Loadings

Scale	Factors			
	1	2	3	4
good-bad	.1439	.3877	.3516	.0547
independent-dependent	.3611	-.1098	.3645	.0528
strong-weak	.3023	-.0989	.3769	.6160
simple-complex	.0715	-.0995	.7006	-.1610
clean-dirty	-.0210	.3816	.3882	.2253
educated-ignorant	.0416	.4275	.0172	.3623
loud-soft	.5793	-.1969	.1095	-.0033
successful-unsuccessful	.2721	.0105	.1790	.6584
pleasant-unpleasant	.0112	.5799	.1951	.1708
passionate-frigid	.6057	.1605	.2614	.1546
happy-sad	.5005	.5657	-.0310	-.0109
sharp-dull	.3759	.3562	.0267	.5691
safe-dangerous	-.1015	.6370	.3213	.1903
artistic-inartistic	.1054	.5971	.0230	-.0230
relaxed-tense	.3664	.2121	.5808	.1855
quick-slow	.3236	.1751	.3009	.6873
brave-cowardly	.5730	.0959	.1629	.4993
thrifty-wasteful	-1607	.5274	.1659	.2255
rich-poor	-.0814	-.0328	-.1701	.6618
trusting-suspicious	-.1704	.4389	.6807	.1497
active-passive	.7136	.1831	.0838	.3059
honest-dishonest	.0267	.3690	.6493	.1321
rugged-delicate	.6292	-.2971	.1430	.1519
sociable-unsociable	.7396	.2491	-.1230	-.0056
friendly-unfriendly	.5096	.4746	.1174	.1016
graceful-clumsy	.0441	.6712	.0396	-.2341
introvert-extrovert	-.6828	-.1034	.1300	-.0912
calm-excited	.0272	.0540	.6321	.0018
intelligent-stupid	.0136	.3348	-.0990	.6135
cooperative-uncooperative	.2586	.4315	-.0803	.1313
Σa_j^2 (The eigenroots or values λ)	7.3572	3.3115	2.2416	2.0123
Percent variance after rotation	14.6455	13.4018	10.6090	11.0852

(2) sex (M/F); and (3) generation of subject (Nisei/Sansei).

RESULTS AND DISCUSSION

Factor 1 (Activity)

There were no significant differences between generations and their interactions with regard to the *activity* factor. Both Nisei and Sansei Japanese–Americans view the Japanese–Americans in general as outgoing and active.

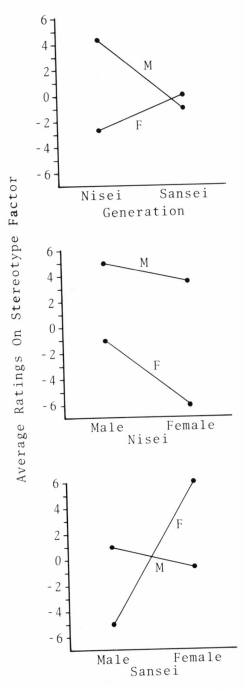

FIG. 15.10. The concept "Americans of Japanese Ancestry" is compared by second and third generation Japanese–Americans and by sex.

Factor 2 (Stereotype)

There was a significant difference between the Niseis' and Sanseis' concept of male and female Americans of Japanese ancestry on the *stereotype* factor (see Fig. 15.10). Second-generation immigrants ranked males very highly, whereas females were ranked very low. However, the third generation ranked both male and female nearly equal, with the female concept being slightly higher than the male.

From the Analysis of Variance there was just one *F* ratio whose probability was less than .05, there were, however, two tests that were close to the .05 level that were worth looking at. For the second generation, both male and female subjects tended to rate male Japanese higher than female Japanese. This result appears to reflect the traditional Japanese value of male superiority. Nevertheless, for the third generation, although both male and female subjects rated the Japanese male only slightly lower than the second generation had rated him, the mean ratings of females by females soared. In fact, the rating was higher than the ratings of males by Nisei males. Meanwhile, the Sansei male tended to rate females lower. Nisei males also tended to rate the concepts of male and female higher than Nisei females, whereas Sansei females tended to rate the concepts higher than Sansei males.

Factor 3 (Goodness)

Two main effects were found to be highly significant under the *calm-goodness* factor. The female subjects, in general, inclined to rate the Americans of Japanese ancestry higher than did male subjects. The Niseis inclined to rate the concepts higher than Sanseis.

Factor 4 (Ability)

Under the *ability* factor there was a significant interaction between the male and female Americans of Japanese ancestry concepts and the second and third generations. Unlike Factor 2, the Niseis rated the female Japanese–Americans higher on the ability factor than the male. However, for the third generation, the ratings of the male Japanese rose while the ratings of the female Japanese declined.

The results of Moriyama's investigation seem to support the hypothesis that attitudinal differences exist between second- and third-generation Japanese–Americans on factors related to females.

Almost all computer packages contain programs to do factor analysis. These include Veldman's FACTOR, BMD's BMDP4M, as well as programs in SPSS and SAS (see Chapter 20).

16 Multidimensional Scaling

Multidimensional Scaling is the name for a number of methods that attempt to represent spatially the proximities between a number of stimuli. The methods can determine metric Euclidian distances between objects with only ordinal assumptions about the data. The method is applicable to a wide number of measures of similarity or dissimilarity and unlike factor analysis can be used on data derived from a small number of subjects and with few assumptions about the data. Its primary purpose is a parsimonious spatial representation of the objects.

THEORY: SHEPARD AND KRUSKAL'S NONMETRIC MONOTONIC

Multidimensional scaling proceeds as follows:

1. There is a given set of n objects.

2. For every two objects (i and j) some measure or function of proximity f (s_{ij}) is obtained. (These measures may be correlations, similarities, associations, distances, etc.) If similarities are obtained (s_{ij}), they are usually converted to theoretical distances ($\hat{d}_{ij}$) by subtracting from a constant.

3. A number of dimensions (t) are selected that may fit the data. The n objects are then placed (randomly or selectively) in one of the dimensional spaces.

4. Multidimensional scaling (MDS) searches for a replotting of the n objects so that physical distances (d_{ij}) between pairs of objects in the plot are related to their measures of proximity $f(s_{ij}) = (\hat{d}i_{j})$. The relation is such that if the distance between two objects is large the expectation is that their original similarity

measure will be small (i.e., distances and similarity measures are related inversely but monotonically [in regular order]). If, for example, the similarity between the words "war" and "peace" is estimated to be small then the two words should be a relatively "large" distance apart, farther apart than the words "lady" and "mother," for example. If d is a measure of distance then its relation to similarity can be stated as

$$d_{ij} < d_{kl} \text{ when } s_{ij} > s_{kl}$$

that is, the distance is greater when the similarity is smaller or specifically:

$$d_{\text{lady}-\text{mother}} < d_{\text{war}-\text{peace}} \text{ when } s_{\text{lady}-\text{mother}} > s_{\text{war}-\text{peace}}$$

The process of arriving at the best spatial configuration to represent the original similarities has been presented by Shepard (1962) and Kruskal (1964a). In Kruskal's method a resolution of the spatial configuration is made by steps (iterations). At each step the objects are moved from their initial placement in the dimensional space and the physical distances between all pairs of objects are calculated. The distances (d_{ij}) between pairs of objects in the new placement are ordered and then compared with the original proximities ($\hat{d}_{ij}$) between the same pairs of objects, which have also been ordered. If the relationship is increasingly monotonic, that is, if the order of the new distances is similar to the order of the original distances, the objects continue to move in the same direction at the next step. If the relationship is not monotonic, changes in direction and step length are made. It is clear that a measure of monotonicity is primary in nonmetric scaling. This measure is provided by ordering the proximity measures ($\hat{d}_{ij}$) on the x-axis and measuring horizontal deviations of the newly obtained distances in the plot (d_{ij}) from the original distances ($\hat{d}_{ij}$). The deviations are squared so they can be summed. The object is to make the sum of the squared deviations as small as possible. That is,

$$\sum_{i<j} (d_{ij} - \hat{d}_{ij})^2 \text{ a minimum.}$$

Suppose the similarities (s_{ij}) among three words are obtained as an average of several subjective estimates as follows:

Similarity Matrix

	Words		
	1 *Athlete*	*2* *Agile*	*3* *Neat*
1. Athlete			
2. Agile	8		
3. Neat	4	3	

By subtracting each of these average estimates from a constant (10) the following proximity values (dissimilarities or theoretical distances $= \hat{d}_{ij}$) are found.

$$\text{proximity} = \hat{d}_{ij}$$
$$(10 - s_{ij})$$

Pairs		$\hat{d}$
1–2	Athlete–agile	= 2
1–3	Athlete–neat	= 6
2–3	Agile–neat	= 7

As an initial step the three objects are *randomly* placed in a two-dimensional space (Fig. 16.1) and the actual distances between pairs (d_{ij}) in the space is calculated (see Table 16.1).

The similarities and distances between the objects are plotted in a two-dimensional diagram, commonly called a Shepard diagram Fig. 16.2. In these diagrams the predicted distances (d_{ij}) will always lie on a smooth line or curve that behaves monotonically. Because the plotted distances (d_{ij}) and the theoretic monotonic distances $(\hat{d}_{ij})$ do not coincide, the initial spatial representation based on random assignment does not fit the basic assumption of monotonicity (i.e., the rank of $\hat{d}_{ij}$ does not equal the rank of d_{ij}).

$\hat{d}_{ij}$	Rank	d_{ij}	Rank
2	1	4	3
6	2	2	1
7	3	3	2

Ranks are not equal

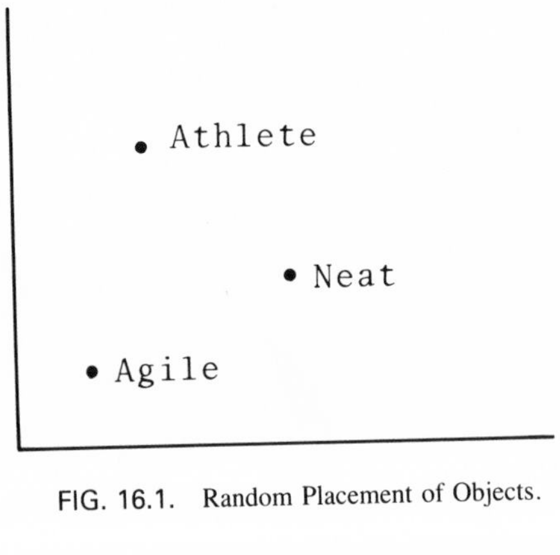

FIG. 16.1.   Random Placement of Objects.

TABLE 16.1
Relationship Between Judged $\hat{d}_{ij}$ and Initial Placement d_{ij} Distances

Pairs	Similarities	Theoretical Distances		Actual Calculated Distances		Difference	D^2
		$\hat{d}_{ij}$	Rank	d_{ij}	Rank		
1-2	8	2	1	4	3	-2	4
1-3	4	6	2	2	1	+4	16
2-3	3	7	3	3	2	+4	16
							$\Sigma = 36$

As measure of how well the points fit the theory, the sum of the squared deviations of d_{ij} from $\hat{d}_{ij}$ is calculated. Kruskal calls this value

$$\text{raw stress} = S^* = \sum_{i<j} (d_{ij} - \hat{d}_{ij})^2$$

For this step $* = (2 - 4)^2 + (6 - 2)^2 + (7 - 3)^2 = 36$

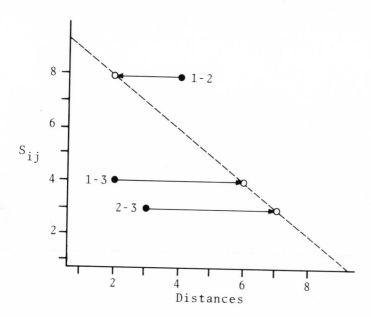

● Plot of similarity s_{ij} and distance d_{ij}.
○ Plot of similarity S_{ij} and monotonic theoretical distance $\hat{d}_{ij}$.

FIG. 16.2. Shepard diagram.

Pairs of words (Athlete [1], Agile [2], and Neat [3]) are plotted as 1–2, 1–3, and 2–3. The horizontal difference between $\hat{d}_{ij}$ and d_{ij} is illustrated.

As a second step the three points are moved in varying small amounts of distance and direction so as to reduce the stress index, as shown in Fig. 16.3. Any two objects of a pair are moved closer together if $\hat{d}_{ij} < d_{ij}$ and farther apart if $\hat{d}_{ij} > d_{ij}$. In the example above, Athlete and Agile are moved closer together, Athlete and Neat farhter apart, and Agile and Neat farther apart.

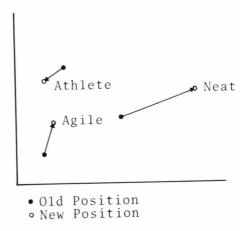

- Old Position
- New Position

FIG. 16.3.   First iteration.

This results in a new set of distances d_{ij} and a new set of differences.

Pairs	Similarity s_{ij}	$\hat{d}_{ij}$	Rank	d_{ij}	Rank	$(d_{ij} - \hat{d}_{ij})^2$
1–2	8	2	1	2	1	0
1–3	4	6	2	5	2	1
2–3	3	7	3	6	3	1
					Raw stress	= 2

This procedure continues until improvement is no longer feasible. In the foregoing example the stress is low and the ranks are equal so the procedure could be conceivably stopped at this point.

Kruskal averages the Raw Stress Sum of Squares by dividing by $\Sigma\, d_{ij}^2$. He then gets the formula back into the original linear units by taking the square root. He calls this index Stress (S).

$$\text{Stress} = S = \sqrt{\frac{\Sigma\,(d_{ij} - \hat{d}_{ij})^2}{\Sigma\, d_{ij}^2}}$$

— In general, minimum stress means better fit.

Stress is a numerical value that denotes the degree of departure of the observed or calculated similarity from the true or judged similarity among objects taken two at a time (Kruskal, 1964a,b). More precisely, stress is analogous to the standard error of estimate in bivariate regression. Note that in linear regression the best line location is fitted to points, whereas in Kruskal's nonmetric the points are best arranged to fit a line. Stress is a normalized sum of squared deviations about a monotonic line fit to the scatter plot of corresponding distances and proximity values. Because of normalization, stress can be expressed as a proportion or a percentage, and the smaller the stress, the better (Subkoviak, 1975).

Although this example has dealt with only two dimensions, distances can be calculated in n dimensions and three or four dimensions may make better fits to the data than one or two dimensions. One way to determine the dimensional space is to plot the stress values for each dimensional solution against the evenly spaced ''number of dimensions'' and test the configuration using Cattell's scree test (see page 180). Because the spatial configuration in MDS is arbitrary with regard to the coordinate axes around which they have been assigned, rotation of these axes is often used to make the spatial representation more clearly recognizable.

METHOD: SUCCESSIVE APPROXIMATION USING STEEPEST DESCENT

In practice, Kruskal's method is one of succession approximation (Kruskal, 1964b). Theoretically the problem is to minimize a stress function involving many variables (x_i) (i.e., the x_i objects in n dimensions). The solution of the problem is found in numerical analysis and is called the ''method of steepest descent.'' In order to understand how the method of steepest descent works for a function involving many variables (the stress function S is a function of the coordinates of all the objects in t dimension), an explanation is given for a simple function involving only two variables.

The graph of a function in two variables is difficult to draw. One can, however, look at such functions by using a topological representation, a representation that map makers use. In mapping mountains, for example, it is common practice to sketch curves at equal points of elevation. A collection of these curves represents the configuration. Lines close together indicate steep declines.

The object is to make the steepest descent from the top of the mountain into the deepest valley. The process has been compared to a skier's return from a mountain to his home in the valley in a heavy fog. Unable to see the goal, the skier starts down this steepest grade. If the path slows or starts to rise he or she changes direction and chooses a new path of steepest descent. The direction is called the negative gradient.

The multidimensional process starts by picking an arbitrary point in the di-

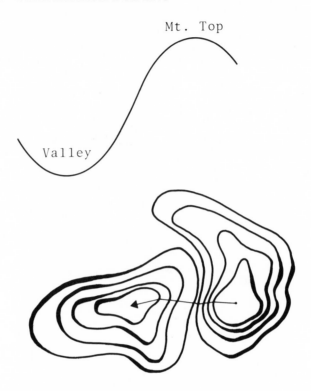

mensional space. The effort is then made to improve the shape of the configuration by moving this point and other points. Improvement is accomplished by finding in which direction the stress function is decreasing most quickly. This direction is called the steepest descent or negative gradient. The negative gradient is found by evaluating the partial derivates of the function with respect to each point and making this gradient negative. This point is then moved a small step in the ''downhill'' direction. After many steps the bottom or minimum is reached.

For example, a function in two variables is used as follows:

$$f(x, y) = x^2 + 4y^2$$

If we plot values of x and y and get the corresponding value of the function (f) we see that the figure is a three-dimensional ''elliptical cup'' as shown in Fig. 16.4.

By letting the function $f(x, y)$ take on constant values, say c, and sketching $f(x, y) = c$, the topological representation of $f(x, y) = x^2 + 4y^2$ can be viewed as Fig. 16.5.

The derivative of an expression like $3x^2$ is found by multiplying the exponent of x, in this case 2, times the coefficient of x and reducing the exponent by 1 or

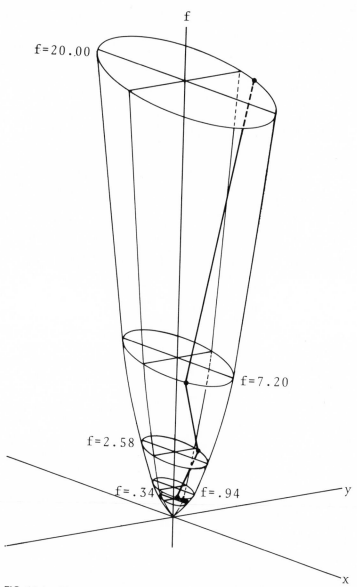

FIG. 16.4. Elliptical paraboloid for $f(x, y) = x^2 + 4y^2$ showing steepest descent line.

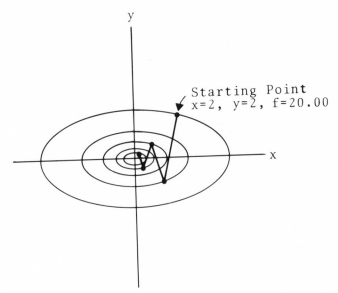

FIG. 16.5.   Topological representation of paraboloid.

$dkx^n = nkx^{n-1}$. Thus the derivative of $3x^2 = 2(3)x^{2-1} = 6x$. The partial derivative of a function of two variables is found for each variable separately by treating the other as a constant. The derivative of a constant is 0. Thus the derivative of $x^2 + 4y^2$ with respect to x is $2x + 0 = 2x$; the derivative with respect to y is $0 + 2(4)y^{2-1} = 8y$. $2x$ and $8y$ are called the partial derivatives of the function and are written as follows:

$$\frac{\partial x}{\partial f} = 2x \qquad \frac{\partial y}{\partial f} = 8y$$

Derivatives are expressions of the rate of change in a function. When both derivations are zero simultaneously the minimum of the function is found. Minimization of the function in the method of steepest descent occurs in a fixed number of steps of varying size. The step size is determined by providing a constant α (alpha = .2, for the example) multiplied times the negative values of the partial derivatives. The derivatives are made negative so that the gradient will be "downhill" or toward a minimum solution. This negative direction is indicated by $\nabla f = -\left(\dfrac{\partial x}{\partial f}, \dfrac{\partial y}{\partial f} \right)$ also known as the delta gradient.

In the present example an arbitrary starting point is taken with $x = y = 2.0$ the function value at that point $f(x, y) = 20.$* Table 16.2 shows the iterative procedure that is followed in reaching an approximate solution, one where $f(x, y)$ is close to zero.

TABLE 16.2
Iterations Method of Steepest Descent Applied to the Function
$f(x,y) = x^2 + 4y^2$ Where $\alpha = 0.2$

Iteration	x	y	$\frac{\partial f}{\partial x} = 2x$	$\frac{\partial f}{\partial y} = 8y$	x Step	y Step	f
			∇f		$(-\nabla f)\alpha$		
Begin	2.0	2.0	4	16	-.8	-3.2	20.00
1	1.2	-1.2	2.4	-9.6	-.48	+1.92	7.20
2	.72	.72	+1.44	+5.76	-.29	-1.15	2.58
3	.43	-.43	.86	-3.46	-.17	+.69	.94
4	.26	+.26					34

*The iterative procedure is as follows: $x_{new} = x_{old} - \alpha\frac{\partial f}{\partial x}$; $y_{new} = y_{old} - \alpha\frac{\partial f}{\partial x}$

Note: In this case $\frac{\partial f}{\partial x}$ depends only on x and $\frac{\partial f}{\partial y}$ depends only on y so that the order of these two steps does not change the solution structure.

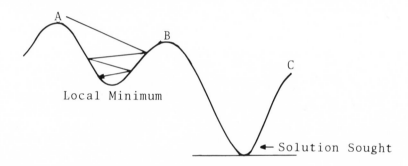

FIG. 16.6. An example of a local minimum.

In this method the beginning arbitrary values of x and y are substituted in the partial derivative. The step values, which are alpha multiplied times the negative values of the derivatives (i.e., $-\alpha\nabla f$) are calculated. These become the new values of x and y. The process continues until no improvement is found or until a solution is "close enough." Close is determined by the experimenter.

Should a function have small valleys known as local minimums, the solution may end up in one of these "holes" and never make its way out. (Fig. 16.6).

This can be solved by starting in a better place to begin with, at points B or C, for example. If no approximate starting position for the variables is available several random starting positions should be tried. New methods, however, ap-

TABLE 16.3

Measures of similarity under template matching (TM) and clustering (C): Upper triangular
matrix shows congruency measures for TM; lower matrix contains proportion
of time two letters were placed in the same cluster ($n=20$)

proximate the initial configuration by techniques such as factor analysis before starting multiple dimensional scaling. Because of the complexity of multidimensional steepest descent problems, solutions are practically restricted to computer solutions. In a problem with seven points and four dimensions, a simultaneous solution of 28 partial derivative equations is required. Furthermore, because the stress function is of the square root form, the partial derivatives are not elementary.

APPLICATION 1: DISCONFIRMING THE LUSCHER COLOR TEST

Gerald Roberts, one of the author's students, studied the *Luscher Color Test,* "the remarkable test that reveals your personality through color." Luscher delineates four bipolar "dimensions" in the colors chosen as test items. Aside from testing the reliability of the test, a validation of the theory was attempted by using MDS (among other measures) in an attempt to reproduce the Luscher dimensions from color preference responses of 34 individual subjects. A *three*-dimensional solution rendered the minimum stress value of .01.

Final configurations for the eight colors were:

	I	*II*	*III*
Grey	.83	.99	−.19
Blue	1.06	.75	.00
Green	−.01	.04	−1.13
Red	.03	.03	−1.11
Yellow	−.48	.05	.59
Violet	−.48	.04	.60
Brown	−.48	.05	.62
Black	−.48	.04	.62

Roberts concluded that although color preference is stable (reliable), the analysis of the underlying structure failed to conform to the Luscher theory of a sophisticated personality predictor.

APPLICATION 2: DIMENSIONS OF HIRAGANA

Dunn-Rankin, Leton, and Sato (1972) studied Typos 35 Hiragana characters. The characters were printed on acetate disks and adult subjects unfamiliar with the Japanese language were asked to group the letters into clusters. The resulting percentage overlap matrix shown in Table 16.3 was analyzed using the KYST MDS program. A three-dimensional solution gave the minimum stress of .11 and

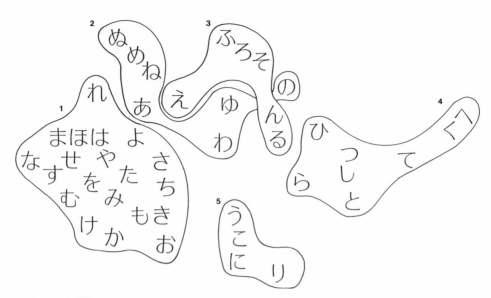

FIG. 16.7. Multidimensional scaling of 46 typos 35 hiragana characters with divisive clustering superimposed. Data were determined by the proportion of times two characters were placed in the same cluster (n = 20). Clusters are identified as: (1) crossed t; (2) circular curve; (3) zigzag; (4) straight line + curve; and (5) simple curve.

the dimensions were readily interpretable as groups of characters with similar features. A two-dimensional solution is presented with a divisive clustering (page 156) superimposed on the scaling in Fig. 16.7.

APPLICATION 3: SCALING COMMON WORDS

For the words that were clustered in Fig. 12.3, (Dunn-Rankin 1978) percentage overlap matrices were formed separately for all words beginning with the letters *a* and *s* (Table 16.4). Multidimensional scaling produced the configurations shown in Fig. 16.8. The attempt was made to determine which dimensions would dominate estimates of word similarity when the initial letter was held constant.

The two-space (two-dimensional) solution for 11 words beginning with the letter *a* produced ''excellent'' fit (stress less than 2½%) and the 12 words beginning with the letter *s* showed ''fair'' fit (stress less than 10%). By ''excellent,'' we mean only that there is an excellent monotone relationship between dissimilarities and the distances (Kruskal, 1964a).

Inspection of Fig. 16.7 shows that the *word length* is definitely one of the two dimensions isolated by MDSCAL. In both the *a* and *s* configurations, the length

TABLE 16.4
Percent Overlap Matrices for 11 Words Beginning With the Letter *a*
Data is Based on 33 Adult Subjects Free Clustering

		a 1	*as* 2	*at* 3	*and* 4	*aged* 5	*areas* 6	*admits* 7	*almost* 8	*aiming* 9	*army* 10
a	1										
as	2	0.394									
at	3	0.273	0.242								
and	4	0.182	0.242	0.212							
aged	5	0.121	0.121	0.121	0.303						
areas	6	0.121	0.000	0.091	0.091	0.333					
admits	7	0.182	0.000	0.030	0.000	0.061	0.091				
almost	8	0.121	0.000	0.030	0.000	0.030	0.061	0.485			
aiming	9	0.000	0.030	0.061	0.030	0.152	0.152	0.303	0.424		
army	10	0.000	0.091	0.030	0.061	0.091	0.030	0.303	0.333	0.414	
away	11	0.000	0.061	0.030	0.061	0.121	0.061	0.273	0.394	0.333	0.606

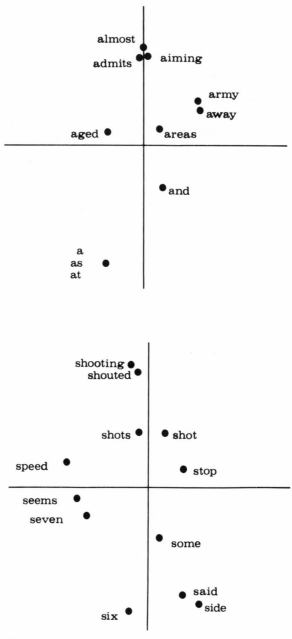

FIG. 16.8.   Rotated two-space multidimensional configurations for words beginning with *a* and *s*. Stresses are .01 for 11 words beginning with *a*, and .07 for 12
words beginning with *s*.

of the word increases from one end of a dimension to the other. The second dimension, however, is not explicitly discernible as relating to a single factor. Rather, the dimension appears to be a mixture of both *proximity of ascenders and descenders* and *unique letter combinations*. Thus, in this case, the results of multidimensional scaling corroborate the results of hierarchical clustering with regard to the bases of perceived word similarity.

Kruskal's KYST may be obtained from the Bell Telephone Laboratory (see also Chapter 20). Guttman and Lingoes (Lingoes, 1970) also have a similar program called SSA (Smallest Space Analysis), which is commonly found in large computer centers. Forrest Young has written a general multidimensional scaling program (ALSCAL) which is found in the latest SAS Software package.

17 Mapping Preference

For almost any entity (Kelso, grape jelly, University of Florida, Enrico Valdes, etc.), a directional identification can be made. That is, given two or more psychological objects, the subject usually prefers one of the elements of the set.

Individual differences in preference are of interest to the behavioral scientist because the interaction between attitude and treatment has not been fully explored. Different people may react differently to the same stimulus. Some people prefer spinach, others dislike it. Some children prefer teacher approval as a reward; others prefer freedom, competitive success, peer approval, or consumable rewards. Children vary in their preferences for reinforcers.

The methods previously discussed have looked at psychological objects from the view of the *average* subject. A unidimensional scale may be thought of as a single axis or vector that represents this average. When all subjects' responses are consistently similar such scaling is reasonable. A multidimensional mapping of objects (like a unidimensional scale) is also represented as the *average* subject's judgment or preference between the pairs of objects. It is important, however, to look at the specific individual's preference.

INCLUSION OF THE IDEAL POINT

A simple way to measure individual preference is to include an "ideal" stimulus among the authentic stimuli and obtain similarity estimates among all the $n + 1$ pairs of stimuli. If, for example, the *ideal professor* is included among the names of the graduate faculty and similarity estimates among faculty members are obtained from each graduate student in a department it is assumed that those professors scaled closest to their ideal are most preferred. The scaling is done using multidimensional methods for each subject.

Configurations of stimuli obtained in this manner, however, are not always meaningful or stable, as they are based on the responses of a single subject. It is also questionable whether similarities between the "ideal" and other stimuli are interpretable as preferences. Nevertheless preference mapping in this manner can yield important results and is thus included.

206

THEORY AND METHOD: CARROLL'S MULTIDIMENSIONAL VECTOR MODEL

The vector model of preference mapping (Carroll, 1972) is analogous to *scoring* a subject's preference on a unidimensional scale in multidimensional space. The process usually starts with a two- or three-dimensional configuration of objects whose interpoint distances have been derived from judgments of their similarity; the subject's preference mapping is then included on that configuration. The results from a multidimensional scaling by an appropriate sample are often used as a starting point.

Suppose, for example, the similarities among four desserts

■ chocolate cake
● chocolate ice cream
□ pound cake
○ vanilla ice cream

were judged by a panel of housewives and the resulting configuration from MDS was as shown in Fig. 17.1.

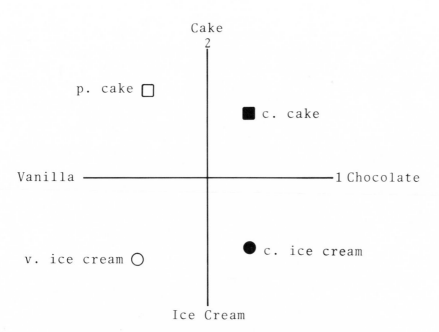

FIG. 17.1. Housewife panel configuration of four desserts.

It is easy to lable the dimensions as (1) chocolate versus nonchocolate and (2) cake versus ice cream. Next, suppose two children were asked to rank order their preference for the four desserts and these results were as follows:

	Preference Scale Values			
Child	*c. cake* ■	*c. ice cream* ●	*p. cake* □	*v. ice cream* ○
A	1	2	3	4
B	3	1	4	2

Surprisingly, the direction and scale scores for each subject can be estimated by the constraints imposed by the initial configuration on the subjects' rank order of preference. In Fig. 17.2, the two vectors are taken as scales upon which the desserts have been projected. In order to accommodate the rank order in each subject's preference the vectors can only be drawn as shown in Fig. 17.2.

Notice that the closest (perpendicular) projection of the stimuli on each vector

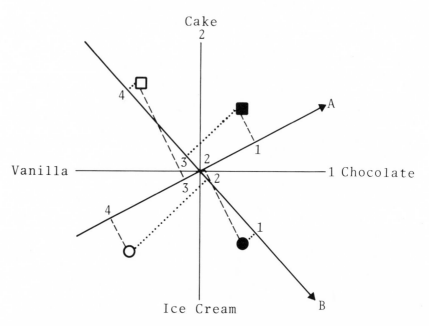

FIG. 17.2.   Subject vectors drawn to accommodate configuration and rank order of preference.

preserves each subject's preference values (rank order). The direction of the vectors is of particular interest because it reveals individual differences in preference with regard to these desserts. A large number of different vectors may be accommodated in a two-dimensional space. When there are several objects and their configuration has been well defined (as by the housewives in this case), the direction of each subject's preference vector is uniquely determined. The case in which the object configuration is determined in advance of the preference mapping has been called *external* analysis.

Preference mapping using the vector model assumes that the stimulus points (objects) are projected onto individual subjects' vectors. If the subject's vectors are of unit length then the projection of an object vector onto the subject vector can be obtained from the scalar product. If, for example, Y_i is the unit length vector for *subject C*, and X_j is the vector for *object j*, then $\hat{S}_{ij}$, the theoretical scale value of X_j for Y_i, is:

$$\hat{S}_{ij} = Y_i Y_j \cos \theta$$

See the figure that follows.

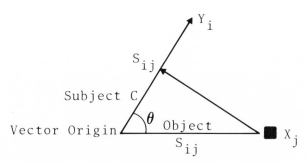

Theoretical Scale Value

Therefore, given a subject's preference for a set of stimulus objects such as

Objects	■	●	□	○
Preference rank	1	2	3	4

the problem is to find the directional vector that best fits the stimulus projections. The stimulus or object projection (scalar products) onto any specific vector is proportional to the distance between the vector's terminus and the stimulus point. Therefore the question can be resolved by determining that specific point where

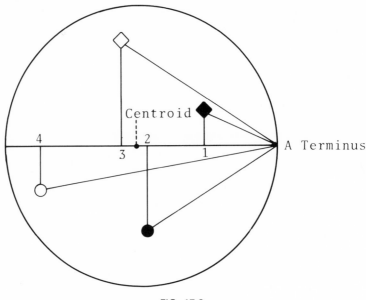

FIG. 17.3.

the vector terminates on a circle enclosing the objects where the circles origin is the centroid of the objects (see Fig. 17.3).

Mathematically the problem of preference mapping is to find the slope of each subject's preference vector. The problem then becomes one of minimizing the sum of the differences between the preference values S_{ij} and distances from the objects to the vector terminus on the circle that are proportional to the projections $\hat{S}_{ij}$ on a vector through the origin; i.e.,

$$\Sigma \ (S_{ij} - \hat{S}_{ij})^2 \text{ is to be minimum,}$$

which is the typical problem in linear prediction.

IDEAL POINT PROJECTION

Finding a subject's ideal point is analogous to finding the vector solution. In this case, however, the *distances* to the ideal point from the stimuli should closely match the preference scale values. The differences between these distances and the scale values are minimized and the location of the ideal point is determined.

In Fig. 17.4, the preference *scale values* $[S_{Aj} = (5 - \text{Rank})]$ for objects X_j for Subject A are

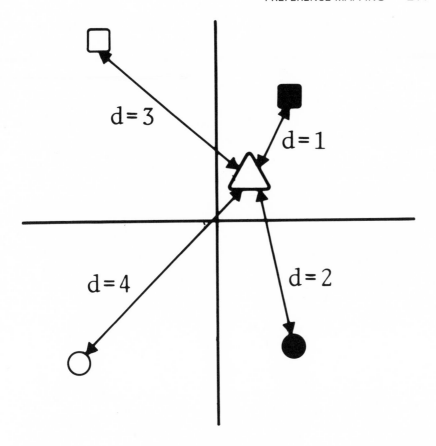

FIG. 17.4.   Ideal point projection.

By placing A's ideal point in the position shown, the distances (d_{Aj}) closely approximate the preference values (S_{Aj}).

PREFERENCE MAPPING

Direct factoring is the name applied to a factor analysis that not only produces the factor structure of the objects but processes the subjects as well. J. J. Chang (1968) has formulized a program called MDPREF that performs a linear factor analysis on the stimuli and fits preference vectors to the object configuration. It has particular usefulness in perception and attitude measurement where rank profiles of preference are available. Chang's program plots the individual's vector direction within the object space. It has the unique advantage of being able to handle a large number of subjects if the number of objects is relatively small.

DISCUSSION

The vector model is often called an unfolding model. Coombs (1964) first talked about unfolding as a way of determining a person's ideal point from *his* rank ordering of the previously ordered or scaled objects. Suppose it has been determined, by some criterion, that five objects are scaled as follows:

$$-A \rightarrow B \rightarrow C \rightarrow D \rightarrow E-$$

Further suppose that a subject indicates his or her preference as

$$B > C > A > D > E$$

By splitting and unfolding the subject's vector as shown in Steps 1 through 4 the ideal point can be fairly accurately approximated on the original scale.

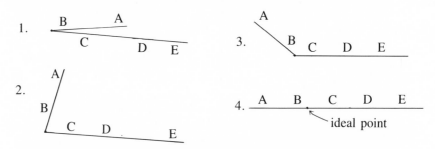

Preference mapping is a form of multidimensional unfolding in which ideal directions and points are determined because of the constraints imposed by the subject's preference interacting with the position of the subjects in space.

More sophisticated programs to do ideal point analysis exist. One of these is PREFMAP, created by Carroll detailed by Green and Carmone (1970). Several nonmetric solutions are possible with this program. The program's vector-fitting options are difficult to interpret for any given problem, as the program allows for flexible weighting and differential rotations of the solution.

APPLICATION 1: COMPARING PSYCHOLOGY AND EDUCATIONAL PSYCHOLOGY STUDENTS

Eddie Wong, one of the author's students, compared psychology and educational psychology students' perception of famous theorists Watson, Thorndike, Skinner, Cattell, Pearson, Carr, Spearman, and Thurstone. Similarity judgments were obtained over the 28 pairs of psychologists. The 14 students then rank ordered the theorists according to how familiar they were with each man.

When the data was analyzed by MDPREF a two-dimensional solution accounting for 88% of the variance was found. The plot of the stimulus objects and subjects is given in Fig. 17.5. This plot reveals that the educational psychology students had a generally different familiarity than the students in psychology (i.e., more knowledgeable about Raymond Cattell and less knowledgeable about the behaviorists).

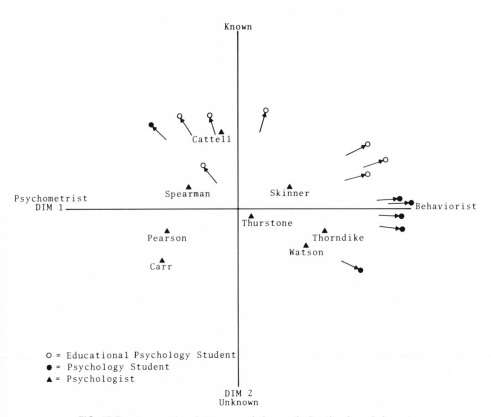

FIG. 17.5.   A comparison between psychology and educational psychology students knowledge about famous theorists.

APPLICATION 2: OCCUPATIONAL RANKING BY JAPANESE AND AMERICANS

Hiraki (1974) studied the relative status of teachers in Japan and in Hawaii by having native Japanese visitors rank order sets of occupations as to prestige. She then compared these ranks with local respondents. Hiraki used a balanced incomplete block design (BIB) with 21 selected occupations ranked in groups of five. Figure 17.6 shows her instrument and Table 17.1 reports the results of the votes for the two groups. The Japanese vote vectors were analyzed by MDPREF and the two-space configuration shown as Fig. 17.7 was the result.

Hiraki also scaled the preference vectors for 21 occupations by Japanese tourists and by Americans of Japanese ancestry.

TABLE 17.1
Occupational Ranking by Subject Response (Japan)

subject	physician	governor	professor	banker	priest	lawyer	artist	factory owner	captain	teacher	official	columnist	electrician	bookkeeper	farmer	policeman	barber	fisherman	singer	taxi driver	janitor
1	20	17	15	16	9	17	11	17	9	8	10	11	14	8	6	6	3	3	2	4	4
2	16	2	13	11	5	16	20	16	3	9	2	19	5	0	18	10	11	11	8	9	6
3	15	9	8	9	14	19	11	6	0	15	2	12	18	5	20	8	15	12	1	6	5
4	12	14	14	12	6	9	7	14	7	9	6	7	14	15	14	7	13	7	6	10	7
5	20	16	15	14	3	18	11	19	12	6	9	10	13	3	17	3	8	0	4	6	3
6	13	7	11	2	0	14	16	6	4	8	14	12	17	1	19	3	9	20	18	11	5
7	19	13	17	13	13	17	11	15	6	3	7	20	11	3	16	7	6	8	1	1	3
8	15	11	5	6	15	19	1	12	9	11	5	15	13	12	14	6	9	5	14	11	2
9	16	20	17	7	18	19	13	9	0	13	6	14	11	11	13	6	4	7	1	3	2
10	15	20	11	10	8	17	10	19	18	6	14	12	12	5	16	1	7	4	0	3	2
11	4	17	17	3	13	7	12	16	17	1	0	20	18	7	12	6	11	9	11	3	6
12	19	11	19	16	14	18	12	12	12	14	6	9	17	8	6	6	4	3	0	3	1
13	20	19	16	10	15	18	7	14	12	5	17	11	13	3	9	8	4	5	3	1	0
14	17	10	5	3	18	15	14	1	0	11	11	13	10	3	20	7	10	19	7	5	11
15	15	17	12	10	15	18	11	19	5	11	7	11	18	6	17	5	5	4	3	1	0
16	17	17	17	13	7	18	14	13	7	15	18	5	9	10	8	8	5	2	6	1	0
17	19	14	18	16	8	16	8	20	10	10	10	12	12	13	8	4	4	2	0	2	4
18	15	11	6	9	10	13	2	9	3	3	5	5	17	7	20	11	14	18	1	14	17
19	16	19	20	13	12	18	10	14	4	17	6	5	8	6	14	12	8	2	0	5	1
20	20	13	11	8	16	19	8	18	0	16	4	9	15	7	13	8	5	10	3	4	3
21	18	15	12	18	5	17	10	17	10	1	10	11	11	6	20	3	7	9	8	1	1
22	14	7	12	11	6	10	7	13	1	15	20	16	18	6	19	0	9	2	3	4	17

TABLE 17.1 (*Continued*)

subject	physician	governor	professor	banker	priest	lawyer	artist	factory owner	captain	teacher	official	columnist	electrician	bookkeeper	farmer	policeman	barber	fisherman	singer	taxi driver	janitor
23	9	20	14	8	7	15	14	15	19	14	6	9	13	3	10	9	1	1	19	4	1
24	16	19	15	8	10	18	14	17	12	13	5	9	11	5	20	6	5	2	0	1	4
25	19	20	14	13	4	18	6	17	12	9	8	15	12	10	7	11	7	3	2	1	2
26	20	16	11	17	4	13	4	17	16	10	9	3	11	12	19	9	8	2	0	6	2
27	17	19	15	6	6	20	1	11	13	15	7	10	18	9	15	12	7	3	0	4	2
28	17	20	15	15	12	18	9	19	0	11	12	7	8	5	12	13	5	5	1	4	2
29	18	16	19	6	14	20	15	12	16	10	10	6	10	3	11	11	2	6	4	1	0
30	20	11	19	10	10	17	4	17	5	14	4	10	14	17	13	5	7	1	1	9	2
31	15	20	17	13	9	18	12	19	4	16	13	8	11	5	11	4	6	2	0	3	4
32	15	20	16	13	6	19	17	17	9	7	11	11	6	10	7	4	4	0	15	1	2
33	17	13	12	14	12	15	15	20	2	8	12	19	8	3	13	1	6	10	1	4	5
34	17	17	18	13	20	17	16	13	5	13	9	9	5	4	10	9	3	5	0	3	4
35	20	13	12	18	0	19	5	15	17	9	8	11	14	14	12	5	2	5	7	3	1
36	18	9	12	13	7	16	19	13	0	9	8	11	16	5	19	6	13	8	1	3	4
37	19	9	20	14	11	18	12	10	12	15	5	10	17	8	10	2	4	3	4	6	1
38	17	10	12	19	16	14	15	20	2	12	0	8	8	6	18	5	8	11	1	3	5
39	17	19	13	8	5	18	8	20	16	12	6	9	15	13	12	1	9	1	4	1	3
40	14	17	15	15	9	19	19	17	6	6	2	5	11	5	11	2	10	8	12	4	3
41	19	15	13	18	9	18	12	19	10	9	3	12	6	5	14	6	4	2	14	1	1
42	15	17	15	4	17	18	12	19	6	14	1	12	5	3	10	5	6	11	10	5	4
43	16	7	19	4	20	14	10	8	11	18	6	5	11	3	12	6	11	14	10	3	2
44	19	13	16	7	9	16	10	11	6	20	6	3	16	5	14	18	11	0	1	6	3
45	9	16	18	3	1	17	7	16	1	13	17	20	15	8	12	7	10	5	4	7	4
46	16	18	12	7	6	17	3	19	1	9	5	16	14	12	19	6	10	11	0	6	3
47	20	7	9	9	7	11	2	6	0	11	10	8	18	17	14	6	15	19	1	6	14
48	13	18	18	14	7	18	16	16	11	10	5	9	12	5	17	9	6	3	0	1	2
49	2	3	4	8	20	5	18	1	0	7	10	11	12	13	6	9	17	19	14	15	16
50	15	14	9	19	9	17	11	20	7	5	4	14	7	14	18	3	4	12	3	0	5

FIG. 17.6.   Example of BIB instrument used to evaluate occupations.

Directions. In each section, rank-order the occupations. Place (1) beside the most prestigious job, (2) beside the next highest in prestige, etc.

SECTION 1.

____ Tenant farmer—one who owns live-
      stock and machinery and manages
      the farm
____ Artist who paints pictures that are
      exhibited in galleries
____ Bookkeeper
____ Owner of a factory that employs
      about 100 people
____ Policeman

SECTION 2.

____ Artist who paints pictures that are
      exhibited in galleries
____ Banker
____ Captain in the army
____ Physician
____ Priest

SECTION 3.

____ Banker
____ Barber
____ College professor
____ Policeman
____ Public school teacher

SECTION 4.

____ Barber
____ Bookkeeper
____ Electrician
____ Priest
____ Singer in a nightclub

SECTION 5.

____ Bookkeeper
____ Captain in the army
____ Fisherman who owns his own boat
____ Public school teacher
____ Taxi driver

SECTION 6.

____ Captain in the army
____ College professor
____ Governor of a prefecture
____ Singer in a nightclub
____ Tenant farmer—one who owns live-
      stock and machinery and manages
      the farm

SECTION 7.

____ College professor
____ Electrician
____ Janitor
____ Taxi driver
____ Artist who paints pictures that are
      exhibited in galleries

SECTION 8.

____ Electrician
____ Fisherman who owns his own boat
____ Lawyer
____ Tenant farmer—one who owns live-
      stock and machinery and manages
      the farm
____ Banker

SECTION 9.

____ Fisherman who owns his own boat
____ Governor of a prefecture
____ Newspaper columnist
____ Artist who paints pictures that are
      exhibited in galleries
____ Barber

SECTION 10.

____ Governor of a prefecture
____ Janitor
____ Official of an international labor
      union
____ Banker
____ Bookkeeper

SECTION 11.

____ Janitor
____ Lawyer
____ Owner of a factory that employs
      about 100 people
____ Barber
____ Captain in the army

SECTION 12.

____ Lawyer
____ Newspaper columnist
____ Physician
____ Bookkeeper
____ College professor

FIG. 17.6.   (*Continued*)

SECTION 13.

____ Newspaper columnist
____ Official of an international labor union
____ Policeman
____ Captain in the army
____ Electrician

SECTION 14.

____ Official of an international labor union
____ Owner of a factory that employs about 100 people
____ Priest
____ College professor
____ Fisherman who owns his own boat

SECTION 15.

____ Owner of a factory that employs about 100 people
____ Physician
____ Public school teacher
____ Electrician
____ Governor of a prefecture

SECTION 16.

____ Physician
____ Policeman
____ Singer in a nightclub
____ Fisherman who owns his own boat
____ Janitor

SECTION 17.

____ Policeman
____ Priest
____ Taxi driver

____ Governor of a prefecture
____ Lawyer

SECTION 18.

____ Priest
____ Public school teacher
____ Tenant farmer—one who owns livestock and machinery and manages the farm
____ Janitor
____ Newspaper columnist

SECTION 19.

____ Public school teacher
____ Singer in a nightclub
____ Artist who paints pictures that are exhibited in galleries
____ Lawyer
____ Official of an international labor union

SECTION 20.

____ Singer in a nightclub
____ Taxi driver
____ Banker
____ Newspaper columnist
____ Owner of a factory that employs about 100 people

SECTION 21.

____ Taxi driver
____ Tenant farmer—one who owns livestock and machinery and manages the farm
____ Barber
____ Official of an international labor union
____ Physician

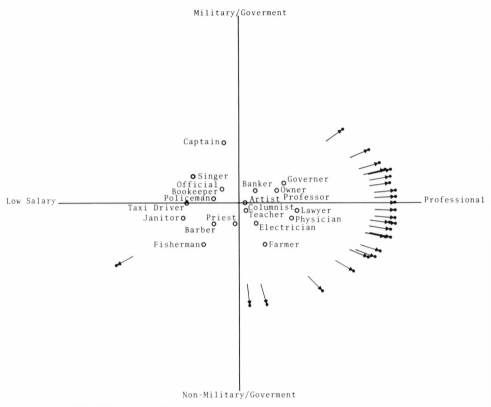

FIG. 17.7.   The MDPREF analysis of Hiraki's data reveals the native Japanese dislike for military occupations and the general desire of most respondants for professional high-salaried occupations. Some specific respondents show a liking for rural occupations frequent in Japanese history.

18 Individual Differences Scaling

The recent development of methodologies that relate differences between individuals to the dimensional aspects of the objects promises to have wide application in the behavioral sciences. In factor analysis and multidimensional scaling (MDS) a description of the objects is the primary purpose. In those methods, an average measure of similarity between pairs of objects is used as the primary data. The subject's individual emphasis is "lost" in the average.

In order to measure individual differences, similarity or preference information between the objects must be obtained for each subject. Each subject responds to the same set of stimuli, for example, "color names" paired in all possible ways. Estimates of the similarity between colors represented by the names are obtained from each subject. Each subject has therefore a matrix of similarity representing all pairs of stimuli. The data can be displayed in a redundant square array or in a lower (or upper) triangular matrix as follows:

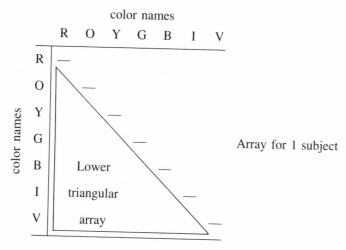

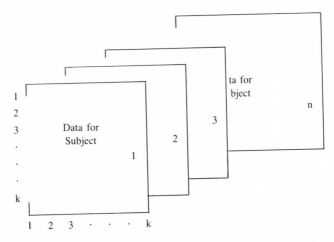

FIG. 18.1.   Individual data sets necessary for individual differences scaling

Thus the input data are a series of object by object matrices of similarity, one for each subject as illustrated in Fig. 18.1.

THEORY: DIMENSIONAL WEIGHTS FOR INDIVIDUALS

The most useful and popular representation of individual differences is a model of a weighted Euclidean space elucidated by Carroll and Chang (1970). Their procedure is called INDSCAL for *In*dividual *D*ifferences *Scal*ing. This model assumes that different subjects perceive stimuli on common sets of dimensions. The authors assume that some dimensions may be more important for one individual than another. It seems clear that a color-blind individual might weight the red–green dimension differently than subjects with normal vision. The importance of a dimension for an individual, however, can be zero. (A weight of zero can occur for an individual who fails to use a dimension in making decisions of similarity, for example.)

Individual differences scaling, like factor analysis, seeks to represent a large body of information in a more parsimonious way. The analysis seeks a small-dimensional solution for the objects and in addition an individual weighting for each subject on these few (t) dimensions.

Once a solution (a set of weights or loadings for each object and subject) is determined, calculated distances (d_{ij}) between the objects are compared with the original or theoretical distances ($\hat{d}_{ij}$) between the objects provided by the proximity data. Pearson's r is used as a criterion in the comparison. If the correlation is too small new weights or dimensions can be tried.

METHOD: CARROLL'S ITERATIVE–ALTERNATING LEAST SQUARES ANALYSES OF SCALAR PRODUCTS

Initially proximities (s_{jk}) of some form are found between all pairs of objects for each subject. These measures are converted to theoretical distances between the objects,

$$\hat{d}^{(i)}_{jk}$$

where j and k stand for stimulus objects and i represents the individual.

In the INDSCAL model scalar products are used to represent distances. The model, therefore, is considered to be metric. It is important to note that the dot product $b_{jk} = \sum_{t} x_{jt}x_{kt}$ between the objects j and k in t dimensions (x_{jt} represents the value of object j on dimension t) is used to represent the distance between two points (See page 35).

Before the scalar products are found proximities are converted to distances in Euclidean space with the addition of a minimum additive constant (C^*), which satisfies any triangle inequalities. (All triples of distances must form triangles in Euclidean space.) If a triangle cannot be formed a constant can be added to the dissimilarities in order to form a triangle (page 146). In addition the scalar products are formed around an origin placed at the centroid of the stimulus points using Torgerson's (1958) formula

$$b^*_{jk} = \frac{1}{2}\left(\frac{1}{n}\sum_{j}^{n} d^2_{jk} + \frac{1}{n}\sum_{k}^{n} d^2_{jk} - \frac{1}{n^2}\sum_{j}^{n}\sum_{k}^{n} d^2_{jk} - d^2_{jk} \right)$$

Carroll (in Shepard 1972) points out that the scalar products are normalized so that each subject has a sum of squares equal to unity or one. In the solution the stimulus dimensions are also normalized with the origin at the centroid and the sums of squares of each dimensional projection is also equal to 1. This allows the subject's distance from the origin to be directly interpreted as variance accounted for in a specific subject by that dimension.

In the INDSCAL model it is assumed that although the stimulus dimensions are common to all subjects they may be differentially important for different individuals. That is, each subject (i) has a weight $\sqrt{(w_{it})}$ for each dimension (t) that is multiplied times the coordinate of each stimulus point (x_{jt}) in that dimension. The weighted values of the subjects for objects j and k are:

$$y^{(i)}_{jt} = \sqrt{w_{it}}x_{jt},$$
$$y^{(i)}_{kt} = \sqrt{w_{it}}x_{kt}, \text{ etc.}$$

The unweighted distance between objects j and k for a single subject is

$$d_{jk}^{(i)} = \sqrt{\sum_t (y_{jt}^{(i)} - y_{kt}^{(i)})^2}$$

and by substitution the weighted distances are equal to

$$d_{jk}^{(i)} = \sqrt{\sum_t (w_{it}^{\frac{1}{2}} x_{jt} - w_{it}^{\frac{1}{2}} x_{kt})^2}$$

or

$$d_{jk}^{(i)} = \sqrt{\sum_t w_{it}(x_{jt} - x_{kt})^2}$$

Using Torgerson's formula the weighted distances are related to the following

$$b_{jk}^{(i)} = \sum_t w_{it} x_{jt} x_{kt}$$

in scalar or dot production notation.
   This equation, however, is of the general form

$$z_{ijk} = \sum_t a_{it} b_{jt} c_{kt}$$

In a method called *canonical decomposition* by Carroll, it is possible, given estimates of two parameters, to find an *accurate* least-squares estimate for the third parameter. Wold (1966) calls the method nonlinear iterative least-squares analysis. If, for example,

$$g_{st} = b_{jt} c_{kt} \text{ and } z_{is}^* = z_{i(jk)}$$

then

$$z_{is}^* = a_{it} g_{st}$$

That is, having values for z and giving values to g we can solve for a. This alternating procedure can be repeated holding values a and c constant and solving for b and then holding a and b constant and solving for c. In each case a solution is found for the coordinates of all the points in t dimensions as well as the individual weights in those dimensions. Once the new values for w_{it}, x_{jt}, and x_{kt} are found, new predicted distances d_{jk} are calculated and compared with the original distances $(\hat{d}_{jk})$. If the correlation is not high the process is repeated (i.e., another iteration occurs). This continues until no further improvement is noted. The process can then be tried in fewer dimensions to see if a better fit between d_{ij} and $\hat{d}_{ij}$ can be obtained. While the alternating least squares approach is not readily demonstrated the reader can gain some appreciation of the method by observing the simplest technique in an *alternating one dimensional* search. In this case all variables except one are held constant while the remaining one varies. Solutions are obtained until a minimum of the equation or function is reached. The remaining variables are treated similarly one at a time. The process is repeated until a desired solution is obtained.

Suppose, for example, one wished to find the minimum of $z = 2x^2 + 4y^2 - 4x$, where x and y are greater than or equal to zero. First x is held constant at some arbitrary value. For example x = 3 is chosen and the values of y are varied over the values 3,2,1,0. Solutions for z are then obtained. In this case the smallest value for z occurs when y = 0. Y is then held constant at zero and x is varied through the values 2,1,0. in this case the minimum value of z occurs when x is equal to one. Holding x constant at one (x = 1) other values of y are tried to assure that the sixth trial values of x = 1 and y = 0 are optimum, that is, result in the minimum value of the function. Figure 18.2 illustrates this solution.

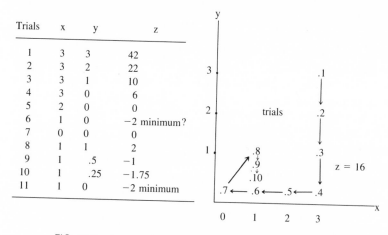

Trials	x	y	z
1	3	3	42
2	3	2	22
3	3	1	10
4	3	0	6
5	2	0	0
6	1	0	−2 minimum?
7	0	0	0
8	1	1	2
9	1	.5	−1
10	1	.25	−1.75
11	1	0	−2 minimum

FIG. 18.2   An example of an alternating one dimensional search.

The reader should consult Kruskal and Wish (1978) for a more complete explication of INDSCAL. See also Carroll (in Shepard, 1972; Carroll & Chang, 1968, 1970.) Pruzansky, (1975) has written a complete program for individual differences scaling called SINDSCAL (see Chapter 20) See also Tucker (1972) and Young, deLoeuw, & Takane (1978).

APPLICATION 1: THE LETTER WHEEL

Several workers have suggested that the processing of the visual features of letters and words is serial, or sequential, but recent research suggests that familiar stimuli are perceived and processed in a parallel, or integrated, fashion.

Evidence for the latter hypothesis is found in an analysis of the reaction times of individual subjects to a complete set of letters paired in all possible ways. The length of time it takes for someone to respond to such stimuli appears to be closely related to reading level, particularly for mature readers. Important findings have resulted from the analysis of the reaction times of 45 children and adults who responded to the question of whether two letters were the same or different. In this experiment two letters, placed side by side on a card, are hidden by a shutter. When they are exposed, a clock starts. As soon as the subject presses a switch indicating that the letters are "different," the clock stops. The length of time it takes the subject to respond is recorded in hundredths of a second. The reaction time then serves as a measure of letter similarity. A matrix of these similarities is analyzed with the aid of a technique called individual-differences scaling.

The 13 letters selected for this study (*f, t, n, h, k, x, z, g, p, q, e, s,* and *c*) were chosen because they could be combined in various ways to form pairs containing similar letter features. More letters were not included because the increase in paired comparisons makes the task too tiring for young children. The multidimensional scaling analysis takes the form of a circular pattern of letters much like a color wheel. This representation suggests that the dimensions of letters are not immutable but integrative; in other words, one letter melds into the next in a continuous way. A general division can be suggested for the 13 letters (in terms of angle versus curve or ascender versus descender). The letter *k* is opposite *e*, and *t* is opposite *g*, for example.

The letter wheel indicates that a parallel processing approach to the perception of familiar letters is preferable to a serial model. Most of the 13 letters contain two or more of the basic constituents, and an analogy between primary-color combinations and letter-feature combinations is strongly suggested. Just as orange is seen as a unique color even though it is a combination of red and yellow, so are the letters of the letter wheel seen as integrated units that are combinations of basic features. In this model *x* combines with *l* to produce *k*, and *l* combines with *n* to produce *h*, yet *h* and *k* are perceived as wholes.

Further reinforcement for an integrative perception of familiar units comes from the fact that the two basic dimensions indicated (curve versus angle, ascender versus descender) are in general relied on equally by all subjects. A unique by-product of the newer scaling methods is that individual weights can be determined for each subject on each dimension found. When the positions of the 45 subjects with respect to the use they made of these two dimensions were plotted, it was clear that none of the subjects, young or old, good reader or poor, chose one feature exclusively. Some subjects, however, recognized the combination of the two basic features more readily than others. These subjects were also the most mature readers in the sample. Such a result might be an artifact of consistency of response, or might reflect the importance of these dimensions to perception in reading, or both.

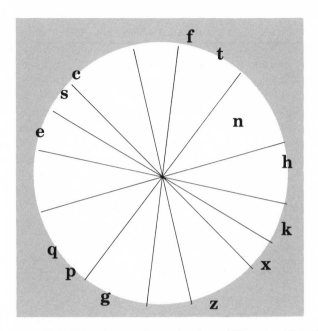

FIG. 18.3.   LETTER WHEEL represents the results of a multidimensional letter-discrimination analysis in which a record was made of the reaction time of 45 children and adults to a set of 13 letters paired in all possible ways. In this experiment the two paired letters were first hidden by a shutter. When they were exposed, a clock was started. As soon as the subject being tested pressed a switch indicating that the letters were "different" the clock stopped. The length of time it took for the subject to respond was then used as a measure of letter similarity. The results suggest that the important visual features of letters are perceived not as being immutable but rather as melding into each other in a continuous way. In this circular representation extremely unlike letters tend to be opposite each other. The letter *n* is not on the circumference of the wheel because it shares certain characteristics with *e*, *s*, and *c;* its left vertical component and its striking similarity to *h*, however, place it closer to the letters with vertically ascending components.

APPLICATION 2: PERCEIVED SIMILARITY AMONG WORDS

In a previous study by Dunn-Rankin (1978), which involved the free clustering of 100 words from a newspaper article, it was demonstrated that adults determine the visual similarity between words on the basis of four characteristics: (1) similar beginning letter; (2) similar word length; (3) similar ending letter; and (4) similar unique letters or letter combinations. The purpose of D. Bennett's study was to determine the nature of the cues upon which similarity is perceived when the first three of these features are held constant. Which unique letters or letter combinations form the basis of perceived similarity among words that have the same beginning letter, the same length, and the same ending letter?

Twenty-three five-letter words starting with the letter *c* and ending with the letter *k* were selected from the dictionary and randomly listed in a free clustering task. Thirty-four college students at the University of Hawaii were asked to group the words 10 separate times on the basis of ''some characteristic which two or more of the words have in common.'' In addition, each respondent was requested to describe the characteristics that formed the basis for the 10 groupings.

In order to determine the measure of similarity between each pair of words, individual percentage overlap matrices were calculated. These 34 matrices were then analyzed using an individual differences scaling technique (INDSCAL, Carroll & Chang, 1968). A three-dimensional solution was calculated that accounted for about 45% of the total variance in individual responses. Each dimension contributed approximately equally to the variance accounted for by the INDSCAL solution (see Tables 18.1 and 18.2).

TABLE 18.1
Coordinates of Objects in a 3 Dimensional INDSCAL Solution

WORD	DIM 1	DIM 2	DIM 3
Check	-0.232	0.140	-0.221
Clock	0.203	0.208	-0.025
Crank	-0.092	-0.041	0.304
Cloak	0.271	-0.204	-0.087
Clack	0.295	0.191	-0.022
Creak	-0.039	-0.292	0.255
Crock	-0.101	0.166	0.275
Clink	0.317	0.018	-0.072
Croak	-0.030	-0.233	0.288
Cluck	0.287	0.196	-0.038
Crack	-0.055	0.136	0.304
Cleek	0.264	-0.321	-0.162
Chuck	-0.231	0.205	-0.216
Chock	-0.227	0.223	-0.154
Click	0.255	0.232	-0.023
Crook	-0.098	-0.247	0.242
Chick	-0.229	0.220	-0.209
Chalk	-0.246	0.005	-0.252
Cheek	-0.213	-0.338	0.290
Chink	-0.163	0.004	-0.219
Creek	-0.106	-0.371	0.176
Clerk	0.281	-0.053	-0.140
Crick	-0.113	0.152	0.285

Correlations between   Normalized Residual
Y (data) and Y = 0.673   Variance = .546

Sums of Products:			
1	5.356	4.394	4.531
2	4.394	5.332	4.003
3	4.531	4.003	4.510

TABLE 18.2
Coordinates of Individuals in a 3 Dimensional INDSCAL Solution

SUBJECT	DIM 1	DIM 2	DIM 3	
1	0.170	0.757	0.391	
2	0.528	0.418	0.533	HIGH
3	0.174	0.234	0.442	
4	0.532	0.557	0.445	HIGH
5	0.407	0.330	0.421	
6	0.290	0.394	0.519	
7	0.200	0.238	0.154	LOW
8	0.433	0.521	0.171	
9	0.412	0.584	0.377	HIGH
10	0.084	0.436	0.099	
11	0.586	0.351	0.295	
12	0.463	0.535	0.556	HIGH
13	0.479	0.433	0.495	HIGH
14	0.214	0.127	0.161	LOW
15	0.182	0.457	0.131	
16	0.244	0.254	0.142	LOW
17	0.511	0.305	0.183	
18	0.551	0.452	0.551	HIGH
19	0.440	0.630	0.379	HIGH
20	0.156	0.135	0.073	LOW
21	0.252	0.421	0.276	
22	0.139	0.232	0.085	LOW
23	0.457	0.191	0.447	
24	0.364	0.778	0.170	
25	0.533	0.092	0.556	
26	0.639	0.250	0.446	
27	0.494	0.129	0.364	
28	0.194	0.238	0.065	LOW
29	0.550	0.171	0.552	
30	0.150	0.133	0.121	LOW
31	0.223	0.234	0.544	
32	0.624	0.175	0.372	
33	0.123	0.156	0.249	LOW
34	0.438	0.550	0.428	HIGH

The three dimensions that emerged from this analysis demonstrated a tendency for the respondents to perceive similarity on the basis of graphic or phonetic units at the beginning and end of the words. Figures 18.2 through 18.4 illustrate the two-dimensional configurations in which each dimension is plotted against each of the other two dimensions. The first dimension, "begins with *cl* versus does not begin with *cl*," and the third dimension, "begins with *cr* versus does not begin with *cr*," suggest the salience of the beginning graphic or phonetic unit in determining similarity. The second dimension, "ends with *ck* versus does not end with *ck*" demonstrates the salience of the ending graphic or phonetic unit.

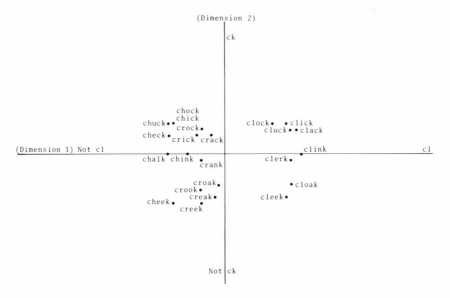

FIG. 18.4.

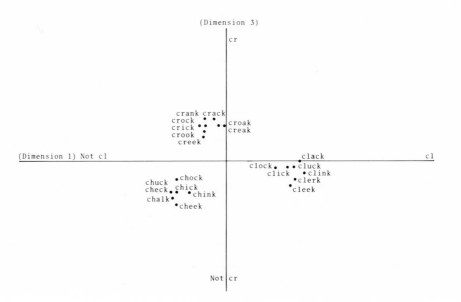

FIG. 18.5.

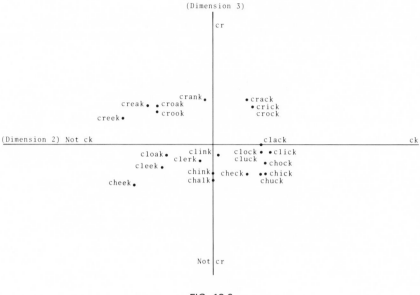

FIG. 18.6.

The appearance of these "dimensions" also lends credence to the idea that individuals may be utilizing a "hidden alphabet" based on higher order graphic or phonetic units when perceiving words. Examination of the frequencies of clustering justifications substantiate this notion. The largest number of reasons for grouping words involved *cl, ch, cr,* or *ck* units.

In order to try to determine an explanation for variance not accounted for by the derived dimensions, a three-dimensional plotting of individuals was examined. Individuals scoring low on all three dimensions (eight respondents with the lowest correlation with the INDSCAL solution) were contrasted against individuals scoring high on all three dimensions. What emerged from this investigation was a nonquantifiable "fourth dimension" that reflected a choice component based on word meaning. All the individuals scoring low on the three graphic or phonetic dimensions were utilizing perceptual choice based on semantics (more than 75% of the responses). Only 3% of the responses of individuals scoring high on all INDSCAL dimensions reflected perceived similarity based on meaning.

Recommendations for an extension of research involving the perceived graphic and phonetic similarities among words include: (1) controlling for salient semantic cues by use of pseudo-words; and (2) allowing perception of similarity to proceed on the basis of more inclusive units (such as syllable) as well as on the basis of the type of unit revealed in this analysis.

SINDSCAL, programmed by Pruzansky can be obtained from Bell Telephone Laboratory, Murray Hill, N.J. A similar program, ALSCAL, has been programmed by Forrest Young and is available in the SAS package of programs.

EXERCISES FOR PART IV

In Table 18.3 are provided the votes for 21 lowercase letters of the English alphabet by 315 second- and third-grade children. Analyze this matrix using multidimensional scaling. Notice the matrix is asymmetric. You can analyze each triangular matrix separately and compare the results.

TABLE 18.3

Dissimilarity Votes for Paired Lower Case Letters by Second and Third Grade Children. Entries Indicate the Number of Times the Letter at the Top of the Table Was Seen as *Least* Like the

Paired Letters

Target Letters	a	b	c	d	e	f	g	h	i	k	l	m	n	o	p	r	s	t	u	w	y
a	12	135	64	119	75	216	112	192	191	225	246	213	144	72	122	144	132	231	86	222	198
b	147	18	129	119	168	149	143	88	213	144	115	214	171	109	81	181	230	178	175	240	218
c	107	118	10	154	51	216	153	173	211	204	248	203	142	63	135	123	110	210	102	230	205
d	151	35	149	21	168	115	135	79	187	128	121	225	191	132	76	204	238	166	190	224	212
e	68	156	43	153	16	187	125	199	188	216	249	203	146	85	146	139	116	211	114	198	198
f	223	118	188	109	192	32	153	103	144	85	64	208	178	250	115	120	207	72	203	222	175
g	119	125	140	120	129	170	19	148	217	168	241	205	177	106	80	171	172	178	151	190	116
h	218	90	210	93	220	126	181	26	176	97	88	139	73	218	127	163	247	117	217	217	175
i	196	160	182	183	183	106	223	121	27	142	52	180	129	213	173	101	227	78	152	195	153
k	210	125	192	125	219	88	173	62	169	18	70	198	177	258	135	148	219	102	193	157	137
l	229	80	225	91	232	61	210	82	101	85	11	193	149	253	135	147	239	95	191	109	160
m	201	184	183	205	175	189	178	103	166	176	198	9	35	202	169	127	193	182	77	58	168
n	155	186	143	197	144	199	212	75	159	198	202	56	9	170	172	83	193	197	54	157	189
o	81	88	62	103	69	229	104	177	222	239	256	192	139	26	82	163	156	223	113	221	206
p	156	53	134	80	166	153	107	129	204	160	149	225	169	102	34	161	214	189	150	242	174
r	173	193	127	207	159	117	201	133	126	173	175	151	90	189	147	37	156	121	112	203	160
s	108	204	70	214	81	168	117	187	208	191	243	161	153	142	173	102	13	180	107	159	164
t	211	131	202	132	222	60	93	101	100	104	86	205	176	242	139	129	198	21	167	208	125
u	146	188	110	168	154	222	194	101	197	218	228	102	43	152	166	131	190	176	19	122	123
w	196	209	169	209	177	191	199	150	150	128	190	31	92	221	208	149	156	160	170	15	80
y	206	185	186	169	186	147	120	116	173	116	161	187	148	216	111	161	218	127	92	105	20

Give the instrument provided in Fig. 18.7 to about 20 subjects; ask for judgment of similarity and for preference. Analyze your data using MDPREF and SINDSCAL.

1-2	1.	banana split vs. strawberry shortcake
3-4	2.	cherry jellow vs. coffee ice cream
5-6	3.	chocolate cake vs. cheesecake
7-8	4.	chocolate marshmallow sundae vs. peaches & cream
2-3	5.	strawberry shortcake vs. cherry jello
4-5	6.	coffee ice cream vs. chocolate cake
6-7	7.	cheesecake vs. chocolate marshmallow sundae
8-1	8.	peaches & cream cs. banana split
2-5	9.	strawberry shortcake vs. chocolate cake
4-7	10.	coffee ice cream vs. chocolate marshmallow sundae
8-3	11.	peaches & cream vs. cherry jello
6-1	12.	cheesecake vs. banana split
7-2	13.	chocolate marshmallow sundae vs. strawberry shortcake
5-8	14.	chocolate cake vs. peaches & cream
3-6	15.	cherry jello vs. cheesecake
1-4	16.	banana split vs. coffee ice cream
5-7	17.	chocolate cake vs. chocolate marshmallow sundae
2-6	18.	strawberry shortcake vs. cheesecake
4-8	19.	coffee ice cream vs. peaches & cream
1-5	20.	banana split vs. chocolate cake
3-7	21.	cherry jello vs. chocolate marshmallow sundae
2-4	22.	strawberry shortcake vs. coffee ice cream
6-8	23.	cheesecake vs. peaches & cream
1-7	24.	banana split vs. chocolate marshmallow sundae
3-5	25.	cherry jello vs. chocolate cake
2-8	26.	strawberry shortcake vs. peaches & cream
4-6	27.	coffee ice cream vs. cheesecake
1-3	28.	banana split vs. cherry jello

FIG. 18.7.

For the correlation matrix presented as Table 11.3, factor analyze the matrix and compare your results with the graphic analyses presented.

For the preference date of Table 18.4, analyze and compare the Hawaii data to that provided on the Japanese sample in Table 17.1. Use MDPREF.

TABLE 18.4

Occupational Ranking by Subject Response (Hawaii)

subject	physician	governor	professor	banker	priest	lawyer	artist	factory owner	captain	teacher	official	columnist	electrician	bookkeeper	farmer	policeman	barber	fisherman	singer	taxi driver	janitor
1	20	19	17	13	15	18	4	11	5	13	4	10	16	10	7	11	7	7	0	1	2
2	12	16	14	10	8	11	5	15	5	17	10	20	8	3	19	11	5	16	0	1	4
3	16	12	11	7	8	20	5	11	7	16	19	18	10	2	14	13	4	13	1	2	1
4	19	18	16	16	15	20	13	9	10	10	7	12	6	6	3	9	4	1	14	1	0
5	19	20	18	11	15	16	12	10	7	15	15	13	9	9	4	5	3	2	6	1	0
6	18	20	17	17	9	16	5	11	13	12	14	15	10	6	7	6	6	5	1	1	1
7	17	19	15	11	18	18	4	11	9	13	17	14	5	10	8	6	3	8	2	1	0
8	18	20	16	15	6	17	7	13	0	14	20	10	11	7	11	4	3	8	8	2	1
9	19	12	17	11	10	18	16	12	5	8	9	14	14	5	4	7	3	2	14	0	2
10	20	20	10	5	10	12	19	10	0	15	1	15	16	4	14	7	4	16	12	3	5
11	16	20	18	16	8	5	3	14	4	19	0	12	10	11	16	9	7	13	1	4	4
12	17	20	14	11	0	19	5	16	14	5	11	17	13	8	10	3	6	13	4	4	1
13	19	20	14	13	7	17	5	16	11	6	18	8	9	3	15	6	1	11	9	2	0
14	15	20	11	15	9	18	6	19	11	7	15	11	17	6	6	13	2	4	3	1	1
15	19	20	16	14	1	16	14	18	0	10	13	9	8	6	7	4	5	13	11	3	3
16	14	20	17	15	9	18	12	14	11	10	19	12	4	3	7	3	3	6	11	2	0
17	17	20	15	15	3	18	3	10	11	10	15	13	11	7	8	6	3	4	19	4	1
18	19	17	20	3	12	16	17	8	1	16	14	8	9	9	13	0	5	11	6	1	0
19	19	20	15	7	1	18	5	16	10	13	17	9	10	7	14	12	3	6	6	3	2
20	13	20	12	5	16	17	10	19	11	7	13	16	6	1	5	7	2	10	17	1	0
21	20	18	17	14	9	19	8	10	6	15	13	16	12	11	6	4	3	5	3	1	0

22	2	3	0	10	2	5	11	3	7	12	14	9	6	16	9	15	20	12	19	18	17
23	0	1	3	8	5	3	6	3	10	13	12	8	15	19	15	10	14	13	14	20	18
24	0	1	10	5	3	11	4	5	6	12	19	7	5	13	10	17	13	15	16	20	18
25	12	8	11	15	6	19	16	2	12	3	5	8	17	0	15	11	17	1	6	6	20
26	0	1	9	4	2	7	5	6	3	9	16	10	11	13	11	18	15	14	17	20	19
27	0	1	12	4	2	11	12	3	7	16	12	5	8	18	11	20	14	6	12	19	17
28	0	1	5	3	2	5	14	7	11	7	9	15	12	13	11	17	19	6	15	20	18
29	0	2	3	10	3	11	6	5	7	12	18	13	14	17	4	16	11	9	14	20	17
30	1	1	0	8	2	9	6	12	10	5	6	16	13	13	5	16	15	13	18	20	19
31	0	1	6	8	2	7	10	3	5	11	19	7	12	14	11	18	11	16	13	20	16
32	0	1	4	6	2	13	11	3	9	8	16	13	6	12	7	18	6	6	15	19	19
33	0	2	18	4	3	7	3	3	9	13	15	12	6	7	9	19	13	13	19	20	17
34	1	1	0	4	2	7	6	13	9	11	12	15	7	13	11	16	13	13	16	20	18
35	0	2	6	3	5	7	5	9	8	15	14	11	4	9	19	18	19	19	14	20	17
36	2	1	0	10	1	20	10	0	12	7	11	12	1	8	8	13	16	8	11	16	18
37	0	5	4	2	3	10	11	4	10	9	17	6	14	10	11	16	20	11	18	20	17
38	0	3	1	8	3	6	1	7	4	14	10	15	6	13	6	20	15	15	17	15	19
39	0	2	13	5	12	9	4	10	12	7	18	8	15	14	7	18	20	15	19	20	18
40	3	4	6	2	1	7	6	10	13	13	13	12	3	18	10	12	18	15	9	10	14
41	0	3	5	3	10	12	4	8	14	13	19	8	13	10	1	18	16	17	11	20	16
42	7	2	10	15	2	8	12	11	7	3	2	15	10	17	15	16	14	12	6	4	20
43	1	6	5	8	1	9	8	11	19	18	18	13	2	18	13	14	17	6	0	20	17
44	0	2	3	5	6	9	4	3	8	9	19	7	5	10	11	17	16	15	12	20	18
45	0	1	13	12	5	13	12	9	8	12	4	13	11	18	14	16	16	7	9	20	19
46	0	1	11	4	2	7	5	2	4	9	12	12	2	12	14	19	13	17	3	18	20
47	4	5	4	10	4	8	17	10	4	13	17	14	13	10	5	10	16	8	20	13	18
48	6	6	16	2	2	7	1	4	10	7	13	9	14	15	13	18	12	17	0	19	20
49	4	1	9	3	2	8	4	9	7	10	18	6	10	12	13	17	19	15	7	20	19
50	0	1	9	6	2	4	5	7	3	9	16	10	10	14	13	16	16	18	13	20	19

V COMPUTER ANALYSIS

19 Computer Usage

Although most unidimensional scaling methods may be solved through hand calculation, all the methods described in this text, with the exception of graphic similarity analyses, have been transcribed into computer programs written in FORTRAN IV. The programs are available from a variety of sources provided at the end of this chapter. Because many of the methods in scaling are possible only because of the speed of computer processing, anybody planning to utilize effective methods of measuring attitudes or reactions to psychological objects must become familiar with: (1) the job control language of the local computer center; (2) program sources; (3) program write-ups; and (4) the writing of simple format statements. While the use of CRT terminals is rapidly replacing cards as a means for handling data input a review of card use is still helpful.

The reader should note that everywhere the word *card* is written the word *line* can be substituted when using a remote terminal.

The familiar computer card contains 80 columns and 12 zones or rows, as shown in the following illustration:

Because of the zones the *bottom* of the card is commonly known as the 9 edge and the top of the card is called the 12 edge. By using the rows singly, the digits from 0 to 9 can be typed and punched into the card. By combining the 10, 11, and 12 zones, letters can also be typed and punched on the card. The letter (A), for example, consists of a 12 zone punch and a row 1 punch in the same column (see illustration).

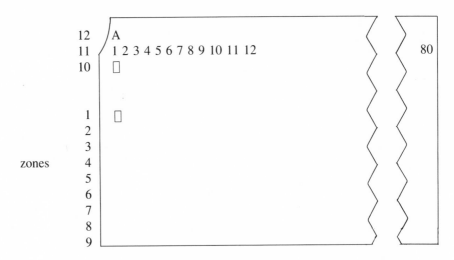

JOB CONTROL LANGUAGE

The Job Control Language or JCL usually consists of two or three computer cards or lines on a video terminal. The first card, or "job" card, contains:

1. A name of the job that is going to be processed.
2. A job number to which the cost of the processing will be charged.
3.* The amount of room or core storage in the computer that the job will take.
4.* Items such as the time the program may take to run, the number of lines of print desired, and the number of copies requested.
5. Finally the name of the user is usually specified.

The second card is called the *execute card* and it contains information that indicates where and what kind of source program will be used to analyze the data. The source programs are sometimes a set of computer cards but more often the computer program deck of cards that will analyze your data has been transcribed and is contained on some library tape or disc pack. The execute card usually defines which library and what program are to be used.

A third card, the *data definition card*, indicates that the data are ready to be analyzed.

---

*These items are usually optional.

After the JCL cards, two or three cards are necessary to provide important information to the source deck such as how many variables or subjects there are and where the raw data are located on the data cards. These cards are called *program cards*. The first or *parameter card* provides the source program with the number of variables and subjects. Sometimes programs contain a great many options such as, ''Should the correlation matrix be printed?'' for example. These options are also answered on the parameter card. The next program card, called the *format card*, indicates what kind of variables are being measured and where they are located. Writing formats for data is not difficult but probably causes beginners more trouble and discouragement than any other part of solving problems by computer processing.

WRITING FORMATS

Three kinds of formats and two location symbols are useful to know: These are:

Format	*I*	Integer Format	(counting numbers)
	F	Floating Point Format	(measurements)
	A	Alphameric Format	(letters and numbers)
Location	*T*	Tab	(variable locator)
	X	Column skipping	

The letter *X* is used to indicate that a *column* of the card is to be skipped. A number placed in front of *X* indicates the number of columns that should be skipped in order. A 10*X*, for example, means to skip 10 columns.

I, F, and *A* stand for *variables* measured in different ways. A number placed in front of these letters indicates how many variables are to be used or read at a time. A 3*I* for example, indicates that three integers should be read.

A number placed after the letter *I, F,* or *A* indicates how many columns of the data card contain the particular variable. If the format is *I*3, it means that one integer variable will occupy three columns of the card. If the format is *A*6, it means that six columns will be read exactly as punched with letters, numbers, or symbols.

If the format is *A*6, 2*X*, 2*I*3, it means that one variable (letters or numbers or both) contained in the first six columns will be read, then two columns (7 and 8) will be skipped, and then two integers each occupying three columns will be read. If your data, for example, consisted of identification information and two integers as shown in the following,

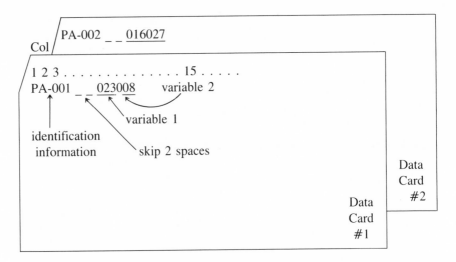

then the format *A*6, *2X*, 213 would correctly pick up the raw data in the correct position.

Most of the time, however, programs deal with measurements and it is the job of the experimenter to indicate how accurately the data have been measured. To do so he or she must indicate where the decimal point is to be placed in the number. Suppose, for example, you have the number

> 137

If no information is given it is assumed that the decimal point comes immediately after the seven as

> 137.

It might be, however, that the number is really measured to the nearest tenth, hundredth, or thousandth and the number should be taken as

> 13.7

or   1.37

or   .137   etc.

F format uses a decimal point and a number placed after the column designating number to indicate the accuracy of the measurement. Suppose, for example, the format is *F*3.1. This format indicates that the variable is going to occupy three columns of the card and that there will be one digit to the right of the decimal point.

If height is measured in inches and tenths of inches then raw data on the card could have two forms, for example

			Format
A	663	no decimal indicated	(*F*3.1)
B	66.3	decimal indicated	(*F*4.1)

Because the decimal point occupies a column of the card, the *B* data occupies four columns of the card. The computer, however, will treat both data equally.

Two examples of coding raw data are given, with their appropriate formats.

Data Card Information	*Columns*
1. Identification of subject	1–6
2. Skip	7–10
3. Responses to 20 item questionnaire	11–30
4. Skip	31–32
5. IQ test score	33–36

Example of data on a card.

1 2 3 4 5 6 7 8 9 10 11 . . .   . 30 31 32 33 34 35 36 . .

P e t e r -   2 3 4 2 3 4 2 3 1 5 2 1 3 5 2 1 3 2 3 3   1 1 7 5

Data Card #1

Format is *A*6, *4X, 20F*1.0 or *20I*1, *2X, F*4.1.

In this case the first six columns are read in alphameric format, four spaces are skipped and the 20 questionnaire responses are treated as variables measured to the nearest whole number, two spaces are skipped and IQ is measured to the nearest tenth (117.5, for example).

Second Example—Reading a row of a similarity matrix

Coding Information	*Column*
1. Identification of objects	1–3
2. Correlation on eight objects measured to use nearest thousandths	4–75

The format could be $A3$, $8F9.3$, in this case. The identification is read in A format and occupies the first three columns of the card, and the correlations occupy eight columns each as follows:

Columns	12	21	30	39	48	57	66	75
003	0.962	−0.341	0.452	0.326	−0.222	−0.001	0.842	−0.023

Data card (first row of correlation matrix)

Data Card #1

Such data might be the first row of a correlation matrix. The parameter card usually indicates how many data cards will be read and the data cards usually follow directly after the format card unless some key cards are necessary to indicate which pairs of objects are to be compared.

T or Tab format is sometimes used to locate a specific column in which to start reading information. If, for example, the identification number for a card is in the last three columns of the card (columns 78, 79, and 80) and it is called to be read in first, then the user can write $T78$, $A3$, $F2.0$, for example.

An example of the three JCL cards used to access programs at the University of Hawaii is:

```
      ⎧ / / RANKO JØB (nnnn,__KR,etc.), 'your name'
JCL  ⎨  / / EXEC EDSTAT, PROGRAM=RANKO,RG=__K
      ⎩ / /GØ.SYSIN DD *

          program control cards
          data deck

    /*RANKO
    / /
    EDSTAT=(Educational Statistics at the University of Hawaii)
```

As time passes more and more algorithms for handling and displaying data of the type described in this text are becoming part of basic software packages that most computer centers purchase and make available. Chief among these well-developed programs are BMD and BMDP-77, which stands for the Biomedical computer program series (Dixon & Brown, 1979); SPSS, the Statistical Package for the Social Sciences (Nie, Hull, Jenkins, Steinbrenner, & Bent, 1975); SAS (Statistical Analysis System, 1979), and the Veldman Package of Computer Programs (Veldman, 1967).

The JCL necessary to retrieve and execute these program packages at the University of Hawaii library is provided in Table 19.1.

TABLE 19.1
Input Setup for Various Source Programs

Examples of JCL to Access Various Computer Programs
Used at University of Hawaii Computer Center

BMD (Biomedical) programs, old version:

Example of cards needed to asses program BMDX72:

```
//BMDΔJØBΔ (nnnn,___KR, etc.), 'your name'
//ΔEXECΔGØLIB, PRØGRAM=BMDX72,RG=___K
//GØ,SYSINΔDDΔ*
       program control cards
       data deck
/*BMDΔJØBΔ (nnnn, KR, etc.), 'your name'
```

where etc. indicates other job parameters
nnnn is replaced by your job (account) number
and Δ indicates 1 or more blanks

The number used to fill in the blanks in lines 1, 2, and 6 (above), the region size, should normally be the same.

Write your name where those words appear.

BMDP (Biomedical Computer Program (P-series) programs:

Example of cards needed for a "regular" run of program BMDP2R:

```
//BMDPΔJØBΔ (nnnn,15OKR, etc.), 'your name'
//ΔEXECΔBIMED, PRØG=BMDP2R
//SYSINΔDDΔ*
       program control cards
       data deck
*BMDPΔJØBΔ (nnnn,150KR, etc.), 'your name'
//
```

SAS (Guide to Statistical Analysis System):

```
//SASΔJØBΔ (nnnn,___KR, etc.), 'your name', CLASS=A
//ΔEXECΔSAS
//SYSINΔDDΔ*
DATA: ΔINPUTΔNAMEΔ$ΔVAR1ΔVAR2;
CARDS:

       Data Cards Follow
       2x BROWN 56 28

PROCΔSORTΔOUT=ALPH;ΔBYNAME; PROC PRINT DATA=ALPH, ETC.
```

SPSS (STATISTICAL PACKAGE FOR THE SOCIAL SCIENCES) includes all SPSS programs:

Example of cards needed to access subprogram GUTTMAN SCALE:

TABLE 19.1 (*Continued*)

```
/ /GUTTMANΔJØBΔ (nnnn,___KR, etc.), 'your name'
/ /ΔEXECΔSPSS,RG=___K
/ /GØ.SYSINΔDDΔ*
        program control cards
        data deck
/*GUTTMANΔJØBΔ (nnnn,___KR, etc.), 'your name'
/ /
```

JCL to Execute Veldman Programs

VELDMAN includes all "regular" runs of Veldman programs:

Example of cards needed to access program DISTAT:

```
/ /DISTATΔJØBΔ (nnnn,150KR, etc.), 'your name'
/ /ΔEXECΔVELDMAN,PRØGRAM=DISTAT
/ /CØ.SYSINΔDDΔ*
        program control cards
        data deck
/*DISTATΔJØBΔ (nnnn,150KR,etc.), 'your name'
```

20 Program Descriptions, Input Directions, Examples, and Listings

COMPUTER SOLUTIONS

Computer algorithms that provide solutions for the methods presented in the text are described in this chapter. Auxiliary programs which provide measures of proximity and which convert preference and proximity data into usable form are also described. Table 20.1 lists all these programs.

Input directions for most of the programs in Table 20.1 are provided in this chapter. For each program an input example and the output from that example is provided. A Fortran source listing is also provided for programs that are not readily available from other sources. Programs for factor analysis and calculating correlations, for example, are routinely provided in the packaged programs at most computer centers. For such programs input directions and Fortran source listings are not provided. For extensive programs such as SINDSCAL, MDPREF, and KYST, the brief "writeups" given do not do justice to the manuals that are provided by the authors. For such programs only an introduction in addition to the examples is provided. For most of the computer programs sample input data are taken from Chapter 2 and Chapter 3 or from tabled data elsewhere in the text. A short instrument (Figure 20.1), however, was given to five adults in order to demonstrate several programs. A description of the data resulting from the administration of the instrument is provided in Table 20.2.

Program Sources

The Fortran source programs provided in this text were written by the author and his students or were solicited from the original authors. A few source programs

Please rate on a scale of 1 to 7 the similarity of the following pairs
of desserts. A rating of 1 indicates that the desserts are highly dissimilar while a rating of 7 indicates that the desserts are highly
similar.

After rating all the pairs, circle one of each pair of desserts that you
most prefer.

chocolate cake--pound cake _____

chocolate cake--vanilla ice-cream _____

chocolate cake--chocolate sundae _____

pound cake--vanilla ice-cream _____

pound cake--chocolate sundae _____

chocolate sundae--vanilla ice-cream _____

FIG. 20.1.   Instrument used to generate similarity and preference data. Sample data derived from this
instrument is presented in Table 20.2.

can be purchased from the Bell Telephone Laboratory. Other programs are
available in the popular software packages such as SAS (Barr et al., 1976),
BMDP (Dixon & Brown, 1979), and SPSS (Nie et al., 1975). Fortran source
programs are provided for all starred items in Table 20.1. The author is indebted
to Professor Donald Veldman for permission to reproduce several programs from
his text (Fortran Programming for the Behavioral Sciences), to Professor Frank
Carmone for permission to reproduce the Large Group Howard Harris Program,
to Douglas McRae for permission to reproduce the program MIKCA, to CACM
for permission to reproduce their SORT subroutine, to IBM for permission to
reproduce their RANK subroutine. TRICIR requires four subroutines from the
IMSL (International Mathematical and Statistical Library). This package is available at most computer centers or can be obtained by writing to: International
Mathematical and Statistical Libraries Inc., Sixth Floor NBC Building, 7500
Bellaire Blvd., Houston, Texas 77036.

Should the reader wish to duplicate the Fortran source, he or she should make
sure to include any necessary subroutines. While most of the programs are self
contained a few DISSIM, GOWER, HGROUP, TESTAT, and TSCALE will
require several of the subroutines listed under the heading SUBROUTINES. The
subroutines are listed alphabetically and are included in that section if they are
called by more than one program. Other specific subroutines are appended to the
main source programs. When using a subroutine the user should check to see that
all the routines called by that specific subroutine are also appended. The author

TABLE 20.1
List of Scaling and Auxiliary Programs

*AVELOMAT	(Averages lower triangular matrices)
*BIB	(Generates paired data from balanced incomplete block data)
BMDP4M	(BMD program for factor analysis)
*CØMPPC	(Complete paired comparison analysis, Case V plus reliability)
*CØNPR	(Creates all the contrast pair cards for k objects)
CORR	(SAS program for Pearson correlations)
*DISSIM	(Calculates distances or scalar products)
*GØWER	(Calculates Gower's similarity index)
GUTTMAN	(SPSS program for Goodenough's Guttman Scaling)
*HGRØUP	(Metric hierarchical clustering)
HICLUST	(Nonmetric hierarchical clustering)
*JUDGED	(Generates interjudge distances)
*KENTAU	(Calculates Kendall's tau and generates matrix)
KYST	(Kruskal-Young-Shepard-Torgerson MDS with initial configuration)
*LOMAT	(Generates lower triangular matrix)
*LRGHWH	(Large group divisive clustering)
MDPREF	(Multidimensional scaling and preference vectors)
MIKCA	(K means interactive clustering)
*PEROVER	(Generates percent overlap matrix from grouped data)
*RANKO	(Variance stable rank scaling)
SINDSCAL	(Symmetric individual differences scaling)
SUBROUTINES	(General subroutines used by several programs)
*TESTAT	(Test statistics)
*TRICIR	(Circular triad analysis)
*TSCALE	(Successive interval scaling)

*The FORTRAN source program is provided.

hopes in the near future to be able to provide an opportunity for the interested reader to obtain by mini tape many of the programs detailed in this chapter.

AVELOMAT (Averages Lower Triangular Matrices)

1. Description and Input Directions.   This is an auxiliary program that averages sets of proximity data and creates a lower triangular matrix of the averages. If individual matrices are averaged, clustering or scaling programs can operate on the group averages provided by this program.

Three program cards follow the JCL cards:

Input Control Cards	Column	Description
Card 1	1–2	Number of variables
	3–4	Number of subjects

TABLE 20.2
Paired Preference and Similarity Data

Data	Description
01 Chocolate cake 02 Pound cake 03 Vanilla ice cream 04 Chocolate sundae	Objects
Key 010201030104020302040304	(Arrangement of pairs: 0102 means chocolate cake (01) is paired with pound cake (02) in that order.)
DS 524225 HA 624327 DB 424424 BB 645336 AF 536325	Paired Similarity Data: number indicates degree of similarity between paired objects. This data is used to demonstrate programs AVELOMAT, HGROUP, LOMAT, and SQMAT.
DS 221212 HA 122221 DB 122221 BB 222112 PD 112212	Paired Preference Data: 1 indicates that the first of each pair of objects was chosen; 2 otherwise. This data is used with programs COMPPC, RANKO, and TRICIR.

Card 3	1–80	Variables format for the data
Card 3 or more	1–80	Pairing keys. Each four columns contains the numbers of the objects which are paired. Thus, columns 1–4 might contain the digits 0102 indicating that object one is paired in order with two. Columns 5–8 might contain 1207, indicating object 12 is paired with object seven, etc. If there are more than nine objects, the pairs continue onto another card.

Next, the data cards are read. These are usually similarity scores of some sort between the paired objects.

2. Input Example for AVELOMAT, *Data from Table 20.2.*

```
//AVELOMAT JOB (2919,250KR,267F,2X),'DUNN-RANKIN'
// EXEC EDSTAT,PROGRAM=AVELOMAT,RG=250K
//GO.SYSIN DD *
0405
(10X,6F1.0)
010201030104020302040304
DS         524225
HA         624327
DB         424424
BB         645336
AF         536325
/*
//
```

3. Output for AVELOMAT, *Data from Table 20.2.*

```
5.20
2.60     3.00
4.60     2.20     5.40
```

4. FORTRAN *Listing for* AVELOMAT.

```
C PROGRAM AVELOMAT
C
C THIS IS A PROGRAM TO FIND THE AVERAGE OF A SET OF SIMILARITY
C   ESTIMATES . THE PROGRAM PUTS THE MEAN IN A LOWER TRIANGULAR MATRIX
C THE PROGRAM READS N (NO OF VARIABLES) AND NS (NO OF SUBJECTS) IN 2I2
C     THE KEY PAIRS ARE READ IN (40I2) INTERNALLY
C   THEN A VARIABLE FORMAT FOR THE DATA
      DIMENSION IKEY (190), JKEY (190), S(25,25), FMT(20), X(190)
     1,SUM(25,25)
      READ (5,900)N,NS
900 FORMAT (2I2)
  25 DO 505 I = 1,N
      DO 505 J = 1,N
      S (I,J) = 0.0
505 SUM (I,J) = 0.0
      M = 0
      READ (5,905) FMT
905 FORMAT(20A4)
      NP=N*(N-1)/2
      READ (5,910) (IKEY(I), JKEY(I), I = 1,NP)
910 FORMAT (40I2)
  20 READ (5,FMT) (X(I), I = 1,NP)
      M = M + 1
      SM = M
      DO 600 I = 1, NP
      IK = IKEY(I)
      JK = JKEY(I)
      IF (IK.LT.JK) GO TO 60
      ITEMP=JK
      JK = IK
      IK=ITEMP
  60 SUM(JK,IK) = SUM(JK,IK) + X(I)
600 S(JK,IK) = SUM(JK,IK)/SM
      IF(M.LT.NS) GO TO 20
```

```
      DO 510 I = 2, N
      JS = I-1
      WRITE(6,930) (S(I,J), J = 1,JS)
  930 FORMAT (1X,10F8.2)
      PUNCH 940, (S(I,J), J = 1,JS)
  940 FORMAT (12F6.2)
  510 CONTINUE
      GO TO 25
      END
```

BIB (Paired Data from Balanced Incomplete Block Data)

1. Description and Input Directions.   This program was written by Burt A. Furuta at the University of Hawaii in 1979. It transforms each subject's partial rankings from a balanced incomplete block design into paired comparison data or preference scores, or both. It punches the transformed data onto IBM cards for analysis by other programs.

For any N objects, more than one BIB design may be employed. Before choosing a design, the user should be sure that all possible paired comparisons can be made. This program will show a '0' for any comparison which cannot be made within a BIB design. If a comparison is made more than once within a BIB design, only the last comparison will be retained.

Output:

1. Prints all parameters, formats, and raw data. Explains output options chosen.
2. Prints a square paired comparison matrix for each subject, including the sum of votes (the preference score) for each object.
3. Prints a vector of preference scores for each subject, if the entire matrix is not desired.
4. Punches paired comparison choices for each subject, including if desired, a key card for the paired comparisons.
5. Punches the preference scores for each subject.

Input:

Input data is rank data from a balanced incomplete block design of R blocks and C items in each block. Ranks are integers from 1 to C, with 1 being the most preferred.

Limitations: maximum number of subjects = 999
maximum number of blocks = 84
maximum number of objects per block = 9

1. Title Card: Any alphanumeric title; up to 80 columns may be used.
2. Parameter Card:

Columns	Description
1–5	Number of objects
6–10	Number of blocks
11–15	Number of objects per block
16–20	Number of subjects
25	1 = Print paired comparison matrix, and the vector of preference scores as the sum of columns
	2 = Print the vector of preference scores only
26	1 = Punch preference scores
27	1 = Punch paired comparison choices AND punch key card(s)
	2 = Punch paired comparison choices BUT DO NOT punch key card(s).

3. Design Format Card: Format for BIB design employed, in I format.
4. Data Format Card: Format for raw data from BIB design, in I format.
5. Design Card: Give the BIB design employed; that is, the order of items in the R × C matrix of R blocks and C items within each block.
6. Data Deck

2. Input Example for BIB, *Data from Partial Ranks in Chapter 2.*

```
//BIB JOB (2919,267F,2X),'DUNN-RANKIN'
// EXEC EDSTAT,PROGRAM=BIB
//GO.SYSIN DD *
   SAMPLE INPUT DATA FROM PARTIAL RANKS IN CHAPTER 2
     7     7     3     1     112
(21I1)
(21I1)
713124235346457561672
132312132132312123312          SUBJECT 1
/*
//
```

3. Output from Program BIB, *Data from Partial Ranks in Chapter 2.*

```
SAMPLE INPUT DATA FROM PARTIAL RANKS IN CHAPTER 2

NUMBER OF OBJECTS =    7
NUMBER OF BLOCKS =     7
OBJECTS PER BLOCK =    3
NUMBER OF SUBJECTS =   2

DESIGN FORMAT (21I1)

RAW DATA FORMAT (21I1)

OUTPUT OPTIONS SELECTED
```

```
1)  PRINT EACH SUBJECTS SQUARE PAIRED COMPARISON MATRIX OF 1'S AND 2'S
            1 = COLUMN OBJECT CHOSEN OVER ROW OBJECT
            2 = ROW OBJECT CHOSEN OVER COLUMN OBJECT
2)  PUNCH EACH SUBJECTS PREFERENCE SCORES
            1 CARDS PER SUBJECT
            FORMAT TO READ CARDS IS (T11,35F2.0) FOR ANY NUMBER OF OBJECTS
            ID CODES, COL.1-10 ON EACH PUNCHED CARD. EXAMPLE: **S 21 C1
                ** - COL.1-2, INDICATES PREFERENCE SCORES
                S 21 - COL.3-6, SUBJECT NUMBER 21
                C1 - COL.8-9, CARD NUMBER 1
3)  PUNCH EACH SUBJECTS PAIRED COMPARISON CHOICES
            1 CARDS PER SUBJECT
            ID CODES, COL.1-10 ON EACH PUNCHED CARD. EXAMPLE: 333  21  1
                333 - COL.1-3, INDICATES PAIRED COMPARISON CHOICES
                21 - COL.6-8, SUBJECT NUMBER 21
                1 - COL.9-10, CARD NUMBER 1
            KEY CARDS NOT PROVIDED

SUBJECT #  1

RAW DATA

        1323121321323121233312

        1  2  3  4  5  6  7

    1 |  0  1  1  1  1  1  1
    2 |  2  0  2  2  2  2  1
    3 |  2  1  0  2  1  2  1
    4 |  2  1  1  0  1  1  1
    5 |  2  1  2  2  0  2  2
    6 |  2  1  1  2  1  0  1
    7 |  2  2  2  2  1  2  0
 SUMS|  0  5  3  1  5  2  5
```

4. FORTRAN *Listing for* BIB

```
        DIMENSION KESIGN(84,9),KRANK(84,9),M(84,84),JSUM(84),NOUT(3),KOUNT
    C(84),FMTK(20),FMTR(20),TITLE(20)
C
C READ AND PRINT PARAMETERS AND CHOSEN OUTPUT OPTIONS
        READ(5,30)  TITLE,NO,NB,K,NS,NOUT,FMTK,FMTR
        PRINT 31,TITLE,NO,NB,K,NS,FMTK,FMTR
        READ(5,FMTK) ((KESIGN(I,J),J=1,K),I=1,NB)
        KK=0
        IF(NOUT(1).NE.1) GO TO 1
        KK=KK+1
        PRINT 32
    1 IF(NOUT(1).NE.2) GO TO 2
        KK=KK+1
        PRINT 33,KK
    2 IF (NOUT(2).NE.1) GO TO 3
        KK=KK+1
        NSPACE=2*NO
        NCPS=NCARDS(NSPACE,70)
        PRINT 34,KK,NCPS
    3 IF (NOUT(3).LT.1) GOTO 7
        DIMENSION LTM(3486)
        KK=KK+1
        NCOMP=(NO*NO-NO)/2
        NCPC=NCARDS(NCOMP,70)
C
C PUNCH KEY CARD
        IF(NOUT(3).NE.1) GOTO 6
        KKK=0
```

```
            DO 4 J=1,NO
            ILO=J+1
            DO 4 I=ILO,NO
            KKK=KKK+1
            LTM(KKK)=J*100+I
         4 CONTINUE
            NSPACE=4*NCOMP
            NCKEY=NCARDS(NSPACE,72)
            DO 5 I=1,NCKEY
            JU=18*I
            JL=JU-17
            IF(JU.GT.NCOMP)JU=NCOMP
            PUNCH 36,I,(LTM(J),J=JL,JU)
         5 CONTINUE
            PRINT 35,KK,NCPC,NCKEY
            GO TO 7
         6 CONTINUE
      C
      C DO NOT PUNCH KEY CARD
            IF(NOUT(3).EQ.2) PRINT 37,KK,NCPC
         7 CONTINUE
      C
      C SET KOUNT FOR LABELS
            DO 10 I=1,NO
            KOUNT(I)=I
        10 CONTINUE
            IF(NOUT(1).EQ.2) PRINT 40,(KOUNT(I),I=1,NO)
            PRINT 41
      C
      C READ DATA FOR EACH SUBJECT, PRINT ORIGINAL INPUT
            DO 25 NSUBJ=1,NS
            READ(5,FMTR)((KRANK(I,J),J=1,K),I=1,NB)
            PRINT 42,NSUBJ
            PRINT 43,((KRANK(I,J),J=1,K),I=1,NB)
      C
      C INITIALIZE MATRIX OF COMPARISONS AND COLUMN SUMS
            DO 11 I=1,NO
            JSUM(I)=0
            DO 11 J=1,NO
            M(I,J)=0
        11 CONTINUE
      C
      C SET UP 3 DO-LOOPS FOR MAKING K(K-1)/2 COMPARISONS WITHIN EACH BLOCK
            DO 13 I=1,NB
            L=K-1
            DO 13 J=1,L
            LL=J+1
            DO 13 JJ=LL,K
      C
      C USE DESIGN TO IDENTIFY OBJECTS AND SET FOR SUBSCRIPT USE
            JONE=KESIGN(I,J)
            JTWO=KESIGN(I,JJ)
      C
      C MAKE COMPARISONS, SCORE OBJECTS, AND ACCUMULATE VOTES PER OBJECT
            IF (KRANK(I,J).LT.KRANK(I,JJ))GOTO 12
            M(JONE,JTWO)=1
            M(JTWO,JONE)=2
            JSUM(JTWO)=JSUM(JTWO)+1
            GO TO 13
      C
        12 M(JTWO,JONE)=1
            M(JONE,JTWO)=2
            JSUM(JONE)=JSUM(JONE)+1
        13 CONTINUE
      C
      C OPTION TO PRINT INDIVIDUAL'S SQUARE MATRICES OF PAIRED COMPARISONS
            IF (NOUT(1).NE.1)GOTO 16
            KT=NO
            IF(NO.GT.42)KT=42
            PRINT 44,(KOUNT(N),N=1,KT)
            PRINT 41
            DO 14 I=1,NO
            PRINT 45, I,(M(I,J),J=1,KT)
```

```
      14 CONTINUE
         PRINT 46,(JSUM(J),J=1,KT)
         IF (NO.LT.43) GOTO 16
         PRINT 44,(KOUNT(N),N=43,NO)
         PRINT 41
         DO 15 I=1,NO
         PRINT 45,I,(M(I,J),J=43,NO)
      15 CONTINUE
         PRINT 46, (JSUM(J),J=43,NO)
C
C   OPTION TO PUNCH INDIVIDUAL SUBJECTS' PREFERENCE SCORES
      16 IF (NOUT(2).NE.1) GOTO 18
         DO 17 I=1,NCPS
         JU=35*I
         JL=JU-34
         IF (JU.GT.NO) JU=NO
         PUNCH 50,NSUBJ,I,(JSUM(J),J=JL,JU)
      17 CONTINUE
C
C  OPTION TO PUNCH PAIRED COMPARISON CHOICES FOR EACH SUBJECT--1'S AND 2'
      18 IF(NOUT(3).LT.1) GOTO21
         KK=0
         DO 19 J=1,NO
         ILO=1+J
         DO 19 I=ILO,NO
         KK=KK+1
         LTM(KK)=M(I,J)
      19 CONTINUE
         DO 20 I=1,NCPC
         JU=70*I
         JL=JU-69
         IF(JU.GT.NCOMP)JU=NCOMP
         PUNCH 51,NSUBJ,I,(LTM(J),J=JL,JU)
      20 CONTINUE
C
C  OPTION TO PRINT EACH SUBJECTS VECTOR OF PREFERENCE SCORES
      21 IF(NOUT(1).EQ.2) PRINT 47,(JSUM(J),J=1,NO)
      25 CONTINUE
         STOP
      30 FORMAT(20A4/5(2X,I3),2I1/20A4/20A4)
      31 FORMAT('0',T20,20A4/'0NUMBER OF OBJECTS =',I4/' NUMBER OF BLOCKS =
        C',I5/' OBJECTS PER BLOCK =',I4/' NUMBER OF SUBJECTS =',I3/'0DESIGN
        C FORMAT ',20A4/'0RAW DATA FORMAT ',20A4/'0OUTPUT OPTIONS SELECTED'
        C)
      32 FORMAT(T16, 69H1) PRINT EACH SUBJECTS SQUARE PAIRED COMPARISON MAT
        CRIX OF 1'S AND 2'S /' ',T24,'1 = COLUMN OBJECT CHOSEN OVER ROW OBJ
        CECT'/' ',T24,'2 = ROW OBJECT CHOSEN OVER COLUMN OBJECT')
      33 FORMAT(' ',T16,I1,') PRINT EACH SUBJECTS VECTOR OF PREFERENCE SCOR
        CES'/)
      34 FORMAT(' ',T16,I1,') PUNCH EACH SUBJECTS PREFERENCE SCORES'/
        C' ',T24,I1,1X,'CARDS PER SUBJECT'/
        C' ',T24,'FORMAT TO READ CARDS IS (T11,35F2.0) FOR ANY NUMBER OF OB
        CJECTS'/
        C' ',T24,'ID CODES, COL.1-10 ON EACH PUNCHED CARD. EXAMPLE: **S 21
        CC1'/' ',T31,'** - COL.1-2, INDICATES PREFERENCE SCORES'/
        C' ',T29,'S 21 - COL.3-6, SUBJECT NUMBER 21'/
        C' ',T31,'C1 - COL.8-9, CARD NUMBER 1')
      35 FORMAT(' ',T16,I1,') PUNCH EACH SUBJECTS PAIRED COMPARISON CHOICES
        C'/' ',T24,I2,1X,'CARDS PER SUBJECT'/
        C' ',T24,'ID CODES, COL.1-10 ON EACH PUNCHED CARD. EXAMPLE: 333  21
        C 1'/' ',T29,'333 - COL.1-3, INDICATES PAIRED COMPARISON CHOICES'/
        C' ',T30,'21 - COL.6-8, SUBJECT NUMBER 21'/
        C' ',T31,'1 - COL.9-10, CARD NUMBER 1'/
        C' ',T24,'KEY CARDS ARE PROVIDED.',1X,I2,1X,'CARDS PUNCHED'/
        C' ',T29,'ID CODES, COL.1-6 ON EACH PUNCHED CARD. EXAMPLE: 999 15'/
        C' ',T34,'999 - COL.1-3, INDICATES KEY CARD'/
        C' ',T35,'15 - COL.5-6, CARD NUMBER 15'/
        C' ',T29,'FORMAT FOR READING KEY CARDS IS (T7,36I2)')
      36 FORMAT('999',1X,I2,18I4)
      37 FORMAT(' ',T16,I1,') PUNCH EACH SUBJECTS PAIRED COMPARISON CHOICES
        C'/' ',T24,I2,1X,'CARDS PER SUBJECT'/
```

```
 C' ',T24,'ID CODES, COL.1-10 ON EACH PUNCHED CARD. EXAMPLE: 333  21|
 C  1'/' ',T29,'333 - COL.1-3, INDICATES PAIRED COMPARISON CHOICES'/
 C' ',T30,'21 - COL.6-8, SUBJECT NUMBER 21'/
 C' ',T31,'1 - COL.9-10, CARD NUMBER 1'/
 C' ',T24,'KEY CARDS NOT PROVIDED')
40 FORMAT('0INDIVIDUAL SUBJECTS PREFERENCE SCORES'//' KEY',2X,42(1X,I
 C2)/' ',5X,42(1X,I2))
41 FORMAT(/)
42 FORMAT(/'0SUBJECT #',I3)
43 FORMAT('0RAW DATA'/'0',(6X,80I1))
44 FORMAT('0',5X,42(1X,I2))
45 FORMAT(' ',I3,1X,'|',42(2X,I1))
46 FORMAT(' SUMS|',42(1X,I2))
47 FORMAT('0PREFERENCE SCORES'//' ',(5X,42I3))
50 FORMAT('**S',I3,1X,'C',I1,1X,35I2)
51 FORMAT('333',2X,I3,I2,70I1)
   END
   FUNCTION NCARDS(NSPACE,NW)
   NCARDS=NSPACE/NW
   IF(NSPACE.GT.NW*NCARDS) NCARDS=NCARDS+1
   RETURN
   END
```

BMDP4M (Factor Analysis)

1. Description and FORTRAN *Source.* Programs for factor analysis are ubiquitous. Most computer centers will have one or more source programs. BMD, SAS, and SPSS all have good programs for doing factor analysis. The Biomedical Program series is presented here analyzing the correlation matrix of Chapter 15 using BMDP4M (Dixon & Brown, 1979).

2. Example Input for Program BMDP4M *(Factor Analysis), Data Is from Correlation Matrix of Fig. 15.1.*

```
//BMDP4M  JOB (2919,267F,400KR,30S),'DUNN-RANKIN'
// EXEC BIMED,PROGRAM=BMDP4M,RG=400K
//GO.SYSIN DD *
/PROBLEM TITLE IS 'ANALYSIS OF SAMPLE MATRIX, FIG. 15.1'.
/INPUT    VARIABLES ARE 5.
          FORMAT IS '(5F3.2)'.
          TYPE=CORR.
          SHAPE=SQUARE.
/FACTOR   FORM=CORR.
          METHOD=PCA.
          NUMBER=2.
/ROTATE   METHOD=VMAX.
/PLOT     INITIAL=2.
          FINAL=2.
/END
100 72 00 18 63
 72100 08 23 56
 00 08100 56 00
 18 23 56100 14
 63 56 00 14100
/*
//
```

3. Output from Program BMDP4M *(Principal Components Factor Analysis), r Matrix Fig. 15.1.*

```
CORRELATION MATRIX
------------------


            X(1)      X(2)      X(3)      X(4)     X(5)
             1         2         3         4        5

X(1)    1    1.000
X(2)    2    0.720     1.000
X(3)    3    0.0       0.080     1.000
X(4)    4    0.180     0.230     0.560     1.000
X(5)    5    0.630     0.560     0.0       0.140    1.000



FACTOR    VARIANCE EXPLAINED    CUMULATIVE PROPORTION OF TOTAL VARIANCE
----------------------------------------------------------------------
   1         2.376652                  0.475330
   2         1.486064                  0.772543
   3         0.452027                  0.862949
   4         0.418859                  0.946720
   5         0.266398                  1.000000

THE VARIANCE EXPLAINED BY EACH FACTOR IS THE EIGENVALUE FOR THAT FACTOR.

TOTAL VARIANCE IS DEFINED AS THE SUM OF THE DIAGONAL ELEMENTS OF THE
CORRELATION MATRIX.


UNROTATED FACTOR LOADINGS (PATTERN)
-----------------------------------
FOR PRINCIPAL COMPONENTS



                  FACTOR    FACTOR
                    1         2

X(1)    1         0.872     -0.242
X(2)    2         0.865     -0.138
X(3)    3         0.226      0.866
X(4)    4         0.431      0.772
X(5)    5         0.795     -0.250

        VP        2.377      1.486

THE VP FOR EACH FACTOR IS THE SUM OF THE SQUARES OF THE
ELEMENTS OF THE COLUMN OF THE FACTOR LOADING MATRIX
CORRESPONDING TO THAT FACTOR.  THE VP IS THE VARIANCE
EXPLAINED BY THE FACTOR.


ROTATED FACTOR LOADINGS (PATTERN)
---------------------------------


                  FACTOR    FACTOR
                    1         2

X(1)    1         0.904      0.037
X(2)    2         0.865      0.134
X(3)    3        -0.051      0.894
```

```
X (4)        4        0.174        0.867
X (5)        5        0.833        0.006

             VP       2.293        1.570
```

THE VP FOR EACH FACTOR IS THE SUM OF THE SQUARES OF THE
ELEMENTS OF THE COLUMN OF THE FACTOR PATTERN MATRIX
CORRESPONDING TO THAT FACTOR. WHEN THE ROTATION IS
ORTHOGONAL, THE VP IS THE VARIANCE EXPLAINED BY THE FACTOR.

ROTATED FACTOR

```
          ....8...6...4...2...0...2...4...6...8....
          .                      *              .
          .                        *            .
          .                                     .
          .                                     .
          5                                     5
          .                                     .
          .                                     .
          .                                  *  .
FACTOR  2 0                                 ** 0
          .                                     .
          .                                     .
          .                                     .
          5                                     5
          .                                     .
          .                                     .
          .                                     .
          ....8...6...4...2...0...2...4...6...8....
```

FACTOR 1

OVERLAP IS INDICATED BY A DOLLAR SIGN. SCALE IS FROM −1 TO +1.

COMPPC (Complete Paired Comparison Analysis)

1. Description and Input Directions.   This is a program originally obtained
from Harold Gulliksen (Gulliksen, 1958) to analyze paired comparison data. It is
based on Thurstone's Case V method, the simplest of Thurstone's various methods. Preference frequencies are converted to proportions, then to normal deviates. Scale values are assigned to the objects by accumulating the differences or
distances between them. Assumptions: normal distribution of reactions to each
object and equal dispersion of reactions. Disadvantage: distortion from proportions greater than .98 and less than .02.

Output:

1. Number of votes of each subject for each object.
2. Matrices of frequency, proportions, normal transform, arcsin transforms
   and logistic transform.

3. Scale values for all three transforms.
4. Theta matrices.
5. Analysis of variance, reliabilities, and variance components analyses, following the Gulliksen and Tukey (1958) procedure.

Input:

The input is paired comparison data. The data is input as a series of 1's and 2's, where 1 indicates the first object of a pair is preferred, while a 2 indicates choice of the second. (This type of input may be used in Knezek's TRICIR program, and Dunn-Rankin's RANKO program.)

Limitations:	max number of subjects = 99999, and max number of stimuli = 70.

Control Cards:

Four or more control cards must always precede the data deck.

1. Parameter Card (1):

Columns	Description
1–2	Number of runs that will use this sequence of pairs. Usually a 1 in col. 2.

2. Parameter Card (2):

Columns	Description
2–4	Identification number for the sequence (key) cards (13).
5–7	Number of stimuli in the questionnaire.

3. Key Card(s):

Columns	Description
1–3	Identification of the key card (equal to the identification number on control card 2, col. 2–4)
4–6	Card number
7–78	Up to 36 two-digit numerical pairings to which the data cards must conform. The pairs are written in 2 digit fields so that a pairing of item 1 with item 2 will be punched as 0102.

Continue for as many cards as need to list N (N − 1)/2 stimuli, with same format as card above.

4. Parameter Card (3):

Columns	Description
1–3	Study code number for data deck (must not equal sequence card number)
6–10	Number of subjects
16–19	Number of cards per subject
20–24	Number of last subject
28	1 = print paired comparison detail
	0 = do not print
29	1 = print analysis of variance
	0 = do not print

Data Cards:

The data cards are read by an internal format, therefore there is no variable format card. The data cards should be set up as follows:

Columns	Description
1–3	Study code number (same as control card 4, col. 1–3)
4–8	Subject number
9–10	Card number within each subject
11–80	Data:
	1 = first object of pair is preferred
	2 = second object of pair is preferred

Continue cards for each subject to include all of the objects.

2. Example Input for COMPPC, *Data from Table 20.2.*

```
//COMPPC JOB (2919,267F,2X),'DUNN-RANKIN'
// EXEC EDSTAT,PROGRAM=COMPPC
//GO.SYSIN DD *
01
  111   4
111   10102010301040203020304030304
222       5        1     5     1
222    01 1221212
222    02 1122221
222    03 1122221
222    04 1222112
222    05 1112212
/*
//
```

3. Output from Program COMPPC, *Paired Preference Data from Table 20.2.*

COMPLETE PAIRED COMPARISONS SCHEDULE

STUDY CODE 222   INDIVIDUAL OUTPUT

LIKE-DISLIKE ITEMS ARE OMITTED

				VOTES FOR EACH OBJECT														
SUBJECT	TCT	L	D	1	2	3	4	5	6	7	8	9	10	11	12	13	14	15
1	2.			1	2	2	1											
2	0.			1	0	3	2											
3	0.			1	0	3	2											
4	0.			0	3	1	2											
5	2.			2	1	1	2											

STUDY CODE 222   SCALE VALUES   NEUTRAL POINT EXCLUDED/

J	NORMAL TRANSFORM	ARCSIN TRANSFORM	LOGISTIC TRANSFORM
1	-0.35733414	-0.27136350	-0.25693250
2	-0.21036875	-0.16086692	-0.15048987
3	0.35733342	0.27136326	0.25693226
4	0.21036845	0.16086686	0.15048981

ANALYSIS OF VARIANCE   NORMAL TRANSFORM WITHOUT NEUTRAL POINT

SOURCE	DF	SUM OF SQUARES	MEAN SQUARE	AV MEAN SQUARE	CHI SQUARE
ALL	6	1.3639	0.2273	0.2356	6.820
COMP JUDG	3	0.8381	0.2794	0.2794	4.191
RESIDUAL	3	0.5753	0.1918	0.1918	2.877

VARIANCE COMPONENTS ANALYSIS

SOURCE	EST. OF VAR. COMPONENT
BINOMIAL SAMPLING	0.19999999
DEV FROM LIN SCALE	-0.00822467
LIN SCALE VALUES	0.02190161

RELIABILITY OF SCALE

R(S) = 0.19269216
R(SS) = 0.15637225
R(B) = 0.12019163

ANALYSIS OF VARIANCE   LOGISTIC TRANSFORM WITHOUT NEUTRAL POINT

SOURCE	DF	SUM OF SQUARES	MEAN SQUARE	AV MEAN SQUARE	CHI SQUARE
ALL	6	1.3639	0.2273	0.2418	6.820
COMP JUDG	3	0.8687	0.2896	0.2896	4.344
RESIDUAL	3	0.5823	0.1941	0.1941	2.911

VARIANCE COMPONENTS ANALYSIS

SOURCE	EST. OF VAR. COMPONENT
BINOMIAL SAMPLING	0.19999999
DEV FROM LIN SCALE	-0.00590140
LIN SCALE VALUES	0.02386948

RELIABILITY OF SCALE

R(S) = 0.21000570
R(SS) = 0.14615214
R(B) = 0.12019163

4. FORTRAN *Listing for Program* COMPPC.

```
C PROGRAM COMPPC
C
C       PUNCHED ON THE 026 KEYPUNCH.    WORKING ON THE IBM 360 COMPUTER.
        DIMENSION KSEQ(4860),KFREQ(71,71),ITEM(2450),LIKE(70)
        COMMON  KSEQ  , ITEM  , LIKE  , KFREQ
        DIMENSION SCN(71),SCA(71),SCL(71),SCN1(71),SCA1(71),SCL1(71),
       1BN(8),BL(8),KA(71),THETA(71,71)
C
   1000 FORMAT (1H1,46X,36HCOMPLETE PAIRED COMPARISONS SCHEDULE//10X,11HST
       1UDY CODE ,I4,5X,17HINDIVIDUAL OUTPUT)
   1001 FORMAT(1H0,9X,30HLIKE-DISLIKE ITEMS ARE OMITTED)
   1002 FORMAT(1H0,9X,31HLIKE-DISLIKE ITEMS ARE INCLUDED)
   1003 FORMAT(1H0,21HSUBJECT   TCT    L    D,48X,21HVOTES FOR EACH OBJECT/
       124X,20I5//)
   1004 FORMAT(1H0,I4,5X,F4.0,10X,20I5/(24X,20I5))
   1005 FORMAT(1H0,I4,5X,F4.0,2I4,2X,20I5/(25X,20I5))
   1006 FORMAT(1H1,9X,11HSTUDY CODE ,I4,5X,31HPAIRED COMPARISON DETAIL OUT
       1PUT///4X1HI,4X1HJ,6X4HFREQ,6X4HPROP,10X6HNORMAL,9X6HARCSIN, 9X8HLOG
       2ISTIC, 7X10HDEN NORMAL,5X10HDEN ARCSIN,5X12HDEN LOGISTIC//)
   1025 FORMAT( 3X3HCOL, 2X3HROW, 6X13H(VOTES FOR I)   )
   1007 FORMAT(2I5,I10,F12.5,3F15.5,3X,3F15.9)
   1017 FORMAT(1H0//)
   1008 FORMAT(1H1,9X11HSTUDY CODE ,I4, 5X38HSCALE VALUES    NEUTRAL POINT
       1EXCLUDED//1H ,3X1HJ,5X16HNORMAL TRANSFORM, 9X16HARCSIN TRANSFORM,
       29X18HLOGISTIC TRANSFORM//(I5,4XF15.8,10XF15.8,10XF15.8) )
   1009 FORMAT(1H1,9X11HSTUDY CODE ,I4,5X50HSCALE VALUES    WITH AND WITHO
       1UT THE NEUTRAL POINT//1H ,3X1HJ,10X16HNORMAL TRANSFORM,19X16HARCSI
       2N TRANSFORM,18X18HLOGISTIC TRANSFORM/14X1HK, 14X3HK+1,2(17X1HK,14X3
       3HK+1)//(I5,2F15.8,5X2F15.8,5X2F15.8))
   4001 FORMAT(1H1,2X5HI COL,1X5HJ ROW,6X6HTHETA ,9X7HTHETAN*,8X7HTHETAL*,
       18X7HTHETAA* //)
   4000 FORMAT(1H ,2I5,4F15.6)
   1010 FORMAT(1H1,63H ANALYSIS OF VARIANCE    NORMAL TRANSFORM WITHOUT NE
       1UTRAL POINT//)
   1011 FORMAT(1H0,65H ANALYSIS OF VARIANCE    LOGISTIC TRANSFORM WITHOUT
       1NEUTRAL POINT//)
   1012 FORMAT(1H1,60H ANALYSIS OF VARIANCE    NORMAL TRANSFORM WITH NEUTR
       1AL POINT//)
   1013 FORMAT(1H0,62H ANALYSIS OF VARIANCE    LOGISTIC TRANSFORM WITH NEU
       1TRAL POINT//)
C
      2 CALL CHECK
        BACKSPACE 2
        READ(2) NR
        NORUNS=1
        REWIND 2
      1 READ(2) IDSEQ,K,KL,KK,(KSEQ(I),I=1,KL)
      3 READ(2) KODE,NGOOD,LD,LS,NPCDT,NTHET
        WRITE (6,1000)            KODE
        GO TO (10,20),LD
     10 WRITE (6,1001)
        GO TO 30
     20 WRITE (6,1002)
     30 WRITE (6,1003)            (I,I=1,20)
        K1=K+1
        XK=K
        XN=NGOOD
        XK1=K1
        DO 40 I=1,K1
        DO 40 L=1,K1
     40 KFREQ(I,L)=0
        DK1=(XK*(XK-1.0)*(2.0*XK-1.0))/12.0
        DK2=(XK*(XK+1.0)*(2.0*XK+1.0))/12.0
C       THIS PART OF THE PROGRAM REPEATS FOR EACH INDIVIDUAL
        DO 200 II=1,NGOOD
        DO 50 I=1,K1
     50 KA(I)=0
        GO TO (55,60),LD
```

```
55      READ(2) ID,(ITEM(I),I=1,KK)
        GO TO 65
60      READ(2) ID,(ITEM(I),I=1,KK),(LIKE(J),J=1,K)
   65 DO 70 J=1,KK
        JJ= ITEM(J)
        I=KSEQ(2*J-1)
        L=KSEQ(2*J)
        GO TO (66,67),JJ
   66 KA(I)=KA(I)+1
        KFREQ(L,I)= KFREQ(L,I)+1
        GO TO 70
   67 KA(L)=KA(L)+1
        KFREQ(I,L)= KFREQ(I,L)+1
   70 CONTINUE
        ASQ= 0.0
        DO 100 J=1,K
        A=KA(J)
  100 ASQ=ASQ +A*A
        D1= DK1 -(ASQ/2.0)
        WRITE (6,1004)              ID,D1,(KA(I),I=1,K)
        GO TO (200,110),LD
  110 DO 120 J=1,K
        JJ= LIKE(J)
        GO TO (111,112),JJ
  111 KA(J)=KA(J)+1
        KFREQ(K1,J)= KFREQ(K1,J)+1
        GO TO 120
  112 KA(K1)=KA(K1)+1
        KFREQ(J,K1)= KFREQ(J,K1)+1
  120 CONTINUE
        ASQ= 0.0
        DO 130 J=1,K1
        A=KA(J)
  130 ASQ=ASQ+ A*A
        KDIS=KA(K1)
        D2= DK2  -(ASQ/2.0)
        KLIK= K - KA(K1)
        WRITF(6,1005)              ID,D2,KLIK,KDIS,(KA(I),I=1,K)
  200 CONTINUE
        GO TO (201,202),NPCDT
C      COMPUTATION OF SCALE VALUES AND TRANSFORMS
  202 WRITE (6,1006)              KODE
        WRITE (6,1025)
  201 GO TO (210,211),LD
  210 K2=K
        GO TO 220
  211 K2=K1
  220 DO 230 L=1,K2
        SCN(L)=0.0
        SCA(L)=0.0
  230 SCL(L)=0.0
        DO 305 L=1,K2
        DO 300 I = 1,K2
        FREQ=KFREQ(I,L)
        IF(I-L) 240,235,240
  235 IF(K2-L) 236,236,300
  236 GO TO (237,238),LD
  237 SCN(L)=SCN(L)/XK
        SCA(L)=SCA(L)/XK
        SCL(L)=SCL(L)/XK
        GO TO 300
  238 SCN1(L)=SCN(L)/XK1
        SCA1(L)=SCA(L)/XK1
        SCL1(L)=SCL(L)/XK1
        SCN(L)=0.0
        SCA(L)=0.0
        SCL(L)=0.0
        GO TO 300
  240 P=FREQ/XN
        IF(P-0.98) 241,241,243
  241 IF(0.02-P) 244,244,242
```

```
  243 P=0.98
      GO TO 244
  242 P=0.02
  244 CONTINUE
      CALL APPROX(P,7.9587,5.8742,11.2502,12.2043,2.5101,DENHN,HN)
      CALL APPROX(P,6.4481,5.4031,8.5359,9.5204,2.0016,DENHA,HA)
      CALL APPROX(P,8.3147,5.9782,6.7602,8.1253,1.7386,DENHL,HL)
      THETA(I,L)= HA
      IF(K2-I)250,250,252
  250 GO TO (255,251),LD
  255 SCN(L)=(SCN(L) +HN)/XK
      SCA(L)=(SCA(L) +HA)/XK
      SCL(L)=(SCL(L) +HL)/XK
      GO TO 254
  251 SCN1(L)=(SCN(L)+HN)/XK1
      SCA1(L)=(SCA(L)+HA)/XK1
      SCL1(L)=(SCL(L)+HL)/XK1
  253 SCN(L)=SCN(L)/XK
      SCA(L)=SCA(L)/XK
      SCL(L)=SCL(L)/XK
      GO TO 254
  252 SCN(L)=SCN(L) + HN
      SCA(L)=SCA(L) + HA
      SCL(L)=SCL(L) + HL
  254 GO TO (300,256),NPCDT
  256 WRITE (6,1007)           L,I,KFREQ(I,L),P,HN,HA,HL,DENHN,DENHA,DEN
     1HL
  300 CONTINUE
      GO TO (305,285),NPCDT
  285 WRITE (6,1017)
  305 CONTINUE
      GO TO(310,311),LD
  310 WRITE (6,1008)           KODE,(L,SCN(L),SCA(L),SCL(L),L=1,K)
      GO TO 312
  311 WRITE (6,1009)           KODE,(L,SCN(L),SCN1(L),SCA(L),SCA1(L),SCL
     1(L),SCL1(L),L=1,K1)
  312 BN(1)=0.50794909
      BN(2)= 0.25801228
      BN(3)= 0.10029399
      BN(4)= 0.03681700
      BN(5)= 0.00492000
      BN(6)= 0.01252400
      BN(7)=-0.00516900
      BN(8)= 0.00176000
      BL(1)= 0.73293560
      BL(2)= 0.53719459
      BL(3)= 0.23181446
      BL(4)= 0.05207900
      BL(5)= 0.00026989
      BL(6)= 0.01203756
      BL(7)=-0.00241953
      BL(8)= 0.00042306
      AN= 1.5707963
      AL= 1.5707963
C     ANALYSIS OF VARIANCE
      IJ=1
      K2=K
  400 ST1= 0.0
      SL1= 0.0
      SD1= 0.0
      SL2= 0.0
      SD2= 0.0
      GO TO (401,402),NTHET
  402 WRITE (6,4001)
  401 DO 500 L=1,K2
      DO 500 I=1,K2
      IF (I-L)405,500,405
  405 FN= SCN(L) - SCN(I)
      FA= SCA(L) - SCA(I)
      FL= SCL(L) - SCL(I)
      THETAN= CONVRT (FN,AN,BN)
```

```
          THETAL= CONVRT (FL,AL,BL)
          GO TO (408,410),NTHET
  410  WRITE (6,4000)            L,I,THETA(I,L),THETAN,THETAL,FA
  408  ST1=ST1+ THETA(I,L)*THETA(I,L)
          SL1=SL1+ THETAN*THETAN
          SD1=SD1+ (THETA(I,L)-THETAN)*(THETA(I,L)-THETAN)
          SL2=SL2+ THETAL*THETAL
          SD2=SD2+ (THETA(I,L)-THETAL)*(THETA(I,L)-THETAL)
  500  CONTINUE
          ST1=ST1/2.0
          SL1=SL1/2.0
          SD1=SD1/2.0
          SL2=SL2/2.0
          SD2=SD2/2.0
          GO TO(501,530),IJ
  501  WRITE (6,1010)
          CALL VAR(ST1,SL1,SD1,XK,XN)
          WRITE (6,1011)
          CALL VAR(ST1,SL2,SD2,XK,XN)
          GO TO(600,510),LD
  510  K2=K1
          IJ=2
          DO 520 L=1,K1
          SCN(L)=SCN1(L)
          SCA(L)=SCA1(L)
  520  SCL(L)= SCL1(L)
          GO TO 400
  530  WRITE (6,1012)
          CALL VAR(ST1,SL1,SD1,XK1,XN)
          WRITE (6,1013)
          CALL VAR(ST1,SL2,SD2,XK1,XN)
  600  IF(NR-NORUNS) 621,621,620
  620  NORUNS=NORUNS+1
          GO TO 3
  621  CONTINUE
          GO TO 2
C                                        $  $  $  $  $  $  $  $  $  $ $$$
C    END OF MAIN PROGRAM PARCOMP / / / / /  END OF MAIN PROGRAM PRCMP
          END
          SUBROUTINE CHECK
          DIMENSION KSEQ(4860),KFREQ(71,71),ITEM(2450),LIKE(70)
          COMMON KSEQ,ITEM,LIKE,KFREQ
C
 1000  FORMAT (I2)
 1001  FORMAT(I4,I3)
 4000  FORMAT(1H1,14HSEQUENCE DECK ,I4,5X,I2,5H RUNS,2X,I3,5H STIM//)
 1002  FORMAT(2I3,36I2)
 1003  FORMAT(1H0,14HSEQUENCE CARD ,I2,35H HAS WRONG ID - CHECKING CONTI
        1NUED)
 1004  FORMAT(1H0,14HSEQUENCE CARD ,I2,37H IS OUT OF ORDER -CHECKING CON
        1TINUED)
 2000  FORMAT(1H0,48HSEQUENCE CARDS DO NOT TALLY - CHECKING CONTINUED)
   73  FORMAT (1X,5H J = I3,5X,5H L = I3,5X,14H KFREQ(J,L) = I3)
 1005  FORMAT(I3,2XI5,I1,2I4,I5,I3,2I1)
 1055  FORMAT(77H CONTROL CARD  KODE,      N,    LD,  NBAD,NCARDS,    LS,
        1KERR, NPCDT, NTHET   / 12X,9I7//)
  111  FORMAT (I3,I5,I2,70I1)
 1151  FORMAT(1H0 49H  SUBJECT NUMBER LARGER THAN LAST SUBJECT NUMBER )
 1109  FORMAT(27H NUM AND NCARD DO NOT MATCH)
 1111  FORMAT(1H0,45H ERROR IN STUDY CODE,SUBJECT NO. OR CARD NO.  )
 1113  FORMAT(1H0,19H STUDY CODE, KODE =I4,7H IDSTU=I4,16HSUBJ. NO, IDSUB
        1=I5,4H ID=I5,2X20HCARD NO. OF SUBJ,NO=I2,2X4HNUM=I2,2X9HNCARDS =
        2I3,2X4HLS =I5//)
 1122  FORMAT(1H0,29H ERROR IN DATA,NOT ALL 1 OR 2//2X
        112H STUDY CODE,6H KODE=I4,7H IDSTU=I4,2X11HSUBJECT NO,7H IDSUB=I5,
        24H ID=I5,2X17HCARD NO. OF SUBJ.3HNO=I2,2X4HNUM=I2//)
 1010  FORMAT(1H0 7H STUDY  I3, 25H     NO. OF GOOD CASES =  I5, 21H
        1TOTAL NUMBER =  I5 )
 1009  FORMAT( 8H0 STUDY ,I3,16H OK FOR ANALYSIS//)
 1011  FORMAT (1H0 12H GOOD STUDY I3, 8H MIKE = I2, 28H BAD SEQUENCE,  NO
        1ANALYSIS  )
```

```
1007 FORMAT(1H0, 6HSTUDY ,I3,61H DOES NOT CHECK - NO ANALYSIS OF THIS S
    1TUDY WILL BE PERFORMED //)
1008 FORMAT(32H DATA IS NOT ABLE TO BE ANALYZED)
C
 900 REWIND 2
     READ (5,1000,END=99)    NORUNS
     NR=1
     NOK = 0
   1 READ (5,1001)          IDSEQ,K
     WRITE (6,4000)          IDSEQ,NORUNS,K
     MIKE=1
  10 KL= K*(K-1)
     KK =KL/2
     II=1
     JJ=36
     NO=1
   2 READ (5,1002)          ID,NUM,(KSEQ(I), I=II,JJ)
     IF(ID-IDSEQ) 5,3,5
   3 IF(NUM-NO) 6,4,6
   5 WRITE (6,1003)         NUM
     MIKE = 2
     GO TO 4
   6 WRITE (6,1004)         NUM
     MIKE=2
   4 NO=NO+1
     II= II+36
     JJ= JJ+36
     IF(KL-II)50,2,2
  50 DO 51 J=1,K
     DO 51 L=1,K
  51 KFREQ(J,L)=0
     DO 60 I=1,KL,2
     J=KSEQ(I)
     L =KSEQ(I+1)
     KFREQ(L,J)=KFREQ(L,J)+1
  60 KFREQ(J,L)=KFREQ(J,L)+1
     DO 75 L=1,K
     DO 75 J=1,K
     IF(J-L)69,68,69
  68 IF(KFREQ(J,L) ) 71,75,71
  69 IF(KFREQ(J,L)-1) 71,75,71
  71 MIKE=2
     WRITE (6,2000)
     WRITE (6,73)          J,L,KFREQ(J,L)
  75 CONTINUE
C    CHECKING OF DATA CARDS                              CHECK DATA
  90 REWIND 3
 100 READ (5,1005)          KODE,N,LD,NBAD,NCARDS,LS,KERR,NPCDT,NTHET
     WRITE (6,1055)         KODE,N,LD,NBAD,NCARDS,LS,KERR,NPCDT,NTHET
     NPCDT = NPCDT+1
     NTHET = NTHET+1
     IF(KODE-IDSEQ) 102,100,102
 102 IDSUB = 0
     NERR=0
     LD= LD+1
     NGOOD=0
 105 II=1
     JJ=70
     NO=1
     IDSUB=IDSUB+1
 110 READ (5,111)          IDSTU,ID,NUM,(ITEM(I), I=II,JJ)
C    TEST FOR PROPER IDENTIFICATION IN FIRST TEN COL
 112 IF(IDSTU-KODE)1110,114,1110
C    IS STUDY CODE CORRECT
 114 IF(NUM-1) 118,116,118
C    IS IT FIRST DATA CARD SET OF ITEMS
 116 IF(ID-IDSUB)1110,120,117
 117 IF(ID-LS)119,119,1150
 118 IF(IDSUB-ID)1110,120,1110
 119 IDSUB=ID
```

```
      120 IF(NUM-NO)1110,122,1110
      122 IF(KK-JJ) 126,126,124
C    INITIALIZE FOR NEXT CARD FOR SUBJECT
      124 II=II+70
          JJ=JJ+70
          NO=NO+1
C    READ NEXT CARD FOR SUBJECT
          GO TO 110
C    TEST FOR  ONLY 1 AND 2 IN ITEMS
      126 NSUM=0
          DO 128 I=1,KK
      128 NSUM =NSUM+IABS (2*ITEM(I)-3)-1
          IF(NSUM)1120,129,1120
C    IS THERE ANOTHER CARD FOR LIKE-DISLIKE
      129 GO TO(136,130),LD
      130 NO=NO+1
C READ ONE LD CARD
      131 READ (5,111)          IDSTU,ID,NUM,(LIKE(I), I=1,K)
C   TEST FOR PROPER IDENTIFICATION OF LD CARD
          IF(IDSTU-KODE)1110,132,1110
      132 IF(ID-IDSUB)1110,133,1110
      133 IF(NUM-NO)1110,134,1110
C    TEST FOR ONLY 1 AND 2 IN L-D ITEMS
      134 NSUM=0
          DO 135 I=1,K
      135 NSUM=NSUM+IABS (2*LIKE(I)-3)-1
          IF(NSUM)1120,136,1120
      136 IF(NUM-NCARDS)1108,138,1108
C
C    THERE ARE ERRORS IN DATA CARDS
     1150 WRITE (6,1151)
          GO TO 1112
     1108 WRITE (6,1109)
          GO TO 1112
     1110 WRITE (6,1111)
     1112 WRITE (6,1113)             KODE,IDSTU,IDSUB,ID,NO,NUM,NCARDS,LS
          GO TO 1116
     1120 WRITE (6,1122)          KODE,IDSTU,IDSUB,ID,NO,NUM
     1116 NERR=NERR+1
          IF(NUM-NCARDS) 1123,1125,1125
     1123 READ (5,111)          IDSTU,ID,NUM,(ITEM(I),I=1,70)
     1124 IF(NUM-NCARDS) 1123,1125,1125
     1125 IF(ID-LS) 1126,151,1126
     1126 IF(NERR-KERR) 1130,1128,1128
     1128 READ (5,111)          IDSTU,ID,NUM,(ITEM(I),I=1,70)
     1129 IF(ID-LS) 1126,1124,1126
     1130 II = 1
          JJ = 70
          NO = 1
     1133 READ (5,111)          IDSTU,ID,NUM,(ITEM(I),I=1,70)
     1134 IF(NUM-1) 1133, 1135, 1133
     1135 IF(IDSTU-KODE)1110,117,1110
C
      138 NGOOD=NGOOD+1
C   IF NO ERRORS IN SUBJECT,BRANCH ON LD TO WRITE DATA ON TAPE 7
      139 GO TO ( 140, 144 ), LD
      140    WRITE(3)ID,(ITEM(I),I=1,KK)
          GO TO 150
      144    WRITE(3)ID,(ITEM(I),I=1,KK)
C   IS IT LAST SUBJECT(LS)
      150 IF(ID-LS) 105,151,1150
      151 WRITE (6,1010)          KODE,NGOOD,N
          IF(N-NGOOD-NBAD)152,152,177
      152 NOK=NOK+1
C  ADD ONE TO NUMBER OF GOOD STUDIES
C    IF GOOD STUDY(IES), ANALYZE DATA,FIRST WRITE OUT ON TAPE 8
          REWIND 3
          GO TO (153,175),MIKE
      153 IF(NOK-1) 177,154,155
C  WRITE OUT SEQUENCE AND GOOD DATA(FIRST STUDY)
```

```
    154 WRITE (2)      IDSEQ,K,KL,KK,(KSEQ(I),I=1,KL)
    155 WRITE (2)      KODE,NGOOD,LD,LS,NPCDT,NTHET
    156 GO TO (160,170),LD
C  WRITE OUT GOOD DATA IF SEQ IS ALREADY WRITTEN OUT
    170 DO 171   J=1,NGOOD
        READ(3)ID,(ITEM(I),I=1,KK),(LIKE(L),L=1,K)
    171 WRITE (2)       ID,(ITEM(I),I=1,KK),(LIKE(L),L=1,K)
        GO TO 173
    160 DO 161   J=1,NGCOD
        READ(3)ID,(ITEM(I),I=1,KK)
    161 WRITE (2)      ID,(ITEM(I),I=1,KK)
C  WRITE NOTE INDICATING IF ANALYSIS IS POSSIBLE
    173 WRITE (6,1009)          KODE
        GO TO 181
    175 WRITE (6,1011)          KODE,MIKE
        GO TO 181
    177 WRITE (6,1007)          KODE
    181 CONTINUE
        IF(NORUNS-NR) 190,190,182
    182 NR=NR+1
        GO TO 90
    190 IF(NOK) 191,191,192
    191 WRITE (6,1008)
        GO TO 900
    192 GO TO (193,900),MIKE
    193 WRITE (2)     NOK
        RETURN
     99 CALL EXIT
C                                          $  $  $  $  $  $  $  $  $$$
C END SUBROUTINE CHECK  /  /  /  /  /  //END OF SUBROUTINE CHECK
        END
        SUBROUTINE VAR(ST,SL,SD,XK,XN)
C
      1 FORMAT(1H ,6X6HSOURCE,10X2HDF,5X14HSUM OF SQUARES,8X11HMEAN SQUARE
      1,7X14HAV MEAN SQUARE,9X10HCHI SQUARE    /8X3HALL,9X15,3(5XF15.4),
      25XF15.3/6X9HCOMP JUDG,5X15,3(5XF15.4),5XF15.3/6X,8HRESIDUAL,6X15,
      33(5X,F15.4),5X,F15.3//)
      2 FORMAT(1H ,4X20HRELIABILITY OF SCALE,35X28HVARIANCE COMPONENTS ANA
      1LYSIS/50X6HSOURCE,14X22HEST. OF VAR. COMPONENT/5X6HR(S) =,F14.8,20
      2X17HBINOMIAL SAMPLING,8XF15.8/5X6HR(SS)=,F14.8,20X18HDEV FROM LIN
      3SCALE,7XF15.8/5X6HR(B) =,F14.8,20X16HLIN SCALE VALUES,9XF15.8/)
C
        XKK= XK-1.0
        T=(2.0*ST)/(XK*XKK)
        XL= SL/XKK
        D= (2.0*SD)/(XKK*(XKK-1.0))
        CHISQT= XN*ST
        CHISQL= XN*SL
        CHISQD= XN*SD
        KFT= XK*XKK/2.0
        KFL= XKK
        KFD= XKK*(XKK-1.0)/2.0
        SIGB = 1.0/XN
        SIGD = D - SIGB
        SIGS = (XL-D)/XK
        RS= SIGS*(2.0/T)
        RSS= (T-D)/T
        RB= (T-SIGB)/T
        AT=2.0*SIGS+SIGD+SIGB
        AL=XK*SIGS+SIGD+SIGB
        AD=SIGD+SIGB
        WRITE (6,1)          KFT,ST,T,AT,CHISQT,KFL,SL,XL,AL,CHISQL,KFD,S
       1D,D,AD,CHISQD
        WRITE (6,2)          RS,SIGB,RSS,SIGD,RB,SIGS
        RETURN
C                                          $  $  $  $  $  $  $  $  $  $ $$$
C   END OF SUBROUTINE VAR  /  /  /  /  /  / END OF SUBROUTINE  VAR
        END
        SUBROUTINE APPROX(P,A,B,C,D,E,DENX,X)
        U=P- 0.5
        U2= U*U
        U4= U2*U2
```

```
        DENX= 1.0 - B*U2 + A*U4
        X= U*(E - D*U2 + C*U4)/DENX
        RETURN
C                                                   $  $  $  $  $  $  $  $  $  $ $$$
C  END OF SUBROUTINE APPROX  /  /  /  /  /  /  END OF SUBROUTINE APPROX
        END
        FUNCTION CONVRT(F,CAPA,B)
        DIMENSION B(8)
        E=1.0
        Y=0.0
        G =ABS(F)
        IF ( F ) 7, 8, 7
     7  H = F/G
     8  DO 10 I=1,8
        E = E*G
    10  Y=Y +B(I)*E
        CONVRT = ( CAPA * Y * H ) / (1.0 + Y )
        RETURN
C                                                   $  $  $  $  $  $  $  $  $  $ $$$
C  END OF FUNCTION CONVRT  /  /  /  /  /  /  END OF FUNCTION CONVRT  ***
        END
/*
//
```

CONPR (Contrast Pair Cards for k Objects)

1. Description and Input Directions.   Sometimes it is useful to punch the complete set of paired objects on cards. The cards can be shuffled as a randomization procedure, can be written on, and if white, can be used as stimulus cards in a variety of ways.

Control Cards

The input consists of a card, or cards, containing (1) the number of objects followed by (2) alphameric symbols representing the objects.

1. Format Card: The number of objects is read in I format and the symbols in A format.
2. Parameter Card and Data Card(s): The number of objects (names) is read first, according to the format, followed by the names of the objects. The present routine is limited to no more than 4 characters representing each object. The output format of the program can be easily changed to accommodate longer names.

2. Example Input for CONPR, *Data Are Dessert Names from Table 20.2.*

```
//CONPR JOB (2919,267F,2X),'DUNN-RANKIN'
// EXEC EDSTAT,PROGRAM=CONPR
//GO.SYSIN DD *
(I2,4A3)
 4 CC PC VI CS
/*
//
```

3. *Output for* CONPR, *Data Represent Desserts from Table 20.2.*

1	0	1	1	CC	CC
2	1	1	2	CC	PC
3	1	1	3	CC	VI
4	1	1	4	CC	CS
5	1	2	1	PC	CC
6	0	2	2	PC	PC
7	1	2	3	PC	VI
8	1	2	4	PC	CS
9	1	3	1	VI	CC
10	1	3	2	VI	PC
11	0	3	3	VI	VI
12	1	3	4	VI	CS
13	1	4	1	CS	CC
14	1	4	2	CS	PC
15	1	4	3	CS	VI
16	0	4	4	CS	CS

4. FORTRAN *Listing for Program* CONPR.

```
C PROGRAM CONPR
C
C       THIS PROGRAM WRITES AND PUNCHES ALL OF THE CONTRAST PAIRS
C                       FOR N OBJECTS.
C
        DIMENSION FMT(20),A(50)
        PRINT 9
        READ (5,900) FMT
  900 FORMAT(20A4)
        READ (5,FMT)N,(A(I),I=1,N)
        M=0
        DO 500 I=1,N
        DO 500 J=1,N
        L=1
        IF(I.EQ.J)L=0
        M=M+1
        PRINT 910,M,L,I,J,A(I),A(J)
  910 FORMAT (2X,2I6,4X,2I3,4X,2A4)
  500 PUNCH 910,M,L,I,J,A(I),A(J)
        PRINT 9
    9 FORMAT('1')
        END
C
```

CORR (SAS)

1. Description and FORTRAN *Source.* All computer centers will have software programs for calculating Pearson's correlation coefficient, r. The SAS package (Barr, Goodnight, Sall, & Helwig, 1976) is used here for illustrative purposes. The data are taken from the imaginary profiles provided under the heading *Correlation* in Chapter 3.

2. Input Example for Program CORR *(r Correlations), Profile Data from Chapter 3.*

```
//CORR JOB (2919,267F),'DUNN-RANKIN'
// EXEC SAS
//SYSIN DD *
DATA DUMMY;
INPUT A B C D;
CARDS;
8 6 8 4
5 2 5 1
9 4 4 4
6 5 4 3
8 2 7 6
5 3 4 3
PROC CORR;
  VAR A B C D;
/*
//
```

3. Example Output from Program CORR (SAS), *Profile Data Chapter 3.*

DISSIM (Calculates Distances or Scalar Products)

1. Description and Input Directions.   This program computes two different measures of dissimilarity—*distances* and *scalar products*. Dissimilarity matrices may be formed between either variables or subjects, or between both individually. The raw data may be either standardized (*z* scores) or unstandardized before the computations are performed. In any case, deletion of missing data may be specified to be either pairwise or casewise. This program was written by Jean Holtz and modified by Martha Crosby. The program uses four of the Veldman (1967) subroutines. These subroutines are provided under the topic SUBROUTINES in this chapter.

The distance is computed as:

$$d(i, j) = \left(\sum_k |x(i, k) - x(j, k)|^r \right)^{1/r}$$

with the value of r specified on the Parameter Control Card. If $r = 1$, the distance calculated is the "city block" distance. Euclidean distance is calculated when $r = 2$. Other values of r can be used, but those which are less than one may create distances that do not conform to the triangular rule.

The scalar product is computed using Torgerson's method. Basically, the scalar product is:

$$b(i, j) = \frac{(d^2(i, k) + d^2(j, k) - d^2(i, j))}{2}$$

where $d(i, j)$ is the Euclidean distance between points *i* and *j*. Point *k* is chosen to be the centroid of the problem space. This computed scalar product is normalized before output.

S T A T I S T I C A L   A N A L Y S I S   S Y S T E M

VARIABLE	N	MEAN	STD DEV	SUM	MINIMUM
A	6	6.8333333	1.7240142	41.0000000	5.0000000
B	6	3.6666667	1.6329316	22.0000000	2.0000000
C	6	5.3333333	1.7519007	32.0000000	4.0000000
D	6	3.5000000	1.6431767	21.0000000	1.0000000

CORRELATION COEFFICIENTS / PROB > |R| UNDER H0:RHO=0 / N = 6

	A	B	C	D
A	1.00000 0.0000	0.33183 0.5205	0.41995 0.4071	0.74200 0.0913
B	0.33183 0.5205	1.00000 0.0000	0.18650 0.7235	0.07454 0.8884
C	0.41995 0.4071	0.18650 0.7235	1.00000 0.0000	0.48653 0.3278
D	0.74200 0.0913	0.07454 0.8884	0.48653 0.3278	1.00000 0.0000

Control Cards:

1. Title Control Card: All 80 columns may be used for a title which will be printed at the beginning of the output. This title may consist of any characters.

2. Parameter Control Card: All values are integer and should be right-adjusted within the specified columns on the card.

Col. 1–5   number of variables

Col. 6–10   number of subjects

Col. 12   dissimilarity measure desired

                   1—distance, 2—scalar product

Col. 13   dissimilarity objects

                   1 = between variables, 2 = between subjects

Col. 14   1 if standardization of variables desired

Col. 15   missing data option

                   1 = pairwise deletion, 2 = casewise deletion

Col. 16–20   value of r for distance measure (read without a decimal point, but with four decimal places, 20000 = 2.0, for example)

Col. 24   blank or 0 default output

                   1 upper triangular matrix with diagonal

                   2 upper triangular matrix without diagonal

                   3 lower triangular matrix with diagonal

                   4 lower triangular matrix without diagonal

                   5 full symmetric matrix

Col. 25   output of dissimilarity matrix

                   0 = none, 1 = print only, 2 = punch only, 3 = both print and punch

2. Input Example for Program DISSIM, *Profile Data from Chapter 3.*

```
//DISSIM JOB (2919,267F,2X),'DUNN-RANKIN'
// EXEC EDSTAT,PROGRAM=DISSIM
//GO.SYSIN DD *
     SAMPLE PROGRAM FOR DISSIM,PROFILE DATA CH.3
    4     6 11112
(A2,8X,4F1.0)
01        8684
02        5251
03        9444
04        6543
05        8276
06        5343
/*
//
```

3. Output from Program DISSIM, *Profile Data from Chapter 3.*

```
        *** OUTPUT FROM PROGRAM DISSIM ***

        SAMPLE PROGRAM FOR DISSIM,PROFILE DATA CH.3

 PARAMETERS
 COL  1- 5 =      4
 COL  6-10 =      6
 COL 11-15 =   1111
 COL 16-20 =  20000
 COL 21-25 =      1

  FORMAT CARD(S)


         (A2,8X,4F1.0)


 V DIST            1          2          3          4

          1      0.0      2.8316     2.6383     1.7595

          2     2.8316     0.0       3.1244     3.3325

          3     2.6383     3.1244     0.0       2.4823

          4     1.7595     3.3325     2.4823     0.0
```

4. FORTRAN *Listing for Program* DISSIM.   Required Subroutines (See SUBROUTINES in this chapter) CCDS, INPUT, PCDS, PRTS, PTMS, RFMT, DYNA, NLOC, PAREN, SINTL, APRINT

Should the reader wish to use the Fortran listing provided he or she should make sure to include the necessary subroutines provided.

```
C PROGRAM DISSIM
C
        EXTERNAL DISTNZ,SCALAR
        COMMON NV, NS, NWAY, NSTD, NMISS, R, NOUT, FMT(80), NV2,NS2
1       CALL CCDS (FMT, NV, NS, NOPTS, NR, NOUT, 8HDISSIMUL)
        R = NR
        R = R / 10000
        NTYPE = NOPTS / 1000
        NOPTS = NOPTS - NTYPE * 1000
        NWAY = NOPTS / 100
        NOPTS = NOPTS - NWAY * 100
        NSTD = NOPTS / 10
        NMISS = NOPTS - NSTD * 10
        IF (NTYPE - 2)  11, 12, 12
C
C                 SETUP FOR DISTANCE MEASURE
C
11        NVS = NV * NS
        IF (NWAY - 2)   111, 112, 112
111         NV2 = NV
            NS2 = NV
            NSIZE = NV * NV
            GO TO 110
```

```
112              NV2 = NS
                 NS2 = NS
                 NSIZE = NS * NS
110          CALL DYNA (DISTNZ, DATA, NVS, D, NSIZE, MISSV, NV, MISS, NS)
             GO TO 19

C                      SETUP FOR SCALAR PRODUCTS
C
12           NVS = NV * NS
             IF (NWAY - 2)  121, 122, 123
121              NSIZE = NV * NV
                 NV2 = NV
                 NS2 = NV
                 GO TO 120
122              NSIZE = NS * NS
                 NV2 = NS
                 NS2 = NS
                 GO TO 120
123              NV2 = MAX0(NV, NS)
                 NS2 = NV2
                 NSIZE = NV2 * NS2
120          CALL DYNA (SCALAR, DATA,NVS, D,NSIZE, MISSV,NV, MISS,NS,
         1       DC, NV2, DR, NS2)
19       GO TO 1
         END
         SUBROUTINE DISTNZ (DATA, NVS, D, NSIZE, MISSV,I, MISS,J)
         COMMON NV, NS, NWAY, NSTD, NMISS, R, NOUT, FMT(80), NV2, NS2
         REAL DATA(NV,NS), D(NV2,NS2), MISSV(NV), MISS(NS)
         REAL*8 ID
         DO 90 I = L, NS
90           MISS(I) = 0
         DO 91 J = 1, NV
91           MISSV(J) = 0
C
C                READ DATA AND STANDARDIZE, IF REQUESTD
C
         DO 1 I = 1, NS
             CALL INPUT (ID, DATA(1,I), I, FMT, NV)
             IF (NMISS . EQ. 1)  GO TO 1
             DO 11 J = 1, NV
                 IF (DATA(J,I) .NE. 0.0)  GO TO 11
                 MISSV(J) = 1
                 MISS(I) = 1
11           CONTINUE
1        CONTINUE
         IF (NSTD .EQ. 1)  CALL STDIZE(DATA, NV, NS)
C
C                CALCULATE DISTANCE MATRIX AND OUPTUT RESULTS
C
             IF (NWAY .EQ. 2)  GO TO 21
             CALL DISTV (DATA, D, NV, NS, R, MISS, NMISS)
             IF (NOUT .LT. 10) GO TO 20
             CALL APRINT(D,NV,NOUT)
             GO TO 21
20           IF (NOUT.EQ.1 .OR. NOUT.EQ.3)  CALL PRTS(D,NV,NV,6HV DIST,NV)
             IF (NOUT .GT. 1)  CALL PTMS(D, NV, 6HV DIST, NV)
21           IF (NWAY .LT. 2)  GO TO 29
             CALL DISTS (DATA, D, NV, NS, R, MISSV, NMISS)
             IF (NOUT .LT. 10) GO TO 22
             CALL APRINT (D,NS,NOUT)
             GO TO 29
22           IF (NOUT.EQ.1 .OR. NOUT.EQ.3)  CALL PRTS(D,NS,NS,6HS DIST,NS)
             IF (NOUT .GT. 1)  CALL PTMS (D, NS, 6HS DIST, NS)
29       RETURN

         END
         SUBROUTINE STDIZE (DATA, NV, NS)
         REAL DATA(NV,NS)
C
C                FOR EACH VARIABLE:
```

```
C
      DO 1 I = 1, NV
C
C               COMPUTE MEAN AND VARIANCE
C
         N = NS
         SUM = 0.0
         SUM2 = 0.0
         DO 11 J=1,NS
            TEMP = DATA(I,J)
          IF (TEMP .NE. 0.0)  GO TO 110
             N = N - 1
             GO TO 11
110         SUM = SUM + TEMP
            SUM2 = SUM2 + TEMP*TEMP
11       CONTINUE
         IF (N .EQ. 0)  GO TO 1
         SUM = SUM / N
         SUM2 = SQRT(SUM2/N - SUM*SUM)
C
C               COMPUTE Z-SCORE FOR EACH SUBJECT
C
         DO 12 J =1, NS
            IF (DATA(I,J) .EQ. 0.0) GO TO 12
            DATA(I,J) = DATA(I,J) - SUM
            IF (SUM2 .NE. 0.0) DATA(I,J) = DATA(I,J) / SUM2
12       CONTINUE
1     CONTINUE
      RETURN
      END
      SUBROUTINE DISTV (DATA, D, NV, NS, R, MISS, NMISS)
      DIMENSION DATA (NV,NS), D(NV,NV), MISS(NS)
C
C     CALCULATE DISTANCE BETWEEN THE VARIABLES IN A DATA SET
C
      NV1 = NV - 1
      DO 1 I = 1, NV1
         I1 = I + 1
         DO 19 J = I1, NV
            SUM = 0.0
C
C               PAIRWISE MISSING DATA DELETION
C
            IF (NMISS.NE.1)  GO TO 14
               DO 12 K = 1, NS
                  IF (DATA(I,K)*DATA(J,K) .NE. 0.0)  SUM =
     1                SUM + ABS(DATA(I,K)-DATA(J,K)) **R
12             CONTINUE
               GO TO 16
C
C               CASEWISE MISSING DATA DELETION
C
14             DO 15 K = 1, NS
                  IF (MISS(K) .EQ. 0)  SUM =
     1                SUM + ABS(DATA(I,K) - DATA(J,K)) ** R
15             CONTINUE
16          SUM = SUM ** (1.0/R)
            D(I,J) = SUM
            D(J,I) = SUM
19       CONTINUE
         D(I,I) = 0.0
1     CONTINUE
      D(NV,NV) = 0.0
      RETURN
      END
      SUBROUTINE DISTS (DATA, D, NV, NS, R, MISSV, NMISS)
      DIMENSION DATA (NV,NS), D(NS,NS), MISSV(NV)
C
C     CALCULATE DISTANCE BETWEEN THE SUBJECTS IN A DATA SET
C
      NS1 = NS - 1
```

```
          DO 1 I = 1, NS1
             I1 = I + 1
             DO 19 J = I1, NS
                SUM = 0.0
C
C                PAIRWISE MISSING DATA DELETION
C
                IF (NMISS .NE. 1)  GO TO 14
                   DO 12 K = 1, NV
                      IF (DATA(K,I)*DATA(K,J) .NE. 0.0)  SUM =
     1                   SUM + ABS(DATA(K,I)-DATA(K,J)) **R
12                    CONTINUE
                      GO TO 16
C
C                CASEWISE MISSING DATA DELETION
C
14                 DO 15 K = 1, NV
                      IF (MISSV(K) .EQ. 0)  SUM =
     1                   SUM + ABS(DATA(K,I) - DATA(K,J)) ** R
15                    CONTINUE
16                 SUM = SUM ** (1.0/R)
                   D(I,J) = SUM
                   D(J,I) = SUM
19           CONTINUE
             D(I,I) = 0.0
1         CONTINUE
          D(NS,NS) = 0.0
          RETURN
          END
          SUBROUTINE SCALAR (DATA, NVS, D, NSIZE, MISSV, I, MISS, J,
     1       DC, K, DR, L)
          COMMON NV, NS, NWAY, NSTD, NMISS, R, NOUT, FMT(80), NV2,NS2
          REAL DATA(NV,NS),D(NV2,NS2), MISSV(NV),MISS(NS), DC(NV2),DR(NV2)
          REAL*8 ID
          DO 10 I = 1, NS
             MISS(I) = 0
             DO 11 J =1, NV
11              MISSV(J) = 0
10        CONTINUE

C                   READ DATA AND STANDARDIZE, IF REQUESTED
C
          DO 2 I =1, NS
             CALL INPUT (ID, DATA(1,I), I, FMT, NV)
             IF (NMISS .EQ. 1) GO TO 2
             DO 21 J = 1, NV
                IF (DATA(J,I) .NE. 0.0)  GO TO 21
                MISSV(J) = 1
                MISS(I) = 1
21           CONTINUE
2         CONTINUE
          IF (NSTD .EQ. 1)  CALL STDIZE(DATA, NV, NS)
C
C                   CALCULATE SCALAR PRODUCTS AND OUTPUT RESULTS
C
          IF (NWAY - 2)  31, 32, 31
31           CALL DISTV(DATA, D, NV, NS, 2.0, MISS,NMISS)
             CALL TORGB1(D, NV, 1, DC, DR)
             IF (NOUT.LT.10)GO TO 33
             CALL APRINT (D,NV,NOUT)
             GO TO 32
33           IF (NOUT.EQ.1 .OR. NOUT.EQ.3)
     1          CALL PRTS (D, NV, NV, 8HV SCALAR, NV)
             IF (NOUT .GT. 1) CALL PTMS (D, NV, 8HV SCALAR, NV)
32        IF (NWAY .LT. 2)  GO TO 39
             CALL DISTS (DATA, D, NV, NS, 2.0, MISSV,NMISS)
             CALL TORGB1 (D, NS, 1, DC, DR)
             IF (NOUT.GT.10)GO TO 34
             CALL APRINT (D,NS,NOUT)
             GO TO 39
```

```
34          IF (NOUT.EQ.1 .OR. NOUT.EQ.3)
     1          CALL PRTS (D, NS, NS, 8HS SCALAR, NS)
            IF (NOUT .GT. 1)  CALL PTMS (D, NS, 8HS SCALAR, NS)
39     RETURN
       END
       SUBROUTINE TORGB1(A, N, IADDC, DC, DR)
C
C                     TORGERSON METHOD TO COMPUTE SCALAR PRODUCT MATRICES
C
       REAL DC(N), DR(N), A(N,N)
       XN = N
       DO 8 I = 1, N
          DC(I) = 0.0
          DR(I) = 0.0
8      A(I,I) = 0.0
       SUMD = 0.0
51     IF (IADDC) 27, 27, 26
26         ADDC = -100.0
           N1 = N - 1
           N2 = N - 2
           DO 30 I = 1, N2
              JJ = I + 1
              DO 30 J = JJ, N1
                 KK = J + 1
                 DO 30 K = KK,N
                    CIJK = A(I,K) - A(J,K) - A(I,J)
                    IF (CIJK .GT. ADDC)  ADDC = CIJK
                    CIJK = A(J,K) - A(I,K) - A(I,J)

                    IF (CIJK .GT. ADDC)  ADDC = CIJK
                    CIJK = A(I,J) - A(J,K) - A(I,K)
                    IF (CIJK .GT. ADDC)  ADDC = CIJK
30         CONTINUE
27     DO 40 I = 2, N
          II = I - 1
          DO 40 J = 1, II
             IF (IADDC .EQ. 0)  GO TO 40
             A(I,J) = A(I,J) + ADDC
             A(J,I) = A(I,J)
40     SUMD = SUMD + A(I,J)**2
       ADIJ = 2.0 * SUMD / XN**2
       DO 7 I = 1, N
          DO 7 J = 1, N
             DC(I) = DC(I) + A(J,I)**2
7      DR(I) = DR(I) + A(I,J)**2
C
C                     COMPUTE B - SCALAR PRODUCT MATRIX
C
       SUM = 0.0
       SUMD = 0.0
       DO 10 I = 1, N
          DO 10 J = 1, I
             QQ = (DR(I) + DC(J)) / XN
             A(I,J) = 0.5 * (QQ - A(I,J)**2 - ADIJ)
             IF (I .EQ. J)  GO TO 11
                SUM = SUM + A(I,J)**2
                GO TO 10
11              SUMD = SUMD + A(I,J)**2
10     CONTINUE
C
C                     NORMALIZE SCALAR PRODUCT MATRIX
C
       Q = 1.0 / SQRT(SUMD + 2.0 * SUM)
       DO 12 I = 1, N
          DO 12 J = 1, I
             A(I,J) = A(I,J) * Q
12     A(J,I) = A(I,J)
500    RETURN
       END
```

GOWER (Calculates Gower's Similarity Index)

1. Description and Input Directions.   The program was written by Jean Holtz using Veldman's (1967) subroutines. GOWER, calculates Gower's Similarity Measure. These subroutines (CCDS, DYNA, INPUT, PRTS, PTMS, PCDS) are under the topic SUBROUTINES in this chapter. The matrices created by the programs can be used as input to other programs or as a final product in themselves.

Control Cards:

1. Title Control Card: All 80 columns may be used for a title which will be printed at the beginning of the output. This title may consist of any characters.

2. Parameter Control Card: All values are integer and should be right-adjusted within the specified columns on the card.

    Col. 1–5   number of variables
    Col. 6–10   number of subjects
    Col. 11–15   data set number for output of original data
    Col. 16–20   output of ranges*
    Col. 24   type of matrix: 1 upper Δ matrix with diagonal
                                       2 upper Δ matrix without diagonal
                                       3 lower Δ matrix with diagonal
                                       4 lower Δ matrix without diagonal
                                       5 full symmetric matrix
    Col. 25   output of similarity matrix*
                   *output options: 0 = none, 1 = print only, 2 = punch
                                       only, 3 = both print and punch

3. Format Control Card: Up to 4 cards may be used to describe the placement of the data on the data cards. The first field may be an A-mode subject identification field, or the data may be read without an ID field.

4. Variable Type Control Card: Beginning with column 1 and continuing one column at a time, the type of each variable is specified. The value to be punched for each variable:

                   1 if the variable is binary
                   2 if the variable is qualitative
                   3 if the variable is quantitative

    All 80 columns of the card are used to specify the variable type (that is, the type of up to 80 variables is specified on a single card). If necessary, additional Variable Type Control Cards may be used to complete the specification of all variables.

2. Input Example for Program GOWER, Data from Gower's Chapter 3.

```
//GOWER JOB (2919),'DUNN-RANKIN'
// EXEC EDSTAT,PROGRAM=GOWER
//GO.SYSIN DD *
SAMPLE DATA ARE FROM GOWER'S CHAPTER 3
     4    5          1    51
(A2,5F3.0)
3312
100 50  1   1
 90 50  2   2
110 45  1   2
115 60  2   3
130 54  1   1
/*
```

3. Output from Program GOWER, *Data from Chapter 3, Gower's Similarity.*

```
        *** OUTPUT FROM PROGRAM GOWERS ***

GOWER TEST

PARAMETERS
COL   1- 5 =     4
COL   6-10 =     5
COL  11-15 =     0
COL  16-20 =     1
COL  21-25 =     1

  FORMAT CARD(S)


        (4F5.0)


MINIMUMS         1         2         3         4
              90.0000   45.0000    1.0000    1.0000


MAXIMUMS         1         2         3         4
             130.0000   60.0000    2.0000    3.0000


RANGES           1         2         3         4
              40.0000   15.0000    1.0000    2.0000


GOWERS           1         2         3         4         5

     1        1.0000    0.4375    0.6042    0.2396    0.7458

     2        0.4375    1.0000    0.5417    0.4271    0.1833

     3        0.6042    0.5417    1.0000    0.2188    0.4750

     4        0.2396    0.4271    0.2188    1.0000    0.3062

     5        0.7458    0.1833    0.4750    0.3062    1.0000
```

4. FORTRAN *Listing for Program* GOWER.   Required Subroutines (See SUBROUTINES in this chapter) CCDS, INPUT, PCDS, PRTS, PTMS, RFMT, DYNA, NLOC, PAREN, SINTL, APRINT.

```
        EXTERNAL GOWERZ
        COMMON NV, NS, NTAPE, NRANG, NSIM, FMT(80)
1       CALL CCDS (FMT, NV, NS, NTAPE, NRANG, NSIM, 6HGOWERS)
        NS2 = NS * NS
        NVS = NV * NS
        CALL DYNA (GOWERZ, SIMLTY,NS2, RANGE,NV, AMIN,NV, AMAX,NV,
     1      DATA,NVS, NTYPE,NV)
        GO TO 1
        END
        SUBROUTINE GOWERZ (SIMLTY,NS2, RANGE,NV1, BMIN,NV2, BMAX,NV3,
     1      DATA,NVS, NTYPE,NV4)
        COMMON NV, NS, NTAPE, NRANG, NSIM, FMT(80)
        INTEGER NTYPE(1)
        REAL SIMLTY(NS,NS), DATA(NV,NS), RANGE(1), BMIN(1),
     1      BMAX(1)
        REAL*8 ID
C
C               READ IN THE DATA AND CALCULATE THE RANGES
C
        READ 10000, (NTYPE(I), I = 1,NV)
        IF (NTAPE .GT. 0)  REWIND NTAPE
        CALL INPUT (ID, DATA (1,1), 1, FMT, NV)
        DO 1 J = 1, NV
            TEMP = DATA(J,1)
            BMIN(J) = TEMP
            IF (TEMP .EQ. 0.0)  BMIN(J) = 90000.
            BMAX(J) = TEMP
            IF (TEMP .EQ. 0.0)  BMAX(J) = -90000.
1       CONTINUE
        IF (NTAPE .GT. 0)  WRITE (NTAPE) ID, (DATA(K,1), K=1,NV)
        DO 2 I = 2, NS
            CALL INPUT (ID, DATA(1,I), I, FMT, NV)
            IF (NTAPE .GT. 0)  WRITE (NTAPE) ID, (DATA(K,I), K=1,NV)
            DO 21 J = 1, NV
                TEMP = DATA(J,I)
                IF (TEMP .EQ. 0.0)  GO TO 21
                IF (BMIN(J) .GT. TEMP)  BMIN(J) = TEMP
                IF (BMAX(J) .LT. TEMP)  BMAX(J) = TEMP
21          CONTINUE
2       CONTINUE
        DO 3 J = 1, NV
3           RANGE(J) = BMAX(J) - BMIN(J)
C
C               CALCULATE GOWER'S SIMILARITY MEASURE
C
        NS1 = NS - 1
        DO 4 I = 1, NS1
            I1 = I + 1
            DO 49 J = I1, NS
                TEMP = 0.0
                N = NV
                DO 45 K = 1, NV
                    IF (DATA(K,I).NE.0.0 .AND. DATA(K,J).NE.0.0)  GO TO 41
                    N = N - 1
                    GO TO 45
41                  IF (NTYPE(K) - 2) 42, 42, 43
42                  IF (DATA(K,I) .EQ. DATA(K,J))  TEMP = TEMP+1
                    GO TO 45
43                  TEMP=TEMP +1.0- ABS(DATA(K,I)-DATA(K,J))/RANGE(K)
45              CONTINUE
                TEMP = TEMP / N
```

```
                    SIMLTY(I,J) = TEMP
                    SIMLTY(J,I) = TEMP
   49        CONTINUE
             SIMLTY(I,I) = 1.0
   4      CONTINUE
          SIMLTY(NS,NS) = 1.0

   C
   C              PRINT AND PUNCH THE RESULTS
   C
          IF (NRANG.EQ.0 .OR. NRANG.EQ.2)  GO TO 51
             CALL PRTS (BMIN, NV, 1, 8HMINIMUMS, NV)
             CALL PRTS (BMAX, NV, 1, 8HMAXIMUMS, NV)
             CALL PRTS (RANGE, NV, 1, 6HRANGES, NV)
   51     IF (NRANG .LE. 1)   GO TO 52
             CALL PCDS (BMIN, NV, 1, 8HMINIMUMS, NV)
             CALL PCDS (BMAX, NV, 1, 8HMAXIMUMX, NV)
             CALL PCDS (RANGE, NV, 1, 6HRANGES, NV)
   52     IF (NSIM .GT. 10) GO TO 53
          IF (NSIM .GT. 1)  CALL PTMS (SIMLTY, NS, 6HGOWERS, NS)
          IF (NSIM.EQ.1 .OR. NSIM. EQ.3)   CALL PRTS (SIMLTY, NS,NS,
         1   6HGOWERS, NS)
          PRINT 50000
          RETURN
   53     CALL APRINT(SIMLTY,NS,NSIM)
          RETURN
   10000  FORMAT (80I1)
   50000  FORMAT (1H1)
          END
```

GUTTMAN (SPSS Program for Goodenough's Guttman Scaling)

1. Description and FORTRAN *Source.* Guttman scaling (Goodenough's Scaling Method) has been programed by Anderson (1966) and is now part of the SSPS (Social Sciences Programming System). Anderson's algorithm determines the scalability of the existing data and indicates divergence from perfect scales. See the SPSS Manual (Nie et al., 1975) for using the software program. The BMD Series of Programs also has extensive programs for doing Guttman Scaling, specifically BMD045–BMD085.

2. Input Example for Guttman Scaling, Data from Table 9.2.

```
//GUTTMAN JOB (2919,267F),'DUNN-RANKIN'
// EXEC SPSS
//GO.SYSIN DD *
VARIABLE LIST   A,B,C,D,E,F
INPUT MEDIUM    CARD
INPUT FORMAT    FIXED (10X,6F1.0)
N OF CASES      12
GUTTMAN SCALE   TABLE9.2=A(2),B(2),C(2),D(2),E(2),F(2)/
READ INPUT DATA
01          122221
```

```
02          222111
03          211112
04          221111
05          112221
06          121221
07          121121
08          122111
09          221222
10          122211
11          112111
12          122121
STATISTICS       ALL
FINISH
/*
//
```

3. Output from Program GUTTMAN (SPSS), *Data from Table 9.2.*

HGROUP (Metric Hierarchical Clustering)

1. Description and Input Directions.   Joe Ward's metric hierarchical clustering program is part of the Veldman (1967) package of programs and listed as HGROUP. HGROUP is a generalized distance analysis to successively cluster subjects or variables. All stages of reduction from N one-person groups to one N-person group are reported.

Control Cards:

1. Title Control Card: Left justified. You can use all 80 columns in any characters.
2. Parameter Control Card:
   - Col. 1–5   number of variables
   - Col. 6–10   number of subjects
   - Col. 11–15   level of grouping at which subject assignments to groups will be printed (typically 10)
   - Col. 20   1 to standardize each variable before analysis to equalize contributions of variables to the profile distance measures.
   - Col. 25   1 to transpose the data matrix, in order to group variables rather than subjects.
3. Format Control Card: First field may be A mode, subject identification or may be read without the subject I.D. field. Data are read in F format.

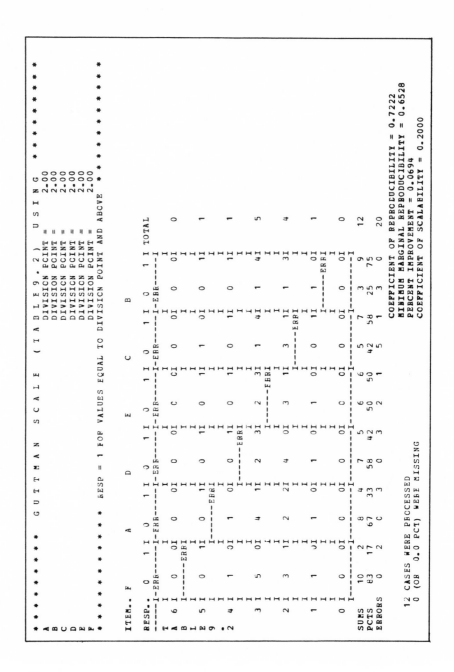

```
*  *  *  *  *  *  *  *    G U T T M A N   S C A L E   ( T A B L E 9 . 2 )   U S I N G   *  *  *  *  *  *  *  *  *  *
*  A                          DIVISION PCINT =    2.00
*  B                          DIVISION PCINT =    2.00
*  C                          DIVISION PCINT =    2.00
*  D                          DIVISION PCINT =    2.00
*  E                          DIVISION PCINT =    2.00
*  F                          DIVISION PCINT =    2.00
*  *  *  *  *  *  *  *  *    RESP = 1 FOR VALUES EQUAL TO DIVISION POINT AND ABOVE  *  *  *  *  *  *  *  *  *  *
```

COEFFICIENT OF REPRODUCIBILITY = 0.7222
MINIMUM MARGINAL REPRODUCIBILITY = 0.6528
PERCENT IMPROVEMENT = 0.0694
COEFFICIENT OF SCALABILITY = 0.2000

12 CASES WERE PROCESSED
0 (OR 0.0 PCT) WERE MISSING

2. Input Example for Program HGROUP, *Preference Data from Table 20.3.*

```
//HGROUP JOB (2919,267F,2X),'DUNN-RANKIN'
// EXEC EDSTAT,PROGRAM=HGROUP
//GO.SYSIN DD *
SAMPLE INPUT DATA IS TAKEN FROM BEGINNING OF CHAPTER 20
     6      5      1      1
(A2,8X,6F1.0)
DS        524225
HA        624327
DB        424424
BB        645336
AF        536325
/*
//
```

3. Output from Program HGROUP, *Using Paired Data of Table 20.3 as Profiles.*

```
        *** OUTPUT FROM PROGRAM HGROUP ***

SAMPLE INPUT DATA IS TAKEN FROM BEGINNING OF CHAPTER 20

PARAMETERS
COL   1- 5 =      6
COL   6-10 =      5
COL  11-15 =      1
COL  16-20 =      1
COL  21-25 =      0

 FORMAT CARD(S)


        (A2,8X,6F1.0)

  4 GROUPS AFTER COMBINING G  1 (N=  1) AND G  2 (N=  1). ERROR =    4.0659

  3 GROUPS AFTER COMBINING G  4 (N=  1) AND G  5 (N=  1). ERROR =    6.0611

  2 GROUPS AFTER COMBINING G  1 (N=  2) AND G  3 (N=  1). ERROR =    8.9927

  1 GROUPS AFTER COMBINING G  1 (N=  3) AND G  4 (N=  2). ERROR =   10.8802
G  1 (N=  5)  DS        HA        DB        BB        AF
```

4. FORTRAN *Listing for Program* HGROUP.   Required subroutines (See SUBROUTINES in this chapter.) CCDS, INPUT, RMFT, PAREN, NLOC, SINTL.

```
C
C
C
C    PROGRAM HGRCUP
C
      SUBROUTINE HGRCUP
      DIMENSION D(100,100), KG(100), W(100), KC(100), IC(100)
      COMMON D, KG, W, KC, IC, KF(80)
      REAL*8  KC, IC, KF*4
      ND = 100
    5 CALL CCDS (KF, NV, NS, KF, KS, KT, 6HHGRCUP)
      T = NS
      DO 10 I = 1,NS
      CALL INPUT (KC(I), W, I, KF, NV)
      DO 10 J = 1,NV
   10 D(I,J) = W(J)
      IF (KS .EQ. 0) GC TO 20
      DO 15 J = 1,NV
      A = SUMF(D, J, NS, ND) / T
      S = SQRT(SUMF(D, J, -NS, ND) / T - A * A)
      DO 15 I = 1,NS
   15 D(I,J) = (D(I,J) - A) / S
   20 IF (KT .EQ. 0) GC TO 30
      N = MAX0(NS, NV)
      DO 25 I = 1,N
      DO 25 J = I,N
      X = D(I,J)
      D(I,J) = D(J,I)
   25 D(J,I) = X
      NS = NV
      NV = T
   30 DO 45 I = 1,NS
      DO 35 J = 1,NV
   35 W(J) = D(I,J)
      DO 45 J = I,NS
      D(I,J) = 0.0
      DO 40 K = 1,NV
   40 D(I,J) = D(I,J) + (D(J,K) - W(K))**2
   45 D(I,J) = D(I,J) / 2.0
      DO 55 I = 1,NS
      DO 55 J = I,NS
   55 D(J,I) = 0.0
      NG = NS
      DO 60 I = 1,NS
      KG(I) = I
   60 W(I) = 1.0
   65 NG = NG - 1
      IF (NG .EQ. 0) GC TO 5
      X = 10.0**10
      DO 75 I = 1,NS
      IF (KG(I) .NE. I) GC TO 75
      DO 70 J = I,NS
      IF (I .EQ. J .CR. KG(J) .NE. J) GO TO 70
      DX = D(I,J) - D(I,I) - D(J,J)
      IF (DX .GE. X) GO TO 70
      X = DX
      L = I
      M = J
   70 CONTINUE
   75 CONTINUE
      NL = W(L)
      NM = W(M)
      PRINT 80, NG, I, NL, M, NM, X
   80 FORMAT (/ I4, 25H GROUPS AFTER COMBINING G, I3,
     1 4H (N=, I3, 7H) AND G, I3, 4H (N=, I3, 10H). ERROR =, F10.4)
      WS = W(L) + W(M)
      X = D(L,M) * WS
      Y = D(L,L) * W(L) + D(M,M) * W(M)
      D(L,L) = D(I,M)
      DO 85 I = 1,NS
      IF (KG(I) .EQ. M) KG(I) = L
   85 CONTINUE
      DO 95 I = 1,NS
```

```
      IF (I .EQ. L .CE. KG(I) .NE. I) GO TO 95
      IF (I .GT. I) GC TC 90
      OD(I,L) = (D(I,I) * (W(I) + W(L)) + D(I,M) * (W(I) + W(M))
     1 + X - Y - D(I,I) * W(I)) / (W(I) + WS)
      GO TO 95
  900 OD(L,I) = (D(L,I) * (W(I) + W(I)) + (D(M,I) + D(I,M))
     1 * (W(M) + W(I)) + X - Y - C(I,I) * W(I)) / (W(I) + WS)
   95 CONTINUE
      W(L) = WS
      IF (NG .GT. KP) GC TC 65
      DO 115 I = 1,NS
      IF (KG(I) .NE. I) GC TC 115
      L = 0
      DO 100 J = I,NS
      IF (KG(J) .NE. I) GC TC 100
      L = L + 1
      LC(L) = KC(J)
      IF (KT .EQ. 1) LC(L) = J
  100 CONTINUE
      IF (KT .EQ. 1) PRINT 105, I, I, (IC(J), J = 1,L)
  105 FORMAT (2H G, 13, 4H (N=, 13, 2H) , 25F4.0 / (14X, 25F4.0))
      IF (KT .EQ. 0) PRINT 110, I, I, (IC(J), J = 1,L)
  110 FORMAT (2H G, 13, 4B (N=, 13, 2H) , 10A9 / (14X, 10A9))
  115 CONTINUE
      GO TO 65
      END
```

5. FORTRAN *Listing for Function* SUMF, *Used with Program* HGROUP.

```
      FUNCTION SUMF (X, KK, NN, ND)
      DIMENSION X(ND,1)
      SUMF = 0.0
      N = IABS(NN)
      K = IABS(KK)
      IF (NN) 5,55,10
    5 IF (KK) 15,55,25
   10 IF (KK) 35,55,45
   15 DO 20 I = 1,N
   20 SUMF = SUMF + X(K,I)**2
      RETURN
   25 DO 30 I = 1,N
   30 SUMF = SUMF + X(I,K)**2
      RETURN
   35 DO 40 I = 1,N
   40 SUMF = SUMF + X(K,I)
      RETURN
   45 DO 50 I = 1,N
   50 SUMF = SUMF + X(I,K)
   55 RETURN
      END
```

HICLUST (Nonmetric Hierarchical Clustering)

1. Description, FORTRAN *Source, and Input Directions.*   This program was written by Stephen C. Johnson of Bell Telephone Laboratories, Murray Hill, New Jersey (Johnson, 1967). Agglomerative methods begin with N entities or taxonomic units, each its own cluster, then combine units into clusters until only one cluster exists; i.e., clustering proceeds from K = N to K = 1 clusters, where K denotes the number of clusters. In this nonmetric method, two dendrograms are constructed, one by the single linkage method (AKA: minimum connectedness and nearest neighbor), where an entity is joined to a cluster if it has a certain level of similarity with at least one member of the cluster. The other is constructed by the complete linkage method (AKA: maximum diameter and furthest neighbor), where an entity must achieve a certain level of similarity with all members of the cluster in order to join it. The single linkage method has a stronger theoretical rationale in the biological sciences; whereas, practice shows that the complete linkage method is more effective, with social science data.

FORTRAN *Source*.   Johnson's program is now part of the SAS software package of programs. The reader may be able to purchase the source from the Bell Telephone Laboratories, Murray Hill, New Jersey.

Output:

1. Two dendrograms: (a) one by the single linkage method, (b) the other by the complete linkage method. The entities are rearranged where necessary.
2. Correlation level for each clustering. This number gives the "strength" or "value" of the clustering.
3. A list of how many and which entities are clustered at the various strength levels.
4. A cluster statistic is computed. This statistic is still experimental insofar as its usefulness is concerned and is meaningless if the data has only rank order structure. However, if the data is on an interval scale and is transformed to ranks, the cluster statistic may be considered a kind of "z score" (when $n > 20$ or 30). To interpret this "z score" one can say that the proportion of clusters better than this one is less than $1/z*z$ ($z*z = z$ squared).

The data is input in the form of:

1. A full or lower triangular matrix of either distances (e.g., coefficients of alienation), or proximities (e.g., coefficients of correlation);
2. or, as an R × C raw data matrix (e.g., a subject by variable score matrix). This program clusters the column entities.

Limitations: max number of row entities (R) = 9999, and max number of entities to be clustered (C) = 100.

To cluster entities >100 and <230, see Program HICLUSTL, EXEC LIBJB, which is a revision by Jerry Brennan of the Psychology Dept., University of Hawaii. HICLUSTL constructs a dendrogram only by the complete linkage method.

Control Cards:

This program requires a parameter card, a format card, and a blank card after the data deck.

1. Parameter Card:

Columns	Description
1–3	Number of variables or objects
4–5	+1 = input is matrix of distances
	−1 = input is matrix of proximities, or raw data.
6–7	Blank or 0 = input is lower triangular matrix
	1 = input is full matrix
	2 = input is raw data
8–11	Number of subjects (only if input is raw data)

2. Format Card(s): Must have ID has first field in A format. Data in F format. There may be as many as 4 format cards.
3. Blank Card: There should be a blank card after the data deck.

3. Input Example for Program HICLUST, Averaged Data from Table 20.2.

```
//HICLUST JOB (2919,267F,150KR),'DUNN-RANKIN'
// EXEC,EDSTAT,PROGRAM=HICLUST,RG=150K
//GO.SYSIN DD *
  4 1
(4F8.2)
    5.20
    2.60    3.00
    4.60    2.20    5.40
/*
//
```

4. Output from Program HICLUST.

```
POINTS IN A CLUSTER    CLUSTER STATISTIC
-------------------    -----------------

  2 PTS.               1.2772855759

  2    4

  2 PTS.               1.0598726273

  1    3

CONNECTEDNESS METHOD
                       0  0  0  0
                       1  3  2  4

  0.21999998E 01       .  .  XXX
  0.25999994E 01       XXX XXX
  0.30000000E 01       XXXXXXX
```

```
END OF METHCD

DIAMETER METHOD
                        0  0  0  0
                        1  3  2  4


      0.21999998E 01      . .  XXX
      0.25999994E 01      XXX XXX
      0.53999996E 01      XXXXXXX


END OF METHCD


POINTS IN A CLUSTER      CLUSTER STATISTIC
-------------------      -----------------


     2 PTS.                 1.2772855759

      2   4


      2 PTS.                 1.0598726273

      1   3
```

JUDGED (Generates Interjudge Distances from Free Clustering)

1. Description and Input Directions.   This program calculates the similarity between judges following their free sorting of objects in categories. The output is a lower triangular matrix of proximities between all pairs of judges. This matrix can then be analyzed by multidimensional scaling or by clustering.

Output:

1. The matrix of free sort data consisting of group or cluster numbers for each subject is repeated in the output as a check.
2. This is followed by a matrix of interjudge distances.

Input:

Data is in the form of cluster numbers, one for each object or variable. A set of numbers is read for each subject. Maximum number of variables is 300 and subjects is 50.

Cards:

1. A variable format card is read which indicates how to read the input data cards.

2. Parameter Card:

Columns		Description
1–5	NS	The number of subjects is read.
6–10	NV	The number of variables is read.

2. Input Example for Program JUDGED, *Data from Association, Chapter 3.*

```
//JUDGED JOB (2919,267F,2X),'DUNN-RANKIN'
// EXEC EDSTAT,PROGRAM=JUDGED
//GO.SYSIN DD *
(10X,5F1.0)
     5    5
S1        11223
S2        11232
S3        11112
S4        11221
S5        13122
/*
//
```

3. Output from Program JUDGED, *Data from Associations, Chapter 3.*

```
10X,5F1.0)
     5    5
 1.00   1.00   2.00   2.00   3.00
 1.00   1.00   2.00   3.00   2.00
 1.00   1.00   1.00   1.00   2.00
 1.00   1.00   2.00   2.00   1.00
 1.00   3.00   1.00   2.C0   2.00



    2.
    4.     6.
    2.     4.     6.
    4.     4.     6.     6.
```

4. FORTRAN *Listing for Program* JUDGED.

```
C PROGRAM JUDGED
C
C     THIS IS A ROUTINE TO CALCULATE THE DIFFERENCE MATRIX
C     FOR (NS)SUBJECTS FOLLOWING THEIR FREE CLUSTERING.
      DIMENSION X(50,50), S(50,300), SUM(50,50),FMT(20)
      READ(5,901) FMT
  901 FORMAT(20A4)
      WRITE(6,901) FMT
      READ(5,900) NS,NV
  900 FORMAT(4I5)
      WRITE(6,900) NS,NV
```

```
      KNS=(NS*NS-NS)/2
      KNV=(NV*NV-NV)/2
      NS1=NS-1
      NV1=NV-1
      DO 550 I=1,NS
      DO 550 J=1,NV
      S(I,J)=0.0
  550 SUM(I,J)=0.0
      DO 500 I=1,NS
      READ(5,FMT) (X(I,J),J=1,NV)
      WRITE(6,950) (X(I,J),J=1,NV)
  950 FORMAT(20F6.2)
  500 CONTINUE
      DO 510 M=1,NS
      L=1
      DO 510 I=1,NV1
      II=I+1
      DO 510 J=II, NV
      IF (X(M,I).EQ.X(M,J)) S(M,L)=1.0
      L=L+1
  510 CONTINUE
      DO 520 M=1, NS1
      MM=M+1
      DO 520 L2=MM, NS
      DIF2=0.0
      DIF=0.0
      DO 520 KC=1, KNV
      DIF=ABS(S(M,KC)-S(L2,KC))
      DIF2 = DIF2+DIF
      SUM(M,L2)=DIF2
  520 CONTINUE
      DO 560 I=1,NS
      DO 560 J=1,NS
      SUM(J,I)=SUM(I,J)
  560 CONTINUE
      WRITE(6,970)
  970 FORMAT(1H1)
      DO 530 I=2,NS
      II=I-1
      WRITE(6,960)  (SUM(I,J),J=1,II)
  960 FORMAT(1X,20F6.0)
  530 CONTINUE
      STOP
      END
```

KENTAU (Calculates Kendall's Tau)

1. Description and Input Directions. This program was written by Bob Bloedon and Ruth Norton at the Education Research and Development Center, University of Hawaii. It computes a matrix of Kendall's tau, a coefficient of rank correlation.

Output:

1. A matrix, the lower triangle of which consists of Kendall's taus, and the upper triangle of which consists of S's. Kendall's coefficients of rank correlation, tau, is defined as the value of the measure of disarray, S, divided by its maximum possible value, i.e.,

$$tau = \frac{S}{(N(N-1)/2)}$$

where N = number of objects ranked, and S = the measure of disarray. S, the measure of disarray, is defined as the maximum number of rank comparisons minus twice the number of inversions, i.e.,

$$S = N(N - 1)/2 - 2I$$

where, I = number of rank inversions.

2. S is used to reference the significance of the obtained taus. Significance at the .05 and .01 levels are indicated by asterisks in the matrix.

Input:

Data is in the form of scores or ranks for each variable by each subject. If, for example, there were 5 variables (scores or ranks) by 20 subjects, the input would be a 20 × 5 matrix.

Limitations: max number of subjects = 200, and max number of variables = 50.

Control Cards:

A parameter and variable format card are required.

1. Parameter Card:

Columns	Description
1–4	Number of subjects
5–8	Number of variables

2. Variable Format Card: Data is read in F format with no ID field.

2. *Input Example for* KENTAU, *Profile Data from Chapter 3, Page 46.*

```
//KENTAU JOB (2919,267F,2X),'DUNN-RANKIN'
// EXEC EDSTAT,PROGRAM=KENTAU
//GO.SYSIN DD *
    6    4
(10X,4F1.0)
01        8684
02        5251
03        9444
04        6543
05        8276
06        5343
/*
//
```

3. *Output from* KENTAU, *Profile Data from Chapter 3, Page 46.*

KENDALL'S TAU CORRELATION MATRIX

	1	2	3	4
1	0.0	4.0000	0.0	11.0000
2	0.2965	0.0	0.0	3.0000
3	0.0	0.0	0.0	3.0000
4	0.8462*	0.2224	0.2402	0.0

* SIGNIFICANT AT THE .05 LEVEL

** SIGNIFICANT AT THE .01 LEVEL

S IN UPPER TRIANGULAR MATRIX

TAU IN LOWER TRIANGULAR MATRIX

4. FORTRAN *Listing for* KENTAU.   Required subroutines (See SUBROU-
TINES in this chapter) RFMT, PAREN.

```
C
      DIMENSION C(200,50),CORR(50,50),A(200),T(200),B(200)
      DIMENSION FMT(200),SIG(11),ZT1(121),ZT5(121)
      DATA ZT5/6.314,2.92,2.353,2.132,2.015,1.943,1.895,1.86,1.833,1.812
     1,1.796,1.782,1.771,1.761,1.753,1.746,1.74,1.734,1.729,1.725,1.721,
     21.717,1.714,1.711,1.708,1.706,1.703,1.701,1.699,1.697,1.695,1.693,
     31.692,1.691,1.690,1.689,1.688,1.686,1.685,1.684,2*1.682,2*1.68,2*1
     4.678,2*1.676,3*1.674,4*1.673,3*1.672,2*1.671,10*1.668,10*1.666,10*
     51.664,10*1.662,10*1.66,10*1.658,1.645/
      DATA ZT1/31.821,6.965,4.541,3.747,3.365,3.143,2.998,2.896,2.821,2.
     1764,2.718,2.681,2.65,2.624,2.602,2.583,2.567,2.552,2.539,2.528,2.5
     218,2.508,2.5,2.492,2.485,2.479,2.473,2.467,2.462,2.457,2.453,2.449
     3,2.445,2.441,2.437,2.434,2.43,2.428,2.426,2.423,2.42,2.418,2.415,2
     4*2.412,3*2.41,3*2.407,2*2.405,3*2.4,1*2.397,2.393,2.390,10*2.384,1
     50*2.378,10*2.373,10*2.368,10*2.363,10*2.358,2.326/
   98 M=0
      X=0.
      Y=0.
      KOUNT1=0
      KOUNT2=0
      L=0
      IX=0
      IY=0
      IZ=0
      K=0
  110 FORMAT (2I4)
  130 FORMAT (20A4)
      READ (5,110,END=99)  N, NV
      CALL RFMT(FMT,10)
   72 NP=N-1
      IF (NP.GT.120) NP=121
      Z5=ZT5(NP)
      Z1=ZT1(NP)
      CALL MCHARS(1H ,1,SIG,1,1)
      ZX=N *(N -1)*(2*N +5)
      ZX=SQRT (ZX/18.)
      DO 25 I=1,NV
   25 CORR (I,I)=0.
      NV2=NV-1
      DO 5 I=1,N
    5 READ (5,FMT) (C(I,J),J=1,NV)
      DO 700 IX=1,NV2
      IZ=IX+1
      DO 700 IY=IZ,NV
      CALL RANK(C(1,IX),A,N)
      CALL RANK(C(1,IY),B,N)
      CALL SORT (A,N,B,DUM,DUM,1,1)
      J=I
      KOUNT1=0
      KOUNT2=0
      DO 7 J=1,N
      DO 7 I=J,N
      IF (B(J)-B(I))  6,7,8
    6 KOUNT1=KOUNT1+1
      GO TO 7
    8 KOUNT2=KOUNT2+1
    7 CONTINUE
      S=KOUNT1-KOUNT2
   18 K=1
      L=0
      M=M+1
      NO=N/2
      DO 3 I=1,NO
    3 T(I)=0.
      DO 13 I=1,N
```

```
         IF (I .EQ. N) GO TO 17
         IF (A(I) .EQ. A(I+1)) GO TO 12
         IF (I .EQ. 1) GO TO 13
   17    IF (A(I) .EQ. A(I-1)) GO TO 14
         GO TO 13
   12    K=K+1
         GO TO 13
   14    L=L+1
         T(L)=K
         K=1
         IF (I .EQ. N) GO TO 15
   13    CONTINUE
   15    IF (M .EQ. 2) GO TO 19
         X=0.
         Y=0.
         DO 16 I=1,L
   16    X=X+T(I)*(T(I)-1.)
         X=X/2.
         CALL SORT (B,N,DUM,DUM,DUM,0,1)
         DO 20 I=1,N
   20    A(I)=B(I)
         GO TO 18
   19    DO 21 I=1,L
   21    Y=Y+T(I)*(T(I)-1.)
         Y=Y/2.
         M=0
         RN=N
         RN=(RN*(RN-1.))/2.0
         TAU=S/SQRT((RN-X)*(RN-Y))
         CORR (IY,IX)=TAU
  700    CORR (IX,IY)=S
  140    FORMAT (1H1,50X,'KENDALL''S TAU CORRELATION MATRIX')
  150    FORMAT (1H0,20X,10I10)
  190    FORMAT (//20X,100('-'))
  160    FORMAT (1H0,18X,I2,10F10.4)
         DO 30 KK=1,NV,10
         WRITE (6,140)
         WRITE (6,190)
         K2=KK+9
         IF (K2.GT.NV) K2=NV
         WRITE (6,150) (J,J=KK,K2)
         DO 31 I=1,NV
         CALL MCHARS (SIG,1,SIG,2,43)
         IJ=1
         DO 40 J=KK,K2
         IJ=IJ+4
         IF(I.LE.J)GO TO 40
         ZY=ABS(CORR(J,I)/ZX)
         IF(ZY.LE.Z5)GO TO 40
         IF(ZY.GT.Z1) CALL MCHARS (2H**,1,SIG,IJ,2)
         IF(ZY.LE.Z1)CALL MCHARS (1H*,1,SIG,IJ,1)
   40    CONTINUE
         WRITE(6,160) I,(CORR(I,J),J=KK,K2)
   31    WRITE(6,161) SIG
         WRITE (6,190)
  161    FORMAT(1H+,A4,18X,10(8X,A2))
  170    FORMAT(//24X,'*  SIGNIFICANT AT THE .05 LEVEL',25X,'S IN UPPER TRI
        1ANGULAR MATRIX')
  180    FORMAT(//23X,'**  SIGNIFICANT AT THE .01 LEVEL',25X,'TAU IN LOWER
        1TRIANGULAR MATRIX')
         WRITE (6,170)
         WRITE (6,180)
   30    CONTINUE
    9    FORMAT (1H1)
         GO TO 98
         WRITE (6,9)
   99    STOP
         END
```

5. *Assembly Language Listing for Subroutine* MCHARS, *Used Only with Program* KENTAU.

```
          ENTRY MCHARS
MCHARS    SAVE  (14,12),,*
          LR    12,15
          USING MCHARS,12
          ST    13,SA+4
          LR    2,13
          LA    13,SA
          ST    13,8(2)
          L     2,0(1)
          L     3,4(1)
          L     3,0(3)
          S     3,ONE
          AR    2,3
          L     4,8(1)
          L     3,12(1)
          L     3,0(3)
          S     3,ONE
          AR    4,3
          L     3,16(1)
          L     3,0(3)
          S     3,ONE
          EX    3,MOVE
          L     13,SA+4
          LM    14,12,12(13)
          BR    14
MOVE      MVC   0(0,4),0(2)
SA        DS    9D
ONE       DC    F'1'
          END
```

6. FORTRAN *Listing for Subroutine* RANK.

```
C A IS INPUT VECTOR, B IS OUTPUT VECTOR, N IS NO OF VALUES
      SUBROUTINE RANK (A,B,N)
      DIMENSION A(1), B(1)
      DO 10 I=1,N
10    B(I)=0.0
      DO 900 I=1,N
      IF (B(I).GT.0.0) GO TO 100
20    LOW=0.0
      SAME=0.0
      T=A(I)
      DO 50 K=1,N
      IF (A(K)-T) 30,40,50
30    LOW = LOW+1.0
      GO TO 50
40    SAME = SAME+1.0
      B(K)=-1.0
50    CONTINUE
      IF (SAME .GT. 1.0) GO TO 70
60    B(I)=LOW+1.0
      GO TO 100
70    W=LOW+(SAME + 1.0)*0.5
      DO 90 K=1,N
      S=B(K)+1.0
      IF(S .NE. 0.0) GO TO 90
80    B(K)=W
90    CONTINUE
900   CONTINUE
      RETURN
      END
```

7. FORTRAN Listing for Subroutine SORT. *(Copyright, Association for Computing Machinery, Inc., by permission.)*

```
          SUBROUTINE SORT (A, N, B, C, D, K, SWITCH )
C
C         THIS ROUTINE SORTS INPUT ARRAY 'A' AND REARRANGES, OPTIONALLY,
C         ARRAYS 'B', 'C', AND 'D', IN ORDER CORRESPONDING TO 'A'.
C         N = NUMBER OF ITEMS IN 'A' (AND 'B', 'C', 'D', IF USED)
C         K = 0--SORT 'A' ONLY, 1--REARRANGE 'B', 2--REARRANGE 'B' AND 'C',
C             3--REARRANGE 'B', 'C', AND 'D'.
C         IF 'SWITCH' IS POSITIVE, SORT WILL BE IN ASCENDING ORDER,
C                      IF ZERO OR NEGATIVE, IN DESCENDING ORDER.
C         ALGORITHM FROM CACM, JULY 1959, PAGE 30 BY D. L. SHELL
C
          DIMENSION A(1),B(1),C(1),D(1)
          INTEGER   SWITCH
    105   KP1=K+1
          IF(N.LE.1) GO TO 999
          M = 1
    106   M = M + M
          IF( M .LE. N ) GO TO 106
          M = M - 1
    994       M = M/2
          IF(M.EQ.0) GO TO 999
          KK = N-M
          J = 1
    992   I = J
    996   IM = I + M
          IF(SWITCH)   810,810,800
    800    IF(A(I).GT.A(IM)) GO TO 110
          GO TO 995
    810   IF(A(I).LT.A(IM))  GO TO 110
    995    J = J+1
          IF(J.GT.KK)   GO TO 994
          GO TO 992
    110   TEMP=A(I)
          A(I) = A(IM)
          A(IM) = TEMP
          GO TO ( 140, 130, 120, 115), KP1
    115   TEMP = D(I)
          D(I) = D(IM)
          D(IM) = TEMP
    120   TEMP=C(I)
          C(I) = C(IM)
          C(IM) = TEMP
    130   TEMP=B(I)
          B(I) = B(IM)
          B(IM) = TEMP
    140       I = I-M
          IF(I.LT.1)   GO TO 995
          GO TO 996
    999    RETURN
          END
```

KYST-2 (Kruskal-Young-Shepard-Torgerson MDS)

1. Description and FORTRAN *Source.*   KYST-2 is the latest version of the multidimensional program made popular by Kruskal (1964a). A Fortran listing for this program can be obtained from the Bell Telephone Laboratory, Murray Hill, N.J. The KYST manual should also be purchased. The directions for input are much too extensive to detail here. An Input and Output example is provided, however, so the reader can obtain some understanding for the program. A similar program is Guttman-Lingoes Smallest Space Analysis (SSA) (Lingoes, 1970). Forest Young also has a general program that performs multidimensional scaling (ALSCAL) which is part of 1980 SAS Software system.

2. Input Example for Program KYST, *Data Are Averaged (by* AVELOMAT) *from Table 20.2.*

```
//KYST JOB (2917,267F,200KR), 'DUNN-RANKIN'
// EXEC EDSTAT,PROGRAM=KYST,RG=200K
//GO.FT08F001 DD DSN=&&CCACT,DISP=NEW,UNIT=S:SVIO,SPACE=(TRK,(1,1)),
// DCB=(RECFM=FB,LRECL=81,BLKSIZE=8100)
//GO.SYSIN DD *
TORSCA
PRE-ITERATIONS=1
DIMMAX=2,DIMMIN=2
COORDINATES=ROTATE
ITERATIONS=15
REGRESSION=ASCENDING
DATA,LOWERHALFMATRIX,DIAGONAL=ABSENT
 KYST TEST USING AVERAGE DATA FROM TABLE 20.1 VIA AVELOMAT
   4   1   1
(4F8.2)
     5.20
     2.60      3.00
     4.60      2.20      5.40
COMPUTE
STOP
/*
//
```

3. Output from Program KYST, *Averaged Data from Table 20.2, via* AVELOMAT.

LOMAT (Generates Lower Triangular Matrices)

1. Description and Input Directions.   This program is an auxiliary program to create the lower triangular matrices which are input into programs such as SINDSCAL.

Output:

The program generates sets of lower triangular matrices, one for each subject. The matrices contain similarity scores for each subject. The data are punched on cards.

Output from Program KYST

```
KYST TEST USING AVERAGE DATA FROM TABLE 20.1 VIA AVELOMAI

INITIAL CONFIGURATION COMPUTATION.  NO. PTS.= 4   DIM= 2

   PRE-ITERATION   STRESS

        0            0.0

THE BEST INITIAL CONFIGURATION OF   4 POINTS IN  2 DIMENSIONS HAS STRESS  0.0   FORMULA 1

HISTORY OF COMPUTATION. N= 4.      THERE ARE    6  DATA VALUES, SPLIT INTO   1  LISTS.

ITERATION STRESS  SRAT  SRATAV CAGRGL COSAV  ACSAV   SFGR    STEP
    0      0.0    0.0   0.800   0.0    0.0    0.0    2.0000   0.0

ZERO STRESS WAS REACHED

THE FINAL CONFIGURATION HAS BEEN ROTATED TO PRINCIPAL COMPONENTS.

THE FINAL CONFIGURATION OF   4 POINTS IN  2 DIMENSIONS HAS STRESS  0.0   FORMULA 1

LABEL FOR CONFIGURATION PLOTS          FINAL CONFIGURATION
                                         1        2
            A                    1    -0.860    0.622
            B                    2     0.646   -0.588
            C                    3    -0.770   -0.540
            D                    4    -0.984    0.507

DATA GROUP(S)

SERIAL  COUNT  STRESS  REGRESSION COEFFICIENTS  (FROM DEGREE 0 TO MAX OF 4)
   1      6     0.0    ASCENDING
```

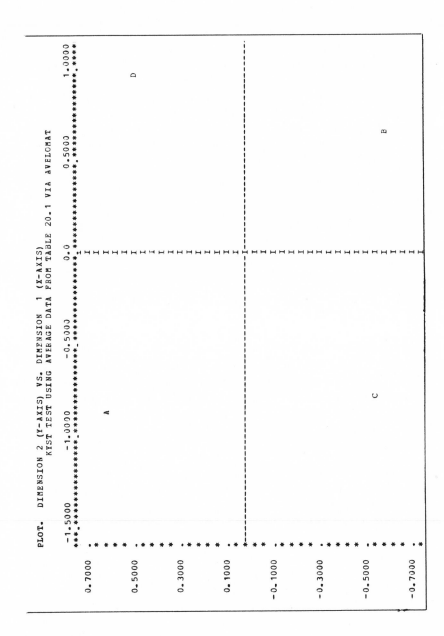

PLOT. DIMENSION 2 (Y-AXIS) VS. DIMENSION 1 (X-AXIS)
KYST TEST USING AVERAGE DATA FROM TABLE 20.1 VIA AVLCMAT

301

Input:

The data is input in the form of scores relating two paired objects.

1. Control Cards:

	Columns	Description
Card 1	1–2	Number of variables

2. Format Card: Variable format for raw data (no ID field is used).
3. Key Card(s): Number of pair objects are listed in columns 1–80, four columns per pair, two columns for each number. For example 0102, 0813, 0702, 1104, etc. . . . .

Data:

Each subject's responses are read separately. A card(s) for each subject.

2. Input for Program LOMAT, *Data Are Similarities in Table 20.2.*

```
//LOMAT JOB (2919,267F,2X),'DUNN-RANKIN'
// EXEC EDSTAT,PROGRAM=LOMAT
//GO.SYSIN DD *
  4
(10X,6F1.0)
010201030104020302040304
DS          524225
HA          624327
DB          424424
BB          645336
AF          536325
/*
//
```

3. Output from Program LOMAT, *Similarity Data from Table 20.2.*

```
5.00
2.00    2.00
4.00    2.00    5.00
6.00
2.00    3.00
4.00    2.00    7.00
4.00
2.00    4.00
4.00    2.00    4.00
6.00
4.00    3.00
5.00    3.00    6.00
5.00
3.00    3.00
6.00    2.00    5.00
```

4. FORTRAN Listing for Program LOMAT.

```
C
C PROGRAM LOMAT
C
C               THIS IS A   ROUTINE TO GENERATE INDIVIDUAL LOWER TRIANGULAR
C               MATRICES OF SIMILARITIES FROM PAIR COMPARISON DATA.
C
C               CARD 1:   N(NO. OF VAR.) IN COL. 1-2.
C               CARD 2:   FORMAT FOR RAW DATA
C               CARD(S) 3:   KEY PAIRS ARE READ IN (40I2).
C               DATA CARDS FOLLOW
C               THEN EACH SUBJECTS RESPONSES ARE FORMED
C               IN A MATRIX SEPARATELY
C
        DIMENSION IKEY (500), JKEY(500),S(30,30),FMT(20), X(500)
        READ (5,900,END=99) N
 900 FORMAT (I2)
        READ (5,905) FMT
        NP=N*(N-1)/2
 905 FORMAT (20A4)
        READ (5,910) (IKEY(I),JKEY(I),I=1,NP)
 910 FORMAT (40I2)
  20 READ (5,FMT) (X(I), I=1,NP)
        DO 600 I=1,NP
        IK=IKEY(I)
        JK=JKEY(I)
        IF (IK.LT.JK) GO TO 600
        ITEMP=JK
        JK=IK
        IK=ITEMP
 600 S(JK,IK) = X(I)
        DO 510 I=2,N
        JS= I - 1
        WRITE (6,930) (S(I,J), J=1,JS)
 930 FORMAT (1X,12F6.2)
        PUNCH 940, (S(I,J), J=1,JS)
 940 FORMAT (12F6.2)
 510 CONTINUE
        GO TO 20
  99 STOP
        END
```

LRGHWH (Large Group Divisive Clustering)

1. Description and Input Directions.   This program was designed by Nigel Howard, programmed by Colin Wordley and modified by Frank Carmone, Computer Program Publishing Company, Malvern, Pa. in 1973. Hierarchical divisive methods start with all entities belonging to one cluster. The cluster is subdivided, then one of these clusters is subdivided, etc.; i.e., the number of clusters proceeds from K = 1 to K = N, or a user-specified number of clusters. LRGHWH superimposes a hierarchical divisive algorithm onto a basic iterative K-means method. The data set is initially partitioned by selection of the entity with the largest variance. The mean of this entity is used as a criterion; all entities with higher means are placed in one cluster, those with lower means in another. A K-means iterative solution is used to stabilize the cluster; that is, the entities are shifted from cluster to cluster until the minimum variance criterion is satisfied. Next the entity in the two clusters with the largest variance is found and that cluster is subdivided at the mean, followed by a K-means iterative pass for a three-cluster solution. The process is repeated until all entities are assigned to the cluster with the nearest centroid.

Following the initial analysis, this program can also do further analyses.

Output:

1. An N × P raw data matrix, with P means and variances.
2. Cluster information: from the first split to the split with the maximum number of groups. For each split, the number of clusters, and their members is given.
3. Cluster summary information: for each number of clusters the cluster membership is given.

Input:

The data is input in the form of an R × C matrix of raw data (e.g., subject by variable score matrix, or observation by object matrix). This program clusters the row entities of the matrix, hence for a subject by variable (R × C) matrix, the taxonomic unit or entity to be clustered will be the subjects not the variables.

Limitations: max number of entities to be clustered = 2000, and max number of variables = 20

1. Title Card: Any alphanumeric title; up to 80 columns may be used.
2. Parameter Card:

Columns	Description
1–5	Max number of groups
6–10	Number of column entities (C)
11–15	Number of entities to be clustered (R)
20	0 = standardize data
	1 = do not standardize data
25	Input tape number
	5 = input on cards
30	1 = read in scaling factors for each variable
	0 = do not read in factors; set = 1.00.

3. Parameter Card (optional): SC(I) = scaling factor for variable 'I', in 16F5.0 format.
4. Variable Card Format: Data should be in F format.
5. Data Cards: Data in format specified on the variable format card.
6. Further Analyses: Repeat control cards and data deck as often as required.

2. *Input Example for Divisive Clustering, Data Are Distances from Chapter 3.*

```
//LRGHWH JOB (2919,267F),'DUNN-RANKIN'
// EXEC EDSTAT,PROGRAM=LRGHWH
//GO.FT02F001    DD    UNIT=SYSDA,DISP=(,DELETE),SPACE=(TRK,(1,1)),
// DCB=(RECFM=VBS,LRECL=3600,BLKSIZE=7204)
//GO.SYSIN DD *
 EXAMPLE FOR DIVISIVE CLUSTERING, DISTANCE DATA FROM CHAPTER 3
    4    6    4    1    5
(10X,6F1.0)
A        859685
B        624523
C        854474
D        414363
/*
//
```

3. *Output from* LRGHWH, *Distance Data from Chapter 3.*

```
              EXAMPLE FOR DIVISIVE CLUSTERING, DISTANCE DATA FROM CHAPTER 3

NO OF OBSERVATIONS OR CASES        4
NO OF VARIABLES PER CASE           6
MAX NO OF CLUSTERS                 4
 FORMAT (10X,6F1.0)

INPUT TAPE NO.    5

SCORE WEIGHTS 1.00 1.00 1.00 1.00 1.00 1.00



                    RAW DATA--MEANS--VARIANCES

      1     2     3     4     5     6
 1  8.00  5.00  9.00  6.00  8.00  5.00
 2  6.00  2.00  4.00  5.00  2.00  3.00
 3  8.00  5.00  4.00  4.00  7.00  4.00
 4  4.00  1.00  4.00  3.00  6.00  3.00


    6.50  3.25  5.25  4.50  5.75  3.75



                    STANDARDIZED   DATA


      1     2     3     4     5     6


    1.66  1.79  2.17  1.12  2.28  0.83


    SPLIT NO.    1
```

```
              GROUP NO.      1
      2    4

              GROUP NO       2
      1    3

NO. IN EACH GROUP
              2           2


        SPLIT NO.     2


              GROUP NO       1
      2    4

              GROUP NO       2
      3

              GROUP NO       3
      1

NO. IN EACH GROUP
              2           1           1


        SPLIT NO.     3


              GROUP NO       1
      2

              GROUP NO       2
      3

              GROUP NO       3
      1

              GROUP NO       4
      4

NO  IN EACH GROUP
              1           1           1           1



    EXAMPLE FOR DIVISIVE CLUSTERING, DISTANCE DATA FROM CHAPTER 3
```

```
        2     3     4
  1     2     3     3
  2     1     1     1
  3     2     2     2
  4     1     1     4
```

FINISHED PROCESSING

4. FORTRAN *Listing for Program* LRGHWH.

```
C           NOTE  REPEAT CONTROL CARDS AND DATA DECK AS OFTEN AS REQUIRED.
C
C     *****************************************************************
C **** ONE SCRATCH FILE ON LOGICAL UNIT 2 IS USED. ****
C
      DIMENSION IVAR(800,20)
C     DIMENSION VAR(500,20),          MTG(2000),UUS(2000) ,
      DIMENSION VAR(800,20),          MTG(2000),UUS(2000) ,
     1 SC (20), GWT (30), AVS (30), NTR (30), UX (30),GSS(30),PXY(30),
     2 GMV(30,20),GSV(30,20),FMT(20) ,   TITLE(20)
      EQUIVALENCE (VAR(1,1), IVAR(1,1))
      COMMON NM, NK, NP, VAR, TW, MTG, UUS, SC, GWT, AVS,
     1 NTR, UX,         GSS, PXY,      GMV, GSV
   40 CONTINUE
      READ(5,15,END=50)  TITLE,NP,NK,NM,IS , INTP, ISC
      WRITE(6,11111)
11111 FORMAT('1'///
     1T40,'LARGE HOWARD HARRIS CLUSTERING PROGRAM'/
     1T40,'        THIS VERSION BY C.P.P.C.'/
     1T40,'           JULY 9, 1973'//)
   15 FORMAT(20A4/6I5)
      DO 71 I=1,NK
      SC(I) = 1.0
   71 CONTINUE
      IF (ISC.EQ.0) G O TO 70
      READ(5,16)       (SC(I),I=1,NK)
   16 FORMAT(16F5.0)
   70 CONTINUE
   72 CONTINUE
      READ(5,17)  FMT
   17 FORMAT(20A4)
      TOL=0.0
      WRITE(6,19)  TITLE,NM,NK,NP, FMT
   19 FORMAT(   30X,  'HOWARD-TYPE CLUSTERING ...PROGRAMMED BY WORDLEY
     1AND MODIFIED BY CARMONE'//10X,20A4//,
     1                          ' NO OF OBSERVATIONS OR CASES',I10/' NO OF V
     1ARIABLES PER CASE',I13/' MAX NO OF CLUSTERS',I19,/'  FORMAT ',
     120A4)
      IF(INTP .EQ. 0) INTP = 5
      WRITE(6,21) INTP, (SC(I),I=1,NK)
   21 FORMAT(/' INPUT TAPE NO.',I5//' SCORE WEIGHTS',20F5. 2)
      DO 90 I=1,NM
   90 READ(INTP,FMT) (VAR(I,J),J=1,NK)
      CALL STD(IS)
      CALL HOW3(TOL,LNN)
      REWIND 2
      NPM1 = NP - 1
      DO 20 J=1,NPM1
      READ(2) (IVAR(I,J),I=1,NM)
   20 CONTINUE
      WRITE(7,15)  TITLE
      WRITE(6,200)  TITLE, (L,L=2,NP)
  200 FORMAT(1H1, 20A4//5X,23I5)
      DO 30 I=1,NM
      WRITE(6,210) I, (IVAR(I,J),J=1,NPM1)
```

```
  210  FORMAT(I5, 23I5)
       WRITE(7,210) I, (IVAR(I,J),J=1,NPM1)
   30  CONTINUE
       GO TO 40
   50  CONTINUE
       WRITE(6,220)
  220  FORMAT(//'  FINISHED PROCESSING')
       STOP
       END
       SUBROUTINE HOW3(TOL,LNN)
C  HOW3 - SUBROUTINE TO SPLIT UNIVERSE INTO GROUPS
C
       DIMENSION IGRPS(800)
       DIMENSION VAR(800,20),           MTG(2000),UUS(2000) ,
      1 SC (20), GWT (30), AVS (30), NTR (30), UX (30),GSS(30),PXY(30),
      2 GMV(30,20),GSV(30,20)
C
       COMMON NM, NK, NP, VAR, TW, MTG, UUS, SC, GWT, AVS,
      1 NTR, UX,       GSS, PXY,       GMV, GSV
       IF (NM-1) 181, 181, 10
C  INITIALIZATION OF PROGRAM AND ARRAYS.
   10  NPM = NP - 1
C  CLEAR ALL WORKING ARRAYS.
C      CALL CLEAR(GMV,600,GSV,600,PXY,30,UUS,NM,GWT,
C     1 NP,AVS,NP,GSS,NP,NTR,NP)
       MGM = 30
       MGP = 20
       DO 11 I=1,MGM
       GWT(I) = 0.0
       AVS(I) = 0.0
       NTR(I) = 0
       GSS(I) = 0.0
       PXY(I) = 0.0
       DO 11 J=1,MGP
       GMV(I,J) = 0.0
       GSV(I,J) = 0.0
   11  CONTINUE
       DO 12 I=1,NM
       UUS(I) = 0.0
   12  CONTINUE
C  SCALE AND WEIGHT VARIABLES, FORM SUMS.
       DO 40 M = 1, NM
C  SUM OBSERVATION WEIGHTS INTO GROUPS 1
   29  GWT (1) = GWT (1) + 1.0
       DO 30 K = 1, NK
C  SCALE VARIABLES AND WEIGHT
       VAR (M, K) = VAR (M, K) * SC (K)
C  GET VARIABLE SUMS
       GMV (1, K) = GMV (1, K) + VAR (M, K)
C  GET SUMS OF SQUARES
       XSQ = VAR (M, K) ** 2
       GSV (1, K) = GSV (1, K) + XSQ
C  GET OBSERVATION VECTOR LENGTHS
   30  UUS (M) = UUS (M) + XSQ
C  GET GROUP VARIANCE FOR GROUP 1
       AVS (1) = AVS (1) + UUS (M)
C  ASSIGN ALL OBSERVATIONS TO GROUP 1
       MTG (M) = 1
   40  CONTINUE
C  GET STARTING VALUE FOR PXY (1, 1)
       DO 50 K = 1, NK
   50  PXY(1)=PXY(1)+GMV(1,K)**2
C  SET OBSERVATION COUNT FOR GROUP 1
       NTR (1) = NM
       GSS(1)=AVS(1)-PXY(1)/GWT(1)
C
C  INITIATE GRAND LOOP OVER REQUIRED NUMBER OF SPLITS
C
       DO 180 LL = 1, NPM
       LN = LL + 1
```

```
C   SEARCH FOR BEST GROUP TO SPLIT, LARGEST GROUP VARIANCE GT 0.
        S = 0.0
        LA = 0
        DO 60 L = 1, LL
        IF (NTR(L) - 1) 60, 60, 51
     51 ST=AVS(L)-PXY(L)/GWT(L)
        IF (ST - S) 60, 60, 52
     52 S = ST
        LA = L
     60 CONTINUE
C   IF ALL GROUP VARIANCES ZERO, EXIT
        IF (LA) 182,182, 61
C   SEARCH FOR BEST VARIABLE TO GOVERN SPLIT, GREATEST VARIANCE
     61 S = 0.0
        KA = 0
        DO 70 K = 1, NK
        ST = GSV (LA, K) - GMV (LA, K) ** 2 / GWT (LA)
        IF (ST - S) 70, 70, 62
     62 S = ST
        KA = K
     70 CONTINUE
C   CALCULATE MEAN OF VARIABLE KA THIS GROUP, AS CRITERION
        AM = GMV (LA, KA) / GWT (LA)
C   SPLIT GROUP LA INTO GROUP LN ON VARIABLE KA
        DO 80 M = 1, NM
        IF (MTG (M) - LA) 80, 71, 80
     71 CONTINUE
     72 IF (VAR (M, KA)          - AM) 80, 80, 73
     73 UX(LA)=0.0
        UX(LN)=0.0
        DO 75 K=1,NK
        UX(LA)=UX(LA)+VAR(M,K)*GMV(LA,K)
     75 UX(LN)=UX(LN)+VAR(M,K)*GMV(LN,K)
        UX(LA)=2.0*UX(LA)
        UX(LN)=2.0*UX(LN)
        CALL ADJ3(LA,LN,IN,M)
     80 CONTINUE
C
C   OPTIMIZE OVER ALL OBSERVATIONS, THIS SPLIT
C
        DO 160 IT=1,10
        IFLAG = 0
C   INITIATE LOOP OVER ALL OBSERVATIONS
        DO 150 M = 1, NM
    101 LA = MTG (M)
        IF (NTR (LA) -1) 150, 150, 102
C   CALCULATE VECTOR PRODUCT FOR OBSERVATION AND PARENT GROUP.
    102 UX(LA)=0.0
        DO 110 K=1,NK
    110 UX (LA) = UX (LA) + VAR (M, K) * GMV (LA, K)
        UX (LA) = 2.0 * UX (LA)
        RW =  1.0  / GWT (LA)
        DISA=(PXY(LA)*RW+UUS(M)/RW-UX(LA))/(GWT(LA)- 1.0 )
        D = 0.0
        LB = 0
C   SCAN ALL OTHER GROUPS FOR POSSIBLE TRANSFER.
        DO 130 L = 1, LN
        IF (L - LA) 111, 130, 111
    111 BW = GWT (L) +  1.0
        UX (L) = 0.0
        DO 115 K = 1, NK
    115 UX (L) = UX (L) + VAR (M, K) * GMV (L, K)
        UX (L) = 2.0 * UX (L)
        RW =  1.0  / GWT (L)
        DISB=(PXY(L)*RW+UUS(M)/RW-UX(L))/BW
        DIS = DISA - DISB
        IF (D - DIS) 116, 130, 130
    116 D = DIS
        LB = L
    130 CONTINUE
```

```
C   IF TRANSFER IS FINALLY ALLOWED, PERMIT IT.
        IF (LB) 150, 150, 131
    131 CALL ADJ3(LA,LB,LN,M)
        IFLAG = 1
    150  CONTINUE
        IF (IFLAG) 162, 162, 160
    160  CONTINUE
    162 CONTINUE
C   ********CODING TO BE INSERTED FOR OUTPUT****************
C   ***************(**************
        WRITE(6,900) LL
    900  FORMAT(1H1,5X, 'SPLIT NO.', I5/ )
        DO 801 K=1,LN
        WRITE(6,910) K
    910  FORMAT(//10X,'GROUP NO.', I5/)
        L = 1
        DO 802 M=1,NM
        IF(MTG(M) .NE. K) GO TO 802
        IGRPS(L) = M
        L = L + 1
    802  CONTINUE
        LZ1 = L - 1
        WRITE(6,920) (IGRPS(I),I=1,LZ1)
    920  FORMAT(1X, 23I5)
    801  CONTINUE
        WRITE(2) (MTG(L),L=1,NM)
C       WRITE(6,902) ((GMV(L,K),K=1,NK),L=1,LN)
C       WRITE(6,902) ((GSV(L,K),K=1,NK),L=1,LN)
C       WRITE(6,902) (GWT(L),L=1,LN)
    902  FORMAT(1H0,/,(1X,10F12.0))
        WRITE(6,906) (NTR(L),L=1,LN)
    906  FORMAT( //' NO. IN EACH GROUP '/(1X,10I10))
C   OUTPUT CURRENT LIST OF OBS. MEMBERSHIP IN GROUPS
        DO 165 L = 1, LN
    165 GSS(LN)=GSS(LN)+AVS(L)-PXY(L)   /GWT(L)
    180  CONTINUE
        GO TO 183
    181 MTG (1) = 1
        GWT (1) = 1.0
        PXY(1)=0.0
        LN = 2
    182 LN = LN - 1
    183 CONTINUE
C   183 PRINT OUT FINAL SUMMARY OF RUN AND RETURN
C       WRITE(6,902) (GSS(L),L=1,LN)
        LNN = LN
        RETURN
        END
        SUBROUTINE ADJ3(IAA,LBB,LNN,JJ)
C   SUBROUTINE TO ADJUST ARRAYS WHEN ONE OBSERVATION (JJ)
C   IS TRANSFERRED FROM GROUP LAA TO GROUP LBB
        DIMENSION VAR(800,20),        MTG(2000),UUS(2000) ,
       1 SC (20), GWT (30), AVS (30), NTR (30), UX (30),GSS(30),PXY(30),
       2 GMV(30,20),GSV(30,20)
C
        COMMON NM, NK, NP, VAR, TW, MTG, UUS, SC, GWT, AVS,
       1 NTR,UX,GSS,PXY,GMV,GSV
C
        LA = LAA
        LB = LBB
        LN = LNN
        J = JJ
C   ADJUST WEIGHTS, VARIANCES, COUNTS, ASSIGNMENTS
        GWT (LA) = GWT (LA) - 1.0
        GWT (LB) = GWT (LB) + 1.0
        AVS (LA) = AVS (LA) - UUS (J)
        AVS (LB) = AVS (LB) + UUS (J)
        NTR (LA) = NTR (LA) - 1
        NTR (LB) = NTR (LB) + 1
        MTG (J) = LB
```

```
C   ADJUST ARRAYS OF GROUP MEANS AND VARIANCES BY VARIABLES
        DO 20 K = 1, NK
        XSQ = VAR (J, K) ** 2
        GMV (LA, K) = GMV (LA, K) - VAR (J, K)
        GMV (LB, K) = GMV (LB, K) + VAR (J, K)
        GSV (LA, K) = GSV (LA, K) - XSQ
 20     GSV (LB, K) = GSV (LB, K) + XSQ
C   UPDATE MATRICES OF GROUP MEAN CROSS-PRODUCTS AND
C   INTERGROUP DISTANCES
        PXY (LA) =PXY (LA) +UUS (J) -UX (LA)
        PXY (LB) =PXY (LB) +UUS (J) +UX (LB)
        RETURN
        END
        SUBROUTINE STD (IS)
        DIMENSION VAR (800,20),          MTG (2000) ,UUS (2000)  ,
       1 SC (20), GWT (30), AVS (30), NTR (30), UX (30),GSS(30),PXY(30),
       2 GMV (30,20) ,GSV (30,20)
        COMMON NM, NK, NP, VAR, TW, MTG, UUS, SC, GWT, AVS,
       1 NTR, UX,       GSS, PXY,       GMV, GSV
        DIMENSION AMEAN (21) ,ASTD (21)
        KNK=NK
        KNM=NM
C       CALL CLEAR (AMEAN,21,ASTD,21)
        DO 31 I=1,NK
        AMEAN (I) = 0.0
        ASTD (I) = 0.0
 31     CONTINUE
        WRITE (6,18)    (I,I=1,KNK)
 18     FORMAT (1H1,30X,'RAW DATA--MEANS--VARIANCES'//,I8,20I6/I7,20I6//)
        DO 17 I=1,KNM
 17     WRITE (6,15)   I, (VAR (I,J) ,J=1,KNK)
 15     FORMAT (I5, (20F6.2))
        DO 10 J=1,KNK
        DO 11 I=1,KNM
        AMEAN (J) =AMEAN (J) +VAR (I,J) /FLOAT (KNM)
 11     CONTINUE
        DO 12 I=1,KNM
        ASTD (J) =ASTD (J) + (VAR (I,J) -AMEAN (J)) **2/FLOAT (KNM)
 12     CONTINUE
        ASTD (J) =SQRT (ASTD (J))
        IF (IS) 999,999,10
 999    DO 13 I=1,KNM
        VAR (I,J) = (VAR (I,J) -AMEAN (J)) /ASTD (J)
 13     CONTINUE
 10     CONTINUE
        WRITE (6,23)    (AMEAN (I) ,I=1,KNK)
 23     FORMAT (//5X, (20F6.2))
        WRITE (6,19)    (I,I=1,KNK)
        WRITE (6,23)    (ASTD (I) ,I=1,KNK)
        IF (IS .GT. 0) RETURN
 19     FORMAT (1H1,30X,' STANDARDIZED   DATA'///,I8,20I6/I7,20I6//)
        DO 21 I=1,KNM
 21     WRITE (6,15)   I, (VAR (I,J) ,J=1,KNK)
        RETURN
```

MDPREF (Multidimensional Analysis of Preference Data)

1. Description, FORTRAN *Source, and Input Directions.*   This program was written by Jih Jie Chang of Bell Telephone Laboratories, Murray Hill, New Jersey, 1973. The program accepts as input either a) paired-comparison data matrices, one for each subject, or b) a preference score matrix with one row for each subject and one column for each stimulus. The reader should contact Bell Laboratory in order to obtain the source program and accompanying manual.

For paired-comparison data matrices the program derives a "score matrix" whose rows represent subjects and columns represent stimuli. To the score matrix, or alternatively to the preference score matrix if such was input directly, the Eckart-Young (1936) procedure of factorization is applied to yield the best configuration of stimulus points and subject vectors.

That is, the program finds a matrix of projections called the "second matrix" which is as close as possible to the "score matrix" in the sum of squares sense, and generates as output a geometric configuration of stimuli and objects.

The program is capable of processing several independent sets of analyses on one computer run.

Output:

1. Mean of raw scores for each subject, first score matrix, cross product matrices of subjects and stimuli, correlation matrix of subjects, second score matrix, population and stimulation matrices.
2. Geometric configurations of stimuli and subjects for the number of dimensions specified. The projections of stimuli on each subject's vector correspond optimally with the order of preference expressed by the subject for the stimuli.

Input:

Data may be input as:

1. Paired comparison matrices; one matrix for each subject. The row i and column j entry is a preference code indicating the subjects preference between stimulus pair i-j, and may be one of four codes, which can be any alphanumeric symbol of no more than 6 characters. The codes are:
    Code 1 = i preferred to j
    Code 2 = j preferred to i
    Code 3 = no preference
    Code 4 = no response (missing datum)
2. Preference score matrix with one row for each subject and one column for each stimulus, where each entry is a preference rating by the ith subject on the jth stimulus.

If a higher number in the score matrix refers to a higher preference, the subject points in the geometric configuration represent the preferred directions, while if a lower number refers to a higher preference, the subject points represent non-preferred directions.

Control Cards:

1. Title Card: Any alphanumeric title; up to 80 columns may be used.
2. Parameter Card: For all options a blank field (treated as a zero value) is considered a "normal option."

Columns	Description
1–4	NP—Number of subjects (max = 60)
5–8	NS—Number of stimuli (max = 60)
9–12	NF—Number of factors (max = 10)
13–16	NPF—Number of factors to be plotted (max = NF)
17–20	IREAD 0 = paired-comparison matrices 1 = preference score matrix of NP rows and NS columns; program normalizes each row by subtracting the row means. 2 = same as IREAD = 1, except in addition, each row is divided by the standard deviation of values in that row.
21–24	MDATA Required only for paired-comparison data. 0 = no missing data and no weight matrices 1 = missing data and no weight supplied by user 2 = weights supplied by the user 3 = missing data and no weights supplied by the user. The non-empty cells are arranged in block pattern or are treated as such.
25–28	NS1 Required when MDATA = 1 or 2. Number of subjects having same pattern of missing data (or same weight matrices). These subjects matrices must be placed together and ahead of other subjects.
29–32	NPUNCH 0 = do not punch solution on cards 1 = punch solution on cards
33–36	IPUNF 0 = do not punch first score matrix on cards 1 = punch normalized first score matrix
37–40	NORP 0 = normalize subject vectors 1 = do not normalize

3. Paired Comparison Data Matrices: Required only if IREAD = 0; that is, input is in form of paired-comparison data matrices.

3a. Format Card: Format for cards specified in 3b and 3c, should be in A format.

3b. Code Specification Card: Should contain 4 codes, punched in same format as in data cards, and must be arranged in the following order:
1. Code indicating row is preferred to column.
2. Code indicating column is preferred to row.
3. Code indicating no preference.
4. Code indicating missing datum.

3c. Paired-Comparison Data Cards: Each row of the matrix must begin on a new card, but may continue on several cards if necessary. Each subject's data matrix is followed by the next without interruption, except when weights are supplied by user (MDATA = 2); then subjects weight matrix follows its data matrix. Weight matrix format is 10F7.2.

4. Preference Score Matrix: Required only if IREAD = 1 or 2; that is, input is in form of preference score matrix.

4a. Format Card: Format for preference score matrix, in F format.

4b. Preference Score Matrix Data Cards: The matrix is punched as NP by NS; with each subject beginning on a new card.

5. Additional Analysis: Repeat 1 through 4 for each additional analysis.

2. Input Example for Program MDPREF, *Data Are Rank Preferences (by* RANKO) *from Table 20.2.*

```
//MDPREF JOB (2919,400KR,267F),'DUNN-RANKIN'
// EXEC EDSTAT,PROGRAM=MDPREF,RG=400K
//GO.SYSIN DD *
  DATA ARE RANK PREFERENCES FROM TABLE 20.1 VIA RANKO
   5   4   2   2   1
(4F1.0)
2332
2143
2143
1423
3223
/*
//
```

3. Output from Program MDPREF, *Data Are Rank Preferences, Table 20.2,* via RANKO *with Row Mean Substracted*

```
POINT NUMBERS ABOVE 5) IDENTIFIED AS   >
MULTIPLE POINTS IDENTIFIED AS   #


  IN JOINT SPACE PLOT FIRST   4  POINTS ARE STIMULI AND NEXT
                              5 POINTS ARE SUBJECTS
```

```
INPUT FORMAT = (4F1.0)


MEAN OF THE RAW SCORES  (BY SUBJECT)
            2.5000       2.5000       2.5000       2.5000       2.5000

FIRST SCORE MATRIX

SUBJECT    STIMULUS
   1      -0.5000       0.5000       0.5000      -0.5000
   2      -0.5000      -1.5000       1.5000       0.5000
   3      -0.5000      -1.5000       1.5000       0.5000
   4      -1.5000       1.5000      -0.5000       0.5000
   5       0.5000      -0.5000      -0.5000       0.5000

CROSS PRODUCT MATRIX OF SUBJECTS
   1       1.0000       0.0          0.0          1.0000      -1.0000
   2       0.0          5.0000       5.0000      -2.0000       0.0
   3       0.0          5.0000       5.0000      -2.0000       0.0
   4       1.0000      -2.0000      -2.0000       5.0000      -1.0000
   5      -1.0000       0.0          0.0         -1.0000       1.0000

CORRELATION MATRIX OF SUBJECTS
   1       1.0000       0.0          0.0          0.4472      -1.0000
   2       0.0          1.0000       1.0000      -0.4000       0.0
   3       0.0          1.0000       1.0000      -0.4000       0.0
   4       0.4472      -0.4000      -0.4000       1.0000      -0.4472
   5      -1.0000       0.0          0.0         -0.4472       1.0000

CROSS PRODUCT MATRIX OF STIMULI
   1       3.2500      -1.2500      -1.2500      -0.7500
   2      -1.2500       7.2500      -4.7500      -1.2500
   3      -1.2500      -4.7500       5.2500       0.7500
   4      -0.7500      -1.2500       0.7500       1.2500

ROOTS OF THE FIRST SCORE MATRIX
           11.3121       4.4030       1.2850      -0.0000

PROPORTION OF VARIANCE ACCOUNTED FOR BY EACH FACTOR
            1            2            3            4            5
           0.6284       0.2446       0.0714      -0.0000       0.0556

CUMULATIVE PROPORTION OF VARIANCE ACCOUNTED FOR
            1            2            3            4            5
           0.6284       0.8731       0.9444       0.9444       1.0000

SECOND SCORE MATRIX

SUBJECT    STIMULUS
   1      -0.8384       0.4761       0.2303       0.1319
   2      -0.2171      -0.6597       0.6965       0.1803
   3      -0.2171      -0.6597       0.6965       0.1803
   4      -0.6584       0.7424      -0.1188       0.0348
   5       0.8384      -0.4761      -0.2303      -0.1319

POPULATION MATRIX

FACTOR
   1       0.2147      -0.9767
   2      -0.9642      -0.2653
   3      -0.9642      -0.2653
   4       0.6485      -0.7612
   5      -0.2147       0.9767

STIMULUS MATRIX (NORMALIZED)

FACTOR
   1      -0.0104       0.8561
   2       0.7717      -0.3179
   3      -0.6200      -0.3721
   4      -0.1413      -0.1661

STIMULUS MATRIX (STRETCHED BY SQ. ROOT OF THE EIGENVALUES)

FACTOR
   1      -0.0349       1.7964
   2       2.5955      -0.6670
   3      -2.0853      -0.7808
   4      -0.4753      -0.3486
```

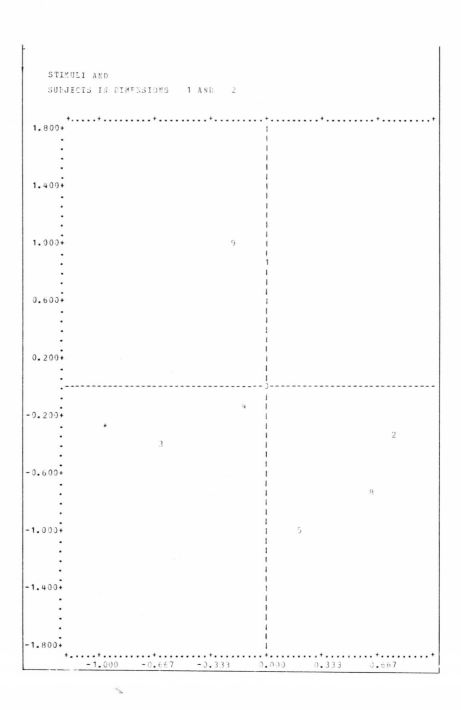

MIKCA (K Means Iterative Clustering)

1. Description, FORTRAN *Source, and Input Directions.* The program partitions an $n \times k$ (observations by variables) data matrix into g disjoint clusters of observations (n) by optimizing in an iterative improvement fashion one of four objective criteria. The iterative K-means procedure attempts to minimize the within cluster variance and consequently to maximize the variance between clusters. Each unit is assigned to one and only one cluster.

MIKCA starts by analyzing three different sets of randomly chosen seed points, then uses an interaction of reassignment and hill climbing passes; that is, it uses both K-means passes by assigning entities to nearest centroid clusters, and also moves an entity from one cluster to another if the particular statistical criterion is better optimized by the individual switches heuristic.

The Fortran listing for this program (McRae, 1971) is produced with permission from Douglas J. McRae, California Test Bureau, Division of McGraw Hill Book Co., Del Monte Research Park, Monterey, California. Several programs similar to MIKCA (Multivariate Iterative K-means Cluster Analysis) have previously been published (Spath, 1980; Anderberg, 1973). A program with nice output can be found in the BMDP (1981) series of programs, specifically BMDPKM.

Control Cards

1. Title Card:
   Cols. 1–80:   Any alphanumeric title
2. Problem Card:
   Cols. 1–3:   The total number of observations (≤ 900) (rows will be clustered).
   Cols. 4–5:   The number of variables (≤ 40).
   Cols. 6–7:   Estimated number of clusters (≤ 15).
   Col. 8:   Criterion to be optimized:
                  1 = min Trace $\mathbf{W}$
                  2 = min $|\mathbf{W}|$
                  3 = max largest root
                  4 = max Hotelling's Trace
   Col. 9:   Standardization parameter:
                  0 = data not standardized before analysis
                  1 = data standardized before analysis
   Col. 10:   Distance parameter:
                  0 = Euclidian distance
                  1 = weighted Euclidean distance
                  2 = Mahalanobis distance

Col. 11:   Data parameter:

0 = data follows VARIABLE FORMAT card

1 = analyzes previously input data

Col. 12:   Timing parameter:

0 = no observation considered by the individual switches heuristic

1–8 = an increasing number of observations considered by the individual switches heuristic

9 = all observations considered by the individual switches heuristic

3. Variable Format Card: (must be present unless Col. 11 in PROBLEM card contains a ''1'' punch).

Cols. 1–72:   The format for each data card.

NOTE: A one to four character identification code in A4 format must be the first item read from each data card.

4. Data Cards:

Cols. 1–80:   Data in format specified on the VARIABLE FORMAT card.

5. For reanalysis of the same data, include new TITLE card and PROBLEM card with a ''1'' punch in Col. 11.

6. For analysis of new data, include TITLE card, PROBLEM card, VARIABLE FORMAT card, and DATA cards.

7. After the last problem include two blank cards for the program to exit normally.

2. Input Example for Program MIKCA, Profile Data from Chapter 3.

```
//MIKCA JOB (2919,250KR,30S,267F),'DUNN-RANKIN'
// EXEC EDSTAT,PROGRAM=MIKCA,RG=250K
//GO.SYSIN DD *
  SAMPLE INPUT FOR MIKCA, PROFILE DATA CH 3
  6 4 311
(A2,8X,4F1.0)
01        8684
02        5251
03        9444
04        6543
05        8276
06        5343

/*
//
```

3. Example Output for Program MIKCA, *Profile Data from Chapter 3.*

```
    SAMPLE INPUT FOR MIKCA, PROFILE DATA CH 3

  THE NUMBER OF OBSERVATIONS IS   6
  THE NUMBER OF VARIABLES IS   4
  THE NUMBER OF GROUPS (INITIAL) IS   3

  THE CRITERION IS TO MINIMIZE TRACE W

  THE VARIABLES WILL BE STANDARDIZED

  EUCLIDIAN DISTANCE WILL BE USED

  THE INPUT FORMAT IS (A2,8X,4F1.0)

  THE TIMING PARAMETER FOR INDIVIDUAL SWITCHES IS 0

  THE VARIABLE MEANS ARE
        6.833        3.667        5.333        3.500

  THE VARIABLE STANDARD DEVIATIONS ARE
        1.722        1.633        1.751        1.643

  THE CROSS-PRODUCTS MATRIX IS
        14.833
         4.667       13.333
         6.333        2.667       15.333
        10.500        1.000        7.000       13.500

   THE FINAL CLUSTER SOLUTION IS

  CLUSTER   1
        SIZE =   2
        CENTER =       8.500        3.000        5.500        5.000
        THE OBSERVATIONS ARE
             03       05

  CLUSTER   2
        SIZE =   1
        CENTER =       8.000        6.000        8.000        4.000
        THE OBSERVATIONS ARE
             01

  CLUSTER   3
        SIZE =   3
        CENTER =       5.333        3.333        4.333        2.333
        THE OBSERVATIONS ARE
             02       04       06

  THE WITHIN CELLS MATRIX IS
          1.167
          2.667        6.667
         -1.833       -4.333        5.167
         -0.333        0.667        1.667        4.667

  THE TRACE OF THE WITHIN-CLUSTERS MATRIX IS 0.176667E 02

   END OF CLUSTER PROBLEM
```

4. FORTRAN *Listing for Program* MIKCA.

```
C
C
C          K-MEANS ITERATIVE CLUSTERING PROGRAM
C          D. J. MCRAE
C          CTB/MCGRAW-HILL
C          DEL MONTE RESEARCH PARK
C          MONTEREY, CALIFORNIA  93940
C
C      REQUIRED INPUT
C
C          TITLE CARD
C              ANY ALPHANUMERIC TITLE IN COLUMNS 1-80
C
C          PROBLEM CARD
C              NUMBER OF OBSERVATIONS IN COLUMNS 1-3
C              NUMBER OF VARIABLES IN COLUMNS 4-5
C              INITIAL NUMBER OF CLUSTERS IN COLUMNS 6-7
C              CRITERION TO BE USED IN COLUMN 8
C                  1 = TRACE W
C                  2 = DETERMINANT W
C                  3 = LARGEST ROOT OF W(INVERSE) * B
C                  4 = TRACE W(INVERSE) * B
C              STANDARDIZATION PARAMETER IN COLUMN 9
C                  0 = DATA NOT STANDARDIZED
C                  1 = DATA STANDARDIZED
C              DISTANCE PARAMETER IN COLUMN 10
C                  0 = EUCLIDIAN DISTANCE
C                  1 = SCALED EUCLIDIAN DISTANCE
C                  2 = MAHALANOBIS DISTANCE
C              DATA PARAMETER IN COLUMN 11
C                  0 = DATA TO BE READ IN
C                  1 = NO DATA READ IN.   PREVIOUS DATA TO BE
C                      REANALYZED USING THE CURRENT PROBLEM CARD.
C              TIMING PARAMETER IN COLUMN 12
C                  0 = NO OBSERVATIONS CONSIDERED IN INDIVIDUAL
C                      SWITCHES
C                  1-8 = AN INCREASING NUMBER OF OBSERVATIONS
C                      CONSIDERED IN INDIVIDUAL SWITCHES
C                  9 = ALL OBSERVATIONS CONSIDERED IN INDIVIDUAL
C                      SWITCHES
C              IN (I3,2I2,5I1) FORMAT
C
C          VARIABLE FORMAT CARD (MUST BE PRESENT UNLESS COLUMN 11 IN
C                      PROBLEM CARD CONTAINS A '1')
C              FORMAT FOR EACH DATA CARD IN COLUMNS 1-72
C
C          DATA CARDS
C
C          FOR REANALYSIS OF THE SAME DATA, INCLUDE NEW TITLE AND
C          PROBLEM CARDS, WITH A '1' IN COLUMN 11 OF THE PROBLEM CARD
C
C          FOR FURTHER PROBLEMS, INCLUDE NEW TITLE CARD, PROBLEM CARD,
C          OPTIONAL CARDS IF APPROPRIATE, VARIABLE FORMAT CARD, AND
C          DATA CARDS
C
C          AFTER LAST PROBLEM, INCLUDE TWO BLANK CARDS FOR THE
C          PROGRAM TO EXIT NORMALLY.
C
   COMMON NOBS,NVARS,NGPS,ICRIT,NOSTAN,IDIST,IFINE,KTIME,IDENT(900),
  1 DATA(900,40),T(40,40),B(40,40),W(40,40),WFCT(40,40),SVCEN(15,40),
  2 IDATA(900),NISV(15),VMEAN(40),SD(40),XVEC(40),YVEC(40),BT(40,40),
  3 NISVT(15),SVCENT(15,40),IDATAT(900),VEC(40,40),EIG(40)
C
C
C      DESCRIPTION OF COMMON AREA:
C
C          NOBS = NUMBER OF OBSERVATIONS
C          NVARS = NUMBER OF VARIABLES
C          NGPS = NUMBER OF CLUSTERS
```

```
C            ICRIT = CRITERION TO BE OPTIMIZED (SEE ABOVE)
C            NOSTAN = STANDARDIZATION PARAMETER (SEE ABOVE)
C            IDIST = DISTANCE PARAMETER  (SEE ABOVE)
C            IFINE = ESCAPE PARAMETER:  IF IFINE IS SET EQUAL TO '1',
C                    SOMETHING IS WRONG AND THE APPROPRIATE ERROR
C                    MESSAGE IS PRINTED OUT; THE PROGRAM GOES ON TO THE
C                    NEXT PROBLEM
C            KTIME = TIMING PARAMETER (SEE ABOVE)
C            IDENT = OBSERVATION IDENTIFICATIONS (A4 FORMAT):  READ FROM
C                    EACH DATA CARD
C            DATA = AREA IN WHICH THE DATA MATRIX IS STORED
C            T = CROSS-PRODUCTS MATRIX
C            B = BETWEEN-CLUSTERS MATRIX
C            W = WITHIN-CLUSTERS MATRIX
C            WFCT = CHOLESKY FACTOR OF THE WITHIN-CLUSTERS MATRIX
C            SVCEN = CLUSTER CENTERS (MEANS)
C            IDATA = CLUSTER IDENTIFICATION FOR EACH OBSERVATION
C            NISV = CLUSTER SIZES (NUMBER OF OBSERVATIONS IN EACH CLUSTER)
C            VMEAN = VARIABLE MEANS
C            SD = VARIABLE STANDARD DEVIATIONS
C            XVEC = TEMPORARY STORAGE
C            YVEC = TEMPORARY STORAGE
C            BT = TEMPORARY STORAGE FOR BETWEEN-CLUSTERS MATRIX
C            NISVT, SVCENT, IDATAT:  TEMPORARY STORAGE SERVING THE
C                 SAME FUNCTIONS AS NISV, SVCEN, AND IDATA
C            VEC = EIGENVECTORS
C            EIG = EIGENVALUES
C
C
  100 CALL PRELIM (CRIT)
C     IFINE IS ESCAPE PARAMETER
      IF (IFINE.EQ.1) GO TO 400
      IF (IFINE.EQ.2) GO TO 500
      CALL RANDST (CRIT)
      IF (IFINE.EQ.1) GO TO 400
  300 CALL KMEANS (CRIT)
      IF (IFINE.EQ.1) GO TO 400
      CALL ISWTCH (CRIT)
      GO TO 100
C     IFINE GOT SET TO 1:  IF DATA HAS BEEN READ IN, RESET DATA AND
C     GO TO NEXT PROBLEM
  400 DO 410 I=1,NOBS
      DO 410 J=1,NVARS
      IF (NOSTAN.EQ.1) DATA(I,J) = DATA(I,J) * SD(J)
  410 DATA(I,J) = DATA(I,J) + VMEAN(J)
      GO TO 100
C     ALL DONE:  WRITE OUT LAST MESSAGE AND EXIT
  500 WRITE (6,900)
  900 FORMAT ('0 END OF ANALYSES.')
      STOP
      END
      SUBROUTINE PRELIM (CRIT)
C
C     THIS SUBROUTINE MAKES THE PRELIMINARY CALCULATIONS.
C     IT INPUTS THE DATA, CALCULATES THE MEANS AND VARIANCES FOR EACH
C     VARIABLE, STANDARDIZES (CONVERTS TO Z-SCORES) EACH VARIABLE IF
C     REQUESTED, AND CALCULATES THE CROSS-PRODUCTS MATRIX
C
      COMMON NOBS,NVARS,NGPS,ICRIT,NOSTAN,IDIST,IFINE,KTIME,IDENT(900),
     1 DATA(900,40),T(40,40),B(40,40),W(40,40),WFCT(40,40),SVCEN(15,40),
     2 IDATA(900),NISV(15),VMEAN(40),SD(40),XVEC(40),YVEC(40),BT(40,40),
     3 NISVT(15),SVCENT(15,40),IDATAT(900),VEC(40,40),EIG(40)
      DIMENSION TITLE(20),IFMT(20),VAR(40)
C
C     INPUT SECTION:  READ IN TITLE CARD, PROBLEM CARD, OPTIONAL CARDS,
C     FORMAT CARD, AND DATA CARDS
C     WRITE OUT SOLUTION SPECIFICATIONS
C
      IFINE = 0
      READ (5,900,END=820) (TITLE(I),I=1,20)
```

```
          WRITE (6,903) (TITLE(I),I=1,20)
          READ (5,901) NOBS,NVARS,NGPS,ICRIT,NOSTAN,IDIST,NODATA,KTIME
          IF (NOBS.EQ.0) GO TO 820
          IF (NOBS.GT.900) GO TO 815
          IF (NVARS.GT.40) GO TO 815
          IF (NGPS.GT.15) GO TO 815
          IF (ICRIT.GT.4) GO TO 815
          IF (NOSTAN.GT.1) GO TO 815
          IF (IDIST.GT.2) GO TO 815
          IF (NVARS.EQ.1) ICRIT=1
          IF (NVARS.EQ.1) IDIST=0
        4 IF (NODATA.EQ.1) GO TO 5
          READ (5,902) (IFMT(I),I=1,18)
        5 WRITE (6,904) NOBS,NVARS,NGPS
          GO TO (10,20,30,40),ICRIT
       10 WRITE (6,920)
          GO TO 50
       20 WRITE (6,921)
          GO TO 50
       30 WRITE (6,922)
          GO TO 50
       40 WRITE (6,923)
       50 CONTINUE
          IF (NOSTAN) 60,60,70
       60 WRITE (6,924)
          GO TO 80
       70 WRITE (6,925)
       80 CONTINUE
          IF (IDIST) 85,85,90
       85 WRITE (6,926)
          GO TO 95
       90 IF (IDIST.EQ.2) GO TO 92
          WRITE (6,936)
          GO TO 95
       92 WRITE (6,927)
       95 CONTINUE
          IF (NODATA.EQ.1) GO TO 101
          WRITE (6,905) (IFMT(I),I=1,18)
          DO 100 I = 1,NOBS
          READ (5,IFMT) IDENT(I),(DATA(I,J),J=1,NVARS)
      100 CONTINUE
          NODATA = 1
          GO TO 102
      101 WRITE (6,937)
      102 WRITE (6,943) KTIME
C
C     CALCULATE VARIABLE MEANS AND VARIANCES
C     SUBTRACT OUT OVERALL MEAN
C
          DO 105 J=1,NVARS
          VMEAN (J) = 0.0
      105 VAR (J) = 0.0
          DO 110 I = 1,NOBS
          DO 110 J = 1,NVARS
      110 VMEAN (J) = VMEAN (J) + DATA(I,J)/NOBS
          DO 120 I=1,NOBS
          DO 120 J=1,NVARS
          DATA(I,J) = DATA(I,J)-VMEAN(J)
      120 VAR(J) = VAR(J) + (DATA(I,J)**2)/(NOBS-1)
          DO 125 J = 1,NVARS
          IF (VAR(J).LE.0.000001) MFLAG=1
      125 SD(J) = SQRT (VAR(J))
          IF (MFLAG.EQ.1) GO TO 825
C
C     CALCULATE T = X'X, THE CROSS-PRODUCTS MATRIX
C
      131 DO 135 K=1,NVARS
          DO 135 J=K,NVARS
      135 T(K,J) = 0.0
          DO 140 K = 1,NVARS
          DO 140 J=K,NVARS
```

```
         DO 140 I = 1,NOBS
   140 T(K,J) = T(K,J) + DATA(I,K)*DATA(I,J)
C
C     OUTPUT SECTION: WRITE OUT MEANS, STANDARD DEVIATIONS, AND CROSS-
C                     PRODUCTS MATRIX T
C
         WRITE (6,908)
         WRITE (6,907) (VMEAN(J),J=1,NVARS)
         WRITE (6,909)
         WRITE (6,907) (SD(J),J=1,NVARS)
         WRITE (6,911)
         DO 810 I = 1,NVARS
         WRITE (6,907) (T(J,I),J=1,I)
   810 CONTINUE
         IF (NOSTAN.EQ.0) GO TO 180
C
C     STANDARDIZE IF REQUESTED
C
         DO 160 J=1,NVARS
         DO 150 I=1,NOBS
   150 DATA(I,J) = DATA(I,J) / SD(J)
         DO 160 K=J,NVARS
   160 T(J,K) = (1.0/SD(J))*T(J,K)*(1.0/SD(K))
   180 RETURN
   815 IFINE = 1
         IF (NODATA.EQ.0) IFINE=2
         WRITE (6,935)
         RETURN
   820 IFINE = 2
         RETURN
   825 WRITE (6,945) J
         IFINE = 1
         RETURN
C
C     FORMAT STATEMENTS
C
   900 FORMAT (20A4)
   901 FORMAT (I3,2I2,5I1)
   902 FORMAT (18A4)
   903 FORMAT ('1',20A4)
   904 FORMAT ('0 THE NUMBER OF OBSERVATIONS IS ',I3,/,' THE NUMBER OF V
     1ARIABLES IS ',I2,/,'  THE NUMBER OF GROUPS (INITIAL) IS ',I2)
   905 FORMAT ('0 THE INPUT FORMAT IS ',18A4)
   907 FORMAT (' ',10(F11.3,1X))
   908 FORMAT ('0THE VARIABLE MEANS ARE')
   909 FORMAT ('0THE VARIABLE STANDARD DEVIATIONS ARE')
   911 FORMAT ('0THE CROSS-PRODUCTS MATRIX IS ')
   920 FORMAT ('0 THE CRITERION IS TO MINIMIZE TRACE W')
   921 FORMAT ('0 THE CRITERION IS TO MINIMIZE DETERMINANT W')
   922 FORMAT ('0 THE CRITERION IS TO MAXIMIZE THE LARGEST ROOT OF W-1B')
   923 FORMAT ('0 THE CRITERION IS TO MINIMIZE THE TRACE OF W-1B')
   924 FORMAT ('0 THE VARIABLES WILL NOT BE STANDARDIZED')
   925 FORMAT ('0 THE VARIABLES WILL BE STANDARDIZED')
   926 FORMAT ('0 EUCLIDIAN DISTANCE WILL BE USED')
   927 FORMAT ('0 MAHALANOBIS DISTANCE WILL BE USED')
   935 FORMAT ('1 ERROR IN PROBLEM CARD.  SKIPPING PROBLEM.')
   936 FORMAT ('0 WEIGHTED EUCLIDIAN DISTANCE WILL BE USED.')
   937 FORMAT ('0PREVIOUS DATA BEING USED ')
   943 FORMAT ('0THE TIMING PARAMETER FOR INDIVIDUAL SWITCHES IS ',I1)
   945 FORMAT ('0 WARNING:  VARIABLE ',I2,' HAS ZERO VARIANCE.')
         END
         SUBROUTINE RANDST (CRIT)
C
C     THIS SUBROUTINE DETERMINES THE INITIAL CLUSTER CONFIGURATION.
C
         COMMON NOES,NVARS,NGPS,ICRIT,NOSTAN,IDIST,IFINE,KTIME,IDENT(900),
     1 DATA(900,40),T(40,40),B(40,40),W(40,40),WFCT(40,40),SVCEN(15,40),
     2 IDATA(900),NISV(15),VMEAN(40),SD(40),XVEC(40),YVEC(40),BT(40,40),
     3 NISVT(15),SVCENT(15,40),IDATAT(900),VEC(40,40),EIG(40)
         DIMENSION ISTRT(15)
C
```

```
C       ONE PASS K-MEANS TO DETERMINE INITIAL CLUSTER SOLUTION
C
C       RANDOM NUMBER STARTER
  200 IX=19739
      NGPST=NGPS
C    DO 260: GETTING THREE INITIAL CONFIGURATIONS; THE ONE WITH THE
C    BEST CRITERION VALUE WILL BE USED
      DO 260 IBSRT = 1,3
      DO 205 M = 1,NGPS
      NISVT(M) =1
C    FIND A RANDOM OBSERVATION TO SERVE AS INITIAL CLUSTER CENTER
C    FOR EACH CLUSTER
  201 RAND = URAND(IX)
      ISTRT(M) = RAND * NOBS
      IF (ISTRT(M).EQ.0) ISTRT(M)=1
      IF (M.EQ.1) GO TO 203
      MM1 = M-1
      DO 204 MM=1,MM1
      IF (ISTRT(M).EQ.ISTRT(MM)) GO TO 201
  204 CONTINUE
  203 I = ISTRT(M)
      DO 205 J=1,NVARS
  205 SVCENT(M,J) = DATA(I,J)
      ITEMP = IDIST
      IDIST = 0
C    DO FOR EACH OBSERVATION
      DO 225 I=1,NOBS
C    FIND EUCLIDIAN DISTANCE TO EACH CLUSTER CENTER
      DO 215 M=1,NGPS
      DO 210 J=1,NVARS
      XVEC(J) =DATA(I,J)
  210 YVEC(J) = SVCENT(M,J)
      CALL DISTCE (XVEC,YVEC,DISTA)
      IF (IFINE.EQ.1) RETURN
      IF (M.EQ.1) GO TO 212
      IF (DISTA.GE.SMDIST) GO TO 215
  212 SMDIST = DISTA
      IDATAT(I) = M
  215 CONTINUE
C    ASSIGN OBSERVATION TO CLOSEST CLUSTER AND UPDATE THAT CLUSTER
C    CENTER
      K = IDATAT(I)
      NISVT(K) = NISVT(K) + 1
      DO 225 J = 1,NVARS
  225 SVCENT(K,J) = ((NISVT(K)-1)*SVCENT(K,J)+DATA(I,J))/NISVT(K)
      IDIST = ITEMP
C    END OF DO FOR EACH OBSERVATION
C    RECALCULATE CLUSTER CENTERS TO ELIMINATE INITIAL RANDOM OBSERVA-
C    TIONS
      DO 230 M=1,NGPS
      NISVT(M) = NISVT(M)-1
      DO 230 J=1,NVARS
  230 SVCENT(M,J)=0.
      DO 235 I=1,NOBS
      M = IDATAT(I)
      DO 235 J=1,NVARS
  235 SVCENT(M,J) = SVCENT(M,J) + DATA(I,J)/NISVT(M)
C
C       CALCULATE THE B AND W MATRICES
C       CALCULATE THE CRITERION VALUE
C
      IDIF=2
      IF (ICRIT.EQ.1) IDIR=1
      CALL WCALC (SVCENT,NISVT,NGPST,IDIR)
      IF (IFINE.EQ.1) RETURN
      CALL CRITON (CRIT)
      IF (IFINE.EQ.1) RETURN
C    WHICH INITIAL CONFIGURATION
      IF (IBSRT.GT.1) GO TO 250
```

```
C     FIRST INITIAL CONFIGURATION: BCRIT IS THE BEST CRITERION
  245 BCRIT = CRIT
C     SAVE CLUSTER SIZES (NISV), CLUSTER CENTERS (SVCEN), CLUSTER
C     LISTS (LSTSV), AND OBSERVATION ID'S (IDATA)
      DO 247 M = 1,NGPS
      NISV(M) = NISVT(M)
      DO 247 L = 1,NVARS
  247 SVCEN(M,L) = SVCENT(M,L)
      DO 249 I=1,NOBS
  249 IDATA(I) = IDATAT(I)
      GO TO 260
C     SECOND OR THIRD INITIAL CONFIGURATION
  250 IF (CRIT.GE.BCRIT) GO TO 260
  255 BCRIT = CRIT
      DO 257 M = 1,NGPS
      NISV(M) = NISVT(M)
      DO 257 L = 1,NVARS
  257 SVCEN(M,L) = SVCENT(M,L)
      DO 259 I=1,NOBS
  259 IDATA(I) = IDATAT(I)
  260 CONTINUE
C     ALL DONE
      RETURN
      END
      SUBROUTINE KMEANS (CRIT)
C
C         K-MEANS.  EACH OBSERVATION IS ASSIGNED TO THE CLOSEST CLUSTER
C         CENTER.
C
C
      COMMON NOBS,NVARS,NGPS,ICRIT,NOSTAN,IDIST,IFINE,KTIME,IDENT(900),
     1 DATA(900,40),T(40,40),B(40,40),W(40,40),WFCT(40,40),SVCEN(15,40),
     2 IDATA(900),NISV(15),VMEAN(40),SD(40),XVEC(40),YVEC(40),BT(40,40),
     3 NISVT(15),SVCENT(15,40),IDATAT(900),VEC(40,40),EIG(40)
C     INITIALIZING FLAGS
C     AND TEMPORARY STORAGE FOR NISV, SVCEN
  200 NGPST = NGPS
      JFLAG = 0
      BCRIT = CRIT
      DO 201 M=1,NGPS
      NISVT(M) = NISV(M)
      DO 201 J=1,NVARS
  201 SVCENT(M,J) = SVCEN(M,J)
C     RECALCULATING WITHIN-CLUSTERS MATRIX
      IDIR=1
      IF (IDIST.EQ.2) IDIR=2
      CALL WCALC (SVCENT,NISVT,NGPST,IDIR)
      IF (IFINE.EQ.1) RETURN
C     INITIALIZING TEMPORARY STORAGE FOR LSTSV, IDATA
      DO 210 I = 1,NOBS
  210 IDATAT(I) = IDATA(I)
C     MAJOR DO LOOP: DO FOR EACH OBSERVATION
      DO 400 I = 1,NOBS
C
C     BEGIN K-MEANS SECTION
C
C     CALCULATE VECTOR OF DISTANCES FROM OBSERVATION TO EACH CLUSTER
C     CENTER
  325 DO 335 M=1,NGPST
      DO 330 J=1,NVARS
      XVEC(J) = DATA(I,J)
  330 YVEC(J) = SVCENT(M,J)
      CALL DISTCE (XVEC,YVEC,DISTB)
      IF (IFINE.EQ.1) RETURN
      IF (M.EQ.1) GO TO 332
      IF (DISTB.GE.SMDIST) GO TO 335
  332 SMDIST = DISTB
      IDGP = M
  335 CONTINUE
```

```
C     IS OBSERVATION ALREADY IN THE CLOSEST CLUSTER? IF YES, SKIP THIS
C     SECTION
      IF (IDGP.EQ.IDATAT(I)) GO TO 360
C     IOLD IS OLD CLUSTER ASSIGNMENT
  346 IOLD = IDATAT(I)
C     INEW IS NEW CLUSTER ASSIGNMENT
      INEW = IDGP
      JFLAG = 1
C     RECALCULATE CLUSTER CENTERS
      DO 348 J = 1,NVARS
      SVCENT(IOLD,J) = (NISVT(IOLD)*SVCENT(IOLD,J)-DATA(I,J))/
     1 (NISVT(IOLD)-1)
  348 SVCENT(INEW,J) = (NISVT(INEW)*SVCENT(INEW,J)+DATA(I,J))/
     1 (NISVT(INEW)+1)
C     ADJUST NISV
      NISVT(IOLD) = NISVT(IOLD)-1
      NISVT(INEW) = NISVT(INEW)+1
C     ADJUST IDATA
      IDATAT(I) = IDGP
C     RECALCULATE WITHIN-CLUSTERS MATRIX FOR USE IN COMPUTING SCALED
C     EUCLIDIAN AND MAHALANOBIS DISTANCE
      IF (IDIST.EQ.0) GO TO 360
      CALL WCALC (SVCENT,NISVT,NGPST,IDIR)
      IF (IFINE.EQ.1) RETURN
  360 CONTINUE
C     DONE WITH MAJOR DO LOOP
  400 CONTINUE
C
C        CALCULATE THE CRITERION
C
C     RECALCULATE SVCEN:   ACCURACY MEASURE
      DO 401 M=1,NGPST
      DO 401 J=1,NVARS
  401 SVCENT(M,J) = 0.
      DO 402 I=1,NOBS
      M = IDATAT(I)
      DO 402 J=1,NVARS
  402 SVCENT(M,J) = SVCENT(M,J) + DATA(I,J)/NISVT(M)
C     RECALCULATE WITHIN-CLUSTERS MATRIX AND CRITERION VALUE BASED ON
C     NEW CLUSTER CENTER VALUES
      IDIR = 2
      IF (ICRIT.EQ.1) IDIR = 1
      CALL WCALC (SVCENT,NISVT,NGPST,IDIR)
      IF (IFINE.EQ.1) RETURN
  405 CALL CRITON (CRIT)
      IF (IFINE.EQ.1) RETURN
C     IF CRITERION BETTER THAN BEFORE? IF YES, THEN ANOTHER ITERATION;
C     IF NO, FINISH KMEANS
      IF (CRIT.GE.BCRIT) GO TO 535
C
C        ANOTHER ITERATION
C
C     PUT TEMPORARY VALUES INTO PERMANENT LOCATIONS
  515 NGPS=NGPST
      DO 520 M = 1,NGPS
      NISV(M) = NISVT (M)
      DO 520 J = 1,NVARS
  520 SVCEN (M,J) = SVCENT (M,J)
      DO 530 I = 1,NOBS
  530 IDATA(I) = IDATAT(I)
      GO TO 200
C
C        FINISH
C
C     JFLAG = 0 MEANS NO CHANGES HAVE BEEN MADE DURING THE LAST
C     ITERATION: ITERATIONS CONVERGED
  535 IF (JFLAG.EQ.0) RETURN
C     JFLAG = 1 MEANS CHANGES HAVE BEEN MADE BUT THE CRITERION VALUE
C     GOT WORSE: ITERATIONS NOT CONVERGING
  540 WRITE (6,940)
```

```
          WRITE (6,942) CRIT
          WRITE (6,943) BCRIT
C     RECALCULATE WITHIN-CLUSTERS MATRIX AND RESET CRIT
          IDIR=2
          IF (ICRIT.EQ.1) IDIR=1
          CALL WCALC (SVCEN,NISV,NGPS,IDIR)
          IF (IFINE.EQ.1) RETURN
          CRIT=FCRIT
          RETURN
  940 FORMAT ('0 ITERATIONS NOT CONVERGING')
  942 FORMAT ('0 THE CRITERION VALUE IS ',E12.6)
  943 FORMAT ('0 THE BEST CRITERION VALUE IS ',E12.6)
          END
          SUBROUTINE ISWTCH (CRIT)
C
C     THIS SUBROUTINE CONSIDERS SWITCHING EACH OBSERVATION TO A
C     DIFFERENT CLUSTER.  THE SWITCH IS MADE IFF A BETTER CRITERION
C     VALUE RESULTS.
C     THIS SUBROUTINE ALSO DEPENDS ON THE PARAMETER KTIME: IT DETERMINES
C     WHICH OBSERVATIONS ARE TO BE CONSIDERED.  FOR COMPLETE EXPLANATION
C     OF THE KTIME PARAMETER, SEE THE PROGRAM DESCRIPTION.
C
          COMMON NOBS,NVARS,NGPS,ICRIT,NOSTAN,IDIST,IFINE,KTIME,IDENT(900),
        1 DATA(900,40),T(40,40),B(40,40),W(40,40),WFCT(40,40),SVCEN(15,40),
        2 IDATA(900),NISV(15),VMEAN(40),SD(40),XVEC(40),YVEC(40),BT(40,40),
        3 NISVT(15),SVCENT(15,40),IDATAT(900),VEC(40,40),EIG(40)
          DIMENSION JFLAG (15)
C     SET UP THE IDIR FLAG
          IDIR=2
          IF (ICRIT.EQ.1) IDIR=1
C     KTIME = 0 MEANS SKIP THIS HEURISTIC
          IF (KTIME.EQ.0) GO TO 750
C     SET UP TEMPORARY STORAGE AREAS FOR NGPS, NISV, AND SVCEN
          NGPST=NGPS
          DO 500 M = 1,NGPS
          NISVT(M)=NISV(M)
          JFLAG(M)=0
          DO 500 J = 1,NVARS
  500 SVCENT(M,J)=SVCEN(M,J)
C     SET IFLAG = 0: WILL BE SET = 1 IF ANY SWITCH IS MADE
  600 IFLAG=0
C     MAJOR DO LOOP: DO 700
          DO 700 M=1,NGPS
C     JFLAG (M) INDICATES WHETHER CLUSTER M HAS BEEN ALTERED
          IF (JFLAG(M).EQ.2) GO TO 700
C     KTIME = 9 MEANS ALL OBSERVATIONS WILL BE CONSIDERED
          IF (KTIME.EQ.9) GO TO 617
C     COMPUTE ALL DISTANCES FROM OBSERVATIONS TO CLUSTER CENTERS FOR THE
C     OBSERVATIONS IN CLUSTER M
          DO 605 J=1,NVARS
  605 YVEC(J)  = SVCEN(M,J)
          BIGDIS = 0.
          DO 615 I=1,NOBS
          IF (IDATA(I).NE.M) GO TO 615
          DO 610 J=1,NVARS
  610 XVEC(J)  = DATA(I,J)
          CALL DISTCE (XVEC,YVEC,DISTA)
C     LOCATE OBSERVATION WITH BIGGEST DISTANCE
          IF (BIGDIS.GE.DISTA) GO TO 615
          BIGDIS = DISTA
  615 CONTINUE
C     DIVIDE BIGDIS BY TIMING PARAMETER KTIME
          TIME = KTIME
          PSME = BIGDIS / TIME
  617 MOLD = M
C     DO FOR ALL OBSERVATIONS IN CLUSTER M
          DO 691 I=1,NOBS
          IF (IDATA(I).NE.M) GO TO 691
          KFLAG = 0
C     KTIME = 9 MEANS CONSIDER ALL OBSERVATIONS
```

```
      IF (KTIME.EQ.9) GO TO 618
C     DO NO  CONSIDER SWITCHING THE OBSERVATION IF THE DISTANCE TO ITS
C     CURRENT CLUSTER CENTER IS LT BIGDIS / KTIME
      DO 619 J=1,NVARS
  619 XVEC(J) = DATA(I,J)
      CALL DISTCE (XVEC,YVEC,DISTA)
      IF (DISTA.LT.PSME) GO TO 691
  618 CONTINUE
      DO 690 MNEW=1,NGPS
      IF (NISV(MOLD).EQ.1) GO TO 690
      IF (MNEW.EQ.MOLD) GO TO 690
      IF (KFLAG.EQ.1) GO TO 690
C     COMPUTE NEW SVCEN BASED ON OBSERVATION BEING SWITCHED
      DO 620 J=1,NVARS
      SVCENT(MNEW,J) = (NISV(MNEW)*SVCEN(MNEW,J)+DATA(I,J))/
     1 (NISV(MNEW)+1)
      SVCENT(MOLD,J) = (NISV(MOLD)*SVCEN(MOLD,J)-DATA(I,J))/
     1 (NISV(MOLD)-1)
  620 CONTINUE
C     ADJUST NISV
      NISVT(MNEW) = NISV(MNEW)+1
      NISVT(MOLD) = NISV(MOLD)-1
C     COMPUTE WITHIN-CLUSTERS MATRIX AND NEW CRITERION VALUE
      CALL WCALC (SVCENT,NISVT,NGPST,IDIR)
      IF (IFINE.EQ.1) RETURN
      CALL CRITON (TCRIT)
      IF (IFINE.EQ.1) RETURN
C     MAKE THE SWITCH IFF NEW CRIT IS BETTER
      IF (TCRIT.GE.CRIT) GO TO 680
C
C     MAKE THE SWITCH
C
C     RESET FLAGS
      JFLAG(M) = 1
      JFLAG(MNEW) = 1
      IFLAG=1
      KFLAG = 1
C     ADJUST CRIT, IDATA, NISV, SVCEN
      CRIT=TCRIT
      IDATA(I) = MNEW
      NISV(MNEW) = NISVT(MNEW)
      NISV(MOLD) = NISVT(MOLD)
  629 DO 630 J=1,NVARS
      SVCEN(MNEW,J) = SVCENT(MNEW,J)
  630 SVCEN(MOLD,J) = SVCENT(MOLD,J)
      GO TO 690
C     SWITCH WAS NOT MADE; RESET NISVT, SVCENT, TO VALUES PRESENT
C     BEFORE THE SWITCH WAS CONSIDERED
  680 NISVT(MNEW) = NISV(MNEW)
      NISVT(MOLD) = NISV(MOLD)
      DO 685 J=1,NVARS
      SVCENT(MNEW,J) = SVCEN(MNEW,J)
  685 SVCENT(MOLD,J) = SVCEN(MOLD,J)
  690 CONTINUE
  691 CONTINUE
C     FINISH WITH CLUSTER M: IF NO SWITCHES HAVE BEEN MADE, SET
C     JFLAG(M) = 2 AND GO TO NEXT CLUSTER;  IF SWITCHES HAVE BEEN MADE,
C     ADJUST LSTSV AND SET JFLAG(M) = 0 AND GO TO NEXT CLUSTER
  695 IF (JFLAG(M).EQ.0) GO TO 699
      JFLAG(M) = 0
      GO TO 700
  699 JFLAG(M) = 2
  700 CONTINUE
C     DONE WITH ALL CLUSTERS: IFLAG = 1 MEANS SOME SWITCHES HAVE BEEN
C     MADE; GO BACK AND ITERATE
      IF (IFLAG.EQ.1) GO TO 600
C
C     ALL DONE: ACCURATELY CALCULATE MEANS AND CRITERION AND OUTPUT
C     THE RESULTS
C
```

```
  750 WRITE (6,900)
  900 FORMAT ('1 THE FINAL CLUSTER SOLUTION IS ')
C    RECALCULATE CLUSTER CENTERS, WITHIN-CLUSTERS MATRIX, AND CRITERION
C    VALUE
      DO 715 M=1,NGPS
      DO 715 J=1,NVARS
  715 SVCEN(M,J) = 0.
      DO 720 I=1,NOBS
      M = IDATA(I)
      DO 720 J=1,NVARS
  720 SVCEN(M,J) = SVCEN(M,J) + DATA(I,J)/NISV(M)
      CALL WCALC (SVCEN,NISV,NGPS,IDIR)
      IF (IFINE.EQ.1) RETURN
      CALL CRITON (CRIT)
      IF (IFINE.EQ.1) RETURN
C    CALL THE OUTPUT ROUTINE
      CALL OUTPUT (CRIT)
      WRITE (6,901)
  901 FORMAT ('0 END OF CLUSTER PROBLEM')
      RETURN
      END
      SUBROUTINE OUTPUT (CRIT)
C
C    THIS SUBROUTINE PRINTS OUT THE CLUSTER SOLUTION
C          FOR EACH CLUSTER - THE CLUSTER SIZE
C                             THE CLUSTER CENTROID
C                             THE OBSERVATIONS BELONGING TO THE CLUSTER
C          THE WITHIN CELLS MATRIX
C          THE CRITERION VALUE
C
      COMMON NOBS,NVARS,NGPS,ICRIT,NOSTAN,IDIST,IFINE,KTIME,IDENT(900),
     1 DATA(900,40),T(40,40),B(40,40),W(40,40),WPCT(40,40),SVCEN(15,40),
     2 IDATA(900),NISV(15),VMEAN(40),SD(40),XVEC(40),YVEC(40),BT(40,40),
     3 NISVT(15),SVCENT(15,40),IDATAT(900),VEC(40,40),EIG(40)
C    UNSTANDARDIZE IF NECESSARY
      IF (NOSTAN.EQ.0) GO TO 40
      DO 20 M=1,NGPS
      DO 20 J=1,NVARS
   20 SVCEN(M,J) = SVCEN(M,J)*SD(J)
      DO 30 J=1,NVARS
      DO 30 K=J,NVARS
   30 T(J,K) = SD(J)*T(J,K)*SD(K)
      IDIR = 2
      IF (ICRIT.EQ.1) IDIR=1
      CALL WCALC (SVCEN,NISV,NGPS,IDIR)
      IF (IFINE.EQ.1) RETURN
      CALL CRITON (CRIT)
      IF (IFINE.EQ.1) RETURN
C    ADD THE OVERALL MEAN BACK INTO EACH OBSERVATION; UNSTANDARDIZE
C    THE DATA IF NECESSARY
   40 DO 80 J=1,NVARS
      DO 50 I=1,NOBS
      IF (NOSTAN.EQ.1) DATA(I,J) = DATA(I,J)*SD(J)
   50 DATA(I,J) = DATA(I,J) + VMEAN(J)
      DO 60 M=1,NGPS
   60 SVCEN(M,J) = SVCEN(M,J) + VMEAN(J)
   80 CONTINUE
C    WRITE OUT NISV, SVCEN
   95 DO 115 M=1,NGPS
      WRITE (6,900) M
      WRITE (6,901) NISV(M)
      WRITE (6,902) (SVCEN(M,J),J=1,NVARS)
      WRITE (6,903)
      LSTNO = NISV(M)
      K = 0
      DO 100 I=1,NOBS
      IF (IDATA(I).NE.M) GO TO 100
      K = K+1
      IDATAT(K) = IDENT(I)
  100 CONTINUE
```

```
C       SORT THE OBSERVATION IDENTIFICATIONS
        L=0
  101 L=L+1
        IF (L.EQ.NISV(M)) GO TO 110
  102 LL=L+1
        IF (IDATAT(L).LE.IDATAT(LL)) GO TO 101
        LTEMP = IDATAT(L)
        IDATAT(L) = IDATAT(LL)
        IDATAT(LL) = LTEMP
        IF (L.EQ.1) GO TO 102
        L=L-1
        GO TO 102
  110 CONTINUE
C     WRITE OUT THE IDENTIFICATIONS
        WRITE (6,904) (IDATAT(K),K=1,ISTNO)
  115 CONTINUE
C     WRITE OUT THE WITHIN-CLUSTERS MATRIX
  119 WRITE (6,905)
        DO 120 J=1,NVARS
        WRITE (6,906) (W(K,J),K=1,J)
  120 CONTINUE
C     ICRIT IS THE CRITERION CHOSEN BY THE USER
        GO TO (150,160,170,170),ICRIT
C     WRITE OUT TRACE W
  150 WRITE (6,907) CRIT
        RETURN
C     WRITE OUT DET W
C     AND LOG (DET T / DET W)
  160 CALL UPRFCT (NVARS,T,M)
        DET = 1.
        DO 165 J=1,NVARS
  165 DET = DET*T(J,J)
        WRITE (6,912) CRIT
        CRIT = ALOG 10 ((DET**2)/(CRIT**2))
        WRITE (6,909) CRIT
        RETURN
C     FOR LARGEST ROOT AND HOTELLING'S TRACE CRITERIA, FIND EIGENVALUES
C     FOR |B-GW|=0.
  170 DO 175 J=1,NVARS
        DO 175 K=J,NVARS
        BT(J,K) = B(J,K)
  175 BT(K,J) = BT(J,K)
        CRIT = 1.0 / CRIT
        CALL UTISUI (NVARS,BT,WFCT)
        CALL EIGN (NVARS,BT,EIG,VEC,IND)
        IF (IND.NE.0) GO TO 180
C     WRITE OUT EIGENVALUES
        WRITE (6,910) (EIG(J),J=1,NVARS)
        IF (ICRIT.EQ.4) GO TO 178
C     WRITE OUT LARGEST ROOT
        WRITE (6,913) CRIT
        RETURN
C     WRITE OUT SUM OF EIGENVALUES
  178 WRITE (6,914) CRIT
        RETURN
C     ESCAPE ROUTE
  180 IFINE = 1
        WRITE (6,911) IND
        RETURN
C
C     FORMAT STATEMENTS
C
  900 FORMAT ('0CLUSTER ',I2)
  901 FORMAT ('      SIZE = ',I3)
  902 FORMAT ('      CENTER = ',10(F9.3,1X))
  903 FORMAT ('      THE OBSERVATIONS ARE ')
  904 FORMAT (8X,10A7)
  905 FORMAT ('0THE WITHIN CELLS MATRIX IS ')
  906 FORMAT ('      ',10(F10.3,1X))
  907 FORMAT ('0THE TRACE OF THE WITHIN-CLUSTERS MATRIX IS ',E12.6)
  908 FORMAT ('0 DETERMINANT T IS ',E12.6)
```

```
      909 FORMAT ('0 LOG (DET T / DET W) = ',E12.6)
      910 FORMAT ('0 THE EIGENVALUES OF W(INVERSE)*B ARE ',10F8.3)
      911 FORMAT ('1 ILL-CONDITIONED W MATRIX -- IND IS',I3)
      912 FORMAT('0THE DETERMINANT OF THE WITHIN-CLUSTERS MATRIX IS ',E12.6)
      913 FORMAT ('0THE LARGEST ROOT IS ',E12.6)
      914 FORMAT ('0THE TRACE OF W(INV)*B IS ',E12.6)
          END
          SUBROUTINE DISTCE (XVECS,YVECS,DIST)
C
C     THIS SUBROUTINE CALCULATES EUCLIDIAN, WEIGHTED EUCLIDIAN, OR
C     MAHALANOBIS DISTANCE (DEPENDING ON IDIST).
C
          COMMON NOBS,NVARS,NGPS,ICRIT,NOSTAN,IDIST,IFINE,KTIME,IDENT(900),
         1 DATA(900,40),T(40,40),B(40,40),W(40,40),WFCT(40,40),SVCEN(15,40),
         2 IDATA(900),NISV(15),VMEAN(40),SD(40),XVEC(40),YVEC(40),BT(40,40),
         3 NISVT(15),SVCENT(15,40),IDATAT(900),VEC(40,40),EIG(40)
          DIMENSION X(40),XVECS(1),YVECS(1)
          IDIR = IDIST+1
          GO TO (100,200,300),IDIR
          WRITE (6,900)
      900 FORMAT ('1 ERROR IN DISTANCE CODE - COLUMN 10 OF PROBLEM CARD')
          IFINE = 1
          RETURN
C
C     CALCULATE EUCLIDIAN DISTANCE
C
      100 DIST=0.
          DO 150 J=1,NVARS
      150 DIST = DIST + (XVECS(J)-YVECS(J))**2
          RETURN
C
C     CALCULATE EUCLIDIAN DISTANCE FOR STANDARDIZED VARIABLES
C
      200 DIST=0.
          DO 205 J=1,NVARS
      205 DIST = DIST + (XVECS(J)-YVECS(J))*(1.0/W(J,J))*(XVECS(J)-YVECS(J))
          RETURN
C
C     CALCULATE MAHALANOBIS DISTANCE AS THE ELEMENTS OF
C     L'(INV)(XVEC-YVEC) SQUARED WHERE L IS THE CHOLESKY FACTOR OF W
C
      300 DIST=0.
          DO 305 J=1,NVARS
      305 X(J) = XVECS(J) - YVECS(J)
          CALL UTIRT (NVARS,1,WFCT,X)
          DO 310 J=1,NVARS
      310 DIST = DIST + X(J)**2
          RETURN
          END
          SUBROUTINE CRITON (CRIT)
C
C     THIS SUBROUTINE CALCULATES THE CRITERIA VALUES
C
          COMMON NOES,NVARS,NGPS,ICRIT,NOSTAN,IDIST,IFINE,KTIME,IDENT(900),
         1 DATA(900,40),T(40,40),B(40,40),W(40,40),WFCT(40,40),SVCEN(15,40),
         2 IDATA(900),NISV(15),VMEAN(40),SD(40),XVEC(40),YVEC(40),BT(40,40),
         3 NISVT(15),SVCENT(15,40),IDATAT(900),VEC(40,40),EIG(40)
          GO TO (100,200,300,400),ICRIT
          WRITE (6,900)
      900 FORMAT ('1 ERROR IN CRITERION CODE, COLUMN 8 IN PROBLEM CARD.')
          IFINE =1
          RETURN
C
C     CALCULATE TRACE W
C
      100 CRIT = 0.
          DO 105 J=1,NVARS
      105 CRIT = CRIT + W(J,J)
          RETURN
C
C     CALCULATE DET W AS THE PRODUCT OF DIAGONAL ELEMENTS OF THE
```

```
C        CHOSESKY FACTOR OF W
C
  200 DET = 1.
      DO 205 J=1,NVARS
  205 DET = DET*WFCT(J,J)
      CRIT = DET
      RETURN
C
C     CALCULATE LARGEST ROOT AS L(INV)*B*L'(INV) WHERE L IS THE
C     CHOLESKY FACTOR OF W
C     CRITERION IS RECIPROCAL OF LARGEST ROOT
C
  300 DO 305 J=1,NVARS
      DO 305 K=J,NVARS
      BT(J,K)  = B(J,K)
  305 BT(K,J)  = BT(J,K)
      CALL UTISUI (NVARS,BT,WFCT)
      CALL EIGN (NVARS,BT,EIG,VEC,IND)
      CRIT = 1.0 / EIG(1)
      RETURN
C
C     CALCULATE HOTELLING'S TRACE AS SUM OF DIAGONAL ELEMENTS OF
C     L(INV)*B*L'(INV)
C     CRITERION IS RECIPROCAL OF THIS SUM
C
  400 DO 405 J=1,NVARS
      DO 405 K=J,NVARS
      BT(J,K)  = B(J,K)
  405 BT(K,J)  = BT(J,K)
      CALL UTISUI (NVARS,BT,WFCT)
      CRIT = 0.
      DO 410 J=1,NVARS
  410 CRIT = CRIT+BT(J,J)
      CRIT=1.0/ CRIT
      RETURN
      END
      SUBROUTINE WCALC (SV,NI,NGP,IDIR)
C
C     THIS SUBROUTINE CALCULATES THE WITHIN-CELLS MATRIX AND, IF
C     NECESSARY, THE CHOLESKY FACTOR OF THE WITHIN-CELLS MATRIX
C
      COMMON NOES,NVARS,NGPS,ICRIT,NOSTAN,IDIST,IFINE,KTIME,IDENT(900),
     1 DATA(900,40),T(40,40),B(40,40),W(40,40),WFCT(40,40),SVCEN(15,40),
     2 IDATA(900),NISV(15),VMEAN(40),SD(40),XVEC(40),YVEC(40),BT(40,40),
     3 NISVT(15),SVCENT(15,40),IDATAT(900),VEC(40,40),EIG(40)
      DIMENSION SV(15,40),NI(15)
C
C     CALCULATE B AND THEN W = T - B
C     B = SUM  NISV(M)*SVCEN(M)**2
C
      DO 100 J=1,NVARS
      DO 100 K=J,NVARS
  100 B(J,K)  = 0.
      DO 105 M=1,NGP
      DO 105 J=1,NVARS
      DO 105 K=J,NVARS
      BT(J,K)  = SV(M,J)  * SV(M,K)
  105 B(J,K)  = B(J,K) + BT(J,K)  * NI(M)
      DO 110 J=1,NVARS
      DO 110 K=J,NVARS
  110 W(J,K) = T(J,K)  - B(J,K)
C
C     CALCULATE CHOLESKY FACTOR OF W IF IDIR = 2
C
      GO TO (120,115),IDIR
  115 DO 116 J=1,NVARS
      DO 116 K=J,NVARS
  116 WFCT(J,K) = W(J,K)
      CALL UPRFCT (NVARS,WFCT,M)
      IF (M.NE.0) GO TO 125
```

```
      120 RETURN
      125 IFINE=1
          WRITE (6,900)
      900 FORMAT ('1 THE WITHIN GROUPS MATRIX IS SINGULAR ')
          RETURN
          END
          FUNCTION URAND(IRAND)
C
C         THIS FUNCTION CALCULATES UNIFORMLY DISTRIBUTED RANDOM NUMBERS.
C         BETWEEN 0 AND 1
C         3**19 CONGRUENTIAL UNIFORM RANDOM NUMBER GENERATOR
C
          IRAND = IRAND*1162261467
          IF (IRAND.GT.0) GO TO 3
    1     IRAND = -IRAND
    3     URAND = FLOAT(IRAND)*0.4656612873E-9
          RETURN
          END
          SUBROUTINE UPRFCT(N,A,M)
C
C         REPLACE UPPER TRIANGLE OF A SQUARE POSITIVE DEFINITE MATRIX A
C         BY ITS CHOLESKI FACTOR
C
          DIMENSION A(40,40)
C         CLEAR THE ERROR INDICATOR
          M=0
          N1=N-1
          IF(N1) 230,100,100
      100 DO 220 K=1,N
          AKK=A(K,K)
          IF(K .EQ. 1) GO TO 120
          DO 110 J=2,K
      110 AKK=AKK-A(J-1,K)**2
      120 IF(A(K,K)) 140,140,130
C         IN THE CASE OF A COVARIANCE MATRIX AKK/A(K,K) IS 1-R**2 WHERE
C         R IS MULT CORRELATION OF VARIABLE K WITH ALL PRECEEDING VARIABLES.
      130 IF(AKK/A(K,K) .GE.    .001) GO TO 150
      140 M=K
          AKK=0.
      150 AKK=SQRT(AKK)
          A(K,K)=AKK
          IF(K .EQ. N) GO TO 230
C
          DO 220 I=K,N1
          AKI=A(K,I+1)
          IF(K .EQ. 1) GO TO 190
          DO 180 J=2,K
      180 AKI=AKI-A(J-1,K)*A(J-1,I+1)
      190 IF(AKK) 210,200,210
      200 A(K,I+1) = 0.0
          GO TO 220
      210 A(K,I+1)=AKI/AKK
      220 CONTINUE
      230 RETURN
          END
          SUBROUTINE UTIRT(M,N,S,B)
C
C         INVERSE OF UPPER (S) TRANSPOSED TIMES RECTANGLE B TRANSPOSED.
C
          DIMENSION S(40,40),B(1,40)
          DO 130 J=1,N
          DO 130 I=1,M
          SUM = 0.0
          IF (S(I,I) ) 90,130,90
   90     SUM = B(J,I)
          IM1 = I-1
          IF(IM1) 120,120,100
      100 DO 110 K=1,IM1
      110 SUM = SUM-S(K,I)*B(J,K)
      120 SUM = SUM/S(I,I)
```

```
      130 B(J,I) = SUM
          RETURN
          END
          SUBROUTINE UTISUI (N,A,B)
C
C         UPPER (B) TRANSPOSE INVERSE TIMES A TIMES UPPER (B) INVERSE.
C
          DIMENSION A(40,40),B(40,40)
C         NOTE THAT POSTMULT IS CARRIED OUT ON FINAL VALUES LEFT BY PREMULT
          DO 200 I=1,N
          I1 = I-1
C         NOTE THAT PREMULT ON RIGHT HALF OF ROW IS SAME AS POSTMULT
C         ON LOWER HALF OF COLUMN - EXCEPT FOR DIAG TERM WHICH IS THE
C         FINAL VALUE LEFT BY PREMULT BEFORE POSTMULT
          DO 130 J=I,N
          IF(I1) 120,120,100
      100 DO 110 K=1,I1
      110 A(J,I) = A(J,I) - B(K,I)*A(J,K)
      120 A(J,I) = A(J,I)/B(I,I)
      130 IF (B(I,I) .EQ. 0.0) A(J,I) = 0.0
C         NOTE THAT ELEMENTS IN LEFT HALF OF ROW ARE FINAL FOR PREMULT
C         NOTE THAT DIAG ELEMENT WAS PREVIOUSLY THE FINAL RESULT OF
C         PREMULT.  NOW WE MAKE THE FINAL RESULT OF POSTMULT.
          DO 200 J=1,I
          J1 = J-1
          IF(J1) 160,160,140
C         HORIZONTAL BRANCH OF INNER PRODUCT EXCLUDING DIAG TERM
      140 DO 150 K=1,J1
      150 A(I,J) = A(I,J) - B(K,I)*A(J,K)
      160 IF(I1-J) 190,170,170
C         VERTICAL BRANCH OF INNER PRODUCT INCLUDING DIAG TERM
      170 DO 180 K=J,I1
      180 A(I,J) = A(I,J) - B(K,I)*A(K,J)
      190 A(I,J) = A(I,J)/B(I,I)
      200 IF (B(I,I) .EQ. 0.0) A(I,J) = 0.0
          RETURN
          END
          SUBROUTINE EIGN(NN,A,EIG,VEC,IND)
C            NN= SIZE OF MATRIX
C            A = MATRIX (ONLY LOWER TRIANGLE IS USED + THIS IS DESTROYED)
C            EIG = RETURNED EIGENVALUES IN ALGEBRAIC DESCENDING ORDER
C            VEC = RETURNED EIGENVECTORS IN COLUMNS
C            IND = ERROR RETURN INDICATOR
C                0 FOR NORMAL RETURN
C                1 SUM OF EIGENVALUES NOT EQUAL TO TRACE
C                2 SUM OF EIGENVALUES SQUARED NOT EQUAL TO NORM
C                3 BOTH OF THESE ERRORS
          DIMENSION A(40,40),GAMMA(40),BETA(40),BETASQ(40),EIG(40)
          DIMENSION W(40),VEC(40,40)
C         THE FOLLOWING DIMENSIONED VARIABLES ARE EQUIVALENCED
          DIMENSION P(40),Q(40)
          EQUIVALENCE (P(1),BETA(1)),(Q(1),BETA(1))
          DIMENSION IPOSV(40),IVPOS(40),IORD(40)
          EQUIVALENCE (IPOSV(1),GAMMA(1)),(IVPOS(1),BETA(1)),
         1(IORD(1),BETASQ(1))
          N=NN
C         RESET ERROR RETURN INDICATOR
          IND=0
          IF(N .EQ. 0) GO TO 560
          N1=N-1
          N2=N-2
C         COMPUTE THE TRACE AND EUCLIDIAN NORM OF THE INPUT MATRIX
C         LATER CHECK AGAINST SUM AND SUM OF SQUARES OF EIGENVALUES
          ENORM=0.
          TRACE=0.
          DO 110 J=1,N
          DO 100 I=J,N
      100 ENORM=ENORM+A(I,J)**2
          TRACE=TRACE+A(J,J)
      110 ENORM=ENORM-.5*A(J,J)**2
          ENORM=ENORM+ENORM
```

```
      GAMMA(1)=A(1,1)
      IF(N2) 280,270,120
120   DO 260 NR=1,N2
      B=A(NR+1,NR)
      S=0.
      DO 130 I=NR,N2
130   S=S+A(I+2,NR)**2
C     PREPARE FOR POSSIBLE BYPASS OF TRANSFORMATION
      A(NR+1,NR)=0.
      IF(S) 250,250,140
140   S=S+B*B
      SGN=+1.
      IF(B) 150,160,160
150   SGN=-1.
160   SQRTS=SQRT(S)
      D=SGN/(SQRTS+SQRTS)
      TEMP=SQRT(.5+B*D)
      W(NR)=TEMP
      A(NR+1,NR)=TEMP
      D=D/TEMP
      B=-SGN*SQRTS
C     D IS FACTOR OF PROPORTIONALITY. NOW COMPUTE AND SAVE W VECTOR.
C     EXTRA SINGLY SUBSCRIPTED W VECTOR USED FOR SPEED.
      DO 170 I=NR,N2
      TEMP=D*A(I+2,NR)
      W(I+1)=TEMP
170   A(I+2,NR)=TEMP
C     PREMULTIPLY VECTOR W BY MATRIX A TO OBTAIN P VECTOR.
C     SIMULTANEOUSLY ACCUMULATE DOT PRODUCT WP,(THE SCALAR K)
      WTAW=0.
      DO 220 I=NR,N1
      SUM=0.
      DO 180 J=NR,I
180   SUM=SUM+A(I+1,J+1)*W(J)
      I1=I+1
      IF(N1-I1) 210,190,190
190   DO 200 J=I1,N1
200   SUM=SUM+A(J+1,I+1)*W(J)
210   P(I)=SUM
220   WTAW=WTAW+SUM*W(I)
C     P VECTOR AND SCALAR K NOW STORED. NEXT COMPUTE Q VECTOR
      DO 230 I=NR,N1
230   Q(I)=P(I)-WTAW*W(I)
C     NOW FORM PAP MATRIX, REQUIRED PART
      DO 240 J=NR,N1
      QJ=Q(J)
      WJ=W(J)
      DO 240 I=J,N1
240   A(I+1,J+1)=A(I+1,J+1)-2.*(W(I)*QJ+WJ*Q(I))
250   BETA(NR)=B
      BETASQ(NR)=B*B
260   GAMMA(NR+1)=A(NR+1,NR+1)
270   B=A(N,N-1)
      BETA(N-1)=B
      BETASQ(N-1)=B*B
      GAMMA(N)=A(N,N)
280   BETASQ(N)=0.
C     ADJOIN AN IDENTITY MATRIX TO BE POSTMULTIPLIED BY ROTATIONS.
      DO 300 I=1,N
      DO 290 J=1,N
290   VEC(I,J)=0.
300   VEC(I,I)=1.
      M=N
      SUM=0.
      NPAS=1
      GO TO 400
310   SUM=SUM+SHIFT
      COSA=1.
      G=GAMMA(1)-SHIFT
      PP=G
      PPBS=PP*PP+BETASQ(1)
```

```
          PPBR=SQRT(PPBS)
          DO 370 J=1,M
          COSAP=COSA
          IF(PPBS .NE. 0.) GO TO 320
          SINA=0.
          SINA2=0.
          COSA=1.
          GO TO 350
      320 SINA=BETA(J)/PPBR
          SINA2=BETASQ(J)/PPBS
          COSA=PP/PPBR
C         POSTMULTIPLY IDENTITY BY P-TRANSPOSE MATRIX
          NT=J+NPAS
          IF(NT .GE. N) NT=N
      330 DO 340 I=1,NT
          TEMP=COSA*VEC(I,J)+SINA*VEC(I,J+1)
          VEC(I,J+1)=-SINA*VEC(I,J)+COSA*VEC(I,J+1)
      340 VEC(I,J)=TEMP
      350 DIA=GAMMA(J+1)-SHIFT
          U=SINA2*(G+DIA)
          GAMMA(J)=G+U
          G=DIA-U
          PP=DIA*COSA-SINA*COSAP*BETA(J)
          IF(J .NE. M) GO TO 360
          BETA(J)=SINA*PP
          BETASQ(J)=SINA2*PP*PP
          GO TO 380
      360 PPBS=PP*PP+BETASQ(J+1)
          PPBR=SQRT(PPBS)
          BETA(J)=SINA*PPBR
      370 BETASQ(J)=SINA2*PPBS
      380 GAMMA(M+1)=G
C         TEST FOR CONVERGENCE OF LAST DIAGONAL ELEMENT
          NPAS=NPAS+1
          IF(BETASQ(M) .GT. 1.E-21) GO TO 410
      390 EIG(M+1)=GAMMA(M+1)+SUM
      400 BETA(M)=0.
          BETASQ(M)=0.
          M=M-1
          IF(M .EQ. 0) GO TO 430
          IF(BETASQ(M) .LE. 1.E-21) GO TO 390
C         TAKE ROOT OF CORNER 2 BY 2 NEAREST TO LOWER DIAGONAL IN VALUE
C         AS ESTIMATE OF EIGENVALUE TO USE FOR SHIFT
      410 A2=GAMMA(M+1)
          R2=.5*A2
          R1=.5*GAMMA(M)
          R12=R1+R2
          DIF=R1-R2
          TEMP=SQRT(DIF*DIF+BETASQ(M))
          R1=R12+TEMP
          R2=R12-TEMP
          DIF=ABS(A2-R1)-ABS(A2-R2)
          IF(DIF .LT. 0.) GO TO 420
          SHIFT=R2
          GO TO 310
      420 SHIFT=R1
          GO TO 310
      430 EIG(1)=GAMMA(1)+SUM
C         INITIALIZE AUXILIARY TABLES REQUIRED FOR REARRANGING THE VECTORS
          DO 440 J=1,N
          IPOSV(J)=J
          IVPOS(J)=J
      440 IORD(J)=J
C         USE A TRANSPOSITION SORT TO ORDER THE EIGENVALUES
          M=N
          GO TO 470
      450 DO 460 J=1,M
          IF(EIG(J) .GE. EIG(J+1)) GO TO 460
          TEMP=EIG(J)
          EIG(J)=EIG(J+1)
          EIG(J+1)=TEMP
          ITEMP=IORD(J)
```

```
        IORD(J)=ICRD(J+1)
        IORD(J+1)=ITEMP
 460 CONTINUE
 470 M=M-1
        IF(M .NE. 0) GO TO 450
        IF(N1 .EQ. 0) GO TO 500
        DO 490 L=1,N1
        NV=IORD(L)
        NP=IPOSV(NV)
        IF(NP .EQ. L) GO TO 490
        LV=IVPOS(L)
        IVPOS(NP)=LV
        IPOSV(LV)=NP
        DO 480 I=1,N
        TEMP=VEC(I,L)
        VEC(I,L)=VEC(I,NP)
 480 VEC(I,NP)=TEMP
 490 CONTINUE
 500 ESUM=0.
        ESSQ=0.
C       BACK TRANSFORM THE VECTORS OF THE TRIPLE DIAGONAL MATRIX
        DO 550 NRR=1,N
        K=N1
 510 K=K-1
        IF(K .LE. 0) GO TO 540
        SUM=0.
        DO 520 I=K,N1
 520 SUM=SUM+VEC(I+1,NRR)*A(I+1,K)
        SUM=SUM+SUM
        DO 530 I=K,N1
 530 VEC(I+1,NRR)=VEC(I+1,NRR)-SUM*A(I+1,K)
        GO TO 510
 540 ESUM=ESUM+EIG(NRR)
 550 ESSQ=ESSQ+EIG(NRR)**2
        TEMP=ABS(512.*TRACE)
        IF((ABS(TRACE-ESUM)+TEMP)-TEMP .NE. 0.) IND=IND+1
        TEMP=1024.*ENORM
        IF((ABS(ENORM-ESSQ)+TEMP)-TEMP .NE. 0.) IND=IND+2
 560 RETURN
        END
```

PEROVER (Generates Percent Overlap Matrix)

1. Description and Input Directions.   This program calculates percent overlap matrices from the results of free clustering. The basic data are group membership numbers assigned to each object by each subject. The program determines the proportion of times any two objects are found to have the same group number.

Output:

1. Prints the original data, format and parameters
2. Prints the matrix of proportions as square symmetric

Input:

After the JCL cards an input format card is read, next a parameter card and then the data.

1. Variable Format Card read in 20A4.
2. Parameter Card read 4I5
   Col. 1–5   number of subjects
   Col. 6–10   number of variables
   Col. 11–15   a positive number one (1) will punch the matrix
3. Data are read by the variable format. Usually they are a series of two digit numbers, one for each object.
4. If another set of data is to be read with the same format and parameters another card is placed after the data with a positive number punched in Col. 1–3 of the card.

2. Input Example for Program PEROVER, *Cluster Data Taken from* ASSO-CIATION, *Chapter 3.*

```
//PEROVER JOB (2919,267F,2X),'DUNN-RANKIN'
// EXEC EDSTAT,PROGRAM=PEROVER
//GO.SYSIN DD *
(10X,5F1.0)
     5    5
            11223
            11232
            11112
            11221
            13122
/*
//
```

3. Output from Program PEROVER.

```
10X,5F1.0)
     5    5
1.00  1.00  2.00  2.00  3.00
1.00  1.00  2.00  3.00  2.00
1.00  1.00  1.00  1.00  2.00
1.00  1.00  2.00  2.00  1.00
1.00  3.00  1.00  2.00  2.00


1.000   0.800   0.400   0.200   0.200
0.800   1.000   0.200   0.200   0.200
0.400   0.200   1.000   0.600   0.200
0.200   0.200   0.600   1.000   0.200
0.200   0.200   0.200   0.200   1.000
```

4. FORTRAN *Listing for Program* PEROVER.

```
C PROGRAM PEROVER
C
C     THIS IS A ROUTINE TO FIND PERCENT OVERLAP VALUES
C
      DIMENSIONX(120,120),Z(120,120),FMT(20)
      READ(5,901)FMT
  901 FORMAT(20A4)
```

```
      WRITE(6,901) FMT
      READ (5,900) NS,NV,NP
900 FORMAT(4I5)
      WRITE (6,900) NS,NV
  5 CONTINUE
      DO 550 I = 1,NV
      DO 550 J = 1,NV
550 Z(I,J) = 0.0
      NV1=NV-1
      AN = NS
      DO500I=1,NS
      READ (5,FMT)(X(I,J), J=1,NV)
      WRITE (6,950)(X(I,J), J = 1,NV)
950 FORMAT(20F6.2)
500 CONTINUE
      WRITE (6,981)
981 FORMAT (1H1)
      DO 505 I = 1,NS
      DO505J=1,NV1
      JJ = J+ 1
      DO505K=JJ,NV
      IF((X(I,J).EQ.X(I,K)).AND.X(I,J).NE.0.0) Z(J,K)=Z(J,K)+1.0
505 CONTINUE
      DO 570 I = 1,NV
      DO 570 J = 1,NV
570 Z(J,I) = Z(I,J)
      DO 510 I = 1, NV
      DO 510 J = 1,NV
      Z(I,J)=Z(I,J)/AN
      IF(I.EQ.J) Z(I,J) = 1.0
510 CONTINUE
      DO515 I=1,NV
      WRITE(6,930) (Z(I,J),J=1,NV )
930 FORMAT(10F8.3)
      IF (NP.NE.1) GO TO 515
      WRITE(7,930) (Z(I,J),J=1,NV)
515 CONTINUE
      READ (5,3) L
  3 FORMAT (F3.0)
      IF (L.GT.0) GO TO 5
 15 CONTINUE
      STOP
      END
```

RANKO (Rank Method of Scaling)

1. Description and Input Directions. This method accepts as input either paired comparison choices or rank orders, and assumes that scale values are proportional to the ranks assigned by the judges to each of the objects. The rank scale is a variance stable scale. Advantages: simplicity, between items significance, scaling continuum with meaningful end points, scale values isomorphic with those obtained by other techniques.

Output:

1. Rank orders of each subject for each item.
2. Rank totals over all subjects; minimum and maximum possible rank totals.
3. Scale scores derived from cumulative rank totals.
4. Linear plot with scale scores indicated.
5. Table of rank differences.

6. Table of critical ranges at .01 and .05 levels where, rows = number of judges (J), and columns = number of items or objects (A).

Input:

Data may be input as,

1. Rank ordering of objects by each judge,
2. or, paired comparison choices made by each judge. The data cards are punched '1' when a judge has chosen the first item in the pair indicated on the key card, and a '0' or '2' when the second was chosen (e.g., judge 4 1101101 . . . , or judge 4 1121121 . . .).

   Limitation: max number of objects = 15.

Control Cards:

This program requires a parameter card, a variable format card, and, if the data are in the form of paired comparison choices, one or more key cards.

1. Parameter Card:

Columns	Description
1–3	Number of judges
4–6	Number of objects (max = 15)
7–9	Number of tests that contribute to the total profile. Usually there is just one test.
10–12	Number of pairs. If just one test, this equals $N(N - 1)/2$ (i.e., all possible pairs), where N = number of objects. If more than one test is included in the total profile, the number of pairs equals $N(N - 1)/2$ multiplied by the number of tests.
	0 = rank order of data
13–15	Positive value = punch cards with subjects rank order.
18	1 = rank order data
	0 = paired comparison data
21	Required only for comparison data
	0 = data coded in 1's and 0's
	1 = data coded in 1's and 2's
22–24	Required only if data not on cards. Unit number from which the data are being read.

2. Variable Format Card: ID is in A format, should precede the data, and should not exceed 8 columns. Data are in I format.
3. Key Card(s): Required only if data are in form of paired comparison

choices. They contain numerical pairings to which the data must conform, usually show all possible pairings, and follow the form:

$$1–2,1–3, \ldots 1–N,2–3,2–4, \ldots 2–N, \ldots (N-1) - N$$

The pairs are written in 2 digit fields so that a pairing of item 1 with item 2 will be punched as 0102. Use up to 80 columns per card. Max number of key cards = 6.

2. Input Example for Program RANKO, *Preference Data from Table 20.2*.

```
//RANKO JOB (2919,267F,2X),'DUNN-RANKIN'
// EXEC EDSTAT,PROGRAM=RANKO
//GO.SYSIN DD *
   5  6  1  6
(A2,8X,6I1)
010201030104020302040304
DS         221212
HA         122221
DB         122221
BB         222112
PD         112212
/*
//
```

3. Output from Program RANKO, *Data from Table 20.2*.

```
     SCALE SCORES FROM PAIRED COMPARISONS
   SUBJECTS =  5
   CATEGORIES =  4
   TESTS =  1
   PAIRS =  6
   PAIRS EACH TEST =  6
   INCREMENT =  1
   STATISTICAL N =    5
   PUNCH =  0
   NOPAIR =  0


   SUBJECT          TEST              RANK  VALUES


 FORMAT CARD(S)

        (A2,8X,6I1)
        DS           1        2  3  3  2
 CUMULATIVE RANK VALUES        2  3  3  2

        HA           1        2  1  4  3
 CUMULATIVE RANK VALUES        2  1  4  3

        DB           1        2  1  4  3
 CUMULATIVE RANK VALUES        2  1  4  3

        BB           1        1  4  2  3
 CUMULATIVE RANK VALUES        1  4  2  3

        PD           1        3  2  2  3
 CUMULATIVE RANK VALUES        3  2  2  3
```

SCALE SCORES DERIVED FROM PAIRED COMPARISONS

ITEM	RANK TOTAL	SCALE SCORE
MIN	5	0
1	10	33
2	11	40
3	15	67
4	14	60
MAX	20	100

0   10   20   30   40   50   60   70   80   90   100

TABLE OF RANK DIFFERENCES

ITEMS

	3	4	2	1
3	0			
4	1	0		
2	4	3	0	
1	5	4	1	0

TAKE CRITICAL RANGE VALUES FROM TABLE

342

4. FORTRAN *Listing for Program* RANKO.

```
C
C PROGRAM RANKO
C
C     THIS IS A PROGRAM TO CONVERT PAIRED COMPARISON CHOICES
C           INTO RANK ORDERS AND THEN TO DERIVE SCALE SCORES
C           FROM THE CUMULATIVE RANK TOTALS.
C           OUTPUT FROM THIS PROGRAM INCLUDES'
C               1. RANK ORDERS FOR EACH SUBJECT FOR EACH ITEM
C               2. RANK TOTALS OVER ALL SUBJECTS
C               3. SCALE SCORES DERIVED FROM PAIR COMPARISONS
C               4. TABLE OF SIGNIFICANT DIFFERENCES
C               5. CRITICAL RANGES AT .10,.05,.01 LEVELS
      REAL*8 CHAR
      DIMENSION FMT(100),KEY(200),JR(100),JA(15,15),NRANK(15),
     1 MRANK(15), KRANK(15), Z(15), Z2(15), RANK(15),LRANK(15,15),
     2JZ2(15),Q1(13),Q2(13),Q3(13),MK(15)
      COMMON N1, NC, NT, NP, NP1, NA, JSUBJ, KEY, JR,
     1    JA,NRANK,MRANK,KOUNT,KRANK,RANK,KO,A,B,AVGR,VAR,S,MAXR,
     2 MINR,Z,Z2,BIGZ,JZ2,NC1,NA1,Q1,Q2,Q3,R1,R2,R3,NR1,NR2,NR3,MK
      NA=0
    1 READ(5,7000,END=947)N,NC,NT,NP,NPUNCH,NOPAIR,NX,NTAPE
 7000 FORMAT (8I3)
      IF (NOPAIR.EQ.0) NA=1
      IF (NTAPE.EQ.0) NTAPE=5
      WRITE(6,7001)
 7001 FORMAT (1H1,5X36HSCALE SCORES FROM PAIRED COMPARISONS )
      NP1=NP/NT
      JSUBJ=N*NT
      N1=N
      WRITE (6,7005) N,NC,NT,NP,NP1,NA,JSUBJ,NPUNCH,NOPAIR
 7005 FORMAT(5X, 10HSUBJECTS = I3/5X12HCATEGORIES =I3/5X7HTESTS = I3/
     1 15X7HPAIRS = I3/5X17HPAIRS EACH TEST = I3/5X11HINCREMENT = I3/
     2 5X15HSTATISTICAL N = I5/5X7HPUNCH = I3/5X8HNOPAIR = I3///)
      WRITE (6,7010)
 7010 FORMAT(7X,7HSUBJECT,9X,4HTEST,18X,4HRANK,2X,6HVALUES,/)
      DO 246 L=1,NC
  246 KRANK(L)=0
      KCUNT = 0
      CALL RFMT(FMT,5)
C     PROGRAM NOW READS THE KEY CARDS AND CONVERTS EACH SET OF DATA
      IF(NOPAIR)  4, 4, 3
    3 ITEN = NC/10
      IONE=NC-(ITEN*10)
    8 READ(NTAPE,FMT) CHAR,(NRANK(N),N=1,NC)
      GO TO 45
    4 NP2 = NP*2
      READ(5,1000)  ( KEY(I), I=1,NP2)
 1000 FORMAT(40I2)
      J = 1
      ITEN= NP/10
      IONE=NP-(ITEN*10)
      GO TO 604
    5 WRITE(6,2000)
 2000 FORMAT(1H )
  604   READ(NTAPE,FMT) CHAR,(JR(I),I=1,NP)
      IF (NX.NE.1) GO TO 601
      DO 600 I=1,NP
      IF (JR(I).EQ.2) JR(I)=0
  600 CONTINUE
  601 DO 500 N=1,NC
      DO 505 M=1,NC
  505 JA(M,N)=0
      MRANK(N)=0
  500 NRANK(N)=0
      KCUNT=0
      I=1
      J=J+1
```

```
     10 DO 510 L=1,NP1
        N=KEY(2*I-1)
        M = KEY(2*I)
        IF (JR(I) .EQ. 1) GO TO 30
     20 JA(N,M) = JA(N,M) + 1
        GO TO 40
     30 JA(M,N)=JA(M,N) + 1
     40 I=I+1
    510 CONTINUE
C       PROGRAM NOW ADDS THE JA(M,N) MATRIX TO GET A RANK ORDER
        DO 520 N=1,NC
    520 NRANK(N)=0
        DO 530 N=1,NC
        DO 535 M=1,NC
    535 NRANK(N)=NRANK(N)+JA(M,N)
    530 CONTINUE
     45 DO 540 N=1,NC
        NRANK(N)=NRANK(N)+NA
        MRANK(N)=MRANK(N)+NRANK(N)
        KRANK(N)=KRANK(N)+NRANK(N)
        RANK(N)=KRANK(N)
    540 CONTINUE
        KCUNT=KOUNT+1
        WRITE (6,979) CHAR,KCUNT,(NRANK(N),N=1,NC)
    979 FORMAT (10X,A8,3X,I5,4X,15I3)
        IF(NOPAIR) 47,47,55
     55 IF(KOUNT-N1) 8,90,90
     47 IF(NPUNCH) 50,50,60
     60 WRITE (7,2020) CHAR,KCUNT,(NRANK(N),N=1,NC),
       1(MRANK(N),N=1,NC)
   2020 FORMAT (A8,3X,I5,5X,15I3/15I3)
     50 DO 545 M=1,NC
        DC 545 N=1,NC
        JA(M,N)=0
    545 CONTINUE
        IF(I-NP) 10, 70, 70
     70 IF((NT .GT. 0) .AND. (KOUNT .EQ. NT)) WRITE(6,7070) (MRANK(N),N=1,
       1NC)
   7070 FORMAT(23H CUMULATIVE RANK VALUES,7X,15I3)
        IF(J-N1) 5, 5, 90
     90 CALL SCORE
        GC TO 1
    947 WRITE (6,447)
    447 FORMAT(1H1)
        END
        SUBROUTINE SCORE
C       THIS SUBROUTINE OBTAINS SCALE SCORES FROM THE RANK TOTALS
        DIMENSION       KEY(200), JR(100), JA(15,15), NRANK(15),
       1 MRANK(15), KRANK(15), Z(15), Z2(15), RANK(15),LRANK(15,15),
       2JZ2(15),Q1(13),Q2(13),Q3(13),MK(15)
        COMMON N1, NC, NT, NP, NP1, NA, JSUBJ, KEY, JR,
       1       JA,NRANK,MRANK,KOUNT,KRANK,RANK,KO,A,B,AVGR,VAR,S,MAXR,
       2 MINR,Z,Z2,BIGZ,JZ2,NC1,NA1,Q1,Q2,Q3,R1,R2,R3,NR1,NR2,NR3,MK
        WRITE (6,7025)
   7025 FORMAT(1H1//)
        WRITE (6,7030)
   7030 FORMAT(9X44HSCALE SCORES DERIVED FROM PAIRED COMPARISONS //)
        WRITE (6,7040)
   7040 FORMAT(14X32HITEM   RANK TOTAL   SCALE SCORE //)
        WRITE (6,7045)JSUBJ
   7045 FORMAT(15X3HMIN,6XI5,13X1H0)
        A=JSUBJ
        B=NC+1
        C=NC
        AVGR=A*B/2.0
        VAR=(A*B*C/12.0)
        S=SQRT(VAR)
        RMAX=JSUBJ*NC
        MAXR=JSUBJ*NC
        MINR=JSUBJ
```

```
      BIGZ=(RMAX-AVGR)/S
      DO 550 N=1,NC
      Z(N)=((RANK(N)-AVGR)/S)+BIGZ
  550 CONTINUE
      DO 555 N=1,NC
      Z2(N)=Z(N)/(2.0*BIGZ)*100.0
      JZ2(N)=Z2(N)+0.5
  555 CONTINUE
      WRITE (6,7050) (N,KRANK(N),JZ2(N),N=1,NC)
 7050 FORMAT(15XI2,7XI5,11XI3)
      WRITE (6,7055) MAXR
 7055 FORMAT(15X3HMAX,6XI5,11X3H100///)
      CALL CRITR
      RETURN
      END
      SUBROUTINE CRITR
C     THIS SUBROUTINE FINDS DIFFERENCES BETWEEN RANK TOTALS AND
C        CALCULATES SIGNIFICANT DIFFERENCES I.E.,CRIICAL RANGES
      DIMENSION        KEY(200), JR(100), JA(15,15), NRANK(15),
     1 MRANK(15), KRANK(15), Z(15), Z2(15), RANK(15),LRANK(15,15),
     2JZ2(15),Q1(13),Q2(13),Q3(13),MK(15),
     2                             JRAY(15),KRAY(102),NTABL(208),
     3 KTABL(182),QTABL1(14,7),QTABL2(14,7),QTABL3(14,7),R(20),NR(20)
      COMMON N1, NC, NT, NP, NP1, NA, JSUBJ, KEY, JR,
     1   JA,NRANK,MRANK,KOUNT,KRANK,RANK,KO,A,B,AVGR,VAR,S,MAXR,
     2 MINR,Z,Z2,BIGZ,JZ2,NC1,NA1,Q1,Q2,Q3,R1,R2,R3,NR1,NR2,NR3,MK
      DATA NTABL             /4*00,12,14,16,18,20,22,24,26,28,2*00,08,10,
     112,14,15,17,19,21,23,25,26,00,09,12,14,16,19,22,24,27,29,32,35,37,
     206,08,10,13,15,17,20,22,25,27,30,32,35,08,11,14,17,20,23,26,29,32,
     335,38,41,45,07,10,12,15,18,21,23,26,29,32,35,38,41,09,12,16,19,23,
     426,29,33,37,40,44,47,51,08,11,14,17,20,23,26,30,34,37,40,43,47,10,
     514,17,21,25,29,33,37,41,45,49,53,57,09,12,15,19,22,26,29,33,37,41,
     643,48,52,11,15,19,23,27,31,36,40,44,49,53,58,62,09,13,16,20,24,28,
     732,36,40,44,48,52,56,12,16,20,25,29,34,38,43,47,52,57,62,67,10,14,
     817,21,25,30,34,38,42,47,51,56,60,12,17,22,26,31,36,41,46,51,56,61,
     966,71,10,14,18,23,27,31,36,40,45,50,54,59,64/
      DATA KTABL  /13,18,23,28,33,38,43,49,54,59,65,70,75,11,15,19,24,28
     1,33,38,43,47,52,57,62,67,14,19,24,29,35,40,46,51,57,62,68,74,78,11
     2,15,20,25,30,35,40,45,50,55,60,65,71,14,20,25,31,36,42,48,54,59,65
     3,71,77,83,12,16,21,26,31,36,41,47,52,58,63,68,74,15,21,26,32,38,44
     4,50,56,62,68,74,80,87,12,17,22,27,32,38,43,49,54,60,65,71,77,16,21
     5,27,33,39,45,52,58,64,71,77,84,90,13,17,23,28,34,39,45,50,56,62,68
     6,74,80,16,22,28,34,41,47,54,60,67,73,80,87,94,13,18,24,29,35,40,46
     7,52,58,64,70,76,83,16,23,29,36,42,49,56,62,69,76,83,90,97,13,18,24
     8,30,36,42,48,54,60,67,73,79,86/
      DATA QTABL1/.0018,.0602,.1994,.3674,.5347,.6913,.8348,.9655,1.085,
     11.193,1.293,1.385,1.470,1.549,.0089,.1348,.3427,.5549,.7490,.9218,
     21.075,1.212,1.335,1.446,1.547,1.639,1.724,1.803,.0177,.1909,.4337,
     3.6650,.8695,1.048,1.205,1.343,1.467,1.578,1.679,1.771,1.856,1.934,
     4.0443,.3031,.5946,.8497,1.066,1.251,1.410,1.550,1.674,1.784,1.884,
     51.976,2.059,2.136,.0887,.4314,.7595,1.030,1.253,1.440,1.600,1.740,
     61.863,1.973,2.071,2.161,2.243,2.319,.1777,.6184,.9794,1.261,1.488,
     71.676,1.835,1.973,2.094,2.202,2.299,2.387,2.467,2.541,.3583,.9001,
     81.286,1.573,1.800,1.985,2.142,2.276,2.394,2.498,2.592,2.677,2.754,
     92.826/
      DATA QTABL2/.5449,1.138,1.531,1.818,2.042,2.224,2.377,2.508,2.623,
     12.724,2.815,2.898,2.973,3.042,.7416,1.363,1.757,2.040,2.260,2.438,
     22.587,2.715,2.826,2.925,3.014,3.094,3.168,3.235,.9539,1.588,1.978,
     32.257,2.472,2.645,2.791,2.915,3.024,3.121,3.207,3.285,3.356,3.422,
     41.190,1.826,2.210,2.482,2.692,2.861,3.002,3.123,3.229,3.322,3.406,
     53.482,3.551,3.615,1.466,2.095,2.469,2.733,2.936,3.099,3.236,3.353,
     63.455,3.546,3.627,3.700,3.767,3.829,1.812,2.424,2.784,3.037,3.232,
     73.389,3.520,3.632,3.730,3.817,3.895,3.966,4.030,4.089,2.326,2.902,
     83.240,3.478,3.661,3.808,3.931,4.037,4.129,4.211,4.285,4.351,4.412,
     94.468/
      DATA QTABL3/2.772,3.314,3.633,3.858,4.030,4.170,4.286,4.387,4.474,
     14.552,4.622,4.685,4.743,4.796,3.170,3.682,3.984,4.197,4.361,4.494,
     24.605,4.700,4.784,4.858,4.925,4.985,5.041,5.092,3.643,4.120,4.403,
     34.603,4.757,4.882,4.987,5.078,5.157,5.227,5.290,5.348,5.400,5.448,
     43.970,4.424,4.694,4.886,5.033,5.154,5.255,5.341,5.418,5.485,5.546,
```

```
     55.602,5.652,5.699,4.654,5.063,5.309,5.484,5.619,5.730,5.823,5.903,
     65.973,6.036,6.092,6.144,6.191,6.234,.999,.995,.99,.975,.95,.90,.80
     7,.70,.60,.50,.40,.30,.20,.10,.05,.025,.01,.005,.001,9*100./
       DO 583I=1,101
       CALL HOLLER(KRAY(I),1H-)
 583 CONTINUE
       DO 585 I=1,NC
       LI=JZ2(I)+1
       CALL HOLLER(KRAY(LI),1H*)
 585 CONTINUE
       WRITE(6,7056)
7056 FORMAT(9X,103H0            10          20         30         40          50
     1        60          70          80          90         100         //)
       WRITE(6,7058) (KRAY(I),I=1,101)
7058 FORMAT(9X,101A1///)
       WRITE (6,7060)
7060 FORMAT(9X32HTABLE OF RANK DIFFERENCES           /)
       WRITE (6,7065)
7065 FORMAT(30X5HITEMS/)
       DO 558 I=1,15
       JRAY(I)=I
 558 CONTINUE
       NC1=NC-1
       DO 560 N=1,NC1
       NA1=N+1
       DO 560 J=NA1,NC
       IF (KRANK(N)-KRANK(J)) 115,560,560
 115 LTEMP=KRANK(N)
       KTEMP=JRAY(N)
       KRANK(N) = KRANK(J)
       JRAY(N)=JRAY(J)
       KRANK(J)=LTEMP
       JRAY(J)=KIEMP
 560 CONTINUE
       DO 575 J=1,NC
       DO 575 N=1,NC
       LRANK(N,J)=KRANK(J)-KRANK(N)
 575 CONTINUE
       WRITE (6,7070) (JRAY(N),N=1,NC)
7070 FORMAT(16X,15(3XI4)/)
       DO 580 N=1,NC
 581 WRITE (6,7075)JRAY(N),(LRANK(N,J),J=1,N)
7075 FORMAT(14XI2,15(3XI4))
 580 CONTINUE
       IF (N1-16) 120, 121, 121
 121 WRITE (6,7078)
7078 FORMAT (1H0)
       WRITE (6,7080)
7080 FORMAT(16X51H              SIGNIFICANCE LEVEL   RANK DIFFERENCE NEEDED)
       DO 610 J=1,7
       I=NC-1
       K=J+7
       R(J)=QTAB11(I,J)*S
       NR(J)=R(J)+.5
       R(K)=QTAB12(I,J)*S
       NR(K)=R(K)+.5
 610 CONTINUE
       DO 620 J=1,5
       K =J+14
       R(K )=QTABL3(I,J)*S
 620 NR(K)=R(K )+.5
       WRITE (6,7085) (QTABL3(I,6),NR(I),I=1,14)
       WRITE(6,7085) (QTABL3(I,7),NR(I+14),I=1,5)
7085  FORMAT(32XF5.3,17XI4)
       GO TO 600
 120 WRITE (6,8005)
8005 FORMAT(1H0,15X39H TAKE CRITICAL RANGE VALUES FROM TABLE    //)
       WRITE (6,8010)
8010 FORMAT (1H1,9X24HTABLE OF CRITICAL RANGES    //)
       WRITE (6,8015)
```

```
8015 FCRMAT (45X5BITEMS/)
     WRITE (6,8020)
8020 FORMAT (     13X60HJ    A    3    4    5    6    7    8    9   10   11   12
    1 13   14   15          / )
     IL2=13
     LI1=1
     DO 590 I=2,9
     WRITE (6,8025) (NTABL(J),J=LL1,LL2)
8025 FORMAT(1HO,16X3H.01,13I4)
     LL1=LL1+13
     LL2=LL2+13
     WRITE (6,8030)  I,(NTABL(J),J=LL1,LL2)
8030 FORMAT(12XI3,2X3H.05,13I4)
     LL1=LL1+13
     LL2=LL2+13
 590 CONTINUE
     LL1=1
     LL2=13
     DO 592 I=10,15
     WRITE (6,8025) (KTABL(J),J=LL1,LL2)
     LL1=LL1+13
     LL2=LL2+13
     WRITE (6,8030)  I,(KTABL(J),J=LL1,LL2)
     LL1=LL1+13
     LL2=LL2+13
 592 CONTINUE
 600 RETURN
     END
```

SINDSCAL (Symmetric Individual Differences Scaling)

1. Description, FORTRAN *Source, and Input Directions.*   The popularity of Individual Differences Scaling has promoted Sandra Pruzanski (1975) to create a modern version of the Carroll and Chang's (1968) INDSCAL program which is faster than the original program and easier to use. Forest Young's general program ALSCAL in the SAS package of programs also performs individual differences scaling. Tucker (1972) has written a general procedure for multimode factor analysis, a form of Individual Differences Scaling.

If your computer center does not have the SINDSCAL program, a tape should be purchased from Bell Telephone Laboratories, Murray Hill, N.J.

Plot

The program generates printer plots of all possible planes (defined by pairs of SINDSCAL coordinates) of the final "group" stimulus space and weights space. The points are labelled with single characters from A–Z then 1–9; this sequence is repeated up to 100 points. It is also possible to suppress all plotting.

Input

An example of an input deck is shown in Appendix A.

CARD 1: Parameter Card—(FORMAT—4I4)
        MAXDIM, MINDIM, NMAT, NSTIM

Column

Column		
1–4	MAXDIM –	maximum number of dimensions (must be ≤ 10)—(See Option B)
5–8	MINDIM –	minimum number of dimensions—(See Option E)
9–12	NMAT –	number of input matrices
13–16	NSTIM –	number of stimuli

CARD 2: Parameter Card—(FORMAT—5I4)
        ITMAX, IRDATA, IPUNCH, IPLOT, IRN

Column

Column		
1–4	ITMAX –	maximum number of iterations If ITMAX = 0 program will solve for weights only. (See Option E)
5–8	IRDATA –	form of input data (See Option A) = 1, similarities, lowerhalf matrices without diagonals = 2, dissimilarities, lowerhalf matrices without diagonals = 3, euclidean distances, lowerhalf matrices without diagonals = 4, correlations, lowerhalf matrices without diagonals = −4, same as 4 but program normalizes each matrix so sum of squares = 1. = 5, covariances, lowerhalf matrices with diagonals = −5, same as 5 but program normalizes each matrix so sum of squares = 1. = 6, similarities, full symmetric matrices (diagonal ignored) = 7, dissimilarities, full symmetric matrices (diagonal ignored)
9–12	IPUNCH –	punch option (See Option G) all punch options except −1 include punching normalized solution = −1, no punched output = 0, punch normalized solution only = 1, punch scalar products matrices

    = 2, punch three unnormalized matrices
    = 3, punch all of the above
13–16   IPLOT − plot options (See Option H)
    = −1, no plotting
    = 0, plot all pairs of planes, points are letters or digits
17–20   IRN − starting configuration (See Option C)
    = 0, user inputs an initial stimulus configuration
    = integer-maximum 4 digits, serves as a primer for generating random starting configuration
CARD 3: Title Card (only one card, 72 columns allowed)
CARD 4: Format of data matrices—enclosed in parentheses (must be F or E format)
CARDS 5 thru N: Data matrices, each card (or cards) contains one row of a proximities matrix of the form specified by IRDATA (col. 5–8, CARD 1) in format as specified on CARD 4.
OPTIONAL CONFIGURATION CARDS—(If IRN = 0)
    CONFIGURATION CARD 1: Format of stimulus configuration (must be F or E format)
    CONFIGURATION CARDS 2 thru N: Initial stimulus configuration in format given on previous card. Each card (or cards) contains one dimension of a dimensions-by-stimulus matrix.
LAST CARD: Must be blank in columns 1–20.

2. Input Example for Program SINDSCAL, *Data from Table 20.3 via* LOMAT.

```
//SINCSCAL JOB (2919,267F),'DUNN-RANKIN'
// EXEC EDSTAT,PROGRAM=SINDSCAL
//GO.SYSIN DD *
    2    2    5    4
   10    1         3333
 SINDSCAL EXAMPLE, INDIVIDUAL MATRICES FROM TABLE 20.1, VIA LOMAT
(4F6.2)
    5.00
    2.00    2.00
    4.00    2.00    5.00
    6.00
    2.00    3.00
    4.00    2.00    7.00
    4.00
    2.00    4.00
    4.00    2.00    4.00
    6.00
    4.00    3.00
    5.00    3.00    6.00
    5.00
    3.00    3.00
    6.00    2.00    5.00
/*
//
```

3. Example Output from SINDSCAL, *Data via* LOMAT *from Table 20.2.*

```
                           SYMMETRIC INDSCAL

        SINDSCAL EXAMPLE, INDIVIDUAL MATRICES FROM TABLE 20.1, VIA LOMAT

   ****************************************************
   PARAMETERS
    DIM  IRDATA  ITMAX IPUNCH  IPLOT     IRN
     2     1      10     0       0      3333
   NO. OF MATRICES =   5  NO. OF STIM. =   4

   ****************************************************

   INITIAL STIMULUS MATRIX
     1 -0.009 -0.191 -0.496  0.349
     2 -0.100  0.366  0.490 -0.078

                           HISTORY OF COMPUTATION
   ITERATION          CORRELATIONS BETWEEN        VAF                   LOSS
                        Y(DATA) AND YHAT          (R**2)             (Y-YHAT)**2
         0                0.350205              0.122644              0.877356
         1                0.935374              0.874925              0.125075
         2                0.952924              0.908064              0.091935
         3                0.953235              0.908656              0.091344
         4                0.953362              0.908899              0.091101
         5                0.953529              0.909218              0.090782
         6                0.953750              0.909639              0.090361
         7                0.954041              0.910195              0.089805
         8                0.954426              0.910930              0.089070
         9                0.954934              0.911900              0.088100
        10                0.955600              0.913171              0.086828
   REACHED MAXIMUM ITERATIONS
      FINAL               0.883055              0.779786              0.220214

                           NORMALIZED SOLUTION

   SUBJECTS WEIGHT MATRIX
    1     0.711  0.709  0.636  0.808  0.805
    2     0.421  0.442  0.654  0.253  0.510

   STIMULUS MATRIX
    1     -0.036 -0.760  0.171  0.625
    2      0.661 -0.187 -0.693  0.219

   NORMALIZED SUM OF PRODUCTS (SUBJECTS)
    1     1.000
    2     0.941  1.000

   SUM OF PRODUCTS (STIMULI)
    1     1.000
    2     0.137  1.000

   APPROXIMATE PROPORTION OF TOTAL VARIANCE ACCOUNTED FOR BY EACH DIMENSION
            1      2
          0.551  0.228

   CORRELATION BETWEEN COMPUTED SCORES AND SCALAR PROD. FOR SUBJECTS


        1     0.833248
        2     0.842745
        3     0.920676
        4     0.850736
        5     0.960731
```

WEIGHTS SPACE   DIMENSION 2 (Y-AXIS) VS. DIMENSION 1 (X-AXIS)
SINDSCAL EXAMPLE, INDIVIDUAL MATRICES FROM TABLE 20.1, VIA LOMAT

STIMULUS SPACE   DIMENSION 2 (Y-AXIS) VS. DIMENSION 1 (X-AXIS)
SINDSCAL EXAMPLE, INDIVIDUAL MATRICES FROM TABLE 20.1, VIA LOMAT

A

D

C

B

0.6000

0.4000

0.2000

0.0

-0.2000

-0.4000

-0.6000

-0.8000

SUBROUTINES

1. Description. While most of the FORTAN programs listed in this chapter are self contained a few require the addition of subroutines that are used by more than one program. These routines were originally written by Bob Bloedon or Donald Veldman. The routines are used to handle control cards, allocate storage, and to handle the reading and printing (or punching) of the results. One routine CCDS, a control subroutine, calls subroutines that also call other routines:

CCDS calls RFMT calls PAREN
      calls INPUT calls NLOC
                    calls SINTL

Therefore, whenever CCDS is used five other subroutines are also called. Therefore these six routines are grouped together under CCDS. Following is a list of the main source programs and the subroutines that they call.

	APRINT	CCDS	DYNA	PCDS	PRTS	PTMS
DISSIM	x	x	x	x	x	x
GOWER	x	x	x	x	x	x
HGROUP		x				
KENTAU	uses PAREN and RFMT only					
TESTAT		x	x	x	x	
TSCALE		x	x		x	
TRICIR	The IMSL routines MDTD, MDBIN, MDCDFI, UERTST are only available from International Mathematical and Statistical Library.					

2. FORTRAN *Listing for Subroutine* APRINT, *Used with Programs* GOWER *and* DISSIM.

```
      SUBROUTINE APRINT(B, N, PTYPE)
C
C     ********* BEGINNING OF SUBROUTINE APRINT*********
C
C     THIS SUBROUTINE PRINTS THE DATA FROM SYMMETRIC ARRAY B
C     AND SETS THE FORMAT FOR THE DIFFERENT TYPES OF VECTOR PRINTING.
C
C        THIS PROGRAM IS DESIGNED TO BE A GENERAL PRINT ROUTINE FOR
C     FOR AN ARRAY.  THE VARIABLE 'TYPE' CONTROLS HOW THE VECTOR WILL
C     BE PRINTED.   THE TYPES ARE:
C        0 = UPPER TRIANGULAR MATRIX WITH THE DIAGONAL ELEMENT
C        1 = UPPER TRIANGULAR MATRIX WITHOUT THE DIAGONAL ELEMENT
C        2 = LOWER TRIANGULAR MATRIX WITH THE DIAGONAL ELEMENT
C        3 = LOWER TRIANGULAR MATRIX WITHOUT THE DIAGONAL ELEMENT
C        4 = FULL SYMMETRIC MATRIX
C
C     VARIABLES PASSED FROM THE MAIN PROGRAM
C        N = NUMBER OF ROWS OR COLUMNS
```

```
C             B = N X N ARRAY PASSED FROM CALLING PROGRAM
C             PTYPE = COMBINED OUTPUT FORMAT AND PRINT AND PUNCH FLAG
C
C        OTHER VARIABLES FOR SUBROUTINE APRINT
C             TYPE EXTRACTED VALUE THAT DETERMINES PRINTING FORMAT
C             PRTPCH = CONTROLS WHETHER PRINTING, PUNCHING, BOTH OR NEITHER
C                      IS DONE. PARAMETERS ARE :
C                      0 = PRINT ONLY
C                      1 = PUNCH ONLY
C                      2 = PRINT AND PUNCH
C             ANY OTHER VALUE IN PRTPCH SUPPRESSES BOTH PRINTING AND
C             PUNCHING.
C             R = ROW POSITION
C             C = COLUMN POSITION
C             K,L,O = CONTROL START & END OF LOOP SO THAT THE DIAGONAL
C                ELEMENT MAY BE EXCLUDED
C
      LOGICAL DEBUG,CONFLG,PRTFLG,PCHFLG
      INTEGER CSIZE,TYPE,PRTPCH,R,C,P,K,L,N,O,LIMIT,PTYPE
      REAL B(N,N)
      DATA DEBUG /.FALSE./
C     ***CHECK FOR ILLEGAL VALUES OF TYPE***********
C
      PRTPCH = MOD(PTYPE,10) - 1
      TYPE = PTYPE/10 - 1
C
      IF ((TYPE .GE. 0 .AND. TYPE .LE. 4).AND.(PRTPCH .GE.0 .AND. PRTPCH
     1 .LE. 2)) GO TO 10
      PRINT 2
      RETURN
   10 CONTINUE
C
C     *****DEBUG PRINT*****
C
      IF (.NOT. DEBUG) GO TO 20
         LIMIT = N*N
         PRINT 1,TYPE,LIMIT
         DO 15 I=1,N
           PRINT 3,(B(I,J),J=1,N)
   15    CONTINUE
   20 CONTINUE
C
      PRTFLG = (PRTPCH .EQ. 0 ) .OR. (PRTPCH .EQ. 2 )
      PCHFLG = (PRTPCH .EQ. 1 ) .OR. (PRTPCH .EQ. 2 )
C
      K=1
      L=0
      O=N
C     **K,L&O CHANGE TO EXCLUDE THE DIAGONAL ELEMENT FOR TYPES 3 & 1**
      IF (TYPE.EQ.3) K=2
      IF (TYPE.EQ.1) O=N-1
      IF (TYPE.EQ.1) L=1
C
C     *****MATRIX PRINT LOOP*****
C
      DO 50 R=K,O
         L=L+1
C
C        **UPPER TRIANGULAR MATRIX OUTPUT**
         CONFLG = (TYPE .EQ. 0) .OR. (TYPE .EQ.1)
         IF (CONFLG .AND. PRTFLG) PRINT 3, (B(R,C),C=L,N)
         IF (CONFLG .AND. PCHFLG) PUNCH 4, (B(R,C),C=L,N)
C
C        **LOWER TRIANGULAR MATRIX OUTPUT**
         CONFLG = (TYPE.EQ.2 .OR. TYPE.EQ.3)
         IF (CONFLG .AND. PRTFLG) PRINT 3, (B(C,R),C=1,L)
         IF (CONFLG .AND. PCHFLG) PUNCH 4, (B(C,R),C=1,L)
C
C        **FULL MATRIX OUTPUT**
         CONFLG = (TYPE.EQ.4)
```

```
            IF (CONFLG .AND. PRTFLG) PRINT 3, (B(R,C),C=1,N)
            IF (CONFLG .AND. PCHFLG) PUNCH 4, (B(R,C),C=1,N)
     50 CONTINUE
C      *****END OF MATRIX PRINT LOOP*****
C
       IF (DEBUG) PRINT 5, PRTPCH,TYPE,PRTFLG,PCHFLG,CONFLG
C
     1 FORMAT(1X,'SUBROUTINE APRINT, TYPE=',I2,'LIMIT=',I2)
     2 FORMAT (1X, 'TYPE EXCEEDS RANGE')
     3 FORMAT (1X,12F10.4)
     4 FORMAT (6(1PE12.6))
     5 FORMAT(2I2,3I2)
C      ****END OF SUBROUTINE APRINT****
       RETURN
       END
```

3. FORTRAN Listing for Subroutine CCDS.

```
       SUBROUTINE CCDS (KF, KI, KJ, KK, KL, KM, KN)
       DIMENSION KH(20),KF(80)
       REAL*4 KF
       REAL KH, KN* 8
       READ(5,10,END=99) KH,KI,KJ,KK,KL,KM
    10 FORMAT(20A4/5I5)
       PRINT 15, KN, KH, KI, KJ, KK, KL, KM
   150 FORMAT (1H1,5X,24H*** OUTPUT FROM PROGRAM ,A6,4H ***//1X,20A4 //
      1 11H PARAMETERS / 13H COL  1- 5 = , I5 /
      2 13H COL  6-10 = , I5 / 13H COL 11-15 = , I5 / 13H COL 16-20 = ,
      3I5/13H COL 21-25 = ,I5)
       CALL RFMT(KF,4)
       CALL INPUT(KN, KH, 0, KF, KI)
       RETURN
    99 CALL EXIT
       RETURN
       END
```

4. Assembly Language Listing for Subroutine PAREN.

```
            ENTRY PAREN
PAREN       STM    14,12,12(13)
            USING PAREN,15
            L     2,0(1)
            L     3,4(1)
            L     3,0(3)
            S     3,=F'2'
            AR    2,3            R2 IS ADDRESS OF FMT
            L     3,8(1)
            L     3,0(3)
            L     8,12(1)
            L     9,16(1)
            L     4,0(8)
            L     5,0(9)
            LA    6,1
            AR    2,3
LOOP        CLI   0(2),X'4D'
            BNE   NEXT
            AR    4,6
NEXT        CLI   0(2),X'5D'
            BNE   INCR
```

```
        AR    5,6
INCR    SR    2,6
        BCT   3,LOOP
        ST    4,0(8)
```

5. FORTRAN *Listing for Subroutine* RFMT.

```
      SUBROUTINE RFMT(FMT,M)
      DIMENSION FMT(1)
      N=1
      IR=0
      IL=0
      I=1
      J=20
      K=0
      PRINT 13
 13   FORMAT('0 FORMAT CARD(S)'//)
 20   IF(K.EQ.M)GO TO 50
      READ(5,100)(FMT(II),II=I,J)
      CALL PAREN (FMT,N,80,IL,IR)
      PRINT 14,(FMT(II),II=I,J)
 14   FORMAT(10X,20A4)
      IF(IR.EQ.IL)RETURN
      K=K+1
      I=I+20
      J=J+20
      N=N+80
      GO TO 20
 50   PRINT 11,FMT
 11   FORMAT (///'  ERROR IN FORMAT STATEMENT---UNBALANCE PARENTHESES'/
     1               '  EXECUTION TERMINATED'//(10X,20A4))
100   FORMAT(20A4)
      CALL EXIT
      STOP
      END
```

6. FORTRAN *Listing for Subroutine* INPUT.

```
      SUBROUTINE INPUT (ID,X,K,KF,N)
      DIMENSION X(N),KF(80),KX(N)
      REAL*4 KF
      REAL ID*8
      IF(K.NE.0)GO TO 5
      L=0
      CALL NLOC (KF,1,20,1HA,M)
      IF(M.GT.16)L=1
      RETURN
 5    IF(L.EQ.1)GO TO 6
      READ KF,ID,X
      RETURN
 6    READ KF,X
      CALL SINTL(ID,1,8,K)
      RETURN
      ENTRY INPIT (ID,KX,K,KF,N)
      IF(L.EQ.1)GO TO 7
      READ KF,ID,KX
      RETURN
 7    READ KF,KX
      CALL SINTL(ID,1,8,K)
      RETURN
      END
```

7. *Assembly Language Listing for Subroutine* NLOC.

C

```
          ENTRY NLOC
NLOC      STM    14,12,12(13)
          USING NLOC,15
          L      4,0(1)
          L      3,4(1)
          L      3,0(3)
          S      3,ONE
          AR     4,3
          L      3,8(1)
          L      3,0(3)
          L      5,16(1)
          ST     3,0(5)
          ST     5,RM
          L      5,12(1)
          SR     6,6
          IC     6,0(5)
          LA     5,TABLE
          AR     5,6
          MVI    0(5),X'01'
          S      3,ONE
          EX     3,TRANS
          BZ     PAU
          SR     1,4
          L      5,RM
          ST     1,0(5)
PAU       LM     14,12,12(13)
          BR     14
TRANS     TRT    0(0,4),TABLE
ONE       DC     F'1'
TABLE     DC     256X'00'
RM        DS     F
          END
```

8. *Assembly Language Listing for Subroutine* SINTL.

```
          ENTRY SINTL
SINTL     STM    14,12,12(13)
          USING SINTL,15
          L      2,0(1)
          L      3,4(1)
          L      3,0(3)
          S      3,ONE
          AR     2,3
          L      3,8(1)
          L      3,0(3)
          L      4,12(1)
          L      4,0(4)
          CVD    4,NM
          S      3,ONE
          LR     7,3
          SLA    3,4(0)
          EX     3,UPCK
```

```
            LR      3,7
            LR      5,3
            AR      5,2
            LR      6,2
BLANKS      CLI     0(2),X'F0'
            BNE     MINUS
            MVI     0(2),X'40'
            A       2,ONE
            BCT     3,BLANKS
MINUS       MVZ     ZN(0),0(5)
            CLI     ZN,X'D0'
            BNE     PLUS
            S       2,ONE
            CR      2,6
            BNM     GO
            STC     7,ERROR+1
ERROR       MVC     0(0,2),AST
            B       PAU
GO          MVI     0(2),X'60'
PLUS        OI      0(5),X'F0'
            CR      2,6
            BE      PAU
            AR      7,6
            SR      7,2
            STC     7,MOVE+1
MOVE        MVC     0(0,6),0(2)
            AR      6,7
            SR      5,6
            S       5,ONE
            STC     5,SPACE+1
            A       6,ONE
SPACE       MVC     0(0,6),BLNK
PAU         LM      14,12,12(13)
            BR      14
UPCK        UNPK    0(0,2),NM
HOLD        DS      D
NM          DS      D
ZN          DC      X'00000000'
ONE         DC      F'1'
BLNK        DC      CL8' '
AST         DC      C'********'
            END
```

9. *Assembly Language Listing for Subroutine* DYNA.   This is a dynamic
core allocation routine that is used with several programs including DISSIM,
GOWER, TESTAT, and TSCALE. The two error subroutines are specific to
DYNA.

```
************************************************************************
*
*          DYNAMIC CORE ALLOCATICN PROGRAM FOR FCRTRAN PROGRAMS
*          USING OS MACRO GETMAIN FOR THE ALLOCATION MECHANISM.
*
*                           2. DOUBLE-WORD BOUNDARIES
*
*              CORE GUESTIMATION ALGORITHM
*
*              LINKAGE EDITOR MAP   TOTAL LENGTH
*              SYSIN/SYSPRINT          4K BYTES
*              FOR N DD CARDS          N*2K BYTES
```

```
*                    SUM (BLKSIZE*BUFNO)          M
*                    TOTAL REQUIREMENTS  (TOTAL LENGTH) +4K+N*2K+M
*
****************************************************************************
DYNA     CSECT
         STM      14,12,12(13)           SAVE THE GENERAL REGISTERS
         LR       12,15                  USE GR 12 AS THE BASE REGISTER
         USING    DYNA,12                TELL THE ASSEMBLER THE BASE IS
         LR       2,1                    SAVE REGISTER 1 FOR LATER.
         LA       0,SAVESIZE             GR 0 HAS THE SIZE OF SAVE AREA
         BAL      1,*+4                  IBM CONVENTION FOR GETMAIN (R)
         SVC      10                     GET MAIN SVC
         USING    DYNASAVE,11
         LR       11,1                   USE GR 11 AS SAVE BASE REGISTER
         LR       1,2                    RESTORE GR 1 TO ORIGINAL VALUE
         ST       13,SAVEAREA+4          SAVE GR 13 FOR LINKAGE
         LA       13,SAVEAREA            RESET THE LINKAGE
         ST       1,SAVEGR1
*
*        INITIALIZATION OF THE PARAMETER LISTS, AND CONSTANTS
*
         LA       3,MINSIZE
         ST       3,GETSIZE
         LA       3,FREEAREA
         ST       3,GETAREA
         ST       3,ERRLIST
         MVI      GETMODE,X'E0'
         MVI      GETSP,X'00'
         XC       FREEAREA(16),FREEAREA
         EJECT
****************************************************************************
*
*        NOW START ALLOCATING THE CORRECT ADDRESSESS.
*
****************************************************************************
         L        5,SAVEGR1
         L        4,0(0,5)               GET ADDRESS OF REAL MAIN PROGRAM
         L        4,0(0,4)               GR 4 HAS THE ADDRESS OF REAL ONE
         ST       4,SAVEMAIN
         LA       5,4(0,5)               GR 5 POINTS TO THE ARRAY ADDRESS
         ST       5,SAVEGR1              SAVE THE NEW PARMLIST PNTR.
*
*        WANDER THRU THE PARAMETER LIST TO DETERMINE THE MAX CORE REQ'D
*
         LA       0,0                    ZERO THE WORK REGISTER.
         LA       4,0                    ZERO THE WORK REGISTER.
LOCATES  EQU      *
         CLI      0(5),X'80'             CHECK FOR ERRONEOUS PARM LIST
         BE       ERROR1
         L        4,4(0,5)               GET THE NUMBER OF WORDS REQ'D
         L        4,0(0,4)               THE ACTUAL NUMBER
         SRL      4,1                    NUMBER OF WORDS/2
         LA       4,1(0,4)               SAFETY FACTOR
         SLL      4,3                    PREPARE FOR DOUBLE WORDS
         AR       0,4                    SUM UP THE NUMBER OF DOUBLE WORD
         CLI      4(5),X'80'             CHECK FOR END OF LIST
         LA       5,8(0,5)               STEP FOR THE EXT SET
         BNE      LOCATES
*
*        FORCING DOUBLE WORD ALIGNMENT FOR DOUBLE PRECISION ARRAYS.
*
         ST       0,MAXSIZE              FOR THE GET MAIN ROUTINE
         LA       1,GETLIST
         SVC      4                      GETMAIN SVC CODE
         L        2,FREEAREA             GR 2 HAS THE ADDRESS OF FREECORE
         L        3,FREESIZE             GR 3 HAS THE AMOUNT OF FREECORE
         C        3,MAXSIZE              TEST IS ALLOCATED ENOUGH
         BL       ERROR
         L        5,SAVEGR1              RESET GR 1
```

```
LOOP      EQU        *
          ST         2,0(0,5)           CHANGE THE OLD ARRAY ADDRESS
          L          6,4(0,5)           PICK UP THE ADDRESS OF =BYTES
          L          6,0(0,6)           GR6 = NUMBER OF WORDS IN ARRAY
          SRL        6,1                =WORDS/2
          LA         6,1(0,6)           =WORD==WORDS+1
          SLL        6,3                =WORDS=MULTIPLE OF 8
          AR         2,6                GR 2-> NEW FREE AREA
          CLI        4(5),X'80'         CHECK IF LAST ARGUMENT
          LA         5,8(0,5)           GR 5 -> NEW ARRAY LIN LIST
          BNE        LOOP
          EJECT
*
*         NOW CALL THE REAL MAIN PROGRAM WITH THE NEW PARAMETER LIST
*
          L          1,SAVEGR1
          L          15,SAVEMAIN
          BALR       14,15              GO TO IT.
*
*         FIRST FREE THE ALLOCATED CORE.
*         RETURN TO THE MAIN CALLER NORMALLY.
*
RETRUNS   EQU        *
          L          0,FREESIZE
          L          1,FREEAREA
          SVC        10                 FREE THE ALLOCATED CORE.
RETURNQ   EQU        *
          L          13,SAVEAREA+4
          LA         0,SAVESIZE         FREE UP THE SAVE AREA
          LR         1,11               RETURN THE ALLOCATED ADDRESS
          SVC        10                 FREE MAIN
          LM         14,12,12(13)
          LA         15,0
          BR         14
*
*         NOT ENOUGH CORE IS ALLOCATED FOR THIS JOB
*
ERROR     EQU        *
          LA         1,ERRLIST
          L          15,=V($ERR1)
          LA         14,RETRUNS
          BR         15
*
*         INCORRECT SETUP OF THE PARAMETER LIST, MISSING =OF BYTES
*
ERROR1    EQU        *
          LA         14,RETURNQ
          L          15,=V($ERR2)
          BR         15
          EJECT
*****************************************************************
*
*         DYNAMIC SAVE AREA AND CONSTANTS FOR PROGRAM
*         THE ADDRESSESES AND CONSTANTS ARE FILLED IN AT EXECUTION TIME.
*
*****************************************************************
          LTORG
DYNASAVE  DSECT
SAVEBEG   EQU        *
          DS         0F
GETLIST   EQU        *
GETSIZE   DS         AL4(MINSIZE)       PARAMETER LIST FOR GETMAIN
GETAREA   DS         AL4(FREEAREA)
GETMODE   DS         XL1'E0'            VC MODE
GETSP     DS         XL1'00'            SP 0
*
          DS         0F
FREEAREA  DS         AL4(0)             ADDRESS OF FREE CORE AREA
FREESIZE  DS         1F'0'              NUMBER OF BYTES ALLOCATED
```

```
MINSIZE    DS      1F'0'              MINIMUM CORE REQUIREMENT
MAXSIZE    DS      1F'0'              MAXIMUM CORE REQUIREMENT
*
ERRLIST    DS      AL4(FREEAREA)
SAVEAREA   DS      18F'0'
SAVEGR1    DS      01F'0'
SAVEMAIN   DS      1F'0'
SAVEEND    EQU     *
SAVESIZE   EQU     SAVEEND-SAVEBEG
           END



      SUBROUTINE $ERR1(ICORE)
      DIMENSION ICORE(4)
      PRINT 10,ICORE(1),ICORE(2),ICORE(4)
   10 FORMAT('ODYNA ERROR: INSUFFICIENT CORE FOR PROGRAM '//
      1' ALLOCATED CORE AT ',Z8,' OF ', I6,' BYTES, BUT REQUIRED '
      2,I6,' BYTES.'//)
      RETURN
      END



      SUBROUTINE $ERR2
      PRINT 10
   10 FORMAT('ODYNA ERROR: INCORRECT PARAMETER LIST SETUP')
      STOP
      END
```

10. FORTRAN Listing for Subroutine PCDS.

```
C
      SUBROUTINE PCDS (X, N, M, KH, ND)
      DIMENSION X(ND, M)
      REAL*8 KH
      IF (M .GT. 1) GO TO 15
      L = 1
      DO 10 I = 1,N,7
      J = MIN0(I + 6, N)
      PUNCH 5, KH, M, L, (X(K,1), K = I,J)
    5 FORMAT (A5, I3, I2, 7F10.4)
   10 L = L + 1
      RETURN
   15 DO 20 I = 1,N
      LL = 1
      DO 20 J = 1,M,7
      K = MIN0(J + 6, M)
      PUNCH 5, KH, I, LL, (X(I,L), L = J,K)
   20 LL = LL + 1
      RETURN
      END
```

11. FORTRAN Listing for Subroutine PRTS.

```
      SUBROUTINE PRTS (X, N, M, KH, ND)
      DIMENSION X(ND, M)
      REAL KH*8
      IF (M .GT. 1) GO TO 20
      PRINT 15
      DO 10 I = 1,N,10
      J = MINO(I + 9, N)
      PRINT 5, KH, (K, K = I,J)
    5 FORMAT (/1X,A8, 10I11)
   10 PRINT 15, (X(K,1), K = I,J)
   15 FORMAT (12X, 10F11.4)
      RETURN
   20 DO 25 K = 1,M,10
      PRINT 15
      L = MINO(K + 9, M)
      PRINT 5, KH, (J, J = K,L)
      DO 25 I = 1,N
   25 PRINT 30, I, (X(I,J), J = K,L)
   30 FORMAT (/I8, 4X, 10F11.4)
      RETURN
      END
```

12. FORTRAN Listing for Subroutine PTMS.

```
      SUBROUTINE PTMS (X, N, KH, ND)
      DIMENSION X(ND,N), A(7)
      REAL KH*8
      L = 1
      K = 0
      DO 15 I = 1,N
      DO 15 J = I,N
      K = K + 1
      A(K) = X(I,J)
      IF (K .LT. 7) GO TO 15
    5 PUNCH 10, KH, L, A
   10 FORMAT (A6, I4, 7F10.4)
      L = L + 1
      K = 0
   15 CONTINUE
      IF (K .GT. 0) PUNCH 10, KH, L, (A(I), I = 1,K)
      RETURN
      END
```

TESTAT (Test Statistics)

1. Description and Input Directions. Scoring and item-analysis of data from choice-response instruments, either right-wrong or item-sum scales. Provision is made for item-scale directionality reversals, sub-scales and replacement of zero item scores.

Control Cards:

1. Title Control Card: Left justified. You may use all 80 columns in any characters.
2. Parameter Control Card:

Col. 1–5	number of items
Col. 6–10	number of subjects
Col. 12	1 to print item-choice percentage table
Col. 13	number of choices per item, only if directionality of scaling is to be reversed for any items. Maximum choices are 9. If the number of choices per item varies, enter the largest number here.
Col. 14	1 if choices are to be converted to right (1)–wrong (0) according to key before summation.
Col. 15	number of sub-scales (Max = 9). If all items are a single scale, enter zero and do not use a key card. Every item must be assigned to a scale; use a dummy scale for filler items.
Col. 16	value to replace zero item scores, to leave them as punched enter zero here.
Col. 17	1 to punch scale scores for subjects

3. Format Control Card: This is the only program that uses I-mode data-field specifications.
4. Special Control Cards: Depending on the options selected in the parameter card, certain control cards must be added after the format, before the data cards, in the following order:

Directionality Key Card (only if col. 13 is non-zero). One column per item: 1 = reverse item scale; 0 = no reversal.

Correct-Choice Key Card (only if col. 14 = 1). One column per item; punch the correct-choice numbers.

Subscale Key Card (only if col. 15 is non-zero). One column per item; punch subscale number for each item.

The last three key cards all begin with column 6 = item 1, col. 7 = item 2, etc. Each may be continued to a second card if necessary (col. 6 = item 76, etc.).

2. Input Example for TESTAT, *Data from Table 8.8.*

```
//TESTAT JOB (2919,267F,2X),'DUNN-RANKIN'
// EXEC EDSTAT,PROGRAM=TESTAT
//GO.SYSIN DD *
INPUT EXAMPLE FROM DATA OF CHAPTER 8, TABLE 8.8
    6   10 15
```

```
(10X,6I1)
01          223325
02          123435
03          111555
04          233225
05          222225
06          222433
07          231324
08          113335
09          123335
10          223435
/*
//
```

3. *Example Output from Program* TESTAT, *Data from Table 8.8.*

```
        *** OUTPUT FROM PROGRAM TESTAT ***

INPUT EXAMPLE FROM DATA OF CHAPTER 8, TABLE 8.8

PARAMETERS
COL  1- 5 =       6
COL  6-10 =      10
COL 11-15 =    1000
COL 16-20 =       0
COL 21-25 =       0

 FORMAT CARD(S)


        (10X,6I1)


ITEM N            1
              6.0000


MEANS             1
             16.8000


SIGMAS            1
              1.2491


ALPHAS            1
             -1.3072


ITEM  SCALE  MEAN  SIGMA  R(TOTAL)  R(SCALE)
  1     0    1.60  0.490  -0.2941   0.0
  2     0    2.00  0.632  -0.2531   0.0
  3     0    2.40  0.800   0.3803   0.0
  4     0    3.30  0.900   0.5871   0.0
  5     0    2.80  0.872   0.5143   0.0
  6     0    4.70  0.640   0.4252   0.0


CHOICE DISTRIBUTIONS (PERCENTAGES).

ITEM  REV  KEY  ZERO   1    2    3    4    5    6    7    8    9

  1    0    0    0     40   60   0    0    0    0    0    0    0
  2    0    0    0     20   60   20   0    0    0    0    0    0
```

3	0	0	0	20	20	60	0	0	0	0	0	0
4	0	0	0	0	20	40	30	10	0	0	0	0
5	0	0	0	0	40	50	0	10	0	0	0	0
6	0	0	0	0	0	10	10	80	0	0	0	0

4. FORTRAN *Listing for Program* TESTAT.   Required Subroutines (See SUBROUTINES in this chapter): CCDS, INPUT, PRTS, DYNA, NLOC, SINTL, RFMT.

```
C
C   PROGRAM TESTAT
C
      CALL TESTA1
      STOP
      END
      SUBROUTINE TESTA1
      EXTERNAL TESTA2
      REAL KF*4
      COMMON KF(80), NI, NS, KA, KB, NUM3
    5 CALL CCDS (KF, NI, NS, KA, KB, 1, 6HTESTA1)
      N1=NI
      N2=10
      N3=(NI+1)/2
      N4=NI*10
      NUM3=N3
      CALL DYNA (TESTA2,KD,N1,KE,N1,KG,N1,KX,N3,KI,N1,KP,N4,
     1 A,N2,F,N2,AT,N2,ST,N2,AI,N1,SI,N1,RT,N1,RS,N1,XT,N2,XI,N1)
      GO TO 5
      END
      SUBROUTINE TESTA2 (KD,M1,KE,M2,KG,M3,KX,M4,KI,M5,KP,M6,
     1 A,M7,F,M8,AT,M9,ST,M10,AI,M11,SI,M12,RT,M13,RS,M14,XT,M15,XI,M16)
      COMMON KF(80), NI, NS, KA, KB, NUM3
      DIMENSION KC(55),KD(NI),KE(NI),KG(NI),KX(NUM3),
     1 KI(NI),KP(NI,10),A(10),F(10),AT(10),ST(10),AI(NI),
     2 SI(NI),RT(NI),RS(NI),XT(10),  XI(NI)
      REAL ID*8, KF*4
      DO 7 I=1,NI
    7 KD(I)=0
      K11 = KA / 10000
      K12 = MOD(KA / 1000, 10)
      K13 = MOD(KA / 100, 10)
      K14 = MOD(KA / 10, 10)
      K15 = MOD(KA, 10)
      K16 = KB / 10000
      K17 = MOD(KB / 1000, 10)
      NC = (NI + 1) / 2
      KT = K15 + 1
      IF (K11 .EQ. 1) READ 10, KC
   10 FORMAT (55A1)
      IF (K13 .GT. 0) READ 15, (KD(I), I = 1,NI)
   15 FORMAT (5X, 75I1)
      IF (K14 .EQ. 0) GO TO 18
      IF (K11 .EQ. 0) GO TO 17
      READ KF, ID, (KX(I), I = 1,NC)
      CALL I230 (KC, KX, KE, NI, ID)
      GO TO 18
   17 READ 15, (KE(I), I = 1,NI)
   18 IF (K15 .GT. 0) READ 15, (KG(I), I = 1,NI)
      DO 20 I = 1,KT
      A(I) = 0.0
      F(I) = 0.0
      AT(I) = 0.0
   20 ST(I) = 0.0
      IF (K15 .EQ. 0) GO TO 30
```

```
      DO 25 I = 1,NI
      K = KG(I)
   25 F(K) = F(K) + 1.0
   30 F(KT) = NI
      DO 35 I = 1,NI
      IF (K15 .EQ. 0) KG(I) = 0
      IF (K14 .EQ. 0) KE(I) = 0
      AI(I) = 0.0
      SI(I) = 0.0
      RT(I) = 0.0
      RS(I) = 0.0
      DO 35 J = 1,10
   35 KP(I,J) = 0
      DO 110 N = 1,NS
      IF (K11 .EQ. 0) GC TC 40
      CALL INPIT (ID, KX, N, KF, NC)
      CALL I230 (KC, KX, FI, NI, IC)
      GO TO 45
   40 CALL INPIT (ID, KI, N, KF, NI)
   45 IF (K12 .EQ. 0) GO TC 55
      DO 50 I = 1,NI
      J = KI(I) + 1
   50 KP(I,J) = KE(I,J) + 1
   55 IF (K13 .EQ. 0) GC TC 65
      DO 60 I = 1,NI
      IF (KI(I) .GT. 0 .AND. KD(I) .EQ. 1) KI(I) = K13 + 1 - KI(I)
   60 CONTINUE
   65 IF (K14 .EQ. 0) GO TC 75
      DO 70 I = 1,NI
      KK = 1
      IF (KE(I) .NE. KI(I)) KK = 0
   70 KI(I) = KK
   75 IF (K16 .EQ. 0) GC TC 85
      DO 80 I = 1,NI
      IF (KI(I) .EQ. 0) KI(I) = K16
   80 CONTINUE
   85 DO 90 I = 1,KT
   90 XT(I) = 0.0
      DO 95 I = 1,NI
      XI(I) = KI(I)
      IF (K15 .EQ. 0) GC TC 95
      J = KG(I)
      XT(J) = XT(J) + XI(I)
   95 XT(KT) = XT(KT) + XI(I)
  100 FORMAT (A8, 2HCS, 1CF7.0)
      IF (K17 .EQ. 1) FUNCH 100, IC, (XT(I), I = 1,KT)
      DO 105 I = 1,KT
      AT(I) = AT(I) + XT(I)
  105 ST(I) = ST(I) + XT(I)**2
      DO 110 I = 1,NI
      AI(I) = AI(I) + XI(I)
      SI(I) = SI(I) + XI(I)**2
      IF (K15 .EQ. 0) GO TC 110
      J = KG(I)
      RS(I) = RS(I) + XT(J) * XI(I)
  110 RT(I) = RT(I) + XT(KT) * XI(I)
      SN = NS
      DO 115 I = 1,KT
      AT(I) = AT(I) / SN
  115 ST(I) = SQRT(ST(I) / SN - AT(I)**2)
      DO 120 I = 1,NI
      AI(I) = AI(I) / SN
      Q = SI(I) / SN - AI(I)**2
      IF (Q .GT. 0.0) GO TC 116
      SI(I) = 0.0
      RT(I) = 0.0
      RS(I) = 0.0
      GO TO 120
  116 SI(I) = SQRT(Q)
      RT(I) = (RT(I) / SN - AT(KT) * AI(I)) / (ST(KT) * SI(I))
      IF (K15 .EQ. 0) GO TC 120
      J = KG(I)
```

```
      RS(I) = (RS(I) / SN - AT(J) * AI(I)) / (ST(J) * SI(I))
      A(J) = A(J) + C
120   A(KT) = A(KT) + C
      DO 125 I = 1,KT
      IF (ST(I) .EQ. 0.0) GO TO 125
      IF ( (F(I) - 1.0) .EQ. 0.0) GO TO 125
      Q = ST(I)**2
      A(I) = (F(I) / (F(I) - 1.0)) * ((Q - A(I)) / Q)
125   CONTINUE
      CALL PRTS (F, KT, 1, 8HITEM N  , KT)
      CALL PRTS (AT, KT, 1, 8HMEANS   , KT)
      CALL PRTS (ST, KT, 1, 8HSIGMAS  , KT)
      CALL PRTS (A, KT, 1, 8HALPHAS  , KT)
      PRINT 130
130   FORMAT ( /45H1ITEM  SCALE  MEAN  SIGMA  F(TOTAL)  F(SCALE))
      PRINT 135, (I, KG(J), AI(I), SI(I), RT(I), RS(I), I = 1,NI)
135   FORMAT (I4, 16, F8.2, F7.3, F9.4, F10.4)
      IF (K12.EQ.0) RETURN
      DO 140 I = 1,NI
      DO 140 J = 1,10
      P = KP(I,J)
140   KP(I,J) = P / SN * 100.0 + 0.4999
      PRINT 145, (I, I = 1,9)
145   FORMAT (36H1CHOICE DISTRIBUTIONS (PERCENTAGES). //
     1 21H ITEM  REV  KEY  ZERO, 9I5 / 1X)
      PRINT 150, (I, KD(I), KE(I), (KP(I,J), J = 1,10), I = 1,NI)
150   FORMAT (I4, 2I5, 2I6, 8I5)
      RETURN
      END
```

TRICIR (Circular Triad Analysis)

1. Description and Input Directions.   This program was written by Gerald A. Knezek at the University of Hawaii in 1978. It records circular triads in paired comparison data, computes circular triad probabilities for individual judges and objects, as well as judge and object groups, performs object scaling according to the simplified rank method, and calculates Kendall's coefficients of consistence and concordance.

Data for the program can take two forms. The first is a complete object by object preference matrix of 1's and 0's, with a 1 in row B, column A indicating object A is preferred to object B. The second form is a series of 1's and 2's, with each number corresponding to a specific pair of objects. A 1 indicates the first object of the pair is preferred, while a 2 indicates choice of the second. This second type of input is allowed because it occupies less physical space (cards) than the first, and it is required for Gulliksen and Tukey's COMPPC program (Gulliksen, 1958; Gulliksen & Tukey, 1958). The present program requires four control cards to run a deck punched for COMPPC. Other formats of 1's and 2's are also allowed.

Three or more control cards must always precede the data deck. The first is the *title card,* which may contain any character and may be up to 80 columns in length. The second is the *parameter card,* where columns 3–5 contain the number of judges (subjects), columns 9–10 contain the number of objects (stimuli), and column 15 contains a 1 if data consisting of 1's and 2's is to be read in. Otherwise, column 15 should be left blank and the data must be read in as a complete preference matrix of 0's and 1's. Column 20 on the parameter card should contain a 1 to suppress circular triad printing for each judge. Any other number in column 20 results in the printing of all circular triads for every judge.

The third card is the *format card* for reading in the data for one judge. This must be in F format, and should contain only the part of a regular FORTRAN format statement written to the right of the word "FORMAT." This is the last control card before the data deck if a complete preference matrix is read in. If column 15 = 1 on the parameter card, a second format card for reading in the key cards must be included after the first. This second format card must be in I format. *Key cards* showing the order of the pairs for one subject must also be included after the second format card. Data consisting of 1's and 2's for the first judge follows the key cards.

The circular triad scaling program will accept no more than 500 judges or 26 objects.

Output:

1. For individual judges:
   a. Total number of circular triads, and number per object.
   b. Absolute Z and absolute probabilities for each object.
   c. Number of votes for each object.
   d. Scaled score for each object according to the simplified rank method.
   e. Kendall's coefficient of consistence.
2. For objects group:
   a. Circular triad distribution.
   b. Preference matrix for circular triads.
3. For judges group:
   a. Total number of circular triads, absolute Z and probabilities, group Z, number of votes and scaled score for each object.
   b. Kendall's coefficient of concordance for judges' votes.
   c. Mean number of circular triads, standard deviation and average consistency.
   d. Significant and critical scale differences among objects.
   e. Number of possible significant pairs, significant pairs and relative scalability index.

Input:

Data may be input as,

1. A complete object by object preference matrix of 1's and 0's with a 1 in row B, column A indicating object A is preferred to object B.
2. or, a series of 1's and 2's, with each number corresponding to a specific pair of objects. A 1 indicates the first object of the pair is preferred, while

a 2 indicates choice of the second. (This type of input is required for Gulliksen and Tukey's COMPPC program, and is also used by Dunn-Rankin's RANKO program.) Other formats of 1's and 2's are also allowed.

Limitations: max number of subjects = 500, max number of objects = 26.

Control Cards:

A title card, a parameter card, variable format card(s) and, if the input is paired comparison data, key card(s) are required.

1. Title Card: Any alphanumeric title; up to 80 columns may be used.
2. Parameter Card:

Columns	Description
3–5	Number of judges (max = 500)
9–10	Number of objects or items (max = 26)
15	1 = data consists of 1's and 2's
	blank = data input as complete preference matrix of 0's and 1's
20	1 = suppress circular triad printing for each judge
	any other number = print circular triad info for each judge.

3. Format Card(s):
   a. This is the format card for reading the data for one subject, and must be in F format. No ID field.
   b. If col. 15 = 1 on the parameter card, then a second format card for reading in the key card(s) must be added. This second format card must be in I format.
4. Key Card(s): If column 15 = 1 on the parameter card, key card(s) showing the order of pairs for each subject must be included next.

2. Input Example for Program TRICIR, *Preference Data from Table 20.2.*

```
//TRICIR JOB (2919,267F,2X),'DUNN-RANKIN'
// EXEC EDSTAT,PROGRAM=TRICIR
//GO.SYSIN DD *
EXAMPLE INPUT DATA IS TAKEN FROM BEGINNING OF CHAPTER 20
    5    4    1    9
(10X,6F1.0)
(12I2)
010201030104020302040304
DS         221212
HA         122221
DB         122221
BB         222112
PD         112212
/*
//
```

3. Output from Program TRICIR, *Preference Data from Table 20.2.*

```
EXAMPLE INPUT DATA IS TAKEN FROM BEGINNING OF CHAPTER 20


JUDGE  1

<  1  3  4
<  2  3  4


OBJECT   # CT'S IN    ABS Z    ABS PROB    # VOTES    SCALED

  1         1         0.33     0.6306       1.        33.33
  2         1         0.33     0.6306       2.        66.67
  3         2         1.67     0.9522       2.        66.67
  4         2         1.67     0.9522       1.        33.33

TOTAL CIRCULAR TRIADS FOR JUDGE  1 =   2.

KENDALL'S COEFFICIENT OF CONSISTENCE = 0.0

PROB(X<=#CT) = PROB(X>=COEF) = .806458294


JUDGE  2


OBJECT   # CT'S IN    ABS Z    ABS PROB    # VOTES    SCALED

  1         0        -1.00     0.1587       1.        33.33
  2         0        -1.00     0.1587       0.        0.0
  3         0        -1.00     0.1587       3.        100.00
  4         0        -1.00     0.1587       2.        66.67

TOTAL CIRCULAR TRIADS FOR JUDGE  2 =   0.

KENDALL'S COEFFICIENT OF CONSISTENCE = 1.0000

PROB(X<=#CT) = PROB(X>=COEF) = .196784914


JUDGE  3


OBJECT   # CT'S IN    ABS Z    ABS PROB    # VOTES    SCALED

  1         0        -1.00     0.1587       1.        33.33
  2         0        -1.00     0.1587       0.        0.0
  3         0        -1.00     0.1587       3.        100.00
  4         0        -1.00     0.1587       2.        66.67

TOTAL CIRCULAR TRIADS FOR JUDGE  3 =   0.

KENDALL'S COEFFICIENT OF CONSISTENCE = 1.0000

PROB(X<=#CT) = PROB(X>=COEF) = .196784914
JUDGE  4


OBJECT   # CT'S IN    ABS Z    ABS PROB    # VOTES    SCALED

  1         0        -1.00     0.1587       0.        0.0
  2         0        -1.00     0.1587       3.        100.00
```

```
   3          0          -1.00      0.1587        1.          33.33
   4          0          -1.00      0.1587        2.          66.67
```

TOTAL CIRCULAR TRIADS FOR JUDGE 4 =   0.

KENDALL'S COEFFICIENT OF CONSISTENCE = 1.0000

PROB(X<=#CT) = PROB(X>=COEF) = .196784914

JUDGE 5

```
>  1   2   4
<  2   3   4
```

OBJECT	# CT'S IN	ABS Z	ABS PROB	# VOTES	SCALED
1	1	0.33	0.6306	2.	66.67
2	2	1.67	0.9522	1.	33.33
3	1	0.33	0.6306	1.	33.33
4	2	1.67	0.9522	2.	66.67

TOTAL CIRCULAR TRIADS FOR JUDGE 5 =   2.

KENDALL'S COEFFICIENT OF CONSISTENCE = 0.0

PROB(X<=#CT) = PROB(X>=COEF) = .806458294

CIRCULAR TRIAD DISTRIBUTION

OBJECTS			>	<	TOTAL	PROB (X<=MIN)
1	2	4	1.	0.	1.	.5000
1	3	4	0.	1.	1.	.5000
2	3	4	0.	2.	2.	.2500

TOTAL CIRCULAR TRIADS ACROSS 5 JUDGES =   4.

PREFERENCE MATRIX FOR CIRCULAR TRIADS

OBJECTS		# A>B	# A<B	TOTAL	PROB(X<=MIN)	VARCOEF
1	2	1.	0.	1.	.5000	2.2361
1	3	0.	1.	1.	.5000	2.2361
1	4	1.	1.	2.	.7500	1.3693
2	3	0.	2.	2.	.2500	1.3693
2	4	3.	0.	3.	.1250	1.4907
3	4	0.	3.	3.	.1250	1.4907
MEANS		0.83	1.17	2.00	.3750	1.6987

ANALYSIS SUMMARY

OBJECT	# CT'S IN	ABS Z	ABS PROB	GRP Z	# VOTES	SCALED
1	2	-0.47	0.3204	-1.22	5.	33.33
2	3	-0.20	0.4207	0.0	6.	40.00
3	3	-0.20	0.4207	0.0	10.	66.67
4	4	0.07	0.5266	1.22	9.	60.00

KENDALL'S COEFFICIENT OF CONCORDANCE (W) FOR JUDGES' VOTES

```
W = .1478    PROB (X>=W) = .5285


PROB NOT ACCURATE FOR SEVEN OR FEWER OBJECTS



JUDGE     # CT      CONSIS     ABS PROB      GRP Z

  1        2.       0.0        0.8065        1.10
  2        0.       1.0000     0.1968       -0.73
  3        0.       1.0000     0.1968       -0.73
  4        0.       1.0000     0.1968       -0.73
  5        2.       0.0        0.8065        1.10


MEAN # CT'S =   0.800

STANDARD DEVIATION =   1.095

AVERAGE CONSISTENCY = 0.6000


PROB(<=    4. CT'S FOR    5 JUDGES) = .3339652



SIGNIFICANT SCALE DIFFERENCES AMONG OBJECTS

OBJECTS     DIFF        P=.1      P=.05      P=.01


CRITICAL DIFFERENCES     63.36      70.83      85.47
   (APPROXIMATE)

MAY NOT BE ACCURATE FOR 16 OR FEWER JUDGES


SIGNIFICANTLY DIFFERENT PAIRS (P=.05) =   0.

POSSIBLE SIGNIFICANT PAIRS (P=.05) =    1.

RELATIVE SCALABILITY INDEX = 0.0

PROBABILITY(X>=INDEX) = 1.0000
```

4. FORTRAN *Listing for Program* TRICIR.   In order to run this program the reader will need four subroutines from the IMSL (1980) package of subroutines. These are MDTD, MDBIN, MDCDFI, UERTST.

```
C
C
C PROGRAM TRICIR
C
C TRICIR    VERSION 5, SEPT., 1978
C FORTRAN PROGRAM WRITTEN BY GERALD A. KNEZEK TO FIND AND RECORD
C CIRCULAR TRIADS IN DATA, COMPUTE CIRCULAR TRIAD PROBABILITIES FOR
C INDIVIDUAL JUDGES AND OBJECTS AS WELL AS JUDGE AND OBJECT GROUPS,
C PERFORM OBJECT SCALING ACCORDING TO THE SIMPLIFIED RANK METHOD, AND
C CALCULATE KENDALL'S COEFFICIENT OF CONCORDANCE FOR JUDGES' SCALES.
C THREE OR MORE CONTROL CARDS MUST PRECEDE THE DATA DECK.
C THE FIRST IS THE TITLE CARD, WHICH MAY CONTAIN ANY CHARACTER AND
C MAY BE UP TO 80 COLUMNS IN LENGTH.
C THE SECOND IS THE PARAMETER CARD, WHERE COLUMNS 3-5 CONTAIN THE
```

```
C NUMBER OF SUBJECTS, COLUMNS 9-10 CONTAIN THE NUMBER OF OBJECTS,
C AND COLUMN 15 CONTAINS A 1 IF DATA CONSISTING OF 1'S AND 2'S IS TO
C BE READ IN..OTHERWISE, COLUMN 15 SHOULD BE LEFT BLANK AND THE DATA
C MUST BE READ IN AS A COMPLETE PREFERENCE MATRIX OF 0'S AND 1'S.
C THE THIRD CARD IS THE FORMAT CARD FOR READING THE DATA FOR ONE
C SUBJECT. THIS MUST BE SPECIFIED IN F FORMAT.
C IF COLUMN 15=1 ON THE PARAMETER CARD, THEN A SECOND FORMAT CARD
C FOR READING IN THE KEY CARDS MUST BE INCLUDED AFTER THE FIRST FORMAT
C CARD. THIS SECOND FORMAT CARD MUST BE IN I FORMAT.
C IF COLUMN 15=1 ON THE PARAMETER CARD, KEY CARDS SHOWING THE ORDER OF
C THE PAIRS FOR EACH SUBJECT MUST BE INCLUDED NEXT.
C WHENEVER COLUMN 20 = 1, CIRCULAR TRIAD PRINTING FOR EACH JUDGE IS
C SUPPRESSED.
      DIMENSION X(26,26),Y(2600,2),TITLE(20),FMT(20),IP(325,2),Z(325)
      DIMENSION INDS(26),INDT(26),W(26,26),SCORE(26,2),RANK(26,2)
      DIMENSION VOTE(26),TVOTE(26),SUBCT(500,3),FMT1(20)
      DIMENSION S(26,26),V(26,26),DUMMY(26),XMEAN(6)
C READ IN TITLE, PARAMETER, AND FORMAT CARDS
      READ 1,(TITLE(I),I=1,20)
    1 FORMAT (20A4)
      PRINT 2,(TITLE(I),I=1,20)
    2 FORMAT ('1',20A4)
      READ 3,NS,N,D,SHORT
    3 FORMAT (2X,I3,3X,I2,4X,F1.0,4X,F1.0)
      READ 5,(FMT(I),I=1,20)
    5 FORMAT (20A4)
C INITIALIZE VARIOUS VARIABLES, VECTORS, AND MATRICES
      RNS=NS
      RK=N
      IC=0
      TIES=0.0
      CTIES=0.0
      N1=N*(N-1)/2*(N-2)/3
      N2=N-1
      N3=N-2
      N4=N*(N-1)/2
      CTMEAN=(RK**2-3.0*RK+2.0)/8.0
      CTSD=SQRT((3.0*RK**2-9.0*RK+6.0)/32.0)
      DF=RK*(RK-1.0)/6.0
      XBAR=RK*(RK-1.0)*(RK-2.0)/24.0
      XBAR=XBAR+.0682662*RK-.109721
      DO 100 I=1,N1
      DO 100 J=1,2
  100 Y(I,J)=0.0
      DO 150 I=1,N
      RI=I
      DUMMY(I)=RNS*(RI-1.0)
      RANK(I,1)=0.0
      RANK(I,2)=0.0
      TVOTE(I)=0.0
  150 INDT(I)=0
      DO 175 I=1,N
      DO 175 J=1,N
      V(I,J)=0.0
  175 W(I,J)=0.0
C READ IN DATA FOR ONE JUDGE (SUBJECT)
  200 IC=IC+1
      IF (IC.GT.NS) GOTO 600
      PRINT 31, IC
   31 FORMAT ('-',6HJUDGE ,I2)
      PRINT 99
   99 FORMAT (1X)
  300 IF(D.NE.1.0) GOTO 350
      DO 310 I=1,N
      DO 310 J=1,N
      S(I,J)=0.0
  310 X(I,J)=0.0
      IF(IC.GT.1) GOTO 315
      READ 5,(FMT1(I),I=1,20)
      READ FMT1,((IP(I,J),J=1,2),I=1,N4)
```

```
315 READ FMT,(Z(I),I=1,N4)
    DO 320 I=1,N4
    IF (Z(I).NE.1.0) GOTO 318
    X(IP(I,2),IP(I,1))=1.0
    GOTO 320
318 X(IP(I,1),IP(I,2))=1.0
320 CONTINUE
    GOTO 360
350 READ FMT,((X(I,J),J=1,N),I=1,N)
C FIND AND RECORD CIRCULAR TRIADS IN ONE JUDGE'S DATA
360 C=0.0
    CT=0.0
    DO 400 I=1,N
    SCORE(I,1)=0.0
    SCORE(I,2)=0.0
    VOTE(I)=0.0
400 INDS(I)=0
    DO 500 I=1,N3
    DO 500 J=2,N2
    DO 500 K=3,N
    IF((I.GE.J).OR.(J.GE.K).OR.(I.GE.K)) GOTO 500
    C=C+1.0
    IF((X(J,I).NE.1.0).OR.(X(K,J).NE.1.0).OR.(X(I,K).NE.1.0)) GOTO 450
    Y(C,1)=Y(C,1)+1.0
    S(J,I)=S(J,I)+1.0
    S(K,J)=S(K,J)+1.0
    S(I,K)=S(I,K)+1.0
    IF (SHORT.EQ.1.0) GOTO 475
    PRINT 37,I,J,K
 37 FORMAT (1X,1H>,3I3)
    GOTO 475
450 IF((X(K,I).NE.1.0).OR.(X(J,K).NE.1.0).OR.(X(I,J).NE.1.0)) GOTO 500
    Y(C,2)=Y(C,2)+1.0
    S(K,I)=S(K,I)+1.0
    S(J,K)=S(J,K)+1.0
    S(I,J)=S(I,J)+1.0
    IF (SHORT.EQ.1.0) GOTO 475
    PRINT 41,I,J,K
 41 FORMAT (1X,1H<,3I3)
475 CT=CT+1.0
    INDS(I)=INDS(I)+1
    INDS(J)=INDS(J)+1
    INDS(K)=INDS(K)+1
500 CONTINUE
C RECORD NUMBER OF VOTES (PREFERENCES) FOR EACH OBJECT & OBJECTS IN CT'S
    DO 540 J=1,N
    DO 535 I=1,N
    W(I,J)=W(I,J)+S(I,J)
    V(I,J)=V(I,J)+(S(I,J)+S(J,I))**2
535 VOTE(J)=VOTE(J)+X(I,J)
540 TVOTE(J)=TVOTE(J)+VOTE(J)
    PRINT 47
 47 FORMAT ('-',6HOBJECT,3X,9H# CT'S IN,3X,7H ABS Z ,3X,8HABS PROB,4X,
   17H# VOTES,6X,6HSCALED)
    PRINT 99
C CALCULATE OBJECT CIRCULAR TRIAD PROBABILITIES AND SCALED OBJECT SCORES
    DO 550 I=1,N
    INDT(I)=INDT(I)+INDS(I)
    SCALE=VOTE(I)/(RK-1.0)*100.0
    RINDS=INDS(I)
    CTZ=(RINDS-CTMEAN)/CTSD
    CTPR=.5*ERFC(-.7071068*CTZ)
    PRINT 51,I,INDS(I),CTZ,CTPR,VOTE(I),SCALE
 51 FORMAT (1X,I2,8X,I4,6X,F7.2,3X,F8.4,6X,F5.0,7X,F6.2)
550 CONTINUE
C CALCULATE PROBABILITY OF TOTAL NUMBER OF CIRCULAR TRIADS FOR ONE JUDGE
    IF (CT.GT.XBAR) GOTO 575
    T=(CT-XBAR)/(SQRT(XBAR))
    CALL MDTD (T,DF,PT,IER)
    PT=PT/2.0
    GOTO 580
```

```
  575 T=(CT-XBAR)/(SQRT(XBAR/2.0))
      CALL MDTD (T,DF,PT,IER)
      PT=1.0-PT/2.0
  580 PRINT 43,IC,CT
   43 FORMAT ('0',32HTOTAL CIRCULAR TRIADS FOR JUDGE ,I2,3H = ,F4.0)
      SWITCH=RK/2.0
      NSWIT=SWITCH
      DSWIT=SWITCH-NSWIT
      IF (DSWIT.NE.0.0) CONSIS=1.0-(24.0*CT/(RK**3-RK))
      IF (DSWIT.EQ.0.0) CONSIS=1.0-(24.0*CT/(RK**3-4.0*RK))
      PRINT 127,CONSIS
  127 FORMAT ('0',39HKENDALL'S COEFFICIENT OF CONSISTENCE = ,F6.4)
      PRINT 129,PT
  129 FORMAT ('0',31HPROB(X<=#CT) = PROB(X>=COEF) = ,F10.9)
      SUBCT(IC,1)=CT
      SUBCT(IC,2)=PT
      SUBCT(IC,3)=CONSIS
      PRINT 99
C COMPUTE OBJECT RANKS, SUMS ACROSS JUDGES
      DO 590 I=1,N
      DUM=VOTE(I)+1.0
  590 SCORE(DUM,1)=SCORE(DUM,1)+1.0
      XRANK=RK
      DO 595 I=1,N
      IF (SCORE(I,1).EQ.0.0) GOTO 595
      IF (SCORE(I,1).GT.1.0) TIES=TIES+SCORE(I,1)
      IF (SCORE(I,1).GT.1.0) CTIES=CTIES+(SCORE(I,1))**3
      SCORE(I,2)=(XRANK+XRANK-SCORE(I,1)+1.0)/2.0
      XRANK=XRANK-SCORE(I,1)
  595 CONTINUE
      DO 597 I=1,N
      DUM=VOTE(I)+1.0
      RANK(I,1)=RANK(I,1)+SCORE(DUM,2)
  597 CONTINUE
      GOTO 200
C PRINT CIRCULAR TRIAD DISTRIBUTION (ACROSS ALL JUDGES)
  600 PRINT 53
   53 FORMAT ('1',27HCIRCULAR TRIAD DISTRIBUTION)
      PRINT 91
   91 FORMAT ('-',2X,7HOBJECTS,19X,1H>,8X,1H<,4X,5HTOTAL,4X,13HPROB (X<=
     1MIN))
      PRINT 99
      TOTAL=0.0
      C1=0.0
      DO 650 I=1,N3
      DO 650 J=2,N2
      DO 650 K=3,N
      IF((I.GE.J).OR.(J.GE.K).OR.(I.GE.K)) GOTO 650
      C1=C1+1.0
      YSUM=Y(C1,1)+Y(C1,2)
      IF(YSUM.EQ.0.0) GOTO 650
      SUCC=Y(C1,1)
      IF (Y(C1,1).GT.Y(C1,2)) SUCC=Y(C1,2)
      NSUC=SUCC
      NT=YSUM
      PX=.5
      CALL MDBIN (NSUC,NT,PX,PS,PK,IER)
      PRINT 57,I,J,K,Y(C1,1),Y(C1,2),YSUM,PS
   57 FORMAT (1X,3I3,17X,F4.0,5X,F4.0,5X,F4.0,5X,F5.4)
      TOTAL=TOTAL+YSUM
  650 CONTINUE
      PRINT 59,NS,TOTAL
   59 FORMAT ('0',29HTOTAL CIRCULAR TRIADS ACROSS ,I3,' JUDGES = ',F6.0)
C PRINT PREFERENCE MATRIX FOR CIRCULAR TRIADS (ALL JUDGES)
      PRINT 99
      PRINT 71
   71 FORMAT ('0',37HPREFERENCE MATRIX FOR CIRCULAR TRIADS)
      PRINT 99
      PRINT 61
   61 FORMAT ('0',7HOBJECTS,4X,5H# A>B,5X,5H# A<B,5X,5HTOTAL,3X,12HPROB(
     1X<=MIN),1X,7HVARCOEF)
```

```
          PRINT 99
          DO 743 I=1,6
  743 XMEAN(I)=0.0
          DO 750 I=1,N
          DO 750 J=1,N
          IF (I.GE.J) GOTO 750
          SUCC=W(J,I)
          IF (W(J,I).GT.W(I,J)) SUCC=W(I,J)
          NSUC=SUCC
          TRSUM=W(J,I)+W(I,J)
          NT=TRSUM
          PX=.5
          CALL MDBIN (NSUC,NT,PX,PS,PK,IER)
          XBARP=TRSUM/RNS
          SDP=SQRT((V(I,J)-TRSUM**2/RNS)/(RNS-1.0))
          VARC=9999.0
          IF (XBARP.EQ.0.0) GOTO 731
          VARC=SDP/XBARP
  731 PRINT 67,I,J,W(J,I),W(I,J),TRSUM,PS,VARC
   67 FORMAT (1X,2I3,1X,3(5X,F5.0),5X,F5.4,5X,F6.4)
          XMEAN(1)=XMEAN(1)+W(J,I)
          XMEAN(2)=XMEAN(2)+W(I,J)
          XMEAN(3)=XMEAN(3)+TRSUM
          XMEAN(4)=XMEAN(4)+PS
          XMEAN(5)=XMEAN(5)+VARC
          XMEAN(6)=XMEAN(6)+1.0
  750 CONTINUE
          DO 753 I=1,5
  753 XMEAN(I)=XMEAN(I)/XMEAN(6)
          PRINT 149,(XMEAN(I),I=1,5)
  149 FORMAT ('0',5HMEANS,4X,3(3X,F7.2),3X,F5.4,5X,F6.4)
C COMPUTE CIRCULAR TRIAD PROBABILITIES & SCALED OBJECT SCORES OVER ALL JUDGES
          PRINT 99
          PRINT 73
   73 FORMAT ('1',16HANALYSIS SUMMARY)
          PRINT 79
   79 FORMAT ('-',6HOBJECT,2X,9H# CT'S IN,2X,7H ABS Z ,3X,8HABS PROB,3X,
     15HGRP Z,4X,7H# VOTES,6X,6HSCALED)
          PRINT 99
          GRPSUM=0.0
          GRPSS=0.0
          RANKSM=0.0
          RANKSS=0.0
          VOTSS=0.0
          DO 725 I=1,N
          GRPSUM=GRPSUM+INDT(I)
          GRPSS=GRPSS+INDT(I)**2
          VOTSS=VOTSS+TVCTE(I)**2
          RANKSM=RANKSM+RANK(I,1)
  725 RANKSS=RANKSS+RANK(I,1)**2
          GPMEAN=GRPSUM/RK
          GPSD=SQRT((GRPSS-GRPSUM**2/RK)/(RK-1.0))
          CTMEAN=CTMEAN*RNS
          CTSD=CTSD*RNS
          DO 700 I=1,N
          SCALE=TVOTE(I)/((RK-1.0)*RNS)*100.0
          RINDS=INDT(I)
          CTZ=(RINDS-CTMEAN)/CTSD
          CTPR=.5*ERFC(-.7071068*CTZ)
          GRPZ=(RINDS-GPMEAN)/GPSD
  700 PRINT 81,I,INDT(I),CTZ,CTPR,GRPZ,TVOTE(I),SCALE
   81 FORMAT (1X,I2,8X,I4,4X,F7.2,3X,F8.4,4X,F5.2,5X,F5.0,7X,F6.2)
C CALCULATE KENDALL'S COEFFICIENT OF CONCORDANCE (W)
          PRINT 99
          VARMAX=RNS**2*(RK**2-1.0)/12.0
          VARMAX=VARMAX-RNS*(CTIES-TIES)/(12.0*RK)
          VARSAM=(RK*RANKSS-RANKSM**2)/RK**2
          WKEN=VARSAM/VARMAX
          CHI=RNS*(RK-1.0)*WKEN
          NDF=N-1
```

```
      CALL MDCDFI (CHI,NDF,Q,IER)
      PRINT 63
   63 FORMAT ('-',58HKENDALL'S COEFFICIENT OF CONCORDANCE (W) FOR JUDGES
     1' VOTES)
      PRINT 89,WKEN,Q
   89 FORMAT ('-',4HW = ,F5.4,4X,14HPROB (X>=W) = ,F5.4)
      IF (RK.LE.7.0) PRINT 77
   77 FORMAT ('-',44HPROB NOT ACCURATE FOR SEVEN OR FEWER OBJECTS)
      PRINT 99
C JUDGE ANALYSIS SUMMARY
      SUMJUD=0.0
      SSJUD=0.0
      DO 800 I=1,NS
      SUMJUD=SUMJUD+SUBCT(I,1)
  800 SSJUD=SSJUD+SUBCT(I,1)**2
      SUBM=SUMJUD/RNS
      SUBSD=SQRT((SSJUD-SUMJUD**2/RNS)/(RNS-1.0))
      PRINT 99
      PRINT 93
   93 FORMAT('-',5HJUDGE,5X,4H# CT,6X,6HCONSIS,4X,8HABS PROB,6X,5HGRP Z)
      PRINT 99
      SUMCON=0.0
      DO 850 I=1,NS
      ZJUD=(SUBCT(I,1)-SUBM)/SUBSD
      SUMCON=SUMCON+SUBCT(I,3)
  850 PRINT 97,I,SUBCT(I,1),SUBCT(I,3),SUBCT(I,2),ZJUD
   97 FORMAT (1X,I2,8X,F5.0,5X,F6.4,5X,F6.4,6X,F6.2)
      APPROX=4.0*(VOTSS-(RNS**2*RK*(RK-1.0)**2/4.0))/(RNS*RK)
      CALL MDCDFI (APPROX,NDF,PCHI,IER)
      PRINT 107,SUBM
  107 FORMAT ('-',14HMEAN # CT'S = ,F7.3)
      PRINT 111,SUBSD
  111 FORMAT ('0',21HSTANDARD DEVIATION = ,F7.3)
      CMEAN=SUMCON/RNS
      PRINT 137,CMEAN
  137 FORMAT ('0',22HAVERAGE CONSISTENCY = ,F6.4)
      PRINT 109,SUMJUD,NS,PCHI
  109 FORMAT ('-',8HPROB(<= ,F6.0,10H CT'S FOR ,I3,10H JUDGES)= ,F8.7)
C CALCULATE SIGNIFICANT SCALE DIFFERENCES FOR OBJECTS
      PRINT 99
      PRINT 99
      PRINT 113
  113 FORMAT ('-',43HSIGNIFICANT SCALE DIFFERENCES AMONG OBJECTS)
      PRINT 117
  117 FORMAT ('0',7HOBJECTS,5X,4HDIFF,8X,4HP=.1,5X,5HP=.05,5X,5HP=.01)
      PRINT 99
      SDRNG=SQRT(RNS*RK*(RK+1.0)/12.0)
      SIG01=(3.44328+.71977*ALOG(RK))*SDRNG
      SIG05=(2.58092+.79297*ALOG(RK))*SDRNG
      SIG1=(2.13762+.83310*ALOG(RK))*SDRNG
      RMAX=(RK-1.0)*RNS
      SINDX=0.0
      DUMRNK=0.0
      DO 900 I=1,N
      DO 900 J=2,N
      IF (I.GE.J) GOTO 900
      STAR1=0.0
      STAR05=0.0
      STAR01=0.0
      VDIF=ABS(TVOTE(I)-TVOTE(J))
      RNKDIF=ABS(DUMMY(I)-DUMMY(J))
      IF (RNKDIF.GE.SIG05) DUMRNK=DUMRNK+1.0
      IF (VDIF.LT.SIG1) GOTO 900
      STAR1=1.0
      IF (VDIF.LT.SIG05) GOTO 875
      STAR05=1.0
      SINDX=SINDX+1.0
      IF (VDIF.LT.SIG01) GOTO 875
      STAR01=1.0
  875 SCLDIF=VDIF/RMAX*100.0
```

```
      PRINT 121,I,J,SCLDIF,STAR1,STAR05,STAR01
121 FORMAT (1X,2I3,3X,F7.2,9X,F2.0,8X,F2.0,8X,F2.0)
900 CONTINUE
      SIG1=SIG1/RMAX*100.0
      SIG05=SIG05/RMAX*100.0
      SIG01=SIG01/RMAX*100.0
      PRINT 123,SIG1,SIG05,SIG01
123 FORMAT ('0',20HCRITICAL DIFFERENCES,2X,F7.2,3X,F7.2,3X,F7.2)
      PRINT 131
131 FORMAT (1X,3X,13H(APPROXIMATE))
      IF (RNS.LE.16.0) PRINT 133
133 FORMAT ('0',42HMAY NOT BE ACCURATE FOR 16 OR FEWER JUDGES)
      RSINDX=0.0
      PRINT 139,SINDX
139 FORMAT ('-',40HSIGNIFICANTLY DIFFERENT PAIRS (P=.05) = ,F4.0)
      PRINT 141,DUMRNK
141 FORMAT ('0',37HPOSSIBLE SIGNIFICANT PAIRS (P=.05) = ,F4.0)
      IF (DUMRNK.EQ.0.0) GOTO 950
      RSINDX=SINDX/DUMRNK
950 PRINT 143,RSINDX
143 FORMAT ('0',29HRELATIVE SCALABILITY INDEX = ,F6.4)
      NSUC=DUMRNK-SINDX
      NT=DUMRNK
      PX=.95
      CALL MDBIN (NSUC,NT,PX,PS,PK,IER)
      PRINT 147,PS
147 FORMAT ('0',24HPROBABILITY(X>=INDEX) = ,F6.4)
      STOP
      END
```

TSCALE (Successive Interval Scaling)

1. Description and Input Directions. Thurstonian successive-intervals scale construction. Categorization data from judges of items are analyzed to yield scale values.

Control Cards:

1. Title Control Card: Left justified. You may use all 80 columns in any characters.
2. Parameter Control Card:
   Col. 1–5   number of items
   Col. 6–10   number of judges
   Col. 11–15   number of judgment categories (Max = 11)
   Col. 20   1 to punch item scale values
   Data cards contain the category number to which the items were assigned. Each judge begins a new card.
3. Format Control Card: First field may be A mode, subject identification or may be read without the subject I.D. field. Data are read in F format.

2. Input Example for Program TSCALE, *Data from Table 8.8.*

```
//TSCALE JOB (2919,267F,2X),'DUNN-RANKIN'
// EXEC EDSTAT,PROGRAM=TSCALE
//GO.SYSIN DD *
EXAMPLE INPUT FOR TSCALE IS FROM TABLE 8.8
      6   10    5
(A2,8X,6F1.0)
01        223325
02        123435
03        111555
04        233225
05        222225
06        222433
07        331324
08        113335
09        123335
10        223435
/*
//
```

3. Output from Program TSCALE, *Data from Table 8.8.*

```
       *** OUTPUT FROM PROGRAM TSCALE ***

EXAMPLE INPUT FOR TSCALE IS FROM TABLE 8.8

PARAMETERS
COL  1- 5 =     6
COL  6-10 =    10
COL 11-15 =     5
COL 16-20 =     0
COL 21-25 =     0

  FORMAT CARD(S)


       (A2,8X,6F1.0)


   S C A L E   V A L U E S    F R E Q U E N C I E S

RANK-ORDERED   ITEM-ORDERED   1   2   3   4   5

     6    4.00      1   0.12   4   5   1   0   0

     4    2.15      2   0.63   2   6   2   0   0

     5    1.61      3   1.18   2   2   6   0   0

     3    1.18      4   2.15   0   2   4   3   1

     2    0.63      5   1.61   0   4   5   0   1

     1    0.12      6   4.00   0   0   1   1   8
```

4. FORTRAN *Listing for Program* TSCALE.   Required Subroutines (See
SUBROUTINES in this chapter.) CCDS, INPUT, PCDS.

```
C
C    PROGRAM TSCALE
C
      SUBROUTINE TSCALE
      EXTERNAL TSCALZ
      REAL KF*4
      COMMON KF(80),NI,NJ,NK,KE,NUM1
    5 CALL CCDS(KF,NI,NJ,NK,KE,I,6HTSCALE)
      N1=NI
      N2=NJ
      N3=NK
      N4=NK*NI
      N5=(NK-1)*NI
      N6=NK-1
      NUM1=N6
      CALL DYNA (TSCALZ,NX,N4,ZX,N5,KI,N1,V,N1,R,N1,B,N6)
      GO TO 5
      END
      SUBROUTINE TSCALZ (NX,M1,ZX,M2,KI,M3,V,M4,R,M5,B,M6)
      COMMON KF(80),NI,NJ,NK,KE,NUM1
      DIMENSION KI(NI),Z(97),C(97),NX(NK,NI),ZX(NUM1,NI),
     1 V(NI),R(NI),B(NUM1)
      DATA Z/-1.96,-1.88,-1.75,-1.64,-1.55,-1.48,-1.41,-1.34,-1.28,-1.22
     1 ,-1.18,-1.13,-1.08,-1.04,-.99,-.95,-.92,-.88,-.84,-.81,-.77,-.74,
     2 -.71,-.67,-.64,-.61,-.58,-.55,-.52,-.50,-.47,-.44,-.41,-.39,-.36,
     3 -.33,-.31,-.28,-.25,-.23,-.20,-.17,-.15,-.13,-.10,-.08,-.05,-.03,
     4 0.0,.03,.05,.08,.10,.13,.15,.17,.20,.23,.25,.28,.31,.33,.36,.39,
     5 .41,.44,.47,.50,.52,.55,.58,.61,.64,.67,.71,.74,.77,.81,.84,.88,
     6 .92,.95,.99,1.04,1.08,1.13,1.18,1.22,1.28,1.34,1.41,1.48,1.55,
     7 1.64,1.75,1.88,1.96/
      REAL ID*8, KF*4
      C(1) = 0.025
      DO 15 I = 2,96
      C(I) = I + 1
   15 C(I) = C(I) / 100.0
      C(97) = 0.975
      DO 25 J = 1,NI
      KI(J) = NJ
      DO 25 I = 1,NK
   25 NX(I,J) = 0
      DO 30 K = 1,NJ
      CALL INPUT (ID, V, K, KF, NI)
      DO 30 J = 1,NI
      I = V(J)
      IF (I .EQ. 0) KI(J) = KI(J) - 1
      IF (I .GT. 0) NX(I,J) = NX(I,J) + 1
   30 CONTINUE
      MK = NK - 1
      DO 50 J = 1,NI
      TJ = KI(J)
      CP = 0.0
      DO 50 I = 1,MK
      FX = NX(I,J)
      CP = CP + FX / TJ
      IF (CP .GT. 0.975 .OR. CP .LT. 0.025) GO TO 40
      DO 35 K = 1,97
      IF (CP .LE. C(K)) GO TO 45
   35 CONTINUE
   40 ZX(I,J) = 10.0
      GO TO 50
   45 IF (C(K) - CP .GT. 0.005) K = K - 1
      ZX(I,J) = Z(K)
   50 CONTINUE
      LK = MK - 1
      B(1) = 0.0
      DO 65 I = 1,LK
```

```
      Q = 0.0
      TN = 0.0
      DO 60 J = 1,NI
      IF (ZX(I,J) .EQ. 10.0 .OR. ZX(I+1,J) .EQ. 10.0) GO TO 60
      D = ZX(I+1,J) - ZX(I,J)
      IF (ABS(D) .LT. 0.00001) GO TO 60
      TN = TN + 1
      Q = Q + D
 60 CONTINUE
      IF (TN.GT.0)   Q = Q / TN
 65 B(I+1) = B(I) + Q
      DO 75 J = 1,NI
      S = 0.0
      X = 0.0
      DO 70 I = 1,NK
      IF (ZX(I,J) .EQ. 10.0) GO TO 70
      X = X + 1.0
      S = S + B(I) - ZX(I,J)
 70 CONTINUE
      KI(J) = J
      V(J) = S / X
 75 R(J) = V(J)
      DO 85 I = 1,NI
      K = I
      DO 80 J = I,NI
      IF (R(K) .LT. R(J)) K = J
 80 CONTINUE
      IF (K .EQ. I) GO TO 85
      KX = KI(K)
      KI(K) = KI(I)
      KI(I) = KX
      X = R(K)
      R(K) = R(I)
      R(I) = X
 85 CONTINUE
      IF (KP .EQ. 1) CALL ECDS (V, NI, 1, 5HIVAI , 200)
      PRINT 90, (I, I = 1,NK)
 90 FORMAT (// 4X, 22HS C A L E  V A L U E S, 5X,
     1 21HF R E Q U E N C I E S // 28H RANK-ORDERED   ITEM-ORDERED,11I5)
      DO 95 I = 1,NI
 95 PRINT 100, KI(I), R(I), I, V(I), (NX(J,I), J = 1,NK)
100 FORMAT (/ I5, F8.2, I7, F8.2, 11I5)
      RETURN
      END
//
```

Appendix A
Tables

TABLE A
Balanced Orders for the Odd Numbers from Five to Seventeen

N = 5	8-6	8-9	7-10	12-1
1-2	7-1	1-4	8-9	7-6
5-3	4-3	3-5	1-3	8-5
4-1	5-2	2-6	2-4	9-4
3-2	6-9	11-7	13-5	10-3
4-5	7-8	10-8	12-6	11-2
1-3	1-4	9-1	11-7	12-13
2-4	3-5	5-4	10-8	1-7
5-1	2-6	6-3	9-1	6-8
3-4	9-7	7-2	4-3	5-9
2-5	8-1	8-11	5-2	4-10
N = 7	5-4	9-10	6-13	3-11
1-2	6-3	1-5	7-12	2-12
7-3	7-2	4-6	8-11	13-1
6-4	8-9	3-7	9-10	7-8
5-1	1-5	2-8	1-4	6-9
3-2	4-6	11-9	3-5	5-10
4-7	3-7	10-1	2-6	4-11
5-6	2-8	6-5	13-7	3-12
1-3	9-1	7-4	12-8	2-13
2-4	5-6	8-3	11-9	*N* = 15
7-5	4-7	9-2	10-1	1-2
6-1	3-8	10-11	5-4	15-3
4-3	2-9	1-6	6-3	14-4
5-2	*N* = 11	5-7	7-2	13-5
6-7	1-2	4-8	8-13	12-6
1-4	11-3	3-9	9-12	11-7
3-5	10-4	2-10	10-11	10-8
2-6	9-5	11-1	1-5	9-1
7-1	8-6	6-7	4-6	3-2
4-5	7-1	5-8	3-7	4-15
3-6	3-2	4-9	2-8	5-14
2-7	4-11	3-10	13-9	6-13
N = 9	5-10	2-11	12-10	7-12
1-2	6-9	*N* = 13	11-1	8-11
9-3	7-8	1-2	6-5	9-10
8-4	1-3	13-3	7-4	1-3
7-5	2-4	12-4	8-3	2-4
6-1	11-5	11-5	9-2	15-5
3-2	10-6	10-6	10-13	14-6
4-9	9-7	9-7	11-12	13-7
5-8	8-1	8-1	1-6	12-8
6-7	4-3	3-2	5-7	11-9
1-3	5-2	4-13	4-8	10-1
2-4	6-11	5-12	3-9	4-3
9-5	7-10	6-11	2-10	5-2
			13-11	

6-15	9-4	10-1	3-7	12-3
7-14	10-3	3-2	2-8	13-2
8-13	11-2	4-17	17-9	14-17
9-12	12-15	5-16	16-10	15-16
10-11	13-14	6-15	15-11	1-8
1-4	1-7	7-14	14-12	7-9
3-5	6-8	8-13	13-1	6-10
2-6	5-9	9-12	6-5	5-11
15-7	4-10	10-11	7-4	4-12
14-8	3-11	1-3	8-3	3-13
13-9	2-12	2-4	9-2	2-14
12-10	15-13	17-5	10-17	17-15
11-1	14-1	16-6	11-16	16-1
5-4	8-7	15-7	12-15	9-8
6-3	9-6	14-8	13-14	10-7
7-2	10-5	13-9	1-6	11-6
8-15	11-4	12-10	5-7	12-5
9-14	12-3	11-1	4-8	13-4
10-13	13-2	4-3	3-9	14-3
11-12	14-15	5-2	2-10	15-2
1-5	1-8	6-17	17-11	16-17
4-6	7-9	7-16	16-12	1-9
3-7	6-10	8-15	15-13	8-10
2-8	5-11	9-14	14-1	7-11
15-9	4-12	10-13	7-6	6-12
14-10	3-13	11-12	8-5	5-13
13-11	2-14	1-4	9-4	4-14
12-1	15-1	3-5	10-3	3-15
6-5	8-9	2-6	11-2	2-16
7-4	7-10	17-7	12-17	17-1
8-3	6-11	16-8	13-16	9-10
9-2	5-12	15-9	14-15	8-11
10-15	4-13	14-10	1-7	7-12
11-14	3-14	13-11	6-8	6-13
12-13	2-15	12-1	5-9	5-14
1-6		5-4	4-10	4-15
5-7	$N = 17$	6-3	3-11	3-16
4-8	1-2	7-2	2-12	2-17
3-9	17-3	8-17	17-13	
2-10	16-4	9-16	16-14	
15-11	15-5	10-15	15-1	
14-12	14-6	11-14	8-7	
13-1	13-7	12-13	9-6	
7-6	12-8	1-5	10-5	
8-5	11-9	4-6	11-4	

(For even numbers of pairs, the next higher odd set is used by striking all pairs containing the nonexistent odd object.)

TABLE B

Critical Lower Tail Values of Circular Triads for k = 5(1)20

k	Probability								
	.20	.15	.10	.05	.01	.005	.001	.0005	.0001
5	0	0	–	–	–	–	–	–	–
	(.1172)	(.1172)							
6	2	2	1	0					
	(.1196)	(.1196)	(.0513)	(.0220)					
7	6	5	4	3	1				
	(.1977)	(.1120)	(.0689)	(.0328)	(.0064)				
8	10	9	9	7	4	3	1	1	0
	(.1528)	(.0938)	(.0938)	(.0370)	(.0057)	(.0025)	(.0004)	(.0004)	(.0001)
9	17	16	15	13	9	6	5	5	4
	(.1846)	(.1377)	(.0946)	(.0449)	(.0077)	(.0011)	(.0004)	(.0004)	(.0001)
10	25	24	22	20	16	14	11	10	8
	(.1726)	(.1342)	(.0752)	(.0388)	(.0082)	(.0037)	(.0010)	(.0004)	(.0000)
11	36	34	33	36	25	23	19	18	14
	(.1924)	(.1233)	(.0956)	(.0414)	(.0079)	(.0039)	(.0008)	(.0005)	(.0001)
12	49	47	45	42	36	34	29	27	22
	(.1887)	(.1274)	(.0832)	(.0417)	(.0081)	(.0048)	(.0009)	(.0004)	(.0001)
13	65	63	61	57	50	48	42	41	36
	(.1946)	(.1369)	(.0958)	(.0416)	(.0082)	(.0045)	(.0009)	(.0005)	(.0001)
14	83	81	79	75	68	64	57	55	48
	(.1774)	(.1320)	(.0944)	(.0449)	(.0099)	(.0042)	(.0008)	(.0004)	(.0001)
15	105	103	100	96	88	84	77	74	68
	(.1803)	(.1374)	(.0862)	(.0454)	(.0095)	(.0042)	(.0008)	(10004)	(.0001)
16	131	128	125	120	111	107	100	98	83
	(.1950)	(.1352)	(.0902)	(.0446)	(.0098)	(.0045)	(.0008)	(.0004)	(.0001)
17	160	157	154	149	138	134	126	122	115
	(.1919)	(.1374)	(.0962)	(.0493)	(.0093)	(.0044)	(.0010)	(.0005)	(.0001)
18	193	190	186	181	169	164	156	152	143
	(.1913)	(.1405)	(.0909)	(.0500)	(.0090)	(.0044)	(.0010)	(.0005)	(.0001)
19	230	227	223	325	205	201	190	185	179
	(.1831)	(.1371)	(0926)	(.0454)	(.0087)	(10049)	(.0009)	(.0004)	(.0001)
20	272	269	264	258	244	239	278	224	216
	(.1893)	(.1451)	(.0913)	(.0489)	(.0092)	(.0046)	(.0010)	(.0004)	(.0001)

TABLE C
Cumulative Probabilities for CT Under Complete Enumeration
when k = 3(1)7

k = 3			k = 6			k = 8	
CT	CP		CT	CP		CT	CP
9	.75		0	.02197		0	.00025
1	1.00		1	.05127		1	.00035
			2	.11963		2	.00090
k = 4			3	.20752		3	.00285
CT	CP		4	.39795		4	.00675
			5	.50928		5	.01220
0	.375		6	.77295		6	.02435
1	.625		7	.91943		7	.03965
2	1.000		8	1.00000		8	.06225
			k = 7			9	.09665
			CT	CP		10	.15380
k = 5			0	.00240		11	.20945
CT	CP		1	.00641		12	.30205
			2	.01682		13	.39421
0	.1172		3	.03284		14	.52596
1	.2344		4	.06889		15	.63001
2	.4688		5	.11199		16	.76791
3	.7031		6	.19771		17	.85626
4	.9766		7	.28743		18	.95141
5	1.0000		8	.41961		19	.98896
			9	.55339		20	1.00000
			10	.73652			
			11	.85294			
			12	.96429			
			13	.99874			
			14	1.00000			

k = 9 20,000 samples			k = 10 30,000 samples			k = 11 30,000 samples	
CT	CP		CT	CP		CT	CP
4	.00005		6	.00003		7	.00003
5	.00035		7	.00003		8	.00003
6	.00105		8	.00003		9	.00003
7	.00220		9	.00020		10	.00003
8	.00390		10	.00043		11	.00003
9	.00765		11	.00100		12	.00003
10	.01250		12	.00173		13	.00006
11	.01885		13	.00266		14	.00009
12	.02965		14	.00369		15	.00019
13	.04485		15	.00526		16	.00022
14	.06630		16	.00819		17	.00025
15	.09455		17	.01239		18	.00045
16	.13765		18	.01936		19	.00082
17	.18455		19	.02726		20	.00132
18	.25155		20	.03876		21	.00172
19	.32285		21	.05386		22	.00255
20	.41130		22	.07519		23	.00385
21	.50230		23	.10106		24	.00528
22	.61380		24	.13419		25	.00788
23	.70495		25	.17259		26	.01211
24	.80130		26	.22402		27	.01634
25	.87790		27	.27919		28	.02211
26	.94395		28	.35099		29	.03021
27	.97970		29	.41799		30	.04141
28	.99765		30	.50489		31	.05618
29	.99990		31	.58492		32	.07461
30	1.00000		32	.67515		33	.09564
			33	.75312		34	:12331
			34	.83112		35	.15464
			35	.89055		36	.19237
			36	.94142		37	.23397
			37	.97179		38	.28700
			38	.99206		39	.34380
			39	.99859		40	.40870
			40	.99999		41	.47417
						42	.54544
						43	.61651
						44	.69081
						45	.75854
						46	.82357
						47	.87757
						48	.92534
						49	.95834
						50	.98197
						51	.99277
						52	.99817
						53	.99967
						54	.99997

k = 12 40,000 samples		k = 13 40,000 samples		k = 13	
CT	CP	CT	CP	CT	CP
20	.00002	34	.00002	84	.98650
21	.00004	35	.00002	85	.99412
22	.00006	36	.00007	86	.99777
23	.00011	37	.00012	87	.99907
24	.00018	38	.00014	88	.99974
25	.00023	39	.00024	89	.99986
26	.00025	40	.00039	90	.99988
27	.00040	41	.00046	91	.99988
28	.00075	42	.00088		
29	.00090	43	.00108		
30	.00130	44	.00135		
31	.00165	45	.00212		
32	.00240	46	.00274		
33	.00335	47	.00334		
34	.00477	48	.00454		
35	.00814	49	.00621		
36	.00814	50	.00816		
37	.01451	51	.01053		
38	.01951	52	.01298		
39	.02558	53	.01638		
40	.03238	54	.02088		
41	.04165	55	.02655		
42	.05270	56	.03325		
43	.06680	57	.04162		
44	.08322	58	.05202		
45	.10482	59	.06437		
46	.12742	60	.07927		
47	.15697	61	.09584		
48	.18874	62	.11629		
49	.22756	63	.13691		
50	.26993	64	.16466		
51	.31868	65	.19461		
52	.37068	66	.22793		
53	.42830	67	.26668		
54	.48680	68	.31018		
55	.55285	69	.35445		
56	.61357	70	.40267		
57	.67627	71	.45377		
58	.73502	72	.50854		
59	.79564	73	.56474		
60	.84709	74	.62024		
61	.84709	75	.67601		
62	.92766	76	.73056		
63	.95711	77	.78258		
64	.97656	78	.82893		
65	.98928	79	.86920		
66	.99605	80	.90710		
67	.99887	81	.93582		
68	.99972	82	.95952		
69	.99989	83	.97515		

	k = 14 50,000 samples		k = 14		k = 15 50,000 samples		k = 15

CT	CP	CT	CP	CT	CP	CT	CP
46	.00004	95	.67976	60	.00002	109	.29392
47	.00004	96	.72792	61	.00002	110	.33046
48	.00008	97	.77268	62	.00002	111	.36742
49	.00012	98	.81646	63	.00004	112	.40658
50	.00016	99	.85418	64	.00004	113	.44756
51	.00020	100	.91756	65	.00004	114	.49166
52	.00024	101	.94258	66	.00004	115	.53666
53	.00032	103	.96092	67	.00008	116	.58346
54	.00034	104	.97516	68	.00008	117	.62844
55	.00042	105	.98540	69	.00012	118	.67236
56	.00054	106	.99224	70	.00016	119	.71436
57	.00082	107	.99650	71	.00032	120	.75512
58	.00106	108	.99854	72	.00034	121	.79504
59	.00130	109	.99938	73	.00038	122	.83148
60	.00158	110	.99992	74	.00044	123	.86410
61	.00188	111	1.0	75	.00054	124	.89156
62	.00264			76	.00068	125	.91640
63	.00326			77	.00078	126	.93790
64	.00416			78	.00110	127	.95532
65	.00514			79	.00142	128	.96952
66	.00632			80	.00178	129	.98004
67	.00790			81	.00230	130	.98802
68	.00992			82	.00272	131	.99328
69	.01242			83	.00330	132	.99648
70	.01590			84	.00416	133	.99836
71	.01958			85	.00506	134	.99936
72	.02406			86	.00632	135	.99972
73	.02938			87	.00752	136	.99994
74	.03692			88	.00948	137	.99998
75	.04486			89	.01196	138	1.0
76	.05460			90	.01494		
77	.06568			91	.01800		
78	.07940			92	.02234		
79	.09444			93	.02700		
80	.11128			94	.03240		
81	.13198			95	.03852		
82	.15374			96	.04540		
83	.17740			97	.05334		
84	.20662			98	.06286		
85	.23728			99	.07362		
86	.27194			100	.08616		
87	.30860			101	.10104		
88	.35086			102	.11760		
89	.39224			103	.13742		
90	.43672			104	.15816		
91	.48162			105	.18030		
92	.53186			106	.20628		
93	.58120			107	.23284		
94	.63312			108	.26248		

k = 16 60,000 samples		k = 16		k = 17 60,000 samples		k = 17	
CT	CP	CT	CP	CT	CP	CT	CP
90	.00002	138	.40488	102	.00002	150	.05683
91	.00004	139	.44175	103	.00002	151	.06495
92	.00006	140	.48063	104	.00002	152	.07367
93	.00006	141	.51995	105	.00004	153	.08424
94	.00016	142	.56090	106	.00004	154	.09616
95	.00019	143	.59957	107	.00004	155	.10839
96	.00026	144	.64097	108	.00004	156	.12191
97	.00036	145	.67842	109	.00004	157	.13738
98	.00044	146	.71679	110	.00004	158	.15415
99	.00059	147	.75239	111	.00004	159	.17305
100	.00079	148	.78771	112	.00006	160	.19190
101	.00079	149	.82096	113	.00006	161	.21367
102	.00142	150	.85221	114	.00008	162	.23747
103	.00177	151	.87894	115	.00010	163	.26250
104	.00222	152	.90394	116	.00015	164	.28858
105	.00279	153	.92521	117	.00020	165	.31683
106	.00351	154	.94436	118	.00025	166	.34645
107	.00446	155	.95884	119	.00030	167	.37833
108	.00558	156	.97126	120	.00033	168	.41096
109	.00685	157	.97994	121	.00036	169	.44533
110	.00815	158	.98696	122	.00049	170	.47945
111	.00982	159	.99193	123	.00064	171	.51453
112	.01185	160	.99541	124	.00069	172	.55153
113	.01415	161	.99758	125	.00079	173	.58761
114	.01672	162	.99885	126	.00097	174	.62483
115	.01999	163	.99945	127	.00110	175	.66195
116	.02392	164	.99980	128	.00135	176	.69710
117	.02797	165	1.0	129	.00170	177	.73078
118	.03277			130	.00208	178	.76308
119	.03830			131	.00250	179	.79423
120	.04462			132	.00297	180	.82393
121	.05155			133	.00359	181	.85088
122	.05888			134	.00436	182	.87650
123	.06803			135	.00534	183	.89842
124	.07870			136	.00666	184	.91812
125	.09017			137	.00784	185	.93614
126	.10400			138	.00931	186	.95161
127	.11892			139	.01108	187	.96354
128	.13515			140	.01310	188	.97334
129	.15322			141	.01530	189	.98132
130	.17367			142	.01760	190	.98777
131	.19502			143	.02028	191	99179
132	.21947			144	.02408	192	.99482
133	.24590			145	.02771	193	.99739
134	.27447			146	.03189	194	.99857
135	.30335			147	.03714	195	.99934
136	.33488			148	.04321	196	.99969
137	.36898			149	.04931	197	.99987
						198	1.0

k = 18 60,000 samples		k = 18		k = 18	
CT	CP	CT	CP	CT	CP
135	.00002	184	.07165	233	.99978
136	.00002	185	.08097	234	.99990
137	.00002	186	.09085	235	.99997
138	.00002	187	.10158	236	.99999
139	.00004	188	.11321		
140	.00004	189	.12596		
141	.00006	190	.14049		
142	.00006	191	.15549		
143	.00008	192	.17314		
144	.00016	193	.19132		
145	.00016	194	.21117		
146	.00024	195	.23204		
147	.00029	196	.25491		
148	.00032	197	.28026		
149	.00034	198	.30481		
150	.00037	199	.33153		
151	.00040	200	.36025		
152	.00050	201	.38978		
153	.00062	202	.41965		
154	.00075	203	.44987		
155	.00083	204	.48144		
156	.00096	205	.51329		
157	.00114	206	.54466		
158	.00146	207	.57789		
159	.00169	208	.61159		
160	.00209	209	.64459		
161	.00267	210	.67617		
162	.00314	211	.70649		
163	.00377	212	.73752		
164	.00442	213	.76775		
165	.00507	214	.79633		
166	.00595	215	.82295		
167	.00677	216	.84757		
168	.00782	217	.86937		
169	.00904	218	.89035		
170	.01056	219	.90953		
171	.01271	220	.92663		
172	.01461	221	.94138		
173	.01716	222	.95486		
174	.01989	223	.96573		
175	.02272	224	.97430		
176	.02605	225	.98128		
177	.02992	226	.98663		
178	.03395	227	.99118		
179	.03873	228	.99425		
180	.04425	229	.99630		
181	.04995	230	.99782		
182	.05600	231	.99885		
183	.06345	232	.99945		

k = 19 60,000 samples			k = 19			k = 19	
CT	CP		CT	CP		CT	CP
172	.00002		220	.06502		268	.99202
173	.00002		221	.07324		269	.99497
174	.00002		222	.08259		270	.99664
175	.00002		223	.09259		271	.99772
176	.00004		224	.10311		272	.99867
177	.00004		225	.11331		273	.99932
178	.00004		226	.12436		274	.99964
179	.00009		227	.13708		275	.99986
180	.00014		228	.15090		276	.99998
181	.00016		229	.16657		277	1.0
182	.00023		230	.18305			
183	.00030		231	.20247			
184	.00035		232	.22130			
185	.00043		233	.24102			
186	.00053		234	.26274			
187	.00058		235	.28467			
188	.00066		236	.30864			
189	.00083		237	.33359			
190	.00093		238	.35967			
191	.00103		239	.38750			
192	.00126		240	.41463			
193	.00148		241	.44226			
194	.00163		242	.47244			
195	.00200		243	.50151			
196	.00237		244	.53048			
197	.00269		245	.56033			
198	.00321		246	.59208			
199	.00369		247	.62238			
200	.00419		248	.65156			
201	.00487		249	.68093			
202	.00559		250	.71026			
203	.00661		251	.73819			
204	.00769		252	.76514			
205	.00874		253	.79071			
206	.01031		254	.81481			
207	.01201		255	.83813			
208	.01391		256	.85981			
209	.01619		257	.87958			
210	.01889		258	.89791			
211	.02139		259	.91504			
212	.02457		260	.92931			
213	.02805		261	.94204			
214	.03168		262	.95367			
215	.03593		263	.96340			
216	.04001		264	.97143			
217	.04543		265	.97865			
218	.05105		266	.98382			
219	.05772		267	.98857			

k = 20	
70,000 samples	
CT	CP
213	.00004
214	.00010
215	.00010
216	.00010
217	.00013
218	.00016
219	.00020
220	.00023
221	.00027
222	.00033
223	.00037
224	.00044
225	.00051
226	.00061
227	.00068
228	.00095
229	.00106
230	.00119
231	.00152
232	.00168
233	.00189
234	.00213
235	.00259
236	.00303
237	.00352
238	.00401
239	.00464
240	.00521
241	.00595
242	.00694
243	.00800
244	.00919
245	.01055
246	.01185
247	.01341
248	.01531
249	.01717
250	.01940
251	.02190
252	.02464
253	.02757
254	.03080
255	.03451
256	.03877
257	.04317
258	.04894
259	.05485
260	.06094
261	.06735

k = 20	
CT	CP
262	.07462
263	.08269
264	.09128
265	.10042
266	.11042
267	.12075
268	.13222
269	.14511
270	.15904
271	.17358
272	.18931
273	.20665
274	.22488
275	.24404
276	.26367
277	.28376
278	.30633
279	.32842
280	.35151
281	.37592
282	.40093
283	.42630
284	.45156
285	.47839
286	.50538
287	.53321
288	.56071
289	.58942
290	.61761
291	.64541
292	.67307
293	.70061
294	.72674
295	.75184
296	.77630
297	.79999
298	.82159
299	.84342
300	.86261
301	.88065
302	.89738
303	.91367
304	.92738
305	.93961
306	.95074
307	.96031
308	.96828
309	.97518
310	.98034

k = 20	
CT	CP
311	.98530
312	.98934
313	.99207
314	.99428
315	.99604
316	.99737
317	.99826
318	.99906
319	.99956
320	.99983
321	.99996
322	1.0

TABLE D
Proportions of Area Under the Normal Curve
If the area under the normal curve is less than .50, prefix z with a negative
sign (e.g., if area = .0495, then $z = -1.65$).

AREA <.50 $p = -z$	z	AREA >.50 $p = +z$	AREA <.50 $p = -z$	z	AREA >.50 $p = +z$
.0202	2.05	.9798	.0455	1.69	.9545
			.0465	1.68	.9535
.0207	2.04	.9793	.0475	1.67	.9525
.0212	2.03	.9788	.0485	1.66	.9515
.0217	2.02	.9783	.0495*	1.65	.9505
.0222	2.01	.9778			
.0228	2.00	.9772	.0505	1.64	.9495
			.0516	1.63	.9484
.0233	1.99	.9767	.0526	1.62	.9474
.0239	1.98	.9761	.0537	.161	.9463
.0244	1.97	.9756	.0548	1.60	.9452
.0250	1.96	.9750			
.0256	1.95	.9744	.0559	1.59	.9441
			.0571	1.58	.9429
.0262	1.94	.9738	.0582	1.57	.9418
.0268	1.93	.9732	.0594	1.56	.9406
.0274	1.92	.9726	.0606	1.55	.9394
.0281	1.91	.9719			
.0287	1.90	.9713	.0618	1.54	.9382
			.0630	1.53	.9370
.0294	1.89	.9706	.0643	1.52	.9357
.0301	1.88	.9699	.0655	1.51	.9345
.0307	1.87	.9693	.0668	1.50	.9332
.0314	1.86	.9686			
.0322	1.85	.9678	.0681	1.49	.9319
			.0694	1.48	.9306
.0329	1.84	.9671	.0708	1.47	.9292
.0336	1.83	.9664	.0721	1.46	.9279
.0344	1.82	.9656	.0735	1.45	.9265
.0351	1.81	.9649			
.0359	1.80	.9641	.0749	1.44	.9251
			.0764	1.43	.9236
.0367	1.79	.9633	.0778	1.42	.9222
.0375	1.78	.9625	.0793	1.41	.9207
.0384	1.77	.9616	.0808	1.40	.9192
.0392	1.76	.9608			
.0401	1.75	.9599	.0823	1.39	.9177
			.0838	1.38	.9162
.0409	1.74	.9591	.0853	1.37	.9147
.0418	1.73	.9582	.0869	1.36	.9131
.0427	1.72	.9573	.0885	1.35	.9115
.0436	1.71	.9564	.0901	1.34	.9099
.0446	1.70	.9554	.0918	1.33	.9082

AREA <.50 p = -z	z	AREA >.50 p = +z	AREA <.50 p = -z	z	AREA >.50 p = +z
.0934	1.32	.9066	.2005	0.84	.7995
:0951	1.31	.9049	.2033	0.83	.7967
.0968	1.30	.9032	.2061	0.82	.7939
.0985	1.29	.9015	.2090	0.81	.7910
.1003	1.28	.8997	.2119	0.80	.7881
.1020	1.27	.8980	.2148	0.79	.7852
.1038	1.26	.8962	.2177	0.78	.7823
.1056	1.25	.8944	.2206	0.77	.7794
			.2236	0.76	.7764
.1075	1.24	.8925	.2266	0.75	.7734
.1093	1.23	.8907	.2296	0.74	.7704
.1112	1.22	.8888	.2327	0.73	.7673
.1131	1.21	.8869	.2358	0.72	.7642
.1151	1.20	.8849	.2389	0.71	.7611
.1170	1.19	.8830	.2420	0.70	.7580
.1190	1.18	.8810	.2451	0.69	.7549
.1210	1.17	.8790	.2483	0.68	.7517
.1230	1.16	.8770	.2514	0.67	.7486
.1251	1.15	.8749	.2546	0.66	.7454
.1271	1.14	.8729	.2578	0.65	.7422
.1292	1.13	.8708	.2611	0.64	.9389
.1314	1.12	.8686	.2643	0.63	.7357
.1335	1.11	.8665	.2676	0.62	.7324
.1357	1.10	.8643	.2709	0.61	.7291
.1379	1.09	.8621	.2743	0.60	.7257
.1401	1.08	.8599	.2776	0.59	.7224
.1423	1.07	.8577	.2810	0.58	.7190
.1446	1.06	.8554	.2843	0.57	.7157
.1469	1.05	.8531	.2877	0.56	.7123
.1492	1.04	.8508	.2912	0.55	.7088
.1515	1.03	.8485	.2946	0.54	.7054
.1539	1.02	.8461	.2981	0.53	.7019
.1562	1.01	.8438	.3015	0.52	.6985
.1587	1.00	.8413	.3050	0.51	.6950
.1611	0.99	.8389	.3085	0.50	.6915
.1635	0.98	.8365			
.1660	0.97	.8340	.3121	0.49	.6879
.1685	0.96	.8315	.3156	0.48	.6844
.1711	0.95	.8289	.3192	0.47	.6808
			.3228	0.46	.6772
.1736	0.94	.8264	.3264	0.45	.6736
.1762	0.93	.8238			
.1788	0.92	.8212	.3300	0.44	.6700
.1814	0.91	.8186	.3336	0.43	.6664
.1841	0.90	.8159	.3372	0.42	.6628
			.3409	0.41	.6591
.1867	0.89	.8133	.3446	0.40	.6554
.1894	0.88	.8106	.3483	0.39	.6517
.1922	0.87	.8078	.3520	0.38	.6480
.1949	0.86	.8051	.3557	0.37	.6443
.1977	0.85	.8023	.3594	0.36	.6406
			.3632	0.35	.6368

AREA < .50		AREA > .50
p = -z	z	p = +z
.3669	0.34	.6331
.3707	0.33	.6293
.3745	0.32	.6255
.3783	0.31	.6217
.3821	0.30	.6179
.3859	0.29	.6141
.3897	0.28	.6103
.3936	0.27	.6064
.3974	0.26	.6026
.4013	0.25	.5987
.4052	0.24	.5948
.4090	0.23	.5910
.4129	0.22	.5871
.4168	0.21	.5832
.4207	0.20	.5793
.4247	0.19	.5753
.4286	0.18	.5714
.4325	0.17	.5675
.4364	0.16	.5636
.4404	0.15	.5596
.4443	0.14	.5557
.4483	0.13	.5517
.4522	0.12	.5478
.4562	0.11	.5438
.4602	0.10	.5398
.4641	0.09	.5359
.4681	0.08	.5319
.4721	0.07	.5279
.4761	0.06	.5239
.4801	0.05	.5199
.4840	0.04	.5160
.4880	0.03	.5120
.4920	0.02	.5080
.4960	0.01	.5040
.5000	0.00	.5000

TABLE E

Significance Tests for Kendall's Tau

Taken from R 73 of The Computation Department of

The Mathematical Center, Amsterdam

TABLE III. Smallest value of S for which P $[\underline{S} \geq S] \leq a$; $S = \binom{k}{2} - 2I$

N	a = 0.005	a = 0.010	a = 0.025	a = 0.050	a = 0.100
4	8	8	8	6	6
5	12	10	10	8	8
6	15	13	13	11	9
7	19	17	15	13	11
8	22	20	16	16	12
9	26	24	20	18	14
10	29	27	23	21	17
11	33	31	27	23	19
12	38	36	30	26	20
13	44	40	34	28	24
14	47	43	37	33	25
15	53	49	41	35	29
16	58	52	46	38	30
17	64	58	50	42	34
18	69	63	53	45	37
19	75	67	57	49	39
20	80	72	62	52	42
21	86	78	66	56	44
22	91	83	71	61	47
23	99	89	75	65	51
24	104	94	80	68	54
25	110	100	86	72	58
26	117	107	91	77	61
27	125	113	95	81	63
28	130	118	100	86	68
29	138	126	106	90	70
30	145	131	111	95	75
31	151	137	117	99	77
32	160	144	122	104	82
33	166	152	128	108	86
34	175	157	133	113	89
35	181	165	139	117	93
36	190	172	146	122	96
37	198	178	152	128	100
38	205	185	157	133	105
39	213	193	163	139	109
40	222	200	170	144	112

Reproduced with permission of the Mathematical Center and A. van Wijngarden.

TABLE F
Number of Judges Needed in Rank Scaling

For the K and alpha levels not listed a solution can be obtained by solving for K in the following formula where Q is taken from the values by Harter (1959b) or Dixon and Massey (1957).

$$N = Q^2(K)\ (K + 1)/12$$

Number of judges necessary to insure the possibility of I items being significantly different.

	Number of Judges		
Items	*.01*	*.05*	*.10*
3	17	11	9
4	33	19	18
5	53	38	31
6	80	57	47
7	112	82	68
8	150	111	92
9	194	145	123
10	244	184	157
11	301	228	195
12	364	278	239
13	434	333	287
14	511	394	341
15	594	461	400

TABLE G
Normalized Range Values
Q_a = W/S Values for 3(1) 15 Items Where a = .01, .05, .10

K		Q_a	
Items	.01	.05	.10
3	4.120	3.314	2.902
4	4.403	3.633	3.240
5	4.603	3.858	3.478
6	4.757	4.030	3.661
7	4.832	4.170	3.803
8	4.987	4.286	3.931
9	5.078	4.387	4.037
10	5.157	4.474	4.129
11	5.227	4.552	4.211
12	5.290	4.622	4.285
13	5.348	4.685	4.351
14	5.400	4.743	4.412
15	5.448	4.796	4.463

df = ∞

From Harter, H. L., Clemm, D. S., & Guthrie, E. H. The probability integrals of the range and the studentized range. WADC Technical Report 58-484, Volume II. Ohio: Wright Air Development Center, 1959, with permission.

TABLE H
Critical Ranges for the Two-Way Classification
Comparing all Possible Pairs of Items:
Judges = 2(1) 15 and Items = 3(1) 15

Judges	A	3	4	5	6	7	8	9	10	11	12	13	14	15
												Items		
2	.01	–	–	–	–	12	14	16	18	20	22	24	26	28
	.05	–	–	8	10	12	14	15	17	19	21	23	25	26
	.10	–	6	8	9	11	13							
3	.01	–	9	12	14	16	19	22	24	27	29	32	35	37
	.05	6	8	10	13	15	17	20	22	25	27	30	32	35
	.10	6	8	10	12									
4	.01	8	11	14	17	20	23	26	29	32	35	38	41	45
	.05	7	10	12	15	18	21	23	26	29	32	35	38	41
	.10	6	9	11	14	17	20	22	25	28	31	34	37	40
5	.01	9	12	16	19	23	26	29	33	37	40	44	47	51
	.05	8	11	14	17	20	23	26	30	34	37	40	43	47
	.10	7	10	13	16	19	22	25	28	32	35	38	42	45
6	.01	10	14	17	21	25	29	33	37	41	45	49	53	57
	.05	9	12	15	19	22	26	29	33	37	41	43	48	52
	.10	8	11	14	17	20	24	27	31	34	38	42	45	49
7	.10	11	15	19	23	27	31	36	40	44	49	53	58	62
	.05	9	13	16	20	24	28	32	36	40	44	48	52	56
	.10	8	11	15	18	22	26	29	33	37	41	45	49	53
8	.01	12	16	20	25	29	34	38	43	47	52	57	62	67
	.05	10	14	17	21	25	30	34	38	42	47	51	56	60
	.10	9	12	16	20	24	27	31	36	40	44	48	52	57
9	.01	12	17	22	26	31	36	41	46	51	56	61	66	71
	.05	10	14	18	23	27	31	36	40	45	50	54	59	64
	.10	9	13	17	21	25	29	33	38	42	47	51	55	60
10	.01	13	18	23	28	33	38	43	49	54	59	65	70	75
	.05	11	15	19	24	28	33	38	43	47	52	57	62	67
	.10	9	13	18	22	26	31	35	40	44	49	54	58	63
11	.01	14	19	24	29	35	40	46	51	57	62	68	74	83
	.05	11	15	20	25	30	35	40	45	50	55	60	65	71
	.10	10	14	18	23	27	32	37	42	46	51	56	61	66
12	.01	14	20	25	31	36	42	48	54	59	65	71	77	83
	.05	12	16	21	26	31	36	41	47	52	58	63	68	74
	.10	10	15	19	24	29	33	38	43	48	54	59	64	69
13	.01	15	21	26	32	38	44	50	56	62	68	74	80	87
	.05	12	17	22	27	32	38	43	49	54	60	65	71	77
	.10	11	15	20	25	30	35	40	45	50	56	61	67	72
14	.01	16	21	27	33	39	45	52	58	64	71	77	84	90
	.05	13	17	23	28	34	39	45	50	56	62	68	74	80
	.10	11	16	21	26	31	36	41	47	52	58	63	60	75
15	.01	16	22	28	34	41	47	54	60	67	63	80	87	94
	.05	13	18	24	29	35	40	46	52	58	64	70	75	83

TABLE I
Selected Balanced Incomplete Block Designs

PLANS

Plan 13.1 $t = 7, k = 3, r = 3, b = 7, \lambda = 1, E = .78$, Type II

		Reps.	
Block	I	II	III
(1)	7	1	3
(2)	1	2	4
(3)	2	3	5
(4)	3	4	6
(5)	4	5	7
(6)	5	6	1
(7)	6	7	2

Plan 13.3 $t = 11, k = 5, r = 5, b = 11, \lambda = 2, E = .88$, Type I

			Reps.		
Block	I	II	III	IV	V
(1)	1	2	3	4	5
(2)	7	1	6	10	3
(3)	9	8	1	6	2
(4)	11	9	7	1	4
(5)	10	11	5	8	1
(6)	8	7	2	3	11
(7)	2	6	4	11	10
(8)	6	3	11	5	9
(9)	3	4	10	9	8
(10)	5	10	9	2	7
(11)	4	5	8	7	6

Plan 13.5 $t = 13, k = 4, r = 4, b = 13, \lambda = 1, E = .81$, Type I

			Reps.	
Block	I	II	III	IV
(1)	13	1	3	9
(2)	1	2	4	10
(3)	2	3	5	11
(4)	3	4	6	12
(5)	4	5	7	13
(6)	5	6	8	1
(7)	6	7	9	2
(8)	7	8	10	3
(9)	8	9	11	4
(10)	9	10	12	5
(11)	10	11	13	6
(12)	11	12	1	7
(13)	12	13	2	8

Plan 13.9 $t = 16, k = 6, r = 6, b = 16, \lambda = 2, E = .89$, Type I

			Reps.			
Block	I	II	III	IV	V	VI
(1)	1	2	3	4	5	6
(2)	2	7	8	9	10	1
(3)	3	1	13	7	11	12
(4)	4	8	1	11	14	15
(5)	5	12	14	1	16	9
(6)	6	10	15	13	1	16
(7)	7	14	2	16	15	3
(8)	8	16	12	2	4	13
(9)	9	15	11	5	13	2
(10)	10	11	6	12	2	14
(11)	11	4	16	3	9	10
(12)	12	3	10	15	8	5
(13)	13	6	9	14	3	8
(14)	14	13	5	10	7	4
(15)	15	9	4	6	12	7
(16)	16	5	7	8	6	11

Plan 13.13 $t = 21, k = 5, r = 5, b = 21, \lambda = 1, E = .84$, Type I

			Reps.		
Block	I	II	III	IV	V
(1)	21	1	4	14	16
(2)	1	2	5	15	17
(3)	2	3	6	16	18
(4)	3	4	7	17	19
(5)	4	5	8	18	20
(6)	5	6	9	19	21
(7)	6	7	10	20	1
(8)	7	8	11	21	2
(9)	8	9	12	1	3
(10)	9	10	13	2	4
(11)	10	11	14	3	5
(12)	11	12	15	4	6
(13)	12	13	16	5	7
(14)	13	14	17	6	8
(15)	14	15	18	7	9
(16)	15	16	19	8	10
(17)	16	17	20	9	11
(18)	17	18	21	10	12
(19)	18	19	1	11	13
(20)	19	20	2	12	14
(21)	20	21	3	13	15

Designs taken from Cochran & Cox, *Design of Experiments,* with permission from the publisher, John Wiley & Sons, Inc. t = treatments; k = number in each block; r = number of times each object appears in the design; b = number of blocks; λ = number of times each object is paired; E = efficiency factor; and Type = type of analysis of variance.

TABLE J
Cumulative Probability Distributions (cp) of Interjudge Differences
(d) for k = 3(1) 20, 25, 30. Distributions Based on 20,000 Random
Differences are Starred (*) in the Table. All Other Values Are
Based on 10,000 Random Differences.

$$\mu = k - 2 + \frac{1}{k} \text{ and } \sigma^2 = k - 4 + \frac{7}{k} - \frac{6}{k^2} + \frac{2}{k^3}$$

k = 3		k = 6		k = 8	
d	cp	d	cp	d	cp
0	1.0000	0	1.0000	0	1.0000
1	.7813	1	.9918	1	.9995
2	.4839	2	.9593	2	.9939
3	.0537	3	.8485	3	.9713
		4	.6287	4	.9034
		5	.3933	5	.7685
		6	.2090	6	.5793
k = 4		7	.0936	7	.3890
		8	.0418	8	.2365
d	cp	9	.0146	9	.1315
0	1.0000	10	.0058	10	.0681
1	.9234	11	.0021	11	.0350
2	.7648	12	.0003	12	.0172
3	.3672	13	.0003	13	.0071
4	.1689	14	.0001	14	.0026
5	.0216			15	.0012
6	.0034			16	.0005
				17	.0003
		k = 7		18	.0001
k = 5*		d	cp		
d	cp	0	1.0000		
0	1.0000	1	.9967		
1	.9730	2	.9847		
2	.8984	3	.9327		
3	.6704	4	.8055		
4	.3865	5	.5986		
5	.1780	6	.3975		
6	.0676	7	.2182		
7	.0207	8	.1217		
8	.0019	9	.0536		
9	.0015	10	.0249		
10	.0002	11	.0092		
		12	.0038		
		13	.0013		
		14	.0006		
		15	.0001		

k = 9			k = 10*			k = 11	
d	cp		d	cp		d	cp
0	1.0000		0	1.0000		1	1.0000
1	.9997		1	.9998		2	.9998
2	.9979		2	.9994		3	.9979
3	.9900		3	.9964		4	.9926
4	.9550		4	.9834		5	.9741
5	.8781		5	.9432		6	.9240
6	.7422		6	.8584		7	.8329
7	.5766		7	.7194		8	.7047
8	.3986		8	.5576		9	.5478
9	.2549		9	.3994		10	.3943
10	.1568		10	.2638		11	.2662
11	.0854		11	.1618		12	.1715
12	.0458		12	.0996		13	.1046
13	.0217		13	.0541		14	.0617
14	.0123		14	.0300		15	.0356
15	.0069		15	.0148		16	.0201
16	.0034		16	.0083		17	.0118
17	.0011		17	.0042		18	.0063
18	.0004		18	.0020		19	.0038
19	.0003		19	.0012		20	.0020
20	.0003		20	.0007		21	.0011
21	.0001		21	.0003		22	.0009
22	.0000		22	.0002		23	.0005
			23	.0000		24	.0005
						25	.0003
						26	.0001
						27	.0001
						28	.0001

k = 12		k = 13		k = 14	
d	cp	d	cp	d	cp
1	1.0000	1	1.0000	3	1.0000
2	.9999	2	.9999	4	.9999
3	.9994	3	.9999	5	.9982
4	.9967	4	.9993	6	.9916
5	.9878	5	.9951	7	.9757
6	.9606	6	.9857	8	.9415
7	.9037	7	.9577	9	.8796
8	.8119	8	.8950	10	.7857
9	.6831	9	.8007	11	.6643
10	.5437	10	.6743	12	.5382
11	.4001	11	.5404	13	.4058
12	.2835	12	.4122	14	.2972
13	.1931	13	.2955	15	.2071
14	.1218	14	.2003	16	.1375
15	.0757	15	.1335	17	.0910
16	.0473	16	.0852	18	.0584
17	.0286	17	.0544	19	.0355
18	.0154	18	.0339	20	.0230
19	.0085	19	.0209	21	.0131
20	.0042	20	.0125	22	.0079
21	.0023	21	.0076	23	.0051
22	.0015	22	.0051	24	.0029
23	.0009	23	.0029	25	.0015
24	.0005	24	.0016	26	.0005
25	.0004	25	.0010	27	.0004
26	.0002	26	.0005	28	.0001
		27	.0001		
		28	.0001		
		29	.0001		

k = 15*			k = 16			k = 17	
d	cp		d	cp		d	cp
3	1.0000		4	1.0000		5	1.0000
4	.9999		5	.9999		6	.9995
5	.9994		6	.9989		7	.9985
6	.9975		7	.9965		8	.9943
7	.9913		8	.9860		9	.9827
8	.9716		9	.9629		10	.9542
9	.0330		10	.9209		11	.9072
10	.8669		11	.8524		12	.8381
11	.7726		12	.7615		13	.7440
12	.6584		13	.6481		14	.6323
13	.5320		14	.5274		15	.5184
14	.4100		15	.4171		16	.4089
15	.3024		16	.3112		17	.3122
16	.2148		17	.2296		18	.2279
17	.1491		18	.1568		19	.1647
18	.1008		19	.1052		20	.1138
19	.0700		20	.0724		21	.0758
20	.0418		21	.0470		22	.0525
21	.0259		22	.0289		23	.0331
22	.0160		23	.0188		24	.0223
23	.0098		24	.0111		25	.0138
24	.0063		25	.0060		26	.0090
25	.0034		26	.0037		27	.0059
26	.0022		27	.0022		28	.0034
27	.0014		28	.0016		29	.0021
28	.0009		29	.0007		30	.0011
29	.0005		30	.0004		31	.0004
30	.0002		31	.0002		32	.0001
31	.0001		32	.0001			
32	.0001		33	.0001			
			34	.0001			

k = 18			k = 19*			k = 20*	
d	cp		d	cp		d	cp
4	1.0000		6	1.0000		7	1.0000
5	.9999		7	.9998		8	.9996
6	.9999		8	.9989		9	.9982
7	.0002		9	.9964		10	.9936
8	.9971		10	.9890		11	.9837
9	.9913		11	.9726		12	.9652
10	.9783		12	.9406		13	.9326
11	.9504		13	.8912		14	.8796
12	.9020		14	.8205		15	.8085
13	.8316		15	.7294		16	.7228
14	.7397		16	.6308		17	.6214
15	.6386		17	.5220		18	.5208
16	.5284		18	.4177		19	.4217
17	.4206		19	.3260		20	.3316
18	.3225		20	.2460		21	.2550
19	.2405		21	.1786		22	.1884
20	.1710		22	.1284		23	.1342
21	.1201		23	.0884		24	.0963
22	.0817		24	.0570		25	.0665
23	.0543		25	.0378		26	.0458
24	.0357		26	.0254		27	.0301
25	.0235		27	.0170		28	.0194
26	.0147		28	.0112		29	.0126
27	.0091		29	.0076		30	.0086
28	.0062		30	.0048		31	.0060
29	.0036		31	.0030		32	.0036
30	.0026		32	.0016		33	.0022
31	.0017		33	.0011		34	.0012
32	.0012		34	.0008		35	.0009
33	.0008		35	.0004		36	.0006
34	.0006		36	.0002		37	.0002
35	.0003		37	.0002		38	.0001
36	.0001		38	.0001		39	.0001
37	.0001					40	.0001

k = 25			k = 30*	
d	cp		d	cp
10	1.0000		12	1.0000
11	.9999		13	.9999
12	.9993		14	.9998
13	.9979		15	.9994
14	.9934		16	.9986
15	.9851		17	.9962
16	.9699		18	.9918
17	.9405		19	.9836
18	.9006		20	.9684
19	.8446		21	.9443
20	.7745		22	.9104
21	.6995		23	.8686
22	.6085		24	.8113
23	.5177		25	.7426
24	.4268		26	.6691
25	.3458		27	.5898
26	.2774		28	.5088
27	.2136		29	.4300
28	.1632		30	.3572
29	.1180		31	.2916
30	.0863		32	.2302
31	.0617		33	.1792
32	.0450		34	.1390
33	.0307		35	.1052
34	.0222		36	.0788
35	.0144		37	.0576
36	.0099		38	.0416
37	.0072		39	.0297
38	.0049		40	.0210
39	.0029		41	.0146
40	.0020		42	.0108
41	.0012		43	.0070
42	.0008		44	.0045
43	.0006		45	.0029
44	.0004		46	.0020
45	.0002		47	.0013
46	.0001		48	.0010
			49	.0007
			50	.0004
			51	.0003
			52	.0002
			53	.0002
			54	.0001
			55	.0001

Appendix B
An Example Using Several Techniques

During the semester students are asked to utilize scaling methods in attacking a problem of their interest. Their grade is primarily based on this major effort. A good example of the type of research that is done is provided in the following paper. Sanford Britton, one of the author's students, made effective use of circular triad analysis and multidimensional preference analysis in his paper concerned with judgments about mainstreaming handicapped students.

Who Should be Mainstreamed? A Multidimensional Scale of Eleven Disabilities

Sanford Britton

INTRODUCTION

Children with educational disabilities have long been segregated into special classes, to be taught by teachers trained to deal with their special needs. Currently, however, the trend has been to integrate (mainstream) many of these children into regular classrooms for some or all of their school day. Specially trained resource teachers work both with the children and the regular teachers to help with individual needs and problems.

As with any educational practice, this integration has been neither uniformly applied, nor uniformly accepted. However, through federal legislation, Public Law 94–142, all children are entitled to education in the "least restrictive environment" that is appropriate for them. The law has led to an increase in mainstreaming throughout the country.

The question which now is being directed at administrators, psychologists, and teachers is: What constitutes a 'least restrictive environment'? This environment differs in each individual case, and with each handicapping condition. The regular classroom may be appropriate for some children, and inappropriate for others. It is important to have some idea of the dimensions of disabilities that are relevant to the decision process related to mainstreaming.

Though mainstreaming has been most often used with children with learning disabilities and those classified as educable mentally retarded (EMR), children with a wide variety of handicaps have been placed in regular classrooms. The physically handicapped have often been educated in regular classrooms (Haring, Stern, & Cruickshank, 1958; Rapier, Adelson, Carey, & Croke, 1972). Children who require full-time assistance due to cerebral palsy have been successfully integrated with non-handicapped children (Huth, 1981). Mainstreaming has also been used with the perceptually impaired. Blind children have been taught in regular classrooms with the addition of special equipment (Ward & McCormick, 1980).

The fact that many children have been mainstreamed does not imply that mainstreaming is a panacea for the problems of educating the handicapped. Professionals in the field of special education feel that we should tread with care in this area, and not overuse the regular classroom for children with special needs (Diamond, 1979; Frostig, 1980). The effects of mainstreaming on exceptional children, teachers and non-handicapped children must be carefully investigated. It has been suggested that mainstreamed children may sometimes take up a disproportionate amount of their teacher's time, causing difficulties with the other children in class (Martin, 1974). Since the goal of PL 94–142 is the education of all children, educational programs must be evaluated in terms of their affect on all of the children involved.

The problems of mainstreaming lead to the question of who is best served by being mainstreamed? Are some disabilities more appropriate for integration than others? What are the characteristics of an individual that make him/her main- streamable? Though no criteria are likely to be universally agreed upon, re- searchers have attempted to investigate attitudes towards the mainstreaming of different disability groups.

Teachers have been found to support mainstreaming of the learning disabled more than the mentally retarded (Moore & Fine, 1978). Research has also found a greater acceptance of physically handicapped and learning disabled than for socially/emotionally disturbed and EMR children (Williams & Algozzine, 1977). A study in Massachusetts has additionally found teachers to be more willing to teach children with orthopedic problems than those with serious per- ceptual problems. In fact, only 13% felt that children with serious visual or auditory problems should be placed in regular classes on a full-time basis (Wechsler, Suarez, & McFadden, 1975).

Harasymiw and Horne (1976) studied the attitudes of teachers toward differ- ent handicaps. The experimental group taught in schools that had integrated classes, while the control subjects taught in schools with no integration. Both groups deemed the epileptics, learning disabled, and retarded as more manage- able in the classroom than the deaf, blind, emotionally disturbed, or multiply handicapped.

An attitude scale was developed to determine people's attitudes toward main- streaming (Berryman, Neal & Robinson, 1980). A factor analysis of the scale found four major factors being tested. These factors were labeled: Learning Capability, Severe Disability, Social Behavior, and General Mainstreaming. Learning capability involved disabilities that don't greatly hinder academic pro- gress. Disabilities in Severe Disability were perceptual impairments and cerebral palsy. Social Behavior involved behavioral disorders or problems. Attitudes toward EMR children loaded highly on the fourth factor, which was concerned with mainstreaming as a whole.

The factors found on this scale separate the major disabilities into four areas. However, the analysis did not attempt to scale the disabilities in terms of their mainstreamability. The purpose of this study is to investigate the scalability of disabilities. It will also look at the salient dimensions used in determining which disabilities are suitable for mainstreaming.

METHOD

A set of eleven handicapping conditions was selected for study. The disabilities chosen ranged in severity from learning disabled to autistic, and included physical, mental, emotional, and perceptual problems. It was expected that learning disabilities and autism would represent the extremes of the scale, providing a basis for comparing the results of the other nine disabilities. Each of the eleven was matched with each other to form 55 pairs. A questionnaire was then formed, consisting of these 55 pairs of disabilities. The eleven chosen disabilities were not considered an exhaustive list, but were chosen as a representative sample. The list was pared to eleven in order to hold the number of pairs to a manageable level. The task required each subject to choose from each pair of disabilities the one that was considered most conducive to integration into regular classrooms.

The questionnaire was administered to 23 graduate students in special education. All of the students were familiar with the disabilities, though they had not necessarily had personal experience with all of them. Some of the subjects had had classroom teaching experience, and all had had a general survey course covering the various handicapping conditions.

The data was analyzed for scalability using a circular triad analysis (TRICIR) (Kneszek, 1978). The analysis checks for both individual and group consistency of response. In a set of three disabilities, the choices should conform to the property of transitivity. That is, if condition A is more suitable (for mainstreaming) than B, and B more than C, then A should also be more suitable than C. A circular triad occurs when this transitivity fails (A > B, B > C, C > A). An abundance of circular triads implies a lack of clear distinction between the objects, and hence low scalability.

The circular triad analysis was used to create a unidimensional scale from the data. The disabilities were arranged in order of their suitability for regular classroom placement. The scale was tested by a relative scalability index, as well as Kendall's coefficient of concordance (Marascuilo & McSweeney, 1977).

The data were then analyzed to find the major dimensions underlying the preferences made. Multidimensional preference mapping (MDPREF) was used. This technique is a form of direct factor analysis (Dunn-Rankin, this volume). In addition to finding factors underlying the data matrix, MDPREF maps both the variables and the subjects into plots of the factors. The importance that each subject placed on each factor can be seen. Factors having eigenvalues greater than one were retained.

RESULTS

The circular triad analysis found the eleven disabilities to be highly scalable relative to mainstreaming. A scale was derived on which disabilities with higher scores were considered more suitable for classroom integration. As expected, the polar items on the scale were learning disabilities and autism, with scale scores of 90 and 9.13, respectively (see Rank Scaling, page 55).

The second most mainstreamable disability was epilepsy, followed by hyperactivity and educable mental retardation. The least mainstreamable, after autism, were severe emotional disorder and blindness. Trainably mentally retarded children were considered better suited to regular classes than were blind children. The severity of the disability appeared to be the major dimension differentiating the handicapping conditions. There were no apparent differences between physical and mental disabilities. Complete scale scores can be found in Table B.1.

Only one of the subjects was found to have a large number of circular triads. Two of the 23 were completely consistent in their responses, with no circular triads. The mean number of circular triads was 5.22, with a standard deviation of

TABLE B.1
Unidimensional Scale of Eleven Disabilities

Disability	Scaled Score
Learning Disability (L)	90.00
Epilepsy (E)	76.96
Hyperactivity (H)	70.00
Educable Mentally Retarded (EM)	61.30
Paraplegia (P)	56.52
Aphasia (A)	54.78
Deaf (D)	37.83
Trainable Mentally Retarded (T)	36.96
Blind (B)	28.70
Severe Emotional Disorder (S)	27.83
Autism (AU)	9.13

Suitability for Mainstreaming

Least   Most

10   20   30   40   50   60   70   80   90

AU   SB   TD   AP EM H E   L

Kendall's Coefficient of Concordance (W) = .59 p < .0001

4.42. The high standard deviation is a result of one subject who had 20 circular triads. No other respondent exhibited more than 11. The median value of 4 is therefore a better index of central tendency than is the mean. All of the subjects had significantly fewer triads than would be expected by chance ($p < .001$).

Similarly, none of the eleven disabilities was found in a significantly large number of circular triads. The two polar items, learning disabilities and autism, were in very few circular triads (19 and 11). The others were all found in circular triads between 30 and 46 times, fewer than would be found if the items were highly ambiguous.

Kendall's coefficient of concordance (W) was calculated for each judge, and for the overall scale. The overall coefficient of concordance was .59, significantly greater than zero ($p < .00001$). This result indicates that all subjects rated the items in a similar fashion. Individual values of W ranged from .64 to 1.0, with 22 of the 23 being greater than .80. All of these were significant, with $p < .01$. These statistics are related to the circularity within the data, and further demonstrate that individuals had little trouble in scaling the data. The circular triad distributions from the sample can be found in Table B.2.

The scalability of the disabilities can be further established by assessing the significance of differences between obtained scale scores. Given the sample size and an alpha level of .05, the difference in the scale scores of two disabilities needed to exceed 31.0 in order to reach significance. It was possible for 28 pairs of disabilities to differ significantly. Of these 28, 22 pairs differed by more than the critical difference of 31.00. The relative scalability index (significant differences/possible significant differences) of .79 is significantly different from chance occurrence ($p < .00001$).

While this initial analysis determined that the chosen disabilities could be

TABLE B.2
Circular Triads Among Eleven Disabilities

Disability	No. Circular Triads
Autism	11
Learning Disability	19
Epilepsy	30
Educable Mentally Retarded	32
Blind	33
Severe Emotional Disorder	34
Trainable Mentally Retarded	36
Aphasia	37
Hyperactivity	37
Deaf	45
Paraplegia	46

Mean = 32.72 S.D. = 10.22
$p < .001$ for all disabilities

scaled, further analysis was desired to determine if there is more than one salient dimension involved in their scaling. Multidimensional preference analysis was used to find the dimensionality of the data matrix.

Initial factoring of the data matrix produced two factors with eigenvalues greater than one. These factors were retained for rotation. The two factors accounted for 75 percent of the variance in the scores.

The first dimension was a Severe-Mild dimension, similar to the unidimensional scale that was found. Disabilities with positive loadings (most severe) on this dimension were autism, blindness, deafness, severe emotional disorder, and trainably mentally retarded. Considered least severe were learning disabled, epilepsy and hyperactivity. EMR and TMR were placed at near equal distances from the origin on this dimension, but in opposite directions. The loading for EMR was $-.16$. while that for TMR was $+.17$.

The second factor was labeled Physical-Mental as it generally differentiated the physical (including perceptual) problems from the psychological. The highest positive (physical) loadings corresponded to paraplegia and blindness, while the highest negative loadings were associated with the two levels of mental retardation. This dimension did not clearly place hyperactivity, aphasia, or severe emotional disorders. Loadings for all three were close to zero on this factor, indicative of the somewhat ambiguous origin of these disabilities. The plot of the disabilities can be seen in Fig. B.1, with the factor coordinates shown in Table B.3.

The judges were also plotted in the two dimensional space. Each point on

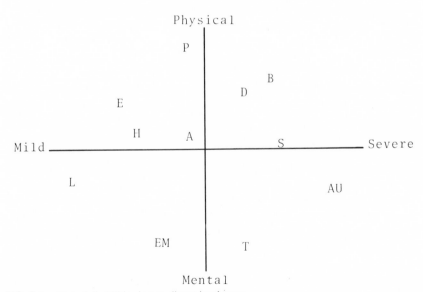

FIG. B.1. Plot of disabilities in two dimensional space

TABLE 3
Matrix of Factor Coordinates

Disability	Factor 1	Factor 2
Epilepsy (E)	−.35	.17
Blind (B)	.28	.36
Deaf (D)	.15	.26
Autism (AU)	.53	−.21
Aphasia (A)	−.07	.07
Hyperactivity (H)	−.26	.08
Learning Disability (L)	−.52	−.21
Educable Mentally Retarded (EM)	−.16	−.46
Trainable Mentally Retarded (T)	.17	−.50
Paraplegia (P)	−.08	.47
Severe Emotional Disorder (S)	.30	−.02
Eigenvalues:	6.62	1.63
Proportion of variance accounted for:	.60	.15

the plot shows the relative value that a subject placed on each dimension, in judging mainstreamability. As expected, all of the subjects consider the less severe disabilities to be more suitable for integration. The Physical-Mental dimension was not so clearly evaluated. The subjects were nearly evenly split on this factor, with 11 viewing the physical handicaps as suitable, and 12 choosing the mentally handicapped. The plot of the subjects can be seen in Fig. B.2.

DISCUSSION

Analysis of people's views on classroom integration of various disabilities yielded some interesting results. If only one dimension is used, people were in general agreement over who is suitable for mainstreaming. The use of multidimensional analysis, however, found that people differed considerably when comparing conditions on two dimensions. The first dimension, that of Severe-Mild, is a fairly obvious one. Certainly all educators would agree that, other things being equal, the less severely handicapped a child is, the more suitable he/she is for mainstreaming. The differences among subjects on the Physical-Mental factor are more remarkable. Classrooms designed for non-handicapped children require adjustments when integration is introduced. The adjustments may involve new equipment, rearranging of the old equipment, or differences in behavior patterns of teachers and students. The extent of consequent disruption of the teacher (and hence, of the class) depend a good deal on attitudes of the teacher. These changes are likely to differ depending upon the nature of the children being integrated. A child in a wheelchair may be better off academ-

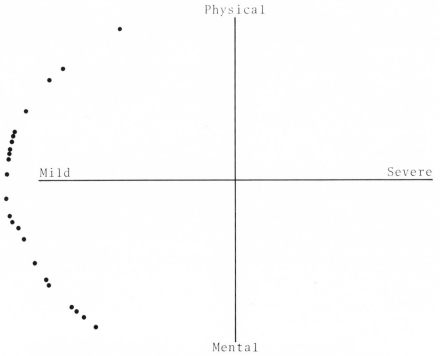

FIG. B.2.   Plot of subjects in two dimensional space. Each point represents a
preference vector for a subject.

ically in a regular class, but may have a great many logistical problems with
which some teachers are uncomfortable. An EMR youngster may be able to be
easily fitted to a classroom, while creating academic problems for the teacher.
Knowledge of the teacher's attitudes, and possible training programs to aid the
teachers, will help to alleviate some of the problems encountered in
mainstreaming.

The question of who to mainstream is not clearly answered. However, the
results of this small study suggest avenues of possible research. It is possible
that responses on the Physical-Mental dimension will differentiate between different subgroups of educators. Perhaps teachers with no experience with special
education place different emphasis on this factor than do those who have taught
the disabled. Administrators may differ from other educators, as may psychologists and other support personnel. With some changes in the list of disabilities
(e.g., elimination of aphasia, perhaps the addition of some others), future research should investigate the values of those directly involved in the decision-
making process. Cross-validation of the dimensionsality of disabilities is also
needed, to confirm the findings of this study. Future research may prove to
benefit educators and children, as the role of mainstreaming becomes more
precisely defined.

References

Anderson, R. E. A computer program for Guttman scaling with the Goodenough technique. *Behavioral Science*, 1966, *11*(3), 235.

Anderberg, M. R. *Cluster analysis for applications*. New York: Academic Press, 1973.

Bashaw, W. L. & Anderson, H. E., Jr. Developmental study of the meaning of adverbial modifiers. *Journal of Educational Psychology*, 1968, Vol. 59, 111–118.

Berryman, J., Neal, W. R. Jr., & Robinson, E. The validation of a scale to measure attitudes toward the classroom integration of disabled students. *Journal of Educational Research*, 1980, *73*, 199–203.

Blashfield, R. K., & Oldenderfer, M. S. The literature on cluster analysis. *Multivariate Behavioral Research*, 1978, *13*, 271–295.

Blumenfeld, W. S. I am never startled by a fish. *Industrial Psychologist Newsletter*, May 1972.

Boorman, S. A. & Arabie, P. Structural measures and the method of sorting. In R. N. Shepard & S. B. Nerlove (Eds.), *Multidimensional Scaling* (Vol. 1). New York: Seminar Press, 1972.

Carroll, J. D. Individual differences and multidimensional scaling. In R. N. Shepard, A. K. Romney & S. B. Nerlove (Eds.), *Multidimensional scaling* (Vol. 1). New York: Seminar, 1972.

Carroll, J. D., & Arabie, P. Multidimensional scaling. *Annual Review of Psychology*, 1980, *31*, 607–649.

Carroll, J. D., & Chang, J. J. *Program INDSCAL*. Murray Hill, N.J.: Bell Telephone Laboratories, 1968.

Carroll, J. D., & Chang, J. J. Analysis of individual differences in multidimensional scaling via an N-way generalization of "Eckart-Young" decomposition. *Psychometrika*, 1970, 35, 283–319.

Cattell, R. B. *Factor Analysis: An Introduction and Manual for the Psychologist and Social Scientist*. New York: Harper & Row, 1952.

Cattell, R. B. The basis of recognition and interpretation of factors. *Educational and Psychological Measurement*, 1962, *22*, 667–697.

Chambers, T. M., & Kleiner, B. *Graphical techniques for multivariate data and clustering*. Paper presented at the June 1980 Annual Meeting of the Classification Society, Boulder, Colorado.

Chang, J. J. *Preference mapping program*. Murray Hill, N.J.: Bell Telephone Laboratories, 1968.

Cliff, N. Scaling. *Annual Review of Psychology*, 1973, *24*, 473–506.

Cochran, W. G., & Cox, G. M. *Experimental designs*. New York: Wiley, 1957.

418

Coombs, H. C. *A theory of data*. New York: Wiley, 1964.

Cronbach, L. J. Coefficient alpha and the internal structure of tests. *Psychometrika*, 1951, *16*, 297–334.

David, H. A. Tournaments and paired comparisons. *Biometrika*, 1959, *46*, 139–149.

David, H. A. *The method of paired comparisons*. New York: Hafner Publishing Company, 1963.

Diamond, B. Myths of mainstreaming. *Journal of Learning Disabilities*, 1979, *12*, 246–250.

Dixon, W. J., & Brown, M. B. *BMD/P-79: Biomedical computer program P series*. Berkeley: University of California Press, 1979.

Dixon, W. J. & Massey, F. J. *Introduction to Statistical Analysis*. New York: p. 79, 81 McGraw-Hill, 1969.

Donovan, M. A. *The relationship between modality preferences and programs used in initial reading instruction*. Unpublished doctoral dissertation, University of Hawaii, 1977.

Dunn-Rankin, P. *The true distribution of the range of rank totals and its application to psychological scaling*. Unpublished doctoral dissertation, Florida State University, Tallahassee, 1965.

Dunn-Rankin, P. An IBM 7040 Fortran IV program for constructing scales from paired comparisons. *Behavioral Science*, 1966, *11*(3), 234.

Dunn-Rankin, P. The similarity of lowercase letters of the English alphabet. *Journal of Verbal Learning and Verbal Behavior*, 1968, *7*, 990–995.

Dunn-Rankin, P. Results of research on the visual characteristics of words. A paper presented to the Far West Regional Conference of International Reading Association, July 1976.

Dunn-Rankin, P. The visual characteristics of words. *Scientific American*, January 1978, *238*(1), 122–130.

Dunn-Rankin, P., & King, F. J. Multiple comparisons in a simplified rank method of scaling. *Educational and Psychological Measurement*, Summer 1969, *29*(2), 315–329.

Dunn-Rankin, P., Knezek, G. A., & Abalos, J. A. *Circular triads revisited*. Paper presented at the Hawaii Psychological Association meeting, Honolulu, Hawaii, May 1978.

Dunn-Rankin, P., Leton, D. A., & Sato, M. The similarity of hiragana characters in typos 35 font. *The Science of Reading*, 1972, *16*(2).

Dunn-Rankin, P., Shimizu, M., & King, F. J. Reward preference patterns in elementary school children. *International Journal of Educational Sciences*, 1969, *31*(1), 53–62.

Dunn-Rankin, P., & Wilcoxon, F. The true distribution of the range of rank totals in the two-way classification. *Psychometrika*, 1966, *31*(4), 573–580.

Edwards, A. L. *Techniques of Attitude Scale Construction*. New York: Appleton-Century-Crofts, 1957.

Edwards, A. L. *Edwards personal preference schedule manual*. New York: The Psychological Corporation, 1959.

Everitt, B. *Cluster analysis*. London: Heinemann, 1974.

Ekman, G. A direct method for multidimensional ratio scaling. *Psychometrika*, Vol. 28, no. 1, March, 1963.

Frostig, M. Meeting individual needs of all children in the classroom setting. *Journal of Learning Disabilities*, 1980, *13*, 51–54.

Fruchter, B. *Introduction to factor analysis*. New York: Van Nostrand, 1954.

Furlong, M. J., Atkinson, D. R., & Janoff, D. S. Elementary school counselors perceptions of their actual and ideal roles. *Elementary School Guidance and Counseling Journal*, 1980.

Gnedenko, B. V., & Khinchin, A. Y. *An elementary introduction to the theory of probability*. Leo F. Born, tr., from Russian 5th ed., 1960. New York: Dover Publications, Inc., 1962.

Goodenough, W. H. A technique for scale analysis. *Educational and Psychological Measurement*, 1944, 179–190.

Gower, J. C. A general coefficient of similarity and some of its properties. *Biometrics*, 1971, *27*, 857–872.

Green, B. F. Attitude measurement. In G. Lindsey (Ed.), *Handbook of Social Psychology*. Reading, Mass.: Addison-Wesley, 1954.

Green, P. E., & Carmone, F. J. *Multidimensional scaling and related techniques in marketing analysis*. Boston: Allyn & Bacon, 1970.

Guilford, J. P. *Psychometric methods* (2nd ed.). New York: McGraw-Hill, 1954.

Gulliksen, H. An IBM 650 program for a complete paired comparisons schedule (Parcoplet 2-21). Tech. Rep. ONR Contract Nonr. 1859(15), 1958.

Gulliksen, H., & Tucker, L. R. A general procedure for obtaining paired comparisons from multiple rank orders. *Psychometrika*, 1961, *26*, 173–184.

Gulliksen, H., & Tukey, J. W. Reliability for the law of comparative judgment. *Psychometrika*, 1958, *23*(2).

Guttman, L. A basis for scaling qualitative data. *American Sociological Review*, 1944, *9*, 139–150.

Guttman, L. The basis for scalogram analysis, in S. A. Stouffer (ed.), *Measurement and prediction*. Princeton, N.J.: Princeton University Press, 1950.

Harasymiw, S. J., & Horne, M. D. Teacher attitudes toward handicapped children and regular class integration. *Journal of Special Education*, 1976, *10*, 393–400.

Haring, N., Stern, G., & Cruickshank, W. *Attitudes of educators toward exceptional children*. Syracuse, N.Y.: Syracuse University Press, 1958.

Harman, H. H. *Modern factor analysis*. Chicago: University of Chicago Press, 1967.

Harshman, R. A. Models for analysis of assymmetrical relationships among n objects or stimuli. Presented at first joint meeting of Psychonomic Society and Society for Mathematical Psychology, Hamilton, Ontario, 1978.

Harter, L. H. *The probability integrals of the range and of the schedulized range*. WADC Technical Report 58-484, Wright Patterson Air Force Base, 1959.

Hiraki, K. *Teacher status in Japan*. A senior honors thesis. College of Education, University of Hawaii, 1974.

Hotelling, H. Analysis of a complex statistical variables into principal components. *Journal of Educational Psychology*, 1938, *24*, 499–520.

Huth, R. "A special class" *Early Years*, 1980, *10*, 54–55.

International Mathematical and Statistical Library (8th ed.) 1980, Houston, Texas.

Johnson, S. C. Hierarchical clustering schemes. *Psychometrika*, 1967, *32*, 241–254.

Kaiser, H. F. The varimax criterion for analytic rotation in factor analysis. *Psychometrika*, 1958, *23*, 187–200.

Kendall, M. G., & Babington–Smith, B. On the method of paired comparisons. *Biometrika*, 1939, *31*.

Kendall, M. G. *The advanced theory of statistics*, Vol. 1 (5th ed.). London: Charles Griffin, 1952.

Kendall, M. G. Further contributions to the theory of paired comparisons. *Biometrics*, 1955, *11*, 43–62.

King, F. J. *A content referenced interpretive system for standardized reading tests*. A final report to the Research Foundation of the National Council of Teachers of English, August 1974.

Knezek, G. A. *Circular triad distributions with applications to complete paired comparisons data*. Doctoral dissertation, University of Hawaii, 1978 (University Microfilms, 1979).

Kruskal, J. B. Multidimensional scaling by optimizing goodness of fit to a nonmetric hypothesis. *Psychometrika*, 1964, *29*, 1–27. (a)

Kruskal, J. B. Nonmetric multidimensional scaling: A numerical method. *Psychometrika*, 1964, *29*(2), 115. (b)

Kruskal, J. B., & Wish, M. *Multidimensional scaling*. Beverly Hills: Sage, 1978.

Levy, S., & Guttman, L. On the multivariate structure of well-being. *Social Indicators Research*, 1975, *2*, 361–388.

Likert, R. A. A technique for the measurement of attitudes. *Archives of Psychology, 1932*, No. 140, 5–53.

Lingoes, J. C. An IBM 360/67 program for Guttman-Lingoes smallest space analysis—PI. *Behavioral Science*, 1970, *15*, 536–540.

Marascuilo, L. A., & McSweeney, M. *Nonparametric and distribution-free methods for the social sciences.* Monterey: Brooks/Cole, 1977.

Martin, E. W. Some thoughts on mainstreaming. *Exceptional Children,* 1974, *41,* 150–153.

McQuitty, L. Elementary linkage analysis for isolating orthogonal and oblique types and typal relevancies. *Educational and Psychological Measurement,* 1957, *17,* 207–229.

McRae, D. J. MIKCA, A Fortran IV iterative k means cluster analysis program. *Behavioral Science, 16,* 423–434, 1971.

Montenegro, X. P. *Ideal and actual student perceptions of college instructors as predictors of teacher effectiveness.* Unpublished doctoral dissertation, University of Hawaii, 1978.

Moore, J., & Fine, M. J. Regular and special class teachers' perceptions of normal and exceptional children and their attitudes toward mainstreaming. *Psychology in the Schools,* 1978, *15,* 253–259.

Moseley, R. L. *An analysis of decision making in the controllership process.* Unpublished doctoral dissertation. University of Washington, Seattle, 1966.

Mosteller, F. Remarks on the methods of paired comparisons: III. A test of significances for paired comparisons when equal standard deviations and equal correlations are assumed. *Psychometrika,* 1951, *16,*

Mosteller, F. The mystery of the missing corpus. *Psychometrika,* 1958, *23*(4),

Napier, D. Nonmetric multidimensional techniques for summated ratings. In R. N. Shepard, A. K. Romney, & S. B. Nerlove (Eds.), *Multidimensional scaling* (Vol. 1). New York: Seminar Press, 1972.

Nie, N. H., Hull, C. H., Jenkins, J. Q., Steinbrenner, K., & Bent, D. H. *SPSS: Statistical package for the social sciences* (2nd ed.). New York: McGraw Hill, 1975.

Osgood, C. E., Suci, G. J., & Tannenbaum, P. H. *The measurement of meaning.* Urbana, Ill.: University of Illinois Press, 1957.

Pruzansky, S. *How to use SINDSCAL: A computer program for individual differences in multidimensional scaling.* Murray Hill, N.J.: Bell Telephone Labs, 1975.

Rapier, J., Adelson, R., Carey, R., & Croke, K. Changes in children's attitudes toward the physically handicapped. *Exceptional Children,* 1972, *39,* 219–223.

Robinson, J. P., Rusk, J. G., & Head, K. B. *Measures of occupational attitudes.* Draft, 1969. (a)

Robinson, J. P., Rusk, J. G., & Head, K. B. *Measures of political attitudes.* Ann Arbori ISR, 1968. (b)

Robinson, J. P., Rusk, J. G., & Head, K. B. *Measures of social psychological attitudes.* Ann Arbor ISR, 1969. (c)

Romney, A. K., Shepard, R. N., & Nerlove, S. B. *Multidimensional scaling* (Vol. 2). New York: Seminar Press, 1972.

Ross, R. T. Optimal orders in the method of paired comparisons. *Journal of Experimental Psychology,* 1934, *25,* 414–424.

Rummel, J. F. *An introduction to research procedures in education.* New York: Harper & Row, 1964.

Rummel, R. J. *Applied factor analysis.* Evanston, Ill.: Northwestern University Press, 1970.

SAS: *A user's guide to SAS 76/* Anthony J. Barr, James H. Goodnight, John P. Sall, & Jane T. Helwig. Raleigh, N.C.: SAS Institute, Inc., 1976.

Shaw, E. M., & Wright, J. M. *Scales for the measurement of attitudes.* New York: McGraw-Hill, 1967.

Shepard, R. N. The analysis of proximities: Multidimensional scaling with an unknown distance function. I. *Psychometrika,* 1962, *27,* 125–140.

Shepard, R. N. Introduction to Volume I. In R. N. Shepard, A. K. Romney, & S. B. Nerlove (Eds.), *Multidimensional scaling* (Vol. I). New York: Seminar Press, 1972. (a)

Shepard, R. N. A taxonomy of some principal types of data and of multidimensional methods for their analysis. In R. N. Shepard, A. K. Romney, & S. B. Nerlove (Eds.), *Multidimensional scaling* (Vol. 1). New York: Seminar Press, 1972. (b)

Smith, C. P. *The distribution of the absolute average discrepancy and its use in significance tests of paired comparison scaling.* Unpublished Master's thesis, University of Hawaii, 1968.

Smith, D. M. Another scaling of arithmetic tests. Unpublished paper, Florida State University, 1971.

Späth, H. *Cluster analysis algorithims.* Chichester: Ellis Harwood, 1980.

Starks, T. H. *Tests of significance for experiments involving paired comparisons.* Unpublished doctoral dissertation, Virginia Polytechnic Institute, 1958.

Starks, T. H., & David, H. A. Significance tests for paired comparison experiments. *Biometrika,* 1961, *48*(1 & 2), 95.

Subkoviak, M. J. The use of multidimensional scaling in educational research. *Review of Educational Research,* 1975, *45*(3), 387–423.

Thurstone, L. L. A law of comparative judgment. *Psychological Review,* 1927, 273–286.

Thurstone, L. L. *Multiple-Factor Analysis.* Chicago: University of Chicago Press, 1947.

Torgerson, W. S. *Theory and methods of scaling.* New York: Wiley, 1958.

Tucker, L. R. Relations between multidimensional scaling and three mode factor analysis. *Psychometrika,* 1972, *37*, 3–27.

Veldman, D. J. *Fortran programming for the behavioral sciences.* New York: Holt, Rinehart & Winston, 1967.

Villanueva, M., & Dunn-Rankin, P. A comparison of ranking and rating methods by multidimensional matching. A paper presented to the 1973 American Educational Research Association.

Waern, Y. Graphic similarity analysis. *Scandinavian Journal of Psychology,* 1972.

Ward, J. H. Hierarchical grouping to optimize an objective function. *Journal of the American Statistical Association,* 1963, *58*, 236–244.

Ward, M. & McCormick, S. "Reading instruction for blind and low vision children in the regular classroom." *The Reading Teacher.* 1981, *34* 372–377.

Wechsler, H., Suarez, A. C. & McFadden, M. Teachers' attitudes toward the education of physically handicapped children: Implications for the implementation of Massachusetts Chapter 766. *Journal of Education,* 1975, *157*, 17–24.

Wilcoxon, F., & Wilcox, R. A. *Some rapid approximate statistical procedures.* New York: Lederle Laboratories, 1964.

Williams, R. J., & Algozzine, B. Differential attitudes toward mainstreaming: An investigation. *Alberta Journal of Educational Research,* 1977, *23* 207–212.

Wold, H. Estimation of principal components and related models by iterative least squares. In P. R. Krishnaiak (Ed.), *Multivariate analysis.* New York: Academic Press, 1966.

Young, F. W., deLeeuw, J., & Takane, Y. Regression with qualitative and quantitative variables: an alternating least squares method with optimal scaling features. *Psychometrika,* 41:505–29, 1976.

Author Index

423

Subject Index

A

Activities
  example of pairing, 84
  preference scale, 85
Additivity, assumption of, 168
Adjectives
  example of pairing, 73, 74
  preference scale, 73
Agglomerative clustering, 136, 287
Alpha, Cronbach's, 92
ALSCAL, 205, 230
APRINT subroutine, listing of, 353
Alternating one dimensional search, 223
Association, measures of, 36
Attitude statements, rules in construction of, 4
Attitude toward reading scale, 91
Attitudinal measurement described, 7, 8
Authority scale, 61
AVELOMAT (averages matrices), description
  of, 247–249
Axes, orthogonal, 177

B

Balanced incomplete block design, 16
  example of, 216
BIB (paired data from incomplete blocks), 17
  description of, 250–254
Binomial test, 72
BMDP, 109, 246
BMDP4M (Factor analysis), 189
  description of, 255–257

C

CACM, 246
Canonical decomposition, 221
Card, computer, 237
Case V unidimensional scaling, 80, 81
  reliability, 83

Categorized ratings, 19
Categories, agreement, 111
Categorizing, 12
CCDS subroutine, listing of, 355
Centroid factor analysis, 170, 173
Centroid, 150
Cheybshev's inequality, 71
Choices, 6
Circularity
  example of, 73
  overall, 73
  pairwise, 75
Circular Triads, 68, 69
Clustering, 136
  free, 36, 41
  k means iterative, 152
  hierarchical-divisive, 156
  instrument, example of, 11
  nonmetric, 144
  partitioning, 149
  pairing and quantifying, 22
  procedures in, 122
  steps in, 10
  when to stop, 139
Clusters
  number of, 158
  graphing of, 158, 159
Cloze tests in reading, 109
Coefficient of,
  reproducibility, 106, 109
  scalability, 107
  variation, 72
COMPPC (paired comparisons scaling), 84
  description of, 257–268
Computer
  algorithms, 245
  card, 237
  programs, list of, 247, Table of Contents
Connectedness, 287, 288
CONPR (contrast pairs), description of,
  270–271